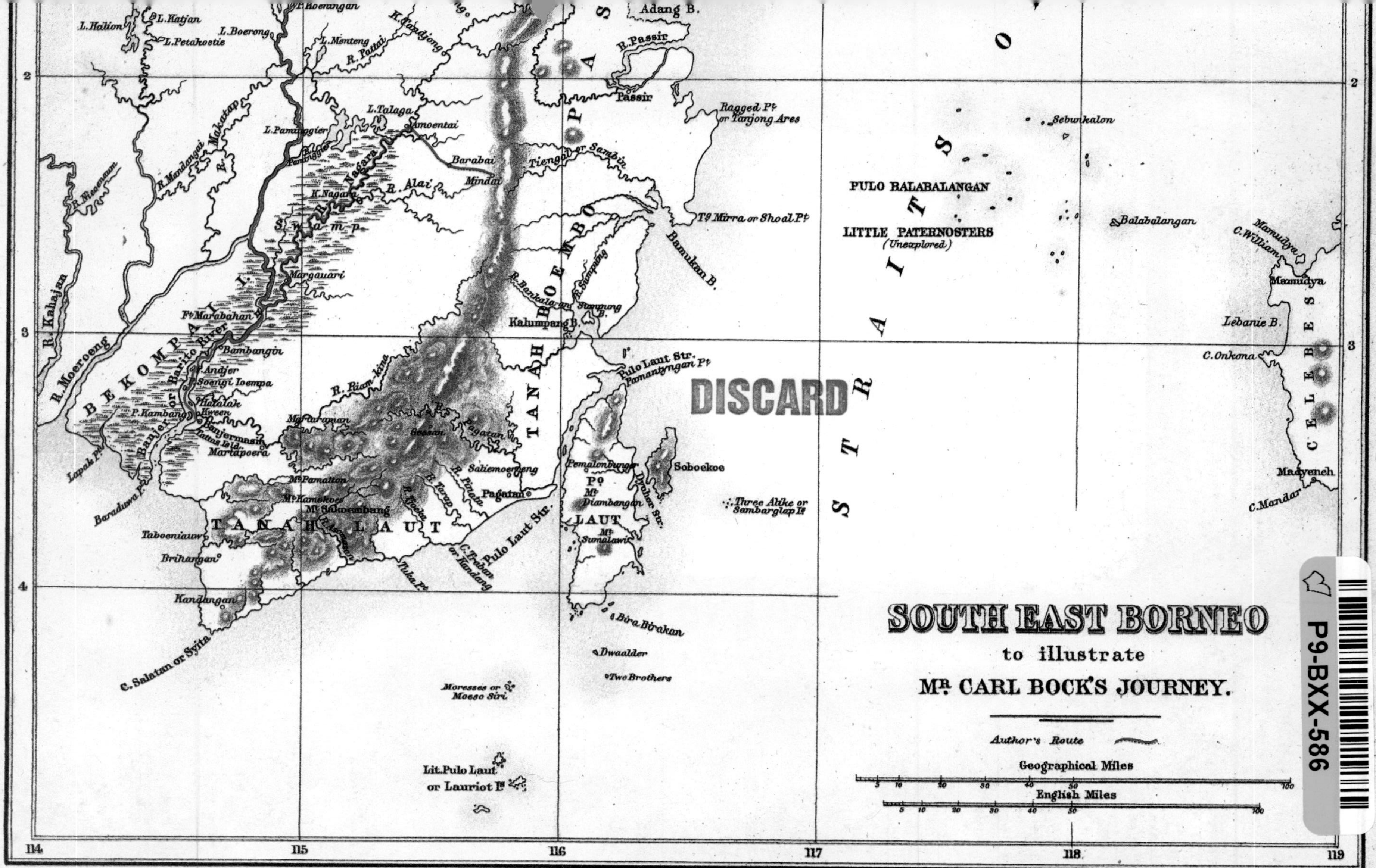

SOUTH EAST BORNEO

to illustrate

MR. CARL BOCK'S JOURNEY.

Author's Route

Geographical Miles

5 10 20 30 40 50 100

English Miles

5 10 20 30 40 50 100

STRAITS OF MACASSAR

CELEBES

PULO BALABALANGAN

LITTLE PATERNOSTERS (Unexplored)

TANAH BOEMBO

TANAH LAUT

BEKOMPAI

PASSIR

Pulo Laut

Swamp

Adang B.
R. Passir
Passir
Ragged Pt. or Tanjong Ares
Tg. Mirra or Shoal Pt.
Bamukan B.
Sebunkalon
Balabalangan
Mamudya
C. William
Lebanie B.
C. Onkona
Madyeneh
C. Mandar
L. Halion
L. Katjan
L. Petakoetie
L. Boerong
L. Menteng
R. Pattai
K. Kandjong
L. Talaga
Amoentai
L. Pamanggier
Barabai
Mindai
Tiengol or Sambin
R. Alai
K. Nagara
R. Nagara
R. Mandangai
R. Makatap
R. Nissenaun
R. Kahajan
R. Moeroeng
Margauari
Ft. Marabahan
Barito River
Bambangin
P. Andjer
P. Soengi Loempa
Halalak
Hween
P. Kambang
Banjer or
Banjermasin
Tattas Isld.
Martapoera
Lapak Pt.
Baraduwa Pt.
R. Riam-kina
Martaraman
Mt. Pamalton
Mt. Kamekoes
Mt. Saloembang
R. Asamasam
Taboeniauw
Brihangan
Kandangan
C. Salatan or Syita
Goesan
Pagatan
R. Pinata
R. Tarap
R. Tjoeka
Saliemoeneng
Pagatan
Tuka Pt.
C. Traban or Kandang
Pulo Laut Str.
Pulo Laut Str.
Panantyngan Pt.
R. Bankalaan
R. Sampang
Sampang B.
Kalumpang B.
Pemalon Bunger
Mt. Diambangan
Mt. Sumalawi
Drohon Str.
Soboekoe
Three Alike or Sambarglap Is.
Bira Birakan
Dwaalder
Two Brothers
Moresses or Moeso Siri
Lit. Pulo Laut or Lauriot Is.

2 3 4

114 115 116 117 118 119

DISCARD

P9-BXX-586

London: Sampson Low, Marston, Searle, & Rivington.

Edwd. Weller, Red Lion Square.

959.8 BOC

Bock, Carl, 1849-

The head-hunters of Borneo

WAYNE PUBLIC LIBRARY
MAIN LIBRARY
475 Valley Road
Wayne, N. J. 07470

Books may be returned at any branch of the library.

MAR 27 1987

THE HEAD-HUNTERS
OF
BORNEO

MAR 27 1937

(courtesy, The Bodleian Library, Oxford)

CARL BOCK

THE HEAD-HUNTERS OF BORNEO:

A NARRATIVE OF TRAVEL UP THE MAHAKKAM AND DOWN THE BARITO;

ALSO,

JOURNEYINGS IN SUMATRA.

BY

CARL BOCK

WITH AN INTRODUCTION BY

R. H. W. REECE

SINGAPORE
OXFORD UNIVERSITY PRESS
OXFORD NEW YORK

Oxford University Press
Oxford New York Toronto
Petaling Jaya Singapore Hong Kong Tokyo
Delhi Bombay Calcutta Madras Karachi
Nairobi Dar es Salaam Cape Town
Melbourne Auckland
and associates in
Beirut Berlin Ibadan Nicosia

OXFORD is a trademark of Oxford University Press

First published by Sampson Low, Marston, Searle & Rivington, London, 1881
First issued as an Oxford University Press paperback 1985
Introduction © Oxford University Press, 1985
Second impression 1986
ISBN 0 19 582629 9

Printed in Singapore by Koon Wah Printing Pte. Ltd.
Published by Oxford University Press Pte. Ltd.,
Unit 221, Ubi Avenue 4, Singapore 1440

INTRODUCTION*

Carl Alfred Bock (1849–1932) was a Norwegian naturalist and explorer who occupies a not unimportant place in the gallery of European officials, merchants, missionaries and adventurers who visited the Malay archipelago in the nineteenth century. He was certainly one of the first European writers to realize and exploit the exotic potential of Borneo.

Born into a merchant family, Bock was brought up and educated in Oslo. In 1868 he went to England and after a year of travel and study there found employment with the Swedish–Norwegian Consul at the north-eastern fishing port of Grimsby. When the Consul died, Bock went to London to pursue his long-standing interest in natural science. In the same year he married Mary Jane Absalon, daughter of a ship's captain.

After a journey through Swedish Lapland in 1877, which probably whetted his appetite for further travel, Bock was commissioned early in the following year by Arthur Hay, ninth Marquess of Tweeddale (1824–78), to make a collecting expedition to Sumatra. Hay was a former military man with a passion for ornithology and possibly visited the Malay archipelago during the early 1840s when he was posted in India. At any rate, in 1844 he described several rare species of birds from the area in the *Madras Journal of Literature and Science*. In retirement at Chislehurst in Kent he pursued his ornithological interests, becoming a Fellow of the Royal Society and the Linnaean Society and President of the Zoological Society of London. It was probably through this latter connection that he met Bock and personally employed him to make the trip to Sumatra. The young Norwegian had evidently been successful in gaining access to scientific and aristocratic circles in the capital.

Bock arrived in Padang, the principal port on the west coast of

*I wish to thank the following people who have assisted me in various ways in the preparation of this introduction: Dr Jan Avé, Dr John Butcher, Dr Peter Carey, the Earl of Cranbrook, Dr Victor King, Professor Rodney Needham and Dr Ida Nicolaisen.

Sumatra, in early August 1878. At this time the Acheh War was at its height and Bock's steamer was crammed with 700 European mercenaries employed to put down the most serious challenge to Dutch power since the Java War. Fluent in Dutch but not Malay, Bock depended very much on his local assistants who included an allegedly 'hermaphrodite' hunter previously employed by the great Italian naturalist, Odoardo Beccari. In just over three months Bock collected 24 mammals, 321 birds, several reptiles and amphibia and 575 insect specimens and prepared them for shipment to England. However the second and more important of his two shipments was later lost in the Red Sea when the steamer taking them to England sank. He also received news of the death of Tweeddale, which forced him to cancel an expedition to Timor.

It was probably on his return to Batavia that Bock met the Governor-General of the Netherlands East Indies, Johan Willem van Lansberge, and was commissioned by him to make an expedition into the little-known interior of south-eastern Borneo. From Bock's own account, he was required to report on the natives of the interior of the east coast kingdom of Kutai and to observe and collect fauna, crossing overland either to Pontianak or Banjarmasin. The fact that he received his final briefing from the Director of Education in Batavia indicates that his commission was semi-official, although, as one reviewer later pointed out, he was hardly justified in styling himself 'Late Commissioner for the Dutch Government'. Apart from the usefulness of any reliable information about the tribes of the interior who had seriously challenged Dutch authority during the Banjarmasin War twenty years earlier, the Governor-General may well have been inspired by the legends of *orang buntut* (men with tails) and cannibals in that part of Borneo.

It was certainly not a commission to be undertaken lightly. An overland expedition from Kutai in 1825 had resulted in the death of its leader Georg Müller and his party at the hands of Dayaks apparently instigated by the Sultan of Kutai. In 1844 the Scottish adventurer Erskine Murray was killed near the mouth of the Mahakam River by the Sultan's Bugis mercenaries after attempting to emulate there James Brooke's earlier exploits in Sarawak. And twenty years later the Dutch Resident of Pelarang died just beyond the borders of Kutai while leading another expedition of 1,500 men. Although there had been earlier journeys up the Mahakam by the first administrator of the East Coast, von Dewall, and the German geologist Dr Schwaner (whose chart Bock took with him), there remained the challenge of returning to the coast by means of one of the other river systems. This was to take him into areas never before penetrated by Europeans and largely unknown to the coastal peoples. His success in persuading the Sultan of Kutai to accompany him was consequently something of a coup and an immense diplomatic advantage in his dealing with the Dayaks.

Bock's official report of his journey was probably written on board ship when he was returning to Europe in early 1880. It was translated into Dutch by P. J. B. C. Robidé van der Aa and in 1881 the first section of 64 pages, together with an historical essay on Kutai by a former Resident, S. W. Tromp, and an 'atlas' or portfolio of thirty coloured plates based on Bock's drawings, was published by Martinus Nijhoff for the Koninklijk Instituut voor de Taal-, Land- en Volkenkunde van Nederlandsch-Indie. For reasons which are not clear, the second part of the text was not published until 1887. Entitled *Reis in Oost- en Zuid-Borneo van Koetei naar Banjermassin*..., the report contained the essence of Bock's ethnographical observations. However, Bock was not content with glory alone and was anxious to capitalize on his unusual achievement. Back in London, where the plates for *Reis* had been prepared at his insistence, he filled out the manuscript with a good deal of anecdotal detail and appended lists of the specimens that he had collected. Before undertaking another expedition to northern Siam and Laos, this time at his own expense, he entrusted all his papers to his friend Charles Fryer, who revised the manuscript for publication and saw it through the press. It is not clear whether Bock chose the title, *The Head-Hunters of Borneo*..., but from what we know of his journalistic leanings we can be fairly confident that he did. The need for a second edition in 1882 certainly justified his optimism about the book's popular appeal. A German edition appeared in 1882 and a Norwegian edition in 1883, just before the publication in London of *Temples and Elephants*... (the account of his Siamese expedition).

Dutch reviewers of *Reis* were favourable on the whole, praising Bock's physical courage and fortitude. However, they unanimously deplored van Lansberge's employment of a foreigner, regarding it as an affront to the initiative and capacity of Dutchmen who had pioneered the colonization of the Indies. Schouw Santwardt, leader of the trans-Sumatran expedition, and van Musschenbroek, explorer of Minahassa in the Celebes, both complained about the lack of co-operation from the Batavia authorities. The preparation of the plates was also seen as a reflection on the capacities of Dutch artists. (Indeed, so strong was the continuing nationalistic resentment that Bock did not earn an entry in the *Encyclopaedie van Nederlandsch-Indië,* although *Reis* was mentioned in the entry for *Dajaks.*) There was also some discussion about whether Bock was the disinterested scientist that he purported to be. Although he told the *Soerabaya–Courant* on his return from Banjarmasin that he would not make a cent out of his journey, there remained a suspicion that his motives were not really so lofty.

The most important review of *Reis* was by M. T. H. Perelaer, a former Dutch soldier and colonial official who had served in the Banjarmasin War of 1859–64 and had published an ethnographic account of the Dayaks in 1870. Returning to Holland in about 1880, he set about writing a number of books, some of them in fictional form, on his experiences in the Indies over twenty-five years. Although he did not know Kutai at first hand and had not met the Dayaks and Punans of the

Mahakam River area, he was familiar with Dayak culture and well qualified to comment on the ethnographic value of Bock's account.

One of his main criticisms was of Bock's linguistic limitations which had played 'some nasty tricks on the gifted writer'. For example, Bock had rendered the title of the Sultan of Kutai as *Haji* rather than *aji* which is the Javanese indicator of royal status (a mistake which was subsequently corrected in *Head-Hunters*). Bock's refusal to eat fruit offered to him by Dayaks on suspicion of being poisoned was also depicted as a mistake, although after what had happened to earlier travellers in the area the Norwegian could hardly be blamed for exercising extreme caution. Perelaer felt that while the thirty coloured plates contained in the atlas greatly enhanced the value of Bock's work, they did less than justice to the beauty of Dayak women. More importantly, Bock's drawings of carved wooden figures with erect phalluses he regarded as presenting the pornography of Kutai as a typical art form. 'The immodest images', he wrote, 'are as seldom shown there as improper photographs [are] in our big cities....' As for Bock's obsession with finding the legendary *orang buntut*, he felt that he had been 'clearly the victim of a joker, whose less than appropriate humour more than once could have given rise to complications'. An English reviewer of *Head-Hunters* in the *Proceedings* of the Royal Geographical Society even made the wry suggestion that Bock's search would almost justify 'an inversion of the title of his book, as no new experience of head-hunters is recorded in it'. However, he believed that the book was of interest for the material it made available to ethnological discussion and for its plates and woodcuts which were 'for the most part very well executed'.

In fact, there was little in Bock's ethnographical accounts that was new and a good deal that was suspect. Earlier accounts of the Dayaks by von Dewall, Schwaner, and Perelaer were more detailed and comprehensive although not so accessible to English readers. Bock made extensive use of them. He was also obliged to depend for his information on the services of two Malay assistants who interpreted for him with Dayak informants and took down notes which were later translated from Malay by Seitz, the Assistant Resident at Kutai, and by Emann, chief clerk to the Resident at Banjarmasin. Of greatest significance is his account of the Medang of Long Wai where he spent about seven weeks.

Bock's main interest was in the exotic and the sensational. Although he made much of his meetings with the Punans, this was almost entirely with groups visiting Kutai and he seems to have spent no more than a day with them in their own territory. It may be true that he was the first European to sight Punan women and his portraits of them are sympathetic and interesting. However, he could hardly be considered as a significant contributor to the ethnography of the Punans. The highlight of his narrative is his meeting with Sibau Mobang, chief of the

Tring Dayaks, who were reputed to be not just head-hunters but cannibals. Although he might well have pursued the veracity of this claim when he visited them, Bock seems to have taken it at face value. His main interest was in providing a description of the Tring chief and of dwelling on the *frisson* of being with people whose main source of protein was human flesh. In fact there is no other firm evidence of cannibalism amongst the Dayaks and Bock was probably doing no more than giving credence to the claims of their enemies. It is just possible that the terrible drought of recent times and the consequent chronic shortage of food had stimulated isolated cases of cannibalism, but the habitual and large-scale cannibalism reported by Bock was almost certainly nonsense. Bock's fellow countryman and explorer, Carl Lumholtz (1851–1922), heard similar stories forty years later about the '*Ulu-Ots*' (people of the headwaters) when travelling through the same area.

Ever in search of the sensational, Bock went to extraordinary lengths to trace the legendary *orang buntut* whose existence was sworn to by the coastal and down-river people. The notion of the 'missing link' between apes and men had received a great deal of publicity in scientific and popular circles since Darwin and was to influence physical anthropology for years to come. Bock was a man of his age and it is natural that he should have written of tailed men as the 'great physiological prize, the missing link in the chain of evidence proving the descent of man from monkey'. However, his efforts to find them were not matched by a scientifically critical attitude to the evidence of their existence. He was so eager to believe in them that he happily accepted hearsay accounts, even to the point of almost causing strife between the Sultan of Kutai and the ruler of the neighbouring kingdom of Pasir where the *orang buntut* were supposed to be found. In a hilarious but certainly dangerous misunderstanding of a letter written on Bock's behalf requesting him to supply a pair of *orang buntut*, the illiterate Sultan of Pasir understood the Sultan of Kutai to be asking him to give up two of his own retainers (tail people) and indignantly replied that anyone who wanted them would have to come and take them by force. It is just possible that Bock was sceptical of the *orang buntut* stories and that his pursuit of them was a device designed to divert his Dutch patrons and a wide audience of European readers. However, this seems to be at odds with the energetic, enthusiastic but not always critical personality which emerges from his writings. Hugh Brooke Low, whose knowledge of Borneo peoples was unrivalled in his day, expressed surprise that Bock had been so ingenuous.

In his own time, Bock's books made him something of a celebrity. He was honoured by the Geographical Societies of Lisbon, Rome and Samarang (Java) as well as the Anthropological Society of Florence and was decorated by Emperor Franz-Josef of Austria, the King of Sweden and the government of Brazil. However the Royal Geographical Society of London, whose accolade would have meant a great deal to him, remained aloof. In Britain the only tribute to his work is his surviving collection of Sumatran bird skins which was eventually donated to the British Museum by Tweeddale's nephew and is now housed at Tring outside London. A collection of 120 Borneo bird skins is held in Leiden and the bronze Buddhas brought back from Laos are in the University Museum in Oslo. Significantly, Bock did not publish any important scientific papers on his collections. His role was to provide material for others. However, his name has been celebrated in that of the hawk-cuckoo, *Cuculus bocki*, which he discovered on the lower Mahakam in 1880.

It is as a travel book that *Head-Hunters* must be judged and from this point of view there is a good deal to be said for it. Bock was a shrewd observer with a nice sense of humour and a journalist's ability to convey his noteworthy experiences. Perhaps the high point of the book is his description of the birthday preparations and celebrations for the Sultan of Kutai whom he portrayed with tolerant good humour. It was this diplomatic ability with indigenous rulers which stood Bock in good stead a few years later in his dealings with the King of Siam who bore much of the expense of his journey to the north-eastern part of the kingdom and to neighbouring Laos which at that time was largely unknown to European travellers. Consequently it is not at all surprising that Bock's subsequent career was as a diplomat in his country's consular service rather than as a scientist, although during this time he secured important botanical collections from China and Africa for Oslo University. Appropriate to his status as an authority on Eastern countries, his first posting was as Norwegian–Swedish Vice-Consul in Shanghai in 1886, where he became Consul in 1893. In 1899 he was transferred to Antwerp and his last post was as Consul-General in Lisbon in 1900–1903, after which he spent his long retirement in Brussels.

Since Bock's visit there has been a veritable flood of travel literature on Borneo, most of it exploiting the perennial popular appeal of head-hunters, bare-breasted women, orang utans, *Rafflesia* and other exotica. Between 1915 and 1917 Carl Lumholtz, a zoological and anthropological collector of rather more significance, retraced Bock's route from the opposite direction, but for some reason failed to make any mention of his countryman's earlier exploits in his own book, *Through Central Borneo*.... Hardly a year has gone by without at least one book describing the adventures of some indefatigable traveller braving the Borneo jungle as if no one had ever done it before. Of these, journeys across the entire island have the greatest cachet, although fact is sometimes liberally garnished with fiction. Bock's book is a pioneering work of this genre and stands up well in any comparison with later travellers' narratives. It has probably had a wider circulation than any other book on Borneo and its colour plates reveal Bock's considerable skills as an artist as well as an observer. Hugh Brooke Low reported roars of appreciation when he showed them to the people of the upper Rejang River a few years after publication.

Murdoch University R. H. W. REECE
Western Australia
March 1985

BIBLIOGRAPHY

Anon., 'Carl Bock Op Borneo', *Aardrijkskundig Weekblad*, No. 30, 8 May 1880.

Bock, Carl, 'Descriptions of two new Species of Shells from China and Japan', *Proceedings* of the Zoological Society of London, 1878, p. 727.

———, 'Letter ... containing remarks upon *Capricornis sumatrensis*' [24 January 1879], *Proceedings* of the Zoological Society of London, 1879, pp. 308–9.

———, 'The Dutch Indian Government Exploring Expedition in Borneo', Transactions of Section E, *Report of the Fiftieth Meeting of the British Association for the Advancement of Science...*, London, John Murray, 1880, pp. 661–2.

———, 'List of Land and Freshwater Shells collected in Sumatra and Borneo, with Descriptions of new Species', *Proceedings* of the Zoological Society of London, 1881, pp. 628–35.

———, *Reis in Oost- en Zuid-Borneo van Koetei naar Banjermassin, Ondernomen op Last der Indische Regeering in 1879 en 1880 door Carl Bock. Met Historische Inleiding over Koetei en de Betrekkingen van dit Leenrijk tot de Regeering van Nederlandsch-Indie. Door P.J.B.C. Robide van der Aa. Met Atlas van 30 Ethnografische Platen in Kleurendruk en Schetskaar*, Uitgegeven door het Koninklijk Instituut voor de Taal-, Land- en Volkenkunde van Nederlandsch-Indie, 's-Gravenhage, Martinus Nijhoff, 1881.
[The second part of *Reis* was published in 1887.]

———, *The Head-Hunters of Borneo: A Narrative of Travel Up the Mahakkam and Down the Barito; Also, Journeyings in Sumatra*, London, Sampson Low, 1881.

———, *Hoved-Jaegerne paa Borneo... Oversat efter den engelske original* ved B. Geelmuyden, Kristiania, 1883.

———, *Temples and Elephants: The Narrative of a Journey of Exploration through Upper Siam and Lao*, London, Sampson Low, 1884.

———, *Templer og elefanter eller beretning om en undersegelse gjennem Siam og Lao...*, Kristiania, 1884.

———, *Orientalske eventyr*, Kristiania, 1885.

Bull, E. *et al.*, *Norsk Biografisk Leksikon*, Oslo, 1925.

Halvorsen, J. B., *Norsk Forfatter-Lexikon 1814–1880*, Kristiana, 1885.

Lumholtz, Carl, *Through Central Borneo: Two Years' Travel in the Land of the Head Hunters*, 2 vols., New York, Charles Scribner's Sons, 1920.

Perelaer, M. T. H., 'Critisch overzicht van Carl Bock's *Reis*', *Indische Gids*, 3 (1881), II, pp. 804–9.

———, *Ethnographische Beschrijving der Dajaks*, ? Amsterdam, 1870.

———, *Ran Away from the Dutch: or Borneo from South to North... Translated by Maurice Block and adapted by A. P. Mendes*, London, Sampson Low [1887].

Ramsay, R. G. Wardlaw, 'Contributions to the Ornithology of Sumatra: Report on a Collection from the Neighbourhood of Padang', *Proceedings* of the Zoological Society of London, 1880, pp. 13–16.

Roth, H. Ling, *The Natives of Sarawak and British North Borneo*, 2 vols., Kuala Lumpur, 1968 (first ed. London, 1896).

Schwaner, C. A. L. M., *Borneo*, 2 vols., Amsterdam, 1853–4.

Smythies, B. E., *The Birds of Borneo*, Edinburgh, Oliver and Boyd, 1960.

PREFACE.

In the spring of 1878, through the liberality of the late and much-lamented Marquis of Tweeddale, I went out to the Dutch Indies with the object of making a collection of the fauna of the western portion of the interior of the Island of Sumatra. The first portion of my collection arrived safe in England, but the second, and by far the larger and better of the two, shared the fate of the Egyptians in the Red Sea. The steamer in which my cases were shipped, sank.

While in Sumatra I was entrusted by his Excellency Van Lansberge, Governor-General of the Dutch Indies, himself a distinguished naturalist, and personally greatly interested in East Indian exploration, with a mission to Borneo. I was commissioned to go first to Koetei, a country enjoying the worst repute among the semi-independent States, and to furnish the Government with a report upon the native races of the interior, and to make observations upon, and collections of, the fauna of that part of the island. I was then to cross the island if possible, either to Pontnianak or Bandjermasin.

The latter journey I successfully accomplished; and the results of my observations on the route from Tangaroeng to Bandjermasin, a distance of over 700 miles, through several dangerous and troublesome Dyak tribes, are given in the first part of this book. My journeyings in Sumatra form the subject of the second portion.

Before leaving these records to receive such recognition as they may deserve at the hands of the public, I must not omit to express my appreciation of the kind services rendered to me by many gentlemen, without whose assistance neither would my travels have been accomplished nor the record of them published.

Foremost in the list stands the name of the late Lord Tweeddale, to whose zoological zeal I owe my original journey to the East.

Next I am indebted to his Excellency Van Lansberge, who entrusted to me the leadership of the Borneo expedition, for his generous personal assistance.

I have to convey my respectful thanks to the Foreign Office for the valuable recommendation to Count Bylandt and to Her Majesty's Consul at Batavia: both were instrumental in facilitating the execution of my travels.

Nor must I forget to express my deep sense of gratitude to his Highness the Sultan of Koetei for his unremitting kindness, and for his personal approbation of, and interest in, my travels; also for his two highly valued gifts—one a sword, presented to me before leaving for the interior—the other a four-and-a-half carat brilliant ring, given to me when taking leave of his Highness at Bandjermasin. Then I have to thank the many gentlemen, official, and non-official in the East, whose hospitality and assistance I enjoyed. Foremost amongst them I must mention Mr. James Waddell, of Soerabaija, and Mr. W. B. Pearson, of Padang, both of whom showed me many acts of favour, which will never be forgotten.

In conclusion, I have to thank Mr. C. E. Fryer—in whose hands, on the eve of my departure for Siam, my papers were left—for the care he has taken in the revision of my manuscript, and in seeing these pages through the press; while the exact reproduction of my coloured drawings by Mr. C. F. Kell, of the smaller sketches and photographs, as woodcuts, by Mr. J. D. Cooper, and of my map by Mr. E. Weller, also deserves frank recognition.

C. BOCK.

April 10, 1881.

CONTENTS.

CHAPTER I.

CHAPTER II.

CHAPTER III.

CHAPTER IV.

CHAPTER IX.

CHAPTER X.

CHAPTER XI.

CHAPTER XII.

CHAPTER XIII.

CHAPTER XIV.

CHAPTER XX.

CHAPTER XXI.

CHAPTER XXII.

CHAPTER XXIII.

PART II.

JOURNEYINGS IN SUMATRA.

CHAPTER I.

CHAPTER II.

CHAPTER III.

CHAPTER IV.

CHAPTER V.

APPENDIX.

LIST OF ILLUSTRATIONS.

DESCRIPTION OF COLOURED PLATES.

(*Between pages 88 and 89*)

LIST OF ENGRAVINGS.

THE HEAD-HUNTERS OF BORNEO.

CHAPTER I.

Introductory—An earthquake—A "universal provider"—Buitenzorg—The Native Agricultural School—Coffee worth more than gold—Rapid growth of eucalyptus—A princely Javanese artist—Nose-rubbing—A new theology—Samarang—Soerabaija—A mountain sanatorium—Raden Adi Patti Pandjie Tjokro Negoro—Curious dyeing process—Fragile pottery—Powdered women—A tragic dance—Chinese traders—Celestial cemeteries—Curious customs in Bali.

In these days of railways and ocean steamers, whose times of departure and arrival on a journey round the world may be calculated as closely as those of a well-appointed coach on a hundred-mile stage forty years ago, a voyage to the East Indies *viâ* the Suez Canal is marked by few adventures or remarkable incidents. Such as they are, so many travellers have experienced the perils or pleasures of a voyage to the East, and so many pens have described them, that it would be vain repetition for me to attempt to give in an introductory chapter even the slightest sketch of the period between my departure from Southampton and my arrival at Batavia. The stories of the tossing in the Bay of Biscay, the call at the historic "Rock," the run down the blue Mediterranean past the island fortress of Malta, the slow progress through the Suez Canal, the horrors of the "Middle Passage" through the Red Sea, the passing call at that other outpost of the British Empire, Aden, the view of the lovely island of Ceylon, and the ultimate landing at Batavia or Padang,—have they not all been written in the Books of the Chronicles of travellers without number? Why should I, then, pause to tell an oft-told tale, while my object is to record events that occurred in less familiar scenes, in some of the bye-paths of travel in the Malay Archipelago?

Suffice it then, for the present, to say that I arrived at Batavia —no matter how—on the 5th June, 1879, and took up my quarters at the Java Hotel, whose worthy hostess, Mrs. Spaanderman, was doing her best to accommodate in comfort an unusually large number of visitors, whose demands strained the resources of the establishment to their utmost.

The day closed eventfully. While the visitors were making the best of that *mauvais quart d'heure* during which the sound of the dinner-bell is anxiously awaited, making believe to read, sipping the national beverage of gin-and-bitters, smoking, chatting, and otherwise killing time, the chairs under the verandah began suddenly to dance, whether empty or not; and while most of us were in doubt whether we were the subjects of some huge practical joke an equally sudden arrest of the movement, following one still more pronounced, forced upon us the conviction that we were experiencing a shock of earthquake. The first impulse was to rush from the building; but before we could do so a third *tremblement* again set the chairs rattling, while the gas flickered as if under a strong wind, although the air was quite still. The sensation was somewhat similar to that experienced in a small boat when it meets the wash from a steamer in a narrow stream. Fortunately no damage was done, and no further disturbance occurred, but the event afforded ample food for conversation during dinner. Some of the company had been witnesses of the recent violent earthquakes at Tjandjoer, only fifty miles distant, and gave most interesting descriptions of the terrible scenes enacted there. For more than two months the whole island, with the two volcanoes at its opposite extremities in violent eruption, and acting as safety-valves, was subject to violent shocks, of which Tjandjoer seemed to be the centre. The town was partially destroyed, and many people were hurried to a sudden and awful death amid the falling ruins.

In order to place myself right with my readers, I will at once explain that, if placed in true chronological order, the two parts of my book would be reversed. It was during a visit to Sumatra, in 1878-9, to make collections of the fauna of the western part of that island, that I received a commission from the Dutch Government to proceed to Borneo and explore the south-eastern portion of that great island; and, as the results of that journey proved more important than those of my journeyings in Sumatra, I have determined to describe the second expedition first.

I was now consequently at Batavia, to receive final instructions for my journey in Borneo from Mr. Stortenbeker, Director of the Educational Department. I was to leave Batavia on the 20th June by steamer for Soerabaija, where I was to be furnished with letters of introduction to the Sultan of Koetei; and then proceed to Macassar to confer with the Governor, who was formerly Resident at Bandjermasin.

The next few days were devoted to the necessary preparations, and to the purchase of stores and provisions for the journey. For these, recourse was had to the store or shop of Lo Po Sing, the principal Chinese merchant of Batavia, who seemed to rival a certain well-known London tradesman in his claim to the title of "Universal Provider." Medicines, tinned provisions of all kinds, clothes and clothing materials of every description, were furnished by this enterprising Celestial, who, in his anxiety to show the vast resources of his establishment, took care that no article that was by any possibility indispensable, or utterly useless, to a traveller like myself should be forgotten.

My greatest difficulty was in engaging servants. The very idea of venturing into the territory of the Head-hunters of Borneo was enough to cool the ardour of those who otherwise professed to be most anxious to accompany me. The offer of high wages, so high as to amount to a positive bribe, was of no avail. Malays, Dutch, half-breeds, Chinese, all valued their heads too highly to risk them among the Dyaks of Borneo. Even the superintendent of police, who might be supposed to be acquainted with all the desperadoes of the place, and who very kindly assisted me in my search, failed to find any one enterprising enough, and in other respects suitable, to accompany me. So in the end I had to take my chance of finding servants at Soerabaija or Macassar.

The remainder of my time was occupied by a short trip inland. At Buitenzorg,[1] where the celebrated botanical gardens are situated,

[1] Buitenzorg = *Sans Souci.*

I had an interview with the Governor-General of Sumatra, Mr. Van Lansberge, an ardent entomologist, and probably the highest living authority on the *coleoptera* of the Malay Archipelago. From this wide field he had formed a magnificent collection of insects, some of them of most beautiful colours and strange forms, and of remarkable size.

Buitenzorg is connected by rail with Batavia, and among the more recent of the many evidences of progress in this part of Java is the Native Agricultural School, founded in 1876, with experimental gardens—not to be confounded with the beautiful botanical gardens—attached. In the school, lectures are given by competent European botanists, and in the gardens lessons are given in practical planting or farming, while, in a museum adjoining, are models of European and American implements. Dr. Scheffer, since dead, was the first Director of this invaluable institution. He told me he found the natives most apt pupils; and under his management the school has proved a great boon to them, and of immense value to the agricultural interests of the colony.

Useful plants and trees from all parts of the world are collected, and experimentally grown in the gardens, their nature and habit of growth carefully studied and exemplified, and seeds or cuttings distributed to those who are willing to take up their cultivation. At the same time the modern methods of agriculture are adapted to the requirements of the soil and climate of the country, and explained to the native planters and others. The native mode of culture consists simply in scratching the earth, scattering a few seeds, and waiting for the harvest; or in the still more simple course of merely collecting such produce as the bounty of nature has placed within reach. But the wealth of the Dutch East India Colonies has not been realized by such measures as these. Skilled planting and organized cropping have been taught, and science has been introduced, to increase the profusion of nature's products. The result is that the resources of the country are being multiplied a hundredfold.

At the time of my visit great excitement existed in regard to the introduction of the Liberian coffee plant. At the first public sale by auction of seeds, single beans had realized the almost fabulous price of two and a half florins (4*s.* 2*d.* sterling). The reports of the wonderfully prolific nature of the Liberian coffee plant had excited the curiosity of the Javanese planters; and the *furore* was intensified by the recent outbreak in the Java plantations of the Ceylon coffee leaf disease (*hemileia vastatrix*), against which the Liberian variety was said to be proof. Some of the coffee plantations were already seriously affected by this destructive disease, the leaves having changed their natural deep lustrous green colour for a murky yellow hue—infallible sign of the existence of the fungus pest. In the experimental gardens at Buitenzorg were 12,000 young plants grown from Liberian seed—all of them so far appearing healthy enough. Among other experimental crops growing here were sugar canes, Bengal grass—the produce of which is too rich for horses if eaten alone, but forms an excellent fodder for cattle—maize, rice of various kinds, vanilla, cocoa, and chinchona. Cocoa is already being grown with success on many private estates, the produce realizing as much as seventy florins (5*l.* 16*s.*) per picol.[2] All the plantations were in excellent condition, with the exception of the chinchona, which looked sickly on account of the heat. At Sindanglaya, however, some twenty miles inland, lying at a considerable altitude, beyond the great Magamendu Pass, I subsequently saw a thriving plantation: the temperature there is much lower than on the sea-coast.

Among the more remarkable specimens of exotic plants growing at the Experimental Gardens at Buitenzorg were a number of eucalypti, the produce of seeds obtained from Timor. Although seedlings only two years old, these trees had already attained the height of twenty feet. Much good is anticipated from the introduction of these trees, on account of their power of absorbing or counteracting malaria, and it is proposed to make large plantations of them at the less salubrious settlements in the Dutch East Indies.

During my stay at Buitenzorg I made the acquaintance of Raden Saleh, the princely Javanese artist, whose reputation as a painter is greater even in Europe than in his native country. The pleasant impressions which I have retained of my interviews with this true nature's painter have been intensified by the melancholy intelligence

[2] One picol = 136 lbs. avoirdupois.

of his death, which I received soon after my return to Europe. Raden Saleh was born in Samarang in 1814. He visited Europe in order to complete his studies, receiving his early education in Holland, but developing his taste for art under the influence of the galleries of Dresden. There he met several German notabilities, with whom he remained all his life on terms of friendship. His reminiscences of European life and habits of thought made a strong impression on his character, and, on the foundation of the superstitious nature of his race, raised the superstructure of the curious beliefs which he maintained and gave expression to in after-life.

When I saw him he was plainly dressed in Javanese style, with a loose green-and-black-striped silk jacket, a dark coloured sarong,[3] and a detta or turban on his head. The features were strongly marked—*markirte züge*, as the Germans would say—the eyes full of vivacity, and the forehead not so flat as in the Javanese generally, but more rounded: as he remarked of himself, "there is Arabian blood in me." Speaking with a certain force, he entered freely into conversation, and talked without reserve of his life, his tastes, his religious feelings. "Europe," he exclaimed, "is for me a heaven on earth." For the Dutch he had a great admiration, intensified, as he was honest enough to admit, by the grant of a pension of five hundred florins a month—"and I do nothing for it." He thought no people were better calculated than the Dutch to govern Java and the Javanese, who were happy under their *régime*—an opinion in which all acquainted with Dutch character and politics and the history of the Dutch settlements in the East will coincide.

The Javanese, as is well-known, are born gamblers; no event is too trivial or too important to excite their gambling propensities; but Raden Saleh hated their gambling as he hated their custom of nose-rubbing in salutations. His European education had taught him to prefer the Western custom of kissing—especially where a lady was concerned—to the native habit of bringing two noses into contact, and keeping opposite lips two nose-lengths apart!

[3] A coloured cloth fastened round the waist, forming a sort of petticoat, almost universally worn by both Malays and Dyaks.

Turning to the Bible and religious belief, he said, "There is no paper manufacture in heaven! My thoughts are quite at variance with the doctrines of the native priests. I don't agree with them. When we die, God does not ask our religion, but what we have done. Still I despise no religion. Sects," he continued, "in religion are the result of different tastes among different people. When I shake hands with a monarch my touch is cold, but with all respect due to his position. When I shake hands with a beggar, I feel in my heart his poor estate, considering we are all alike before God, that we are all God's servants." He said he had influence with the Javanese on account of his "humanity." "When I die," he uttered with a loud voice and a smile upon his face, "there will never be another Raden Saleh—no, never."

The heart of this prince, painter, and philosopher was certainly in his art studies. He showed me many of his pictures, which displayed great talent, and wonderful skill in the expression of truthful feeling.

He was then engaged on a portrait of the Governor-General, for the official residence at Batavia, but his best efforts were in hunting scenes, although he had a passionate taste for natural scenery. "When I see a beautiful landscape," he said, "I ponder over it, and admire it more than the interior of the most magnificent cathedral, because the landscape was made by the Creator Himself." He had presented many of his paintings to European sovereigns, from several of whom he had received decorations. He was especially proud of an autograph letter from the Emperor of Germany, in which that venerable monarch thanked him in flattering terms for a picture from his brush, at the same time conferring upon him the Crown Order of the second class.

Alas for frank, genial, simple, albeit vain and dogmatic Saleh! He probably never wilfully did anybody any harm, and, if his name is not connected with any very distinguished achievement, he at least did much to foster the love of the beautiful among his fellow-countrymen, and assisted by his example and enthusiasm in making known the grandeur of the scenery of his native land. Java is highly favoured by nature with a profusion of all that tends to make the gorgeousness of tropical landscapes: mountains and valleys, rivers and waterfalls, tall trees and many-coloured flowers and shrubs with foliage of infinite variety; and Raden Saleh's pencil could convey the colour and spirit of these with remarkable fidelity.

He leaves behind him a charming young widow, a Javanese princess, daughter of the Sultan of Djokja.

On the 20th June I left Batavia for Soerabaija in the S.S. "Prins Alexander." Amongst the passengers was Mr. James Waddell, Superintendent Engineer to the large fleet of the Nederland Indian Steamship Company, whose memory will always be endeared to me by the recollection of his great hospitality, and of many acts of kindness which he showed to me during my stay in Soerabaija.

The voyage past the beautiful volcanic shores of the island of Java was full of interest, the scenery along the coast being very grand. At Samarang we had the opportunity of landing, the vessel staying there for twenty-four hours, which, however, we were unable to turn to much advantage in sight-seeing, as heavy rain began to fall as we landed, and the views inland were obscured by thick mist. Next day, however, we had a fine view of Smero, an active volcano, and the highest mountain in Java, 12,500 feet above the level of the sea.

On the 24th the steamer dropped anchor in the roads of Soerabaija. I passed the first night as the guest of Mr. Waddell, at his residence at Gedong Doro; and the next day, at the invitation of Mr. Connington, I went to Priggen, a favourite resort on the slope of the Arjoeno mountain, thirty-two miles from the port. There is a railway for twenty miles of the distance, passing through flat, uninteresting, but fertile country, devoted to rice-fields and sugar-plantations, with here and there large sugar-mills, indicating the progress which this industry has made in the country. The next stage of the journey had to be performed in a dog-cart, driven in Javanese style, *i.e.* at full gallop; the driving of the Javanese is like the driving of Jehu, the son of Nimshi, for they drive furiously. The six miles were covered in half an hour; and then, as the ground began rapidly to rise, we exchanged the chariot for nimble, but sure-footed ponies, by whose help we accomplished the remainder of our journey in little more than an hour. From the hill-side a splendid view was obtained of the rich alluvial plain over which we had just passed, with the sea beyond, out of which rose the rich, undulating island of Madoera.

The altitude of the settlement of Priggen is about 1700 feet; the climate is bracing and healthy, affording a pleasant retreat from the enervating effects of the high temperature and moist air of the low-lying shores. Near Priggen is an interesting cascade, of no great width, but falling 150 feet in perpendicular height, without a break.

Having seen the sights of this pleasant place, I returned to the town to have an audience of the Regent of Soerabaija, Raden Adi Patti Pandjie Tjokro Negoro, and solicit the favour of letters of introduction to the Sultan of Koetei, to whose son his eldest daughter is married.

On arriving at the Residency, three doors leading out on to the spacious verandah were opened, and I was ushered into a large, marble-paved saloon, handsomely furnished in European style. Presently the Regent entered, and the Controlleur, Mr. Van Meverden, who accompanied me as the representative of the Dutch Government, introduced me to him. He is a man of about forty years of age, handsome, and with quite European manners. I told him the object of my visit, and he said he would be glad to give letters of introduction to the Sultan of Koetei, as well as to his son-in-law, and would send them to-morrow. During the conversation two of his sons came in. One, a lad of perhaps eighteen, who conversed fluently in English, had been three years near Manchester, and had only lately returned. The other was a charming, handsome, lively little boy of eight summers, whose beauty was enhanced by his fair complexion, which was very light for a Javanese. He spoke Dutch, and entered into conversation with natural grace and freedom, his large, luminous eyes beaming with delight as he mounted a diminutive pony, no bigger than a Newfoundland dog, which was brought into the saloon for our edification.

The Regent receives a salary from the Dutch Government of 1200 florins (100*l.*) a month, besides certain percentages on coffee, with a free residence, and exemption from taxes. Still he complained that his allowance was not enough, for, like all natives of high rank in Java, he had a great entourage to support. Besides paid servants and courtiers, a large circle of relations made a heavy call upon him. Not only had he his "mother and his sisters, and his cousins and his aunts" to provide for, as well as sisters-in-law by the dozen, and half-cousins by the score; but he had to maintain a numerous array of wives, with their children. The two sons just referred to had fourteen brothers and sisters, or half-brothers and sisters.

Under the guidance of Mr. Waddell I had excellent opportunities of seeing all the sights of Soerabaija, for, notwithstanding the muddy state of the kampongs, or native quarters, he insisted on accompanying me to every point of interest. The principal industry among the women is the making of coloured prints, called Battikken. Seated on a low footstool, with a small fire by their side, on which is placed a pot containing wax, the women hold before them a large square frame or stretcher, resting on four wheels, which serves as an easel for a piece of unbleached calico. On this material the artist draws imaginary designs in endless variety—not with pencil or brush, but with a curious instrument consisting of a tiny copper pot or vessel, fitted on one side with a fine, sharp-pointed tube, and on the other with a straight handle. The pot or reservoir being filled with wax, this curious drawing instrument is placed on the fire till the contents are melted, when a design is drawn on the sheet of calico with the point of the tube, from which runs the melted wax, hardening as it touches the cloth. When the design is complete, the cloth is put into a tub of dye, those parts to which the wax adheres not taking the colour, while the rest of the fabric is dyed to the desired tint.

If it is desired to have several colours in the cloth, portions of the wax are removed from time to time, according to the pattern, and the cloth dipped in different dyes, care being taken to protect each time with a coating of wax all those parts which have been already dyed, or which have to be dipped in a different colour. The effect of the cloths thus treated is very pretty, many of the designs being both quaint in idea and clever in execution.

As in almost every other native industry, whether in the East or the West, imitation is going on in this branch too. The European merchants employ Chinamen to draw the Javanese patterns on paper, and these are forwarded to Manchester or Switzerland, to be reproduced on the cloth by machinery, thousands of yards at a time. The difference between the hand-drawn and the machine-made cloths is easily distinguished. The native work is rougher, and the artistic effect better; but the best way is to smell the cloth, for the waxy scent never seems to leave the real battiks, however often they are washed. The greater cheapness of the machine-made article has not so far ruined this national industry, for all the better classes of Javanese, as well as Europeans, prefer to buy native cloth, although it is considerably dearer. I have seen battikken used for sarongs sold for twenty-five or thirty florins, which, in a stranger's eyes, would hardly look worth one tenth of that price.

In another kampong nothing but pottery and bricks were being manufactured. As every European house has a collection of plants, flower-pots have a ready sale. The native pottery work is very brittle, and falls to pieces with a slight knock, owing to its not being burnt sufficiently long, and to the fires not being hot enough. Still the natives, like more civilized and "skilled" workmen nearer home, see the advantage of not making their pottery-ware too strong, for were the pots to last too long it would not be "good for trade."

The girls, women, and children powder their faces with rice powder (*poudre de riz*), not merely for the sake of beautifying themselves, but to prevent perspiration by artificially closing the pores of the skin with the powder. European ladies who are addicted to the free use of powder, and who doubt this effect of the practice, should see the faces of the powdered Javanese women. On the fair skin of a European the presence of powder, clogging the minute openings in the skin, is not noticed; but on the yellowish-brown ground of a Javanese woman's face the snow-white specks of powder are easily distinguishable. The effect is very curious, and reminded me of the ochred and powdered face of a clown in a circus.

One evening I went in company with the Whodono (the officer next in rank to the Regent) to hear and see a *gamallang* and *tandak,* that is, a native music-band and dancers. During my travels in Sumatra I had occasion to see many dancers—who were all men, as the Malay women never dance. Here, however, in Java, both sexes join in the pastime. The performance took place under a covered "tent." The poles supporting the roof, which consisted of a stuffed mattress, were painted white with red stripes, and the sides of the tent were of calico similarly striped. The band consisted of twenty-four performers, the instruments comprising drums, fiddles, tom-toms, cymbals, harmonicons, &c. The "guests," who, by the way, had to pay for the invitation, numbered about fifty. There was a slightly raised platform occupied by the dancers and musicians; the first dancer was a girl, dressed in a red-striped sarong and a violet *slendang* or shawl across the right shoulder, with natural flowers in her hair, scented like jasmine, gold bangles round her arms, several diamond rings ornamenting her tiny fingers, and diamond earrings; a broad silver belt to uphold the sarong, completed the list of her ornaments. The girl threw herself into different attitudes, and the dancing was rather a series of gesticulations than the graceful bodily movements which Europeans associate with the name. She took a red shawl and twisted it round her waist and arms, occasionally chanting a few words, and sometimes covering her face up to the eyes with the shawl. The greater part of the performance, however, consisted of merely twisting her fingers and hands in such positions as to make them appear out of joint. The dance was supposed to represent some tragical history; after the girl had finished her act, three others came on dressed in a similar fashion, and they were presently joined by two men. The gesticulations were the same as before, with the difference that, several glasses of gin-and-bitters having been served to the performers, they now began to shout louder, and gesticulate more violently; eventually the two men kissed, *à la Javanaise*, the two female dancers. As the Whodono told me that if we stayed longer we should be compelled to dance, I thought the best thing we could do was to depart at this stage of the performance.

Here, as everywhere else in the East, the Chinamen are numerous and form the great majority of the business people. I bought some additional goods for my journey, especially a quantity of beads and buttons for the Dyaks, at the Chinese *tokos* (stores), and found every article much cheaper than in any European shop; the Chinaman's principle seems to be "small profits and quick returns." His staff is cheaper, and his living far less expensive than is the case with the European traders. John Chinaman's dress again is very inexpensive:—a white loose jacket, a pair of wide dark-coloured trousers, both of some thin material, and a pair of felt shoes. Near the harbour are immense fish-ponds belonging to Chinamen, the produce of which forms a considerable portion of their diet. The greatest luxury a Chinaman has is a fine carriage and pair of good horses; the handsomest turnouts in Soerabaija belong to the wealthy Chinamen. Their houses are nicely furnished, grotesque to the European eye, it is true, though the Oriental style seems to be at the height of fashion in England just now.

There are many Chinese cemeteries in Soerabaija, irregularly scattered in and about the town, and covering a large area of land. The Chinese display the deepest veneration for the dead, and each departed Celestial is allotted a very large space of ground to rest in. The Chinamen are the principal source of profit to the Dutch Government, as they are the opium farmers. The contractor for Soerabaija Residency has to pay 1000 florins (90*l.*) per day to the Government, while in Kediri the enormous rental of 80,000 florins a month is paid for the monopoly of this trade.

The "Schout" or Superintendent of Police, to whom I applied for some servants to accompany me to Borneo, succeeded in engaging three lads, good wages and three months' advance being the best terms on which their services could be secured: and on Thursday morning, 3rd July, I left Soerabaija in the steamer "Baron Mackay," for Macassar. Up to the last moment I was in trepidation lest Ali, Sariman, and Siden should fail to appear on board at the time of starting, for it is a common occurrence for servants who have secured an advance to run away, and indulge their native propensity for gambling with the money;

when once they have disappeared in any of the dessa (villages), there is no chance of getting them back. I was fortunate, however, in this respect, and my three attendants came on board together just as I was giving up all hope of seeing them.

The following day we arrived at Bali Bolélèng, the chief port of Bali Island. The steamer anchored close to the shore, and I took the opportunity of landing to examine the place. The town is situated close to a small river or creek: the great bulk of the houses are low dirty structures of mud and brick; black pigs, goats, and dogs run about the streets, and have free *entrée* to the houses, where they seem just as much at home as the Irishman's proverbial lodger. The women do all the trading. Their dress consists merely of a sarong fastened round the waist. The coiffure is the same as in Java and Sumatra, the hair being allowed to grow to its full length, and twisted round in a knot. The chief cultivation is rice and coffee, the latter of inferior quality, and worth only from twenty-five to thirty florins the picol. I saw a number of men coming into town, leading ponies laden with rice, with women, young and old, following, carrying on their heads baskets containing coffee.

Close to the town was a curious Balinese temple, merely a square enclosure surrounded by a red brick wall, falling into ruins. Entering through a high narrow gateway, the arch of which was carved with rough designs of various animal forms, I observed in the centre of the opposite wall a structure consisting of a shed with an attap roof supported by two carved tigers, and a red brick floor. This was the high altar, and on each side of this "altar" were a number of smaller ones. In the middle of the square stood an old tree, the "Varingin" (*ficus religiosa*), sacred to the Balinese; a little to the left was a large pool of muddy water. The majority of the population in the island profess the Hindoo religion, but there are many curious customs in Bali connected with their religious rites which have been grafted on to the original ceremonies. The people have an ancient literature, and a calendar of their own with thirty-five days to the month, and but six months to the year; though some Balinese assert that this period comprises only half a year. Again, the year is divided into thirty *woekoes* or weeks of seven days, and the day and night are divided into eight hours each, reckoning from sunrise to sunset and from sunset to sunrise respectively. Tigers and wild cattle are plentiful in the island; the latter keep up in the hills, but the former are often shot from boats, when, towards sunset, they come down to the river-side to drink.

The captain bought a few black pigs and a couple of cows before we left. The cattle are a small breed, and cost from 18 to 20 florins (nearly 2*l.*) a head, but form an article of export. The pigs cost 4 dollars (16*s.*) each, a price certainly out of all proportion to that of the cattle. As the pigs were being tied together, their squealing protestations brought down their late associates, who manifested a wonderful affection, and not only showed their sympathy by joining in chorus, but actually followed the coolies who carried the pigs down to the water's edge. When their comrades were in the boat, they quietly turned round, and went back unconcernedly to their homes.

The steamer left in the evening, and arrived at Macassar on Sunday, 6th of July.

CHAPTER II.

Macassar—Its markets and produce—Abnormal nail-growth—Troublesome servants—A visit to Ghoa—A sporting Rajah—Deserters—A cruise along Celebes shores—A slave nest—Fast on a mudbank—Custom-house officers at Pelaroeng—Arrival at Samarinda—My Chinese host—Undesirable neighbours—The Living associate with the Dead—Floating houses—Important officials—Turtle eggs—A Chinese bill of fare—Tame orang utans.

MACASSAR is one of the oldest and most important commercial settlements in the East Indies. The town, built on a large plain, is divided into three parts, called "Kampong Baroe" (the new village), "Kampong Malajoe" (the Malay village), and "Kampong Boegis" (the Boegis village). In the first, which is the European settlement, the streets are broad and straight, crossing each other at right angles, and lined with fine avenues of trees. On the seaward side the town is defended by the Fort Rotterdam, outside which and running parallel with the beach are a number of bamboo huts, whose occupants I was informed all get a living by fishing. Nowhere in the East have I seen such a vast quantity and strange variety of fish as were in the market at Macassar. There were dozens of different kinds, of all shapes, and sizes, and colours. A large export trade is done in dried, smoked, and salted fish. A small fish (a species of *Engraulis*) is prepared somewhat like anchovies, and exported in large quantities under the name of *red fish*. It makes one of the many different agreeable ingredients in the popular dish of rice and curry. The natives also consume locally a large quantity of fish, sometimes "fresh," but more often in a putrid state.

The principal street, where all the warehouses and shops are situated, runs along the beach for more than two miles. Beginning at the southern end are a row of white-washed brick stores, mostly belonging to Chinese traders. Spread out in front of the premises in nearly every case are many hundredweight of *tre-pang*, or *bêche-de-mer* (*Holothuria*, sea-slug), which are being dried in the sun previous to shipment. By degrees the brick houses give place to rudely constructed bamboo sheds or huts, occupied by Boegis, *i. e.* natives of Celebes, most of whom are traders, chiefly dealing in the daily necessaries—rice, fish, fruit, and fowls. Bird-fanciers' shops are not wanting, in which large assortments of talking parrots are offered for sale; and at short distances apart are open shops or workrooms, in which women may be seen weaving the well-known Macassar cloths. Towards the northern end of the street a large boat-building industry is carried on, where vessels of considerable size and of curious shapes are constructed by the native workmen, such as "*prahoe betri-pangs*" (for the trepang fisheries), "*padoeakans*," "*sampangs*," and others, all bearing different names, and designed for special services.

I noticed several peculiarities amongst the Boegis women; one very common practice is to let the nail on the left thumb grow to an abnormal length, over one inch beyond the tip. This incon-venient growth is considered an ornament, and is protected by a neatly-plaited cover, called "*sarong koekoe*."[1] The women also shave the hair from the forehead when it grows too low, and covers the forehead too much; and they paint the eye-lashes and eye-brows black.

The day after my arrival I paid an official visit to the Governor, Mr. Tromp, to hand him my letter of introduction, and consult him about my journey to Koetei. He did not think the zoological results would be rich, and he laid great stress on the drought which had visited both the east coast of Borneo and Celebes during the year 1877-8. As for making the overland journey to Band-jermasin, he smiled at the idea, and did not think it possible, the natives in the interior of Koetei being dangerous and hostile. Mr. Tromp kindly furnished me with a letter of introduction to the Sultan of Koetei.

Here I already began to have some trouble with the three

[1] *Sarong* = cover : *koekoe* = nail.

servants I had engaged at Soerabaija. Two of them came to me and asked for money, a request which I thought very unreasonable, as only a week ago I had given them three months' advance. They said they had given their wives nearly all the money, with the exception of some with which clothes had been bought. Knowing the gambling propensities of the Javanese, I refused to give them any more, but offered to buy for them anything they wanted. They did not seem very pleased with this proposal, but asked me to buy some tobacco for them. I engaged here—also under three months' advance of wages—a Boegis lad, named Laban, who turned out to be the most dirty, lazy, cowardly, and troublesome fellow I ever came across.

While staying in Macassar I had the opportunity of paying a visit, accompanied by the Assistant Resident, Mr. Bensbach, to the Rajah of Ghoa, whose territory begins only half an hour's drive from the town. The short journey was performed in grand style, for Mr. Tromp very kindly placed at our disposal his four-in-hand, which the brave little native horses rolled along as if coaches were of every day occurrence in Celebes. The Rajah is reputed to be worth eight and a half million guilders (about 700,000*l.*), all of which are popularly believed to be stored in hard cash in his palace. His fortune has been chiefly amassed by a monopoly of the coffee trade in his territory. He buys the produce at from fifteen to twenty florins per picol, and sells it again to the Macassar merchants at a profit of about 100 per cent. But neither "Rajah" nor "Palace" bore out in appearance the reputation of wealth or grandeur. The palace was a large bamboo structure, elevated, like the rest of the native dwellings, on posts, some ten or twelve feet above the ground. The owner was a feeble-looking old man, whose beauty was entirely spoiled by the protruding lower lip, which was bulged out of all shape by the long-continued habit—practised, perhaps, during at least fifty of the sixty-two years of his life—of packing his "quid," when sirih-chewing, in front of his teeth. The old man was evidently very ill, and spoke in a very low tone of voice; so that, as he was a little deaf into the bargain, conversation was not very easily carried on. After the usual introductions we were asked to be seated, and the Rajah, in deference to the custom of his white visitors, elevated himself on a chair, on which he sat cross legged, instead of taking his usual seat on the floor.

The aspect of the audience-chamber and its occupants was picturesque, if ludicrous. On one side of a table sat the old Rajah, perched on his chair, clothed in blue striped sarong and loose jacket, with a pretty cap on his head, neatly woven of various fibres and fitted with a rim of gold. The Crown Prince and half-a-dozen other princes, wearing a similar cap or coronet, with a sarong round the waist and a kris, or dagger, attached, but the rest of the body bare, squatted on the floor, each with his large silver-gilt sirih-box, and a huge brass spittoon in their midst; here, there, and everywhere, flitting about like brown butterflies, were a swarm of naked children, while through an open door could be seen a number of women, mostly slaves, some of whom presently came forward to hand round coffee and cakes. Against the wall facing the entrance stood what I at first took for a "throne," but which Mr. Bensbach subsequently explained was a bedstead, specially erected in honour of one of the Rajah's daughters, who had lately been married. The bedstead was covered with red cloth; on the vallance in front were painted two crocodiles, between which was the representation of a crowned being. The tester, or canopy, was supported by eight bamboos. On the bed itself were no less than eight short pillows, and one long one—known familiarly to all travellers in the East under the name of a "Dutch wife." On a large baulk of timber supporting the roof were hung a number of stags' horns, trophies of the chase in the Rajah's deer forest. One of his favourite amusements is deer-stalking; all Boegis are fond of hunting the deer on horseback; they are splendid horsemen. Speaking of hunting, his Highness said he remembered Mr. Wallace, who went out deer hunting one day with him. Along one side of the room was a long row of wicker covers, or cages, under each of which stood a fighting-cock, keeping up a continual chorus. These birds are another indication of the sporting proclivities of the old Rajah and his sons. The principal cock-fights take place on Sundays, and he was very anxious that I should pay him a visit on the next Sunday, when I should be able to select a bird, and bet on its chance of success.

On the 14th July I left Macassar in the steamer "Karang,"

Capt. Steurs, for Samarinda, minus two of my men, Ali and Siden, who had at last taken it into their heads that their skulls were too valuable to risk among the bloodthirsty Dyaks of Borneo. Sariman, the only one of the trio I had engaged in Soerabaija who remained true to me, told me of their intended desertion, but not till just as the steamer was starting, when it was too late to do more than send a polite note to the chief constable, recommending the runaways to his particular attention.

The weather was lovely ; not a breath of wind ruffled the surface of the ocean as the steamer kept its course close along the shores of Celebes, of whose mountain-range a splendid view was afforded.

At Paré Paré we stayed for an hour, and the vessel was at once surrounded by a numerous fleet of native canoes, laden with cocoa nuts and bananas.

This is a regular slave nest. Good-looking young girls fetch from twenty to fifty guilders each. I went ashore in a canoe, and paid my respects to the Rajah, a mild-looking man over seventy years of age, who lived in a miserable bamboo structure, by courtesy styled a palace. He was ill, but received me in audience, and I found him supported on cushions, with an old wife of his, poulticing his forehead with some green clay-like mixture. The old Rajah was not equal to talking much, and when I asked for specimens of native workmanship, he called a number of women out of their seclusion, who brought neatly-made boxes of coloured straw, plaited into regular patterns. Some of these I bought for a dollar apiece, and a drawing of one is given in Plate 20, Fig. 5. While bargaining with the men for some *toemba* (lances) and knives, I was warned by the bell of the steamer that it was time to depart. On getting on board I found as fellow-passengers some forty or fifty Boegis traders, all with a quantity of their famous cloth which they were taking to Koetei for sale.

The next day was passed in slowly steaming towards the coast of Borneo. On the 16th we sighted Koetei, and soon afterwards entered the delta of the river Mahakkam, its low-lying banks thickly clothed with forests. Navigation was difficult owing to the multitude of shifting channels, and at times we came so close in shore that the great leaves of the nipa palms brushed us as we passed. Incessantly were the captain's orders, uttered and passed from mouth to mouth in Malay, changed as the vessel was turned now to the right, now to the left. Keenly was the look-out kept for possible shoals ahead; but, notwithstanding all precautions, about midday, just as we were within hail of our destination, Pelaroeng, the steamer went softly, quietly, but fast into a mud bank. All efforts to get her off were in vain, and we had to wait till Nature, the all-powerful goddess, came to our assistance in the person of the Flood-tide. Eventually, after four hours' delay, the vessel was lifted from the bed of mud, and in a few minutes we were off Pelaroeng.

As soon as the anchor was down a large prau with covered cabin came alongside, bringing the Sabandar or Harbour-Master, with several customs officers. Now began a general over-hauling of goods; bales of cloth were unpacked and carefully inspected by the zealous officials, who noted down their contents and the estimated value of the goods, together with the names of the owners, and demanded immediate payment of the ten per cent. import duty.

Fortunately I escaped this ordeal. My commission under the Dutch Government was sufficient to allow my goods to pass free. The captain advised me to proceed in the steamer to Samarinda, an hour further up the river, whither he was going in search of a cargo, and, as I had a letter of introduction to a Chinese merchant there, I decided to avail myself of his offer. The broad river was now nearly full, it being nearly high tide, and ten miles' run up stream was accomplished without incident.

Kwé Ké Hiang received me most cordially, storing my baggage in his warehouse, and telling me all the news of the place. Of Koetei, generally, he gave a very bad account. The Malays altogether were a pack of thieves, while the Boegis would occasionally enliven the proceedings by running a-muck generally after their custom; as for the interior, the Dyaks were perfect savages and inveterate Head-Hunters. Altogether the good Chinaman's narrative was forcible, and the picture he drew of the country graphic and interesting if not prepossessing; and on the first night of my visit to Koetei my ideas were not of a sort likely to foster the most pleasant dreams.

Samarinda, the chief trading-port of Koetei, is situated at the mouth of the Mahakkam, and occupies a considerable area on both banks of the river, which is here nearly a mile wide.

That portion of the town which lies on the right bank is inhabited by Boegis of whom a large settlement has existed here for many years; they are in great force here and have at their head a "kapitan" or chief, whose rank is officially recognized by the Sultan of Koetei. That potentate, indeed, through his agents, has induced a large number of Boegis to settle at Samarinda, and also in other parts of his territory, by promising greater advantages than they possess in their original home at Celebes, and every month sees a further influx of new arrivals. There is little doubt that the Boegis have been wise in their generation and chosen the better part in seeking the protection of the Sultan of Koetei, as they are much oppressed by the unreasonable taxes imposed by the Rajahs in their native country, and made the subjects of a harassing slave-trade, all the less endurable because surreptitiously carried on. I have spoken to many of these people but never yet heard one of them express a wish to return to Celebes. With their greater liberty and their annually increasing numbers they are, however, assuming too much power in Koetei, and, as they are a treacherous race, they will probably one day turn round and bite the hand that has fed them. Indeed they have already made an attempt to gain the upper hand at Samarinda, and for a time established a semi-independence, refusing to admit the authority of the Sultan and his Government. They are, however, apparently acquiescent in the present state of affairs, being permitted the administration of their own local laws called "Towadjoe."

The Boegis have an ugly habit of suddenly giving way to an uncontrollable fit of rabid fury, known as "amok," generally prompted by jealousy. If one of these amiable people is put out by any little domestic difficulty, or by any other cause, he is seized with the "amok" fever. "Running-a-muck" is the nearest English equivalent (curiously enough, as similar in sound as in meaning) for the native term. Friend or foe, man or woman, old or young, it makes little difference to the apparently demented savage whom he may meet. He will furiously attack without the slightest provocation and without discrimination whosoever crosses his path, and woe betide the unfortunate beings among whom a Boegis takes it into his head to "run-a-muck." Armed with fine krisses stuck in their waist-cloths, these Boegis are ugly customers to meet even on the best of terms; but, when "amok," they will kill or wound perhaps twenty or thirty people before they are secured, disarmed, or killed. In Macassar and other large towns the native police are armed with a long, two-pronged fork of bamboo, something like the humble "clothes-prop;" and when they see an "amok" Boegis, they place the fork against his throat, and hold him at bay till he can be secured. The tragic scene assumes a ludicrous aspect, when the frantic savage is seen firmly pinned by the neck against a wall or tree, vainly endeavouring to release his head from the uncomfortable position, or being ignominiously forced along the street by an active policeman, skilled in the use of this bloodless weapon of defence.

A few, very few, Koetei Malays, and not more than a dozen Chinamen, and two or three Klings are found settled among these very unneighbourly neighbours. On the left bank of the river the bulk of the Koetei people, and the Chinese merchants, of whom there are about a hundred, are settled. None of these ever think of venturing across the river after dusk without being well armed —the Malay with his mandau, the Chinaman with his revolver. The two towns have between them a population of some 10,000, or exactly twice as many inhabitants as when Mr. H. Von Dewall visited the place in 1846.[2]

Samarinda itself has not the appearance which might be expected of so important a settlement. The entry I made in my diary at the time was that "This is the most miserable place I have ever seen; the natives and their buildings correspond in squalor." The buildings are mostly bamboo structures, with an "attap" cover or roof—most wretched habitations. Here and there are a few wood-built edifices, so few, however, that their rare occurrence only serves to increase the miserable appearance of the surrounding dwellings. The sense of oppression caused by the poverty-stricken look of the place, is increased by the fact that the living

[2] *Indisch Archief.* 1849.

here seem to associate with the dead. The dwellings are everywhere surrounded by tombs. Although there is plenty of land available for the purpose of a burial-ground, the Malays do not trouble themselves to consecrate a piece of ground, according to the Mohammedan principles which they profess, for the purpose of depositing the remains of the departed, but dig a hole anywhere, and hurry the dead ones under the soil without ceremony, or apparent regard for sentiment, and certainly in defiance of all sanitary laws. The houses are all—even the most ricketty—raised on bamboo posts, the floor being at a height of eight or ten feet from the ground, which is perhaps some compensation for their undesirable position among the tombs. In plate 1, figure 2, is shown one of the better class of ordinary dwelling houses, with the tombstones dotted around.

Besides these land habitations, many of the people dwell in huts built on rafts floating on the water, and anchored by means of rattan ropes to the shore. Communication from one point to another is maintained by praus, and every one has one or more of these handy craft. There are literally no roads or paths of any description, the houses are nearly all crowded down to the water's edge, and there seems to be no reason for inland communication. The people grow a very little rice, but depend upon trade for nearly all their supplies. I managed to follow a muddy channel, which did duty for a path, for some little distance behind the row of houses next the shore, but saw nothing to indicate the existence of any traffic inland. A few children were playing about, but ran away to hide the moment they perceived a stranger approaching. The women, a few of whom were engaged in pounding rice with wooden pestle and mortar, did the same, rising hurriedly from their work and going indoors as if they took me for the ghost of one of their departed neighbours from the surrounding tombs.

Amid all this squalor, there are one or two pretentious buildings. The Sultan's palace, for instance—a large, white-painted structure, with a galvanized iron roof—has the very uncommon feature of two storeys, and a verandah upstairs. It is, however, seldom occupied by the Sultan, who has no taste for living in too close proximity to his Boegis subjects, and is consequently in a rather dilapidated condition. As a symbol of authority, there stand in front of the palace a dozen dismounted, rusty guns and mortars, dating from the last century.

The residence of the Governor of the town, the Pangeran Bandahara, is a really well-appointed, comfortable house, furnished throughout in European style. This "Prince" may be termed the Sultan's Minister for Foreign Affairs. A shrewd, clever man, tall and slightly built, with a very intelligent face which proclaims his Arabian descent, Bandahara has great influence over the natives. The Assistant Resident told me he was the only official that was not afraid of the Sultan, who generally left to him the settlement of any difficult question, such, for instance, as the treatment of the Boegis.

Next in importance to Bandahara is the Sabandar, or harbour-master, whose duty it is to collect the import and export duties on all merchandise entering and leaving the port. The post is a lucrative one—(consider the opportunities it offers for the giving and receiving of bribes!)—but the present Sabandar, like any other official, holds it on the favour of his master, with whom he has more than once been in disgrace. The last dispute was about one of the Sabandar's wives, whom the Sultan took a fancy to, and induced to go with him to Tangaroeng. The Sabandar had words with his Highness over this little matter, and was dismissed; but through the good offices of the Assistant Resident he was lucky enough not only to be reinstated in his post, but to have his wife returned to his bosom.

Samarinda is the residence of the Imam, or upper priest, who has established here a school, where the children are taught writing in Arabic characters, and instructed in the tenets of the Koran. He has charge of all ecclesiastical matters in the kingdom, and receives an annual income from the Sultan.

The commerce of Samarinda is very considerable. Every one is a trader, even the Pangerans and the Hadjis.[3] Here, as everywhere, John Chinaman musters in great force, and the greater part of the export trade is in his hands. At the time of my arrival there were

[3] Those who have performed the pilgrimage to Mecca.

five vessels—three of them barques of considerable size—all belonging to Chinamen, being loaded with the produce of the country, which is brought down the river on long rafts. Rattan is the staple product; but gutta-percha, timber, beeswax, and edible birds' nests (*Sarong boeroeng*) from the interior, and trepang, tortoise-shell, and turtle eggs from the coast, are also exported in considerable quantities.

The Badjoes, or coast Malays, are principally engaged in the fishing industries; and are very clever in finding the "nests" of the turtles in the sand, from a single one of which sometimes as many as a hundred eggs may be taken. These were recommended to me as a great luxury, but I was prejudiced, perhaps, by the leathery-looking shells, reminding one of large snakes' eggs, and found the flavour to resemble that of dried, and very "strong" fish-roe.

The imports are rice, salt, opium, gambier, coffee, petroleum, coloured prints, white and black calico, iron and brass wire, and cocoa-nuts and cocoa-nut oil—the two last principally for Celebes.

There is at present only one European merchant in the place, and he complained very much of the dishonesty of the natives, and the loose methods of doing business generally among them; and of the absence of any law or authority to protect the foreigner. The natives always expect ready money for their produce, but demand long credit for all their own purchases. The "nobles" especially seem to have a particular fancy for rooting themselves deeply into the traders' books.

The country is, however, undoubtedly rich, and if the trade were protected by a regular administration, and some greater semblance to law and order, there is no doubt that a larger number of Europeans, and of Chinese especially, would be attracted to it, and develope its resources. The soil is everywhere fertile, the natural productions are abundant, and all that is wanted is greater honesty among the people, from the highest to the lowest, for the land to be able to support ten times its present population.

At the hospitable board of my Celestial friend, Kwé Ké Hiang, who had, for Samarinda, a very good wooden house and extensive warehouses, I was able to taste the various gastronomic luxuries of a well-to-do Chinaman. He used to complain that he could get nothing in "this dirty place," and that everything had to be ordered from Singapore or Soerabaija two or three months beforehand; but he kept an excellent Chinese cook, and I am sure that when he was grumbling he was only fishing for a compliment. The edible birds' nests soup I found excellent, and would recommend it as a nutritious food for delicate people. Somewhat similar was the chicken broth with *agar-agar*—a sort of seaweed. Rice curry was of course a standing dish. Fish, fresh, dried, salted, and—well, "high," was in abundance, and, cooked in various forms, generally (always excepting the high game) proved excellent. Delicious fried cray-fish and prawns formed a most appetizing *plat:* but the *pièce de résistance*, stewed cuttle-fish, was beyond my powers of appreciation.

Dear old Kwé Ké Hiang was a general favourite; and many a pleasant hour have I spent with him under the verandah in front of his house, as he sat smoking his opium-pipe. His friends and acquaintances, his customers and his clerks, would come in every day—several times a day indeed, especially about luncheon and dinner-time—and, with the excuse of having a chat, help themselves to the inevitable "bite" of gin and bitters.

Kwé Ké Hiang was very fond of animals, and had among other household pets a couple of large orang utans, male and female, which had been caught in the interior. The big male was in a consumption, and lay most of the day wrapped up in a blanket, his great frame shaken incessantly by a terrible cough, which soon carried him off. His mate, which Kwé Ké Hiang kindly presented to me, was apparently in good health, but on my return three months afterwards, she too had gone the way of all orangs.

The Malays of Samarinda catch the orangs near the small creeks and streams falling into the Mahakkam near the town. They told me that the animals only come to the banks early in the morning, returning during the day to the jungle. When they catch one alive they sell it for three dollars to the Chinese, who feed the animals first on fruit and afterwards on rice, but never succeed in inducing them to live long in confinement. The captive animals seem capable of little or no activity, sitting for an hour or longer in the same position, so still that they could be photographed with the greatest ease, then slowly turning on one side and sleeping with the arm under the head. Their eyes are very keen, and give them a very intellectual and human-like appearance. The remarkable listlessness of the orangs in captivity made me extremely anxious to see them in their native woods and jungles, but I was never fortunate to see a single orang utan alive or dead in any part of the interior, though the Dyaks of Long Wai said they were found further north and on the Teweh; I also heard that they were by no means rare in the Doesoen district, where they are called "keoe." It is only among the Malays that they are known as orang utan (literally "wild men"). Dr. Solomon Müller in his "Travels" says the natives have distinct names for the sexes; the male being called "Salamping," and the female "Boekoe."

CHAPTER III.

Unseaworthy craft—A forest solitude—Coal-mines—Fish and fisheries—The capital of Koetei—Sultan Mohamad Soleman Chaliphat oel Moeminin—An interview in the palace—A hideous idol—Princely treasures—A mania for diamonds—The Government of Koetei—Revenue—Financial abuses—Royal executioners—A much-married man—Cock-fighting—A cock-crowing contest—Funeral rites—A royal gambling hell.

On Sunday, July 20th, 1879, I started from Samarinda with two praus for Tangaroeng, a distance of thirty miles by river. The larger of the two vessels, twenty-five feet long, and hewn out of a single tree, was so well laden with provisions and other baggage that its ordinary crew of seven men had to be reinforced by my two personal followers before it could be safely trusted to stem the rapid current of the river Mahakkam. Thus loaded its gunwale was within a few inches of the water, and it seemed as if the slightest disturbance of its "trim" would be fatal to the success of its voyage: but the Malay boatmen had never heard of Mr. Plimsoll, and seemed to think more of the risks of a land journey than of any perils by water. It was, however, a long time before I got accustomed to travelling in the frail craft. The second prau, which was fitted with a covered cabin, was much smaller, and with its crew of five, and two passengers—for I was accompanied by my hospitable friend, Kwé Ké Hiang—appeared even more ready to founder on the slightest provocation than its companion. To me it was very irksome to be obliged to sit motionless for hours at a time, although to the Oriental constitution such a necessity appeared a luxury; I gradually, however, got accustomed to the position, as the little bark proved its buoyancy and stability, and was able to take note of the surrounding scenery. To avoid the strong current the praus were kept as close as possible to the shore, and, as both banks of the river were covered to the water's edge with forest, we frequently came into uncomfortable proximity to the overhanging branches of the trees, which, however, afforded a pleasant shade. Here and there a break in the forest revealed a patch of rice-field, and a little distance in the background a low range of wooded hills. Occasionally the stillness of the everlasting forest would be broken by the sound of a monkey sitting chattering at us for intruding on his privacy, or springing from branch to branch, startled by our sudden approach. Of the feathered tribe there was next to nothing to be seen, while in the water an occasional crocodile was the only visible sign of animal life.

At Batu Pangal, a short distance above Samarinda, however, we came to an unexpected symptom of future life and commercial activity, in the shape of a coal-mine, which is occasionally resorted to by Dutch steamers, but is worked principally for the purpose of supplying the steam yacht belonging to the Sultan of Koetei. The mine is not a hundred yards from the river, and if properly developed might prove a valuable property.

The soil along the banks of the river here appears to be rich and capable of easy and remunerative cultivation, but the land is practically uninhabited, and the whole distance between Samarinda and Tangaroeng there are not more than a couple of dozen small huts of most miserable appearance. The few settlers are Boegis, who cultivate *pisangs* (bananas), but depend chiefly upon fishing for the means of subsistence. The people everywhere in the east are fond of fish; whether owing to actual gastronomic preference, or because the capture of the finny prey is a matter involving less labour than the cultivation of the fields, or the hunting of animals and birds, I will not attempt to decide. It is certain, however, that in many parts of the East the demand for fish is so great, and the methods adopted for catching them with the least trouble so destructive—thousands of small fish being captured in a basket or a "net" made of a sheet of calico, from which the smallest fry cannot escape—that in the more populous districts this source of food supply is rapidly failing. The Mahakkam itself, however, swarms with fish, of which a large species of *silurus* is the commonest and most usually eaten. There are also delicious crayfish, gigantic freshwater shrimps, and turtles.

Between three and four in the afternoon we arrived at Tangaroeng—a second Samarinda, only on a smaller scale. The population is about 5000, all of them located on the right bank of the river, which is here over 1000 yards wide. There are three classes of habitations, as shown in Plate 2: those built on dry land, those built on the foreshore, where, at high tide, they are only a few inches above the level of the water; and those built on floating rafts in the river itself. The houses in the first two categories are erected on high posts. The place has the advantage over Samarinda in the fact that it can boast of a road, though a bad one, into the neighbouring country; but it surpasses the latter place, if possible, in filthiness. All the refuse from the houses—floating or not—is thrown on to the foreshore, where, as the river is tidal, it lies often for six or eight hours in the hot sun, quite long enough to evolve a most loathsome effluvium. This is increased by the quantity of stinking fish, salted eggs, also decidedly "high," dried fish, prawns, &c., not over fresh, and other savoury provisions offered for sale, alongside of fruits and sirih, and different kinds of cakes (*kwé kwé*). Most of the smaller houses are shops. The larger store-keepers deal in European manufactures, such as prints, iron-ware, &c., and in Chinese crockery and Boegis cloth. The houses are most of them dirty, both inside and outside, and round them may be seen, at all hours of the day, equally dirty children—whose brown skins fortunately (?) do not "show the dirt"—flying kites, or playing "heads and tails" with cents.

This is the capital town of Koetei, and the residence of his Highness the Sultan Mohamad Soleman Chaliphat oel Moeminin, one of the most intelligent rulers in the Malay archipelago.[1]

[1] According to Von Dewall,* Mohamad Soleman is descended from Maharadja Deewa Gong Sakhtie, who, in response to the continued supplication of one Panggawa Besar, residing in Koetei, came down from heaven to earth. Panggawa Besar had a number of children, grandchildren, and great-grandchildren, and was anxious to have a king to reign over them, and prayed to one of the gods to send a ruler who might

* "*Overzigt van het Rijk van Koetei.* 1846-7."

Immediately on landing at the ricketty structure which did duty for a pier or landing-stage I went in search of the Sultan, asking to be directed to the "Palace." I was shown a large, square, wooden building, approached through a long covered courtyard, with two openings for doorways, and covered with a corrugated galvanized iron roof. (See Plate 1.) A crowd of ill-looking Malays surrounded the premises, some of whom ushered me into what appeared to be the hall, or rather, perhaps, the reception-room. It was half an hour before any one came to receive me, and I had an opportunity of studying the architecture of the place. This Pandoppo, as it is called, looked for all the world like a Methodist chapel. It had large side galleries running along the whole length, and another facing the door over a raised platform; while part of the floor was occupied by subdivisions, or "rooms," resembling pews. A few lamps, suspended from the lofty roof, which was supported by massive pillars of iron-wood, completed the resemblance to a chapel. I looked in vain, however, for chairs or seats of any kind; and the side galleries were occupied, not by a congregation of worshippers, but by a number of fat-tailed sheep. In the left-hand corner, near the entrance, was a large wooden idol of hideous appearance. This figure is shown in Plate 27, Fig. 1, and gives a good idea of the prevailing style of carving adopted for idols among the Long Wahou Dyaks in the interior of the island of Borneo. These figures are not exactly idols, in the ordinary sense of the word, as they are not directly worshipped, although representing the religious beliefs of the Dyaks, and regarded with superstitious veneration;[2] they should, perhaps, rather be called talismans, as they are looked upon as charms to keep away evil spirits and ill-luck.

marry one of his children. Maharadja Deewa Gong Sakhtie consequently came and married Poetrie Karang Mélènesh. From this union have sprung all the rulers of Koetei, who at first assumed the title of "Ratoe;" then that of "Adjie" (a corruption of the word Rajah); later that of "Pangeran;" and for the last four generations that of "Sultan." Under the reign of Adjie di Méndirsa the Mohammedan religion was introduced into Koetei by an Arab named Tosan Toengkang Parangan—this name being derived, as the legend runs, from the fact of the Arab having come into the country riding on a Parangan (fish).

[2] *Vide infra*, p. 189.

Presently the eldest son of the Sultan, the Pangeran (Prince) Praboe, came in, and said the Sultan was at prayer, but would not keep me waiting much longer. Hardly had he spoken, when his Highness himself entered—a well-built man of gentlemanly bearing, about the middle height, and apparently about forty years of age.[3] A clean-shaved, fleshy, and rather heavy-looking face was set off by a pair of extraordinarily bright eyes, flashing like fire. The lips were parted by a pleasant smile as he advanced to greet me, and revealed a set of teeth as black as Whitby jet from betel chewing. He wore a semi-European costume of long black cloth coat, and black cotton trousers; and an ordinary Cashmere travelling-cap on his head completed his attire. Holding out his hand, he at once made me feel at home with him, and ordering chairs and table to be brought forward, he proceeded with a business-like air to read the letters of introduction which I presented to him. The one from the Governor of Macassar, Mr. Tromp, was sewn up in an orange silk cover, which was carefully cut open by one of the attendants, while his Highness read the epistle from his relative at Soerabaija. He seemed pleased with the contents of the letters, and when he had finished them he said in English, putting his right hand to his breast, "All right;" and then, shaking hands again with me, added,—

"Me do all; me do everyting for you."

Then, probably thinking it the proper thing to seal our incipient friendship by pouring out a libation in European fashion, he inquired, "Vat you like to drink?" mentioning by name a long list of beverages, from foaming champagne down to equally foaming, but more modest, seltzer-water. Knowing that the Sultan, like all Malays, was a "teetotaller," I thought it wise to suggest the last-named non-alcoholic drink, in which we could pledge each other. On the order being given accordingly, there was a general bustle among the servants, one of whom brought in a huge brass vessel, which he placed by the Sultan's side. The use of this curious addition to the ordinary drinking paraphernalia was soon made apparent, for the Sultan, instead of drinking the

[3] His Highness was born on 28th October, 1836. For an account of his *fête*, or birthday feast, which occurred during my stay in Koetei, see p. 97.

PANGERAN SOSROE. THE SULTAN OF KOETEI. PANGERAN SOKMAVIRO. MANTRIE KADATAN. PANGERAN PRABOE (Crown Prince).

seltzer, merely rinsed his mouth with it, ejecting it into the brass pot, and immediately filling his mouth again with sirih. His inveterate habit of betel-chewing did not tend to lessen the difficulty which I felt in understanding his remarks, when, having exhausted his small stock of English expressions, he relapsed into the Malay tongue. There were, he told me, "plenty of birds, plenty of insects; all I could wish for; also, just now, *banja soesa*" (plenty of trouble)—a favourite expression of his, for it was proverbial that he was always complaining of "trouble" of one kind or another. He had reason, just then, perhaps, for the remark, since he had lost his second son only a few days previously. He then questioned me about my proposed expedition into the Interior, and suddenly said he would go with me, for he was afraid to trust me alone among the Dyaks. At the close of a lengthened interview, he asked me to take up my quarters with his second surviving son, the Pangeran Sosro, the same one to whom I had a letter of introduction from the Regent of Soerabaija, to whose daughter he was married.

The Pangeran received me most kindly. His house, a neatly built structure in the grounds of the palace, was most tastefully decorated in light blue and gold, and furnished after the European style.

The Sultan, I found, had no accommodation for visitors, although he had plenty of room and a quantity of furniture stored in his warehouse. He has, in fact, a mania for collecting all kinds of miscellaneous objects, few, if any, of which he ever uses himself, though he takes delight in exhibiting them to visitors. He has such a rich and varied store that he could at any time open an exhibition of valuable, curious, and useful articles, which would attract much attention if shown in London. Among them I noticed several splendid silver tea and coffee services; glass and china services of an expensive description; valuable watches without number; many very valuable krisses both ancient and modern, and other articles of *virtu* that would set Wardour Street in a fever of excitement.

Jewellery generally, and especially diamonds, are his particular passion. Of the latter he has a splendid collection, whether for the number of specimens it contains, or for the size and variety of the stones, which range from the purest water to yellow, green, and grey-blue or black. The whole of these diamonds were found in Borneo. The Emperor of Siam, he told me, was anxious to buy them, and had sent an influential officer for the purpose of negotiating the sale. The Sultan is in a perpetual state of negotiation with merchants and others for the purchase of diamonds, and his passion for them has more than once involved him in difficulties. One large stone of the purest water, weighing fifty-five carats, he bought from the Dutch Indian Commercial Company, the directors of which gave him credit for the amount. The money, however, amounting to a very large sum, was not forthcoming, and after waiting for eighteen months they became impatient, and induced the Dutch Government to send a war-steamer up the Mahakkam to enforce payment. After some little trouble the money was paid, but it was generally understood that rather than open his money-chests, the Sultan disposed of large quantities of jewellery and other goods to Malay merchants and others, in order to "raise the wind."

The Sultan has six or eight Chinamen on his premises, goldsmiths by profession, who are employed making different gold and silver articles for him—mostly bracelets—studded with hundreds of diamonds. A few days after my arrival I saw a couple of bracelets, some earrings, and gold and silver tankards, which the Chinamen had just finished.

But the Sultan's time is not altogether taken up in business transactions of this nature. He has, on the one hand, to find time for more serious matters connected with the administration of his kingdom, and, on the other hand, for amusement pure and simple. His government is that of an absolute, or rather, despotic monarchy, and the Sultan's interpretation of his "administrative duties" is, that he should increase his revenue by all possible means. He is, however, of progressive principles, and has done much to make his province prosperous and contented. Chief among the many services he has rendered has been the suppression of the slave-trade. In this he met with much opposition from the Boegis population, though themselves the victims of slavery;

but he has so far succeeded that it is very rarely that a slave prau is successfully smuggled into his dominions.

His income is derived from three recognized sources: first, a duty of ten per cent. on all articles imported or exported; second, a monopoly of the salt and opium trade; and third, the produce of the coal-mines at Pelaroeng and Batu Pangal. The export duty is collected in a rough and ready manner by his financial officers stationed at different posts throughout the country, who simply take a tithe of all goods produced. Rattan is the staple article of trade, the value of which is very considerable. The monopoly of the salt and opium trade is also a source of considerable profit, both these revenues being farmed out for annual payments. The Sultan has no great scruple about breaking an agreement made with one contractor if he can afterwards get a better bid from another. An instance of this occurred at the time of my visit, when, the tender of one Chinaman having been duly accepted, the bargain was repudiated by the Sultan, who had subsequently received an offer of better terms from another Chinaman. The coal-mine at Batu Pangal, already referred to, and another at Pelaroeng, are the property of the Sultan, who employs over a hundred men, mostly convicts, as miners. The Dutch Government is his best customer, and a very considerable trade is done at the Pelaroeng mines. Besides these recognized official sources of revenue, the Sultan receives a considerable income from practising the business of a banker, or money-lender. He charges interest at the rate of twenty-four per cent. per annum, and always takes care to have good security. His gross annual income is generally estimated to amount to from 50,000 to 60,000 guilders (about 5000*l.*) per month. I once put the question plainly to him, and he stated that these figures were not quite high enough, adding that when he first came to the throne his income did not exceed 3000 guilders (under 300*l.*) per month.

Notwithstanding all these facts, his Highness is, I am sorry to have to state it, deficient in many of those virtues which facilitate the transaction of commercial business, and tend to national as well as personal progress and prosperity. Besides, he has many difficulties to contend with in the supineness of his officials, though many of them loyally support him; still he is apt to leave too much to his Pangerans, or "Raad," as he calls them, and they are his inferiors both intellectually and physically.

It must not be forgotten, again, that his subjects are still in a low state of civilization, and it will be a work of time to raise them in the scale of humanity.

The Sultan himself is a really well-informed man, and is fairly well acquainted with the different forms of government and the customs of the different European States. In the course of conversation with me he was very fond of asking questions about the different countries of Europe, their people, industries, &c., but above all he delighted in talking about "Men of the Times," such as Bismarck, Moltke, Garibaldi, Napoleon, and MacMahon. Of them, as well as of most of the crowned heads in Europe, he had photographs, including of course a good stock of the King of Holland, and the newest member of the royal family, Queen Emma. He was much interested in the Russo-Turkish war, and I happened to have by me some numbers of the *Illustrated London News*, and *Illustrirte Zeitung*, giving sketches from the seat of war, with which he was highly delighted, and under the illustrations he used to write his remarks, in Arabic characters. He knew all about Plevna, Osman Pacha and Skobeloff, the Czar and the Sultan; but when I told him the war was over, and the two monarchs were now friends, he was surprised, and could not credit that this should be the case, after so many of his co-religionists had been killed by the Russians!

"Very much rotten in the States," says Mr. Money; and these words apply with far greater force, to compare small things with great, to Koetei. It is a curious fact that the Oriental nature is not compatible with financial progress, or good government generally. As it is with Turkey, so it is more or less with all Oriental—certainly with all Mohammedan—States.

Financial disorganization is the great blot in Koetei. The coal-miners at Pelaroeng are about the only men of the lower order of servants who are paid their wages regularly; and the Sabandars, or harbour-masters, are the only men of any official rank who receive their salaries when due. Neither the Pangerans nor the *Mantries* are paid properly. But they not only must live, but must, like the nobles in more civilized countries, keep up an appearance; and corruption and extortion, not to call it robbery, are the order of the day. The result is, that chiefs and Mantries are being continually disgraced and dismissed, and replaced by others. Of the numerous household servants of the Sultan not one is paid regular wages; they get food and clothes, and on great *fêtes* a little money, but that is all. And yet the Sultan is popular. All the people are obedient to him in a remarkable degree. They come when called, and work when wanted. Perhaps one reason for this is the fact that every one can speak to his Highness at any time; no formal audience is required. The native simply approaches the Sultan, in such a way that he is always nearer to the ground than his ruler; then, saluting with folded hands to his forehead, he sits down on the ground. The chiefs and Hadjis have the privilege of kissing the Sultan's right hand. This ceremony over, the conversation begins.

The following facts may serve as an illustration of the autocratic authority exercised by the Sultan:—Some years ago his brother was murdered by a Boegis, who had associated with his wife. No steps were taken to punish the man, but the woman was instantly ordered by the Sultan to be drowned at Pulo Tangaroeng, the long island in the river before the capital, where the execution took place at once.

Again, one day during my stay in Koetei two Malays stole 3500 florins from a wooden chest in which the Sultan kept his "gambling money." By-and-by the thieves were caught, and were sentenced to be flogged at once—fifty lashes with a rattan each. To my great astonishment, the executioners were the Sultan's two eldest sons, Praboe and Sosroe, who undertook the task in order that there should be no fear that the executioners would sympathize with the culprits and weaken the strokes. When the flogging was over, the thieves were brought into the palace, their hands bound, and each led by two men; immediately after followed the two Pangerans with a numerous suite. It was a pitiful sight to see them, and I thought the punishment inflicted on them far too severe. Blood flowed in streams from their backs and heads, and they had to be dragged—almost carried—along, being unable to walk. One of them died the same evening. A few days later I saw the Sultan go down in a hurry to the river, accompanied by a number of men, one of whom went in the water, and in a moment brought up a bag full of money. This was part of the stolen coin. The surviving thief had confessed where he had concealed the bag. The Sultan, with a smile on his face, hurried back, bag in hand, to his palace; and in the evening he told me he had recovered 2500 florins of the stolen property, and he would not trouble himself about the rest. A guard, with a loaded gun, is now placed at night over the Sultan's treasures, and if he is caught asleep at his post he gets seven days' imprisonment.

The Sultan's leisure time is pretty equally divided between the hareem and the cock-pit. He boasts of having forty-two wives, *i.e.* four privileged wives and thirty-eight concubines, the latter of whom he can remove at his pleasure. The number of children born to him averages just two to each wife and concubine, or eighty-four altogether, most of whom are still alive. These children are a practical commentary on an observation which the Sultan once made to me when speaking of the politics of his country,—

"Me want Koetei make big country; want plenty people."

Like Santa Anna, the wretched Mexican President, and like nearly every Malay that ever breathed, he takes the greatest delight in cock-fighting. Not a day passes but some important contest takes place on his premises. The crowd, with their cocks, generally begin to assemble between two and three in the afternoon, and his Highness is soon on the spot closely examining the birds that are going to fight, the owners of which bring them to him, grovelling at full length on the ground. The Sultan puts the spurs—curved steel blades, three inches long, and as sharp as a razor—on his own birds, rubs the blade with lemon, in order that any wound inflicted by the combatants may smart the more, and does not scruple to show his confidence in his birds by betting on them to any extent. Birds pitted against each other under such conditions are very soon *hors de combat*. As soon as one of the combatants is declared to be defeated, the executioner—

a functionary as necessary to a properly conducted cock-pit as a time-keeper to a prize-fight—decapitates it with his mandau, first, however, allowing the conqueror to give it a final *coup* by biting it with its beak on the neck or head.

The Sultan has over sixty large fighting cocks, each of which is kept in a room in the Palace under an oval wicker cage, somewhat resembling a lobster-pot with the bottom taken out. Every day these birds, or such of them as survive the daily contests, are taken to the river to be washed, being afterwards fed on maize and rice.

The loud and pertinacious crowing of the cocks in almost every village in Borneo, Java, Sumatra, or indeed any of the islands of the Indian Archipelago, is an experience not likely to be forgotten by any European traveller there. Before sunrise every day one restless bird utters his long drawn out clarion cry of challenge, which is taken up by dozens, by scores, by hundreds of birds throughout the village, who then continue the crowing exercise, in detachments, volley firing as it were, or singing in a discordant chorus, till such time as the whole village is awake. As soon as the inhabitants begin to move about these very undesirable neighbours seem satisfied with the result of their performance, and are silent. The effect of sleeping in close contiguity to a select company of sixty of the finest, strongest, heartiest, and gamest of the game cocks of Koetei may be imagined. I have many a day suffered severe headache as a result of the combined inharmonious battle-cries of these birds.

Like most Mohammedans, the Sultan is very punctual in the performance of his religious duties. Although a Hadji he has never performed the Mecca journey, but has sent his representative to offer prayer at the Kaba and kiss the feet of the Shereef of Mecca. Every year he gives large sums of money for pilgrims to offer at the shrine of the Prophet.

As I have already stated, the Sultan had shortly before my arrival lost his second son, and the mourning solemnities were still uncompleted. Twice daily, at eight a.m. and four p.m., a large procession of men and women enveloped in white garments, the former carrying white flags, spears, shields, and other ornaments, all of which were also covered with white calico, and the latter bearing rice and sirih on trays, proceeded to the grave of the lately deceased Pangeran (Prince), to offer up their prayers and strew flowers and water on the grave, as a substitute for the rice and sirih, which should properly, I believe, be offered at the grave. This ceremony is performed twice a day for twenty-one days after the death of any one, prince or peasant. It is repeated on the fortieth day, and again on every anniversary.

A guard of six men keeps watch day and night over the royal tomb, which is situated within the Palace enclosure. Several of the Sultan's wives rest there, and with them a high priest, said to be "positively a descendant of Mohammed."

Next to cock-fighting, the principal amusement of the Sultan, as of every one of his subjects, is gambling. Every evening at eight o'clock the covered courtyard of the Palace is turned into a gaming saloon, where the people congregate together, sit or squat on the floor, and play a game which, to an ordinary observer, seems to be very similar to "heads and tails," having all the elements of chance, with the absence of any requirements of skill or science, peculiar to that dignified game—so far, at least, as I am acquainted with its rules. Sometimes a soiled and dog's-eared pack of cards—generally Chinese—will take the place of the jingling coins, and bets are freely laid on the skill or luck of this player or that. The Princes (Pangerans) will associate with the people, and not disdain to stake their fifty dollars at a time. Even the little sons of the Sultan, barely eight years of age, and of course the children of persons of lower degree, may be seen taking an eager part in the all-absorbing pastime, their faces aglow with excitement. The Sultan himself sometimes pays a visit to this "hell," and generally indulges in high play himself, with his nobles, or visitors in the Pandoppo. To do him justice, he can play a very good game of chess or whist: but he always prefers that it should be for a high stake.

In the meantime the Sultan's Javanese musicians (gamallang) discourse music of doubtful sweetness on their primitive instruments; and occasionally his *danseuse* performs privately before him, dressed in a magnificent sarong covered with diamonds and bangles, that sparkle like the golden drops that glittered upon Danaë after the Olympian shower.

So the amusement goes on all night, and till the small hours of the morning. One noticeable feature in all these gatherings is that no drinking of intoxicating liquors takes place. Neither Dyak nor Malay is ever seen to touch alcoholic drinks. Hence they do not artificially stimulate the excitement which naturally supervenes on high play, and quarrels are seldom if ever witnessed. Not even high words are exchanged. They play till their last cent is lost, and then either quietly retire, or watch the luck of others.

But the taste for gambling in all its varieties leads to much dishonesty among the people, and also tends to demoralize them in other respects, increasing the natural love of idleness and dislike for labour, and leading to deception and fraud. If a man or boy raises a dollar—especially if he gets a "windfall" or unexpected reward—he must try his luck at gambling. The taste is spreading from the Malays to the Dyaks. I one day made a drawing of a Dyak lad, and gave him a dollar as his "sitter's fee:" the same evening I found him gambling with the money—he was winning, for a wonder, and wanted me to join.

CHAPTER IV.

Doubts and delays—Off at last—Up the Mahakkam—More deserters—A dead forest—Monotonous travelling—A whirlpool—Midnight foes—Hindoo remains—Moeara Klintjouw—Short rations—A microcephalous boy—Coal in process of formation—A Borneo landscape—Interview with a Dyak Radenajo—A war-dance—Doctoring the Dyaks—Dangerous practice.

I SPENT nearly a fortnight in this gay yet miserable capital of Koetei, waiting partly for the Sultan to make up his mind whether or not he would accompany me into the interior, and partly for the completion of certain official arrangements for my journey. As the time was passing rapidly and uselessly away, I determined to make a preparatory trip up the Mahakkam, to get accustomed to this country, and to endeavour to add to my natural history collection. Even this could not be done without the Sultan's help; and he was endowed with such a wonderful faculty for making promises and breaking them that I might have stayed in Tangaroeng to this day, listening to his daily excuses for delay, had I not threatened to return to Macassar.

I had engaged two Chinese servants, Tan Bon Hijok and Tan He Wat, and was agreeably surprised one day when Sariman came and said the two runaways, Ali and Siden, had arrived, and were waiting to see me. The chief of the police at Macassar had very promptly arrested them, and sent them on by the next steamer.

At last, after much vacillation and procrastination, it was definitely arranged that I should start on August 10th. After the collapse of so many promises I was somewhat doubtful whether this engagement would be kept, and it was with relief that I saw signs of real preparation being made. The Sultan had promised not only to supply me with men, but to accompany me in person; but some of his courtiers had evidently been working upon his fears, by descanting on the dangers of the journey, and the ferocity of his "subjects" in the hills and forests of the interior, and I doubted whether he would leave Tangaroeng. Still, as the appointed day approached there were indications that the august resolve to allow me to start had been fixed. His Highness presented me with a very fine mandau (or sword), which he generally wore. This mandau has served me as a subject for illustration in describing the nature of these weapons (see Plate 18, Figs. 1, 2, 3, 4; and p. 191). He also ordered his best prau to be got ready, and appointed a picked crew of twenty men, including two mantries to act as guides. This prau was a fine boat, 56ft. in length and 4ft. 6in. wide, the hull being cut out of a single tree, with upper bulwarks, 6 inches high, added from end to end; and was provided with a small cabin in the centre, the covering of which was made of attap, and could be removed at will.

Notwithstanding these outward and visible manifestations I was still doubtful about the real intentions of the Sultan. There had been too many requests to "wait a little," too many excuses, for me to be perfectly satisfied till the day of departure arrived, and I found myself actually embarked. There was considerable excitement in the town as, early in the morning, I went down to the river with my men to see that all was ready for the start. There, in all the glory of a new jacket and bright new silver buttons, were the mantries—one of them freshly appointed, as I afterwards discovered, only the previous day to his high office. They said the Sultan would not accompany me, but assured me that everything was finally settled for the start to take place as soon as I was ready. I almost feared to go and take leave of the Sultan and his sons; but found him quite enthusiastic. He walked down to the quay with the Pangerans Praboe and Sosroe to wish me a "*slaamat jallan*"—*bon voyage;* and with a hearty shake of the hand bade me good-bye.

With twenty stout rowers we quickly left Tangaroeng behind, having the benefit of the flood tide, and soon the last traces of human habitation died away, leaving before us nothing but the broad expanse of river, here some thousand yards wide, lined on each side with forest growth, backed by low hills in the distance.

Along the banks were frequent outcrops of coal strata, suggestive of a not far distant future when the river would be crowded with smoke-begrimed "colliers," sending forth their long track of black smoke across the clear blue sky.

At sunset we reached Pulo Juboe, where a sabandar or harbour-master is appointed to collect customs duties, but we were fortunately exempt from the ordeal of a general overhauling of our luggage. Here we stayed for the night, starting again early on the following morning; when, instead of twenty of the Sultan's men, only twelve mustered to their work; instead of two mantries, only one—he who had been promoted but the day before yesterday—Ké Patti by name, an innocent old fool of perhaps sixty years of age, nothing but skin and bone to look at when his insignia of office were removed, very talkative for a Malay, but speaking only the Koetei dialect, of which I understood so little that I was obliged to get one of my men to act as interpreter. Here was a pretty start! Still, my own men had not deserted, and I thought it better to make the best of the matter and go on than to risk the loss of more men by protesting.

Beyond Pulo Juboe the country became dull and uninteresting. The excessive drought of the previous year had told with terrible effect on the trees in the forest. Many of them were dead—large patches at a time—stretching their bare arms like so many skeletons over the scene. Of animal life there was little to be seen. Occasionally a happy family of monkeys would glare at us; or a pair of snake darters—the *boeroeng dandang* of the Malays—might be espied sitting on the topmost branches of a tree in an attitude of repose resembling the letter S. For ten hours we paddled along the mighty river, meeting not a single vessel, and seeing not a single dwelling on shore. Yet the country is rich and fertile, and could support a large agricultural and manufacturing population.

Under such circumstances the unbroken succession of forest upon forest, refreshing though such a sight is to the brick-weary eyes of the jaded dweller in towns, becomes after a time absolutely monotonous, especially to a traveller seated "cribbed, cabined, and confined" beneath the awning of a small canoe, with no legroom, and no companion capable of exchanging an intelligent remark, save in a foreign tongue and through the intermediation of an interpreter. Towards evening on the 12th we came upon a couple of miserable huts, where my men asked leave to cook their frugal fare—rice with a little dried fish, seasoned with *lombock* (pepper), and rested for the night. Tan Bon Hijok, whom I had made my mandoer, or headman, busied himself with cleaning his revolver, and asked if mine was ready. He and all my men were astonished to be told that it would be time enough to look to our arms when we came among the Dyaks. They declared that the Malays living up the river were great thieves, with few scruples about spilling blood. This was nothing new, but the oft-repeated statement gained force in our present surroundings.

At five p.m. we arrived at Moeara Kaman, the point of junction of the River Kaman with the Mahakkam. The tributary stream is very large, and flows with great force, causing a great whirlpool, through which it was difficult to navigate the prau without risk. Moeara Kaman is a small village consisting of but eleven houses, five of which are built on rafts (*lantings*) in the river. The country all around is flat, covered with immense forests; at least one-third of the trees were dead, owing to the drought of 1878, which lasted here, the inhabitants told us, between eight and nine months. Here we stayed for the night, the mantrie meanwhile arranging for a reinforcement of men for me. These officials are unpaid, but can demand "statute labour" from the people in the villages for cultivating the rice-fields, building praus, erecting dwellings, or other work.

There was little rest for any of us that night, for we were secretly attacked by hosts of bloodthirsty enemies, who stole upon us unawares—the terror that walketh by darkness assuming the form, not of Dyak head-hunters or Malay robbers, but of myriads of mosquitoes.

Hindoo remains have been found in this village: amongst other things a well-executed figure of a goddess, in solid gold, weighing eight thails (314 grammes), which is now in the possession of the Sultan. The people were still busy searching for further relics, and had come upon a number of cut stones, probably belonging to a tomb, similar to some inscribed tombstones, of undoubted Hindoo origin, found at Sankolirang, a village on the coast, and now preserved by the Sultan at Tangaroeng.

A few miles further, the Mahakkam receives a larger tributary, known as the Telén, of which the Kaman is really a branch channel. Up this our course now lay. Again the whole day long we paddled up-stream without encountering a soul. Every now and then we paused amid the solemn stillness to listen for the sound of voices, or other indications of human existence in the boundless forest. But no sign met either ear or eye, and towards sunset the prau was moored to an overhanging tree, and the crew landed and made a fire to cook their supper. Ké Patti said there was no settlement of any kind between this and Moeara Klintjouw, and that we could not arrive there before Monday evening. On looking at the map it seemed to me that this was a long time to take to accomplish the distance, as this was only Friday, and I told the men that if they reached Moeara Klintjouw by Sunday afternoon I would give them a dollar apiece. This offer threw a somewhat more pleasant expression over their grim faces, and they answered cheerfully, "*Boele, toewan, harie mingo surrie di Moeara Klintjouw*" (To be sure, sir, Sunday afternoon at Klintjouw).

So they were up early next morning, and pulled with a will. The river gradually became narrower and more winding. Soon after starting I saw a proboscis monkey sitting alone on a lofty tree—the first I had come across—its prominent and very human-like nose greatly increasing the general resemblance to the human form. This was, for many hours, the nearest approach to humanity that we met: and it was not till past six in the evening, as it was rapidly getting dark, that we came to a bamboo house, the sight of which my men hailed with delight, as they would be able to prepare their food there with little trouble. Like all Malays they were lazy, and glad of any opportunity to save themselves a little labour. Often when we came to a hut would they beg to be permitted to leave off rowing an hour or two earlier than I wished, in order to save themselves the trouble of hunting for sufficient dry wood in the forest to make their fires; while they would even sometimes lengthen their day's work in the hope of reaching a hut, where they might find a fire ready lighted for them.

Here, two large rafts of rattan, each fifty feet long, passed us, quietly floating down stream towards Samarinda, which they would reach in about four or five weeks.

The next day my crew seemed tired of rowing, after their unusual exertions of the two previous days, and as the banks just here were comparatively free from trees they adopted the expedient of making two stout ropes of rattan, which they fastened to the boat, while three of the crew took it in turns to go ashore and tow.

We passed a small tributary—the Moeara Sui—on the right bank of the Telén, across the mouth of which was slung a line of rattan. This my guide told me was a sign that the natives were forbidden to cut rattan in that river, which was reserved for the Sultan's use.

At sunset we arrived at the confluence of the Moeara Klintjouw with the Telén, where the village of the same name, sometimes called Moeara Tjaloeng, is situated.

This village is surrounded by the best cultivated district I have seen in any part of the interior. The natives—all Malays—farm cocoa-nuts, pisangs, maize, and rice.

The settlement has historical associations. Here it was that the Pangeran Pandjie, brother of the then Sultan, lived in exile for many years. He had been condemned to death in 1846, for having committed adultery with one of the Sultan's wives, but escaped to Tjaloeng, and remained there till pardoned.

According to Von Dewall, the people of this village have adopted some of the superstitious customs of the Dyaks, such as recourse to "balians,"[1] or sorcerers, in the case of sickness. The witch, or sorceress, dances round the sick person till she falls down exhausted, and then prays to her *Deewa* (God), and is inspired with the knowledge of the manner in which the disease is to be treated, and prescribes accordingly.

As soon as the prau was made fast to a kind of rude pier in front of the mantrie's house, Ké Patti and his men went ashore

[1] See p. 219.

and had a "bitchara" with the mantrie. My headman and I soon followed, but the landing was by no means easy: the pier, or landing-place, consisted simply of the trunk of a tree, not a foot wide, with the upper side roughly squared off, and with thirty-one notches cut into it which did duty for steps; one end rested on the bank and the other in the muddy river-bed: nothing in the shape of a handrail existed to guide a stranger's doubtful steps.

Beyond this again were two immense trees, placed end to end, leading directly to the ladder at the entrance to the house. Ké Patti introduced me to the mantrie and the people present, saying he had the Sultan's orders that every assistance should be rendered me; that I had come as a friend of the Sultan, to see the country, collect all sorts of animals, and make drawings of the Dyaks. The idea of any sane man coming so far for such a purpose amused them highly, and somebody suggested that I was a spy, come to spy out, not "the nakedness of the land," but its wealth. But Ké Patti reassured them on that point, and the judicious distribution of a few presents set their minds at rest as to my good intentions.

Ké Patti then ordered ten fresh men to be ready to start with me on Tuesday morning, and we set about procuring provisions. These were not easily obtained. My mandoer and I went from house to house trying to buy fowls, eggs, lombock, and dried fish, but had the greatest difficulty in purchasing a few fowls and a little lombock. The whole attention of the people seemed to be devoted to agriculture. My men were grumbling at getting no fish, when I saw a small sampang coming down the stream, and signalled to the occupants that I wanted to buy their fish. They shook their heads, answering "Nda, nda," but the offer of a quantity of tobacco was too tempting, and they gladly gave their fish in exchange.

While passing from house to house with Ké Patti I saw a microcephalous boy—*affenmensch*, as Carl Vogt would call him. He was standing in the corner of a room, making a continuous humming noise, "uh—uh—uh," staring at me, and apparently somewhat afraid of me. But Ké Patti took him in his arms and nursed him, so that I had a good opportunity of examining him. He was apparently between six and eight years of age, with a small oval face, and the top part of the head very much flattened and shallow. His head was twisted to the right, and his throat entirely on the right side. He kept gazing at me, and blinking his eyes as though the light was too strong for him. He could not speak, but occasionally uttered a sound like a grunt, and now and then gave a frantic laugh. In all other respects his body was well formed; but when Ké Patti put him down, he would either crawl on all-fours, or walk with his feet very far apart, waddling like a duck, with his elbows stuck out, and his arms half bent.

On the morning of August 19th I left Klintjouw with a crew of eighteen men, who made rapid progress against the stream, which was now gradually lessening in volume and velocity; and at seven in the evening we reached the kampong, or village, of Binjau. Habitations now became more frequent, and Ké Patti amused me very much by representing every house on the way up as belonging to either a son, a brother, a sister, or other relative of his. Indications of coal were plainly visible at many places on the banks of the river. Indeed the process of coal formation was even then being carried on—masses of decayed leaves, broken branches, grasses, and undergrowth, several feet in thickness, had collected together, and were being compacted by the heavy rains, and gradually covered by alluvial deposits. Enormous trees, with massive straight stems, rising sixty or eighty feet from the ground before throwing out a single branch, overshadowed the rank vegetation beneath, the thickness of which rendered it impossible to penetrate into the forest more than a few yards from the river-side. Innumerable orchids covered many of the trees, those that were dead looking at the distance like so many birds' or wasps' nests. Every tree in the forest was linked to its neighbour by fairy chains of festooned creepers, on which, now and again, might be seen a monkey swaying to and fro. I believe I should be within the truth in saying that a monkey might pass from one end of Borneo to the other without once touching the ground, along the branches of the trees and the creepers that hang between them.

Still the scenery could not be called really beautiful. Though the harmony of colour in the forest leaves, and the graceful shape of many single plants or groups of trees, form a series of pretty pictures, the landscape is not striking. There is nothing that the Germans would call *grossartig* or *wunderschön;* nothing that approaches the idea of grandeur. Nowhere in the East Indies did I see such romantic spots as are to be found in Norway and Sweden, or even in wild, rocky Lapland. What the landscapes seem to lack is foreground. The background is pretty enough, consisting generally of low hills, to which distance lends that soft depth of tone which only dense wood can give, but there is no variety of incident, no striking character, in the immediate foreground.

I only stayed at Binjau to sleep, being anxious to reach Dyak country. The first Dyak village is at Melan, about two hours by water above Binjau, where a tribe of Modang Dyaks has established itself. Rajah Dinda, the most powerful Dyak chief in the territory of the Sultan of Koetei, has a house here, and, accompanied by Ké Patti and my mandoer, I landed to see if by any chance the Rajah, whose principal residence is at Long Wai, might be on a visit here. The " road " to the house was better adapted for a rope-dancer than for an ordinary traveller. Across the muddy beach was a small tree, in which a dozen irregular steps were cut, similar to that at Moeara Tjaloeng. At the end of this again was the trunk of a long tree, with the bark removed, but in the rough, which was very slippery, as it was raining at the time. Luckily I had no boots on, and so was able to accomplish this " middle passage " in safety. Then again came a Dyak ladder—a plank with notches for steps—almost upright, which led to a platform under the house. Arrived here, I sent word that I would speak to the Rajah, or to the Radenajo, if her husband were not there. Still another ladder had to be ascended, when I was ushered into the presence of a tall plain-looking woman, of about thirty-five years of age, sitting in a corner of the room, arrayed in a blue-and-red striped jacket, with a blue sarong. From her ears, the lobes of which, according to the Dyak standard of beauty, were elongated and split to form a long fleshy loop, hung two pairs of weighty silver rings, stretching the ears till they reached an inch below the level of the chin. In holes in the upper part of the ears were fastened tassels made of cotton wool. The hands, fingers, arms, and ankles were all tattooed in plain bands of blue. Asking me to be seated on her best mat—a piece of English carpet which she had brought out for the occasion—she placed before me a magnificent gold sirih box, of Malay workmanship; but I gave her to understand that I preferred a cigarette, and lighted one of native make. The Radenajo could speak but half a dozen words in Malay, but she at once utilized her limited knowledge by asking for *obat* (medicine). Ké Patti inquired what her ailment was, when she complained first of asthma, then of rheumatism, and finally pointed to her throat, as a sign that she was suffering from a wen—that complaint so common among the women of Borneo.

I regretted that for none of these disorders had I a proper remedy, but I took the opportunity of presenting to her an embroidered silk scarf and a few strings of beads, with which she was much pleased, promising to give me in return three fowls. The room soon became filled with women and children, and a few old men—the young men being all at work. They manifested the greatest curiosity to see the "white man," and I was as much an object of interest to them as they were to me. They did not show the slightest fear or jealousy of my presence; and when I gave to the crowd of naked, staring, half-begging children who surrounded me a number of indiarubber air-balls, with a whistle attached, showing them how to blow them out, and when they heard the whistle sound as the balls gradually diminished in bulk, their delight knew no bounds.

Ké Patti's ubiquitous relations were to be found even here. He pointed out to me a young Malay in the room, saying, *Saja poenja anak* (this is my child). I laughed, which annoyed him; when he added, *Anak betoel* (really my child), explaining that he was here on a trading journey to buy rattans from the Dyaks.

Finding that Rajah Dinda was not here, I was anxious to get on to Long Wai, and hastened away from Melan, stopping at Longna, to make a passing call on Rajah Sinen, Dinda's brother. Here I was treated to a private rehearsal of a "war-dance," performed at the Rajah's request for my especial benefit. This terpsichorean exercise consisted of a series of loud stampings of the feet, accompanied by quick cries, and threatening attitudes with mandau and shield. Meanwhile another Dyak was fiddling away most vigorously on a two-stringed instrument, a sort of cross between a banjo and a violin. It was roughly carved out of a single piece of wood, the back being hollow and open. The strings, which were made of thin bamboo threads, were played by the fingers, not with a bow. After some bargaining I succeeded in purchasing the fiddle for 10 florins, and it is figured on Plate 19, Fig. 1.

On leaving Rajah Sinen, I was invited to enter a house where a Dyak lay in a corner, groaning loudly, and apparently very ill. The place was full of women and children, who tried to hide themselves behind their elders. On my asking what was the matter, the invalid replied in Malay that about a week ago he had fallen from a tree from a height of some twenty feet, and had injured himself internally. The women had given him some *obat*, and applied hot poultices of minced herbs, but all without avail, and were going to have recourse to *pomali*, or incantation, to drive the evil spirit away, when they heard the white man had arrived, and so they applied to me for relief, asking for medicine, which they offered to pay for. My Chinese head servant reminded me that if the man was really dying—and it looked like it—and my medicine did not cure him, his death would be attributed to me, and not to natural causes; that I should be looked upon with suspicion, and the consequences might be very serious. I found on inquiry that all the man really wanted was some aperient medicine, and offered to give some obat, but took the precaution of saying that he must take it at his own risk. The women made ominous murmurs on hearing my remarks translated to them; but the sick man, who was evidently suffering great agony, said he would gladly try my obat. So I went over to the prau, and looked at my stock of drugs. I had castor oil and pills; but these, I thought, would not be sufficiently rapid in their effects to make any impression on the sceptical minds of the people; so I administered two table-spoonfuls of *cali carbonicum* in water, which, notwithstanding several wry faces at its unpleasant flavour, the patient took to the last drop. An hour or so afterwards I found myself surrounded by a crowd of men, women, and children, all of whom had suddenly discovered that they were dangerously ill, suffering terrible pains in the stomach. My *cali carbonicum* had had the desired effect. I was immediately regarded as a hero, a miracle-worker, by the hitherto suspicious Dyaks, and nothing would do but I must supply them all with unlimited quantities of obat.

CHAPTER V.

Dyak graves—The first skull—Disappearance of Ké Patti—An alarm—A visit from the Rajah's mother—Taking French leave—Bitten by a crocodile—Wild men of the woods—Recruiting for hunters—A beautiful bird—An impostor—Intrusive visitors—Description of Long Wai—A Dyak dictionary—A herculean Rajah—An amorous warrior—Joint captives of Mars and Cupid—The Rajah's wealth—Family cares—Sketching his wife's feet—The manufacture of earrings.

So far, then, my relations with these terrible savages had been satisfactory. I looked anxiously for proof of their head-hunting practices, but saw no skulls ornamenting any of the houses. The Sultan forbids head-hunting in his territory; but Ké Patti assured me that the people were bound by their *adat* (custom) to get heads on certain important occasions in their lives, as before marriage, &c., and that they consequently made inroads into neighbouring territories beyond the Sultan's jurisdiction.

At nine p.m. we arrived at another Modang settlement, called Long Dingen, where we stayed for the night. Next day (August 21) we left at sunrise, and were soon on Dyak territory proper. Along the bank of the river were long bamboo poles, some fifteen feet high, stuck into the ground and ornamented with a few strips of red, blue, and white calico. These served the purpose of tomb-stones, marking the spots where dead Dyaks lay. Besides these ordinary graves, there were, in the neighbourhood of Long Desá, elaborate structures raised on posts eight or ten feet high, in which the bodies of deceased warriors were deposited. And soon afterwards I had the doubtful pleasure of seeing the first human trophy which had come under my observation, in the shape of a skull, bleached and weather-beaten, stuck on a branch of a high tree. This, Ké Patti told me, was the head of one of the enemies of the tribe—a sort of public, as distinguished from a private or personal, trophy—taken, no doubt, in war in *tempo doelo* (times gone by).

Shortly before ten in the morning we reached Long Wai, the capital town of the most powerful Dyak tribe in Koetei, and the residence of the great Rajah Dinda. Here, as at Melan and Longna, the landing-place or pier lay opposite the Rajah's house. When we had made the prau fast to this primitive structure, Ké Patti said it would be better for me to remain on board, while he went ashore to ask permission for me to land and take up my temporary abode in the village. Besides, he said, he must go and find a house, although he had told me beforehand that he had a good house here. This, however, was but another example of the amiable weakness of my good old guide, who seemed to be possessed of a more than usually large share of the "lying spirit" which lies so light on the consciences of Malays in general. Before landing, the old diplomatist arrayed himself in a pair of black cloth trousers, and a white linen jacket with silver buttons bearing the Sultan's initials, and made himself look quite *gentil.* I had been so accustomed to seeing him in his dirty print suits that I hardly knew him as he stepped carefully, yet confidently, along the narrow gangway, and up the steep ladders connecting the low-lying muddy foreshore with the main bank on which the houses were built, which lay from fifteen to twenty feet higher. One false step, oh Ké Patti, and the glory of your newly-donned suit would be dimmed in the mud beneath!

Hours passed, and still no tall figure, arrayed in black unmentionables and white silver-buttoned jacket, could be seen trusting itself to the frail structure which was the only link between the floating habitation from which it had lately emerged, and the, to me, unknown world, into which I had watched it pass. Could Ké Patti have lost his head, as well as his clothes and silver buttons, among these savages? Had Rajah Dinda, or one of his wives, given the order, once so familiar in fiction, if not in fact, among more civilized rulers, "Off with his head!"? I began to be impatient; my men were anxious; and the two Chinamen were afraid. We scanned the habitations on shore most carefully. All the holes which did duty for windows were filled with faces, mostly of women and children, whose eyes seemed to be fixed on us in one concentrated stare. Not a soul could we see on the beach or in what may be called the streets. Presently gongs and drums began to be sounded, in response to which the Dyaks who were at work in the fields and forests came in twos and threes to the town. Then, on the river, prau after prau, filled with armed men, suddenly appeared, all making towards us, some from above, some from below. Some fifteen vessels bore down in succession upon us. The men landed and filed in a long string across the narrow foot-bridge, and joined their comrades ashore. Those who had been indoors now came out, and the whole beach was soon crowded with armed natives. There was an absence of excitement, a method of orderliness about them, which was ominous of something serious. There was no shouting or loud talking that could be heard, but high above the hum of voices on shore resounded the barking of numbers of dogs, who evidently knew that something unusual was happening.

Presently some of the assembled multitude went up to Rajah Dinda's house for a "bitchara;" and, as all this time I could see nothing of Ké Patti, I felt the responsibility lay upon me to do something to ascertain what had become of him. More than half the day had gone, and I did not like the prospect of passing the night in the neighbourhood of what appeared to be a hornet's nest, without knowing something of the intentions of the occupants of the nest. So I sent a messenger ashore, ordering him to approach carefully, and to make every possible sign of friendship, without appearing too submissive. I watched his progress across the landing-place with some anxiety, and was relieved to find that a passage was made for him through the crowd to the Rajah's house. Presently nothing less than the unmistakable black trousers and white jacket were seen slowly descending the ladder. After all, old Ké Patti had lost neither his head nor his buttons. He came with a long story about the difficulty he had had in endeavouring to overcome the scruples of the women of the palace; the Rajah and his brother Sinen were both away, and I could not be permitted to land till one or other of them returned, some days hence.

I took time to consider what I should do: meanwhile the aspect of affairs on shore underwent little change, until, about four o'clock, a procession headed by a woman, escorted by two chiefs, approached my prau. This Ké Patti said was Dinda's mother. I immediately offered to receive her and the two chiefs in my cabin, while her female attendants took their places alongside in praus, changing places from time to time so that they could peep by turns into my cabin.

The Rajah's mother was a tall masculine-looking dame, probably over sixty years of age, but still showing signs of former beauty; for many of the Dyaks have, notwithstanding their high cheek-bones and broad noses, a type of face which is quite in accordance with European ideas of beauty. Taking a seat on the floor of the cabin she scrutinized every object, turning her eyes in all directions. Guns, a nickel-cased clock, a folding chair, cooking utensils—all attracted her attention in turn. Nothing seemed to escape her curious gaze; but as each object caught her eye she turned to me with an inquiring look, and the words "*Mau liat?*" (Permit to look) one of the few Malay expressions with which she was acquainted. The sight of my mandau seemed to reassure her. From the length of the hair tufts and the number of bead ornaments hanging from the sheath, she rightly judged that it belonged to the Sultan. I made her understand it was a present to me from *Toewan Adji*, as the Dyaks all over Koetei call his Highness.

I offered her a cup of cocoa and milk and some biscuits; but she declined the former, though appreciating the tempting-looking mixed biscuits, still as crisp as if fresh from Huntley and Palmer's factory.

Presently an awkward pause occurred. She somehow avoided speaking to Ké Patti, and her stock of Malay was exhausted, while I could not make any attempt to speak in the Dyak tongue. So I thought to improve the occasion by opening one of my boxes, and offering the old lady a couple of silk scarves, and a few strings of red and yellow glass beads. Her face suddenly assumed a bland expression, a slight smile broke from her lips, and with a few nods of the head, and a muttered "h'm h'm" she suddenly rose to leave.

Still I had no permission to land. In the abruptness of the

departure of my visitor, Ké Patti lost the opportunity of asking leave to go ashore; and I saw the procession return as it had come, leaving me none the wiser as to the intentions of the people regarding my landing.

After allowing a decent interval to elapse after the departure of my distinguished guest—or was she my hostess?—I determined to take French leave, and, bidding the rest of my crew stay on board and guard my property, took my two Chinamen on shore with me. My white face, and their yellow skin and pigtails, on which the wondering gaze of the natives had been fixed from a distance, proved irresistibly attractive as we drew nearer. I found it somewhat easier than I had expected to reach *terra firma*, after my recent experience in crossing and recrossing the native landing stages, especially as the ladder leading to Rajah Dinda's house was provided with a light bamboo handrail. By the time I had reached dry land, followed by my Celestial companions, the crowd had concentrated itself round the entrance to the Rajah's house. I went straight to the door, and entered the apartment set apart for the men, giving them to understand that if I could not obtain a small house for my own use I must share their quarters with them. And, as it was now rapidly getting dusk, I asked them, assuming a half air of authority, if they would go and help my men carry my baggage up from the prau, promising them some tobacco when the work was over. Much to my satisfaction, they gave a ready response in the affirmative, and volunteered almost to a man to earn the coveted guerdon of tobacco. While they were gone I had the opportunity of examining my surroundings. The room was but fourteen or fifteen feet long, with a bamboo floor, irregularly laid, with crevices of from half an inch to three inches between each cane. These interstices afforded ample ventilation, and a convenient means of getting rid of dust and dirt; but at the same time they gave free scope for the entry of foul smells, of which there was no lack, especially as in addition to these cracks there were several large holes left in the floor for the purpose of casting down all refuse on to the platform beneath, and of these facilities the inhabitants had availed themselves only too freely. In one corner of the room was a young Dyak, whose leg was terribly swollen, and pierced with half a dozen large holes—the result of a bite from a crocodile, by which he had been attacked about a month previously while bathing. The smell from the ulceration of the wounds was so exceedingly offensive that I lost no time in getting the poor fellow carried to another house.

Some of the men soon set to work to split a quantity of bamboo, for the purpose of making a partition to divide the room into two.

Among the occupants of the place were some dozen men, who, I could see at a glance, belonged to an entirely different tribe. Their skin was somewhat fairer than that of the other Dyaks, and their features were of a different cast, with an obliqueness of the eye and a coarseness in the hair, which gave them some resemblance to the Mongolian type. Their headdress and *tjawat* or waist-cloth, instead of being made of cotton, were of a brown material made from bark, somewhat resembling tappa. They spoke a different language, too, from the others. On inquiry I was told that they were members of the tribe or race known as "Orang Poonan," or Forest People—a community dwelling in the forest, always in the open air, except when the men came on a visit to Long Wai. The women of the tribe had never been seen at Long Wai, and never left their homes in the depth of the forest. The men were on a visit to Rajah Dinda, with whom they were on terms of friendship; and they had to share with the other Dyaks the back portion of the large room in which I was, while I and my men were to occupy the improvised chamber facing the river. "Adversity makes us acquainted with strange bedfellows," says the proverb; and, if in this case I had no cause to complain of ill-luck generally, I had some reason to question the fortune which had doomed me to sleep in close proximity to such wild men of the woods as these.

I had often heard of the Orang Poonan, and of their alleged ferocity, and the state of utter savagedom in which they lived; and, though I had hoped to be able to see them in the course of my journey, I little expected to have been confronted with them so early. I was comforted, however, with the reflection that they were in Rajah Dinda's confidence, and that I was still in territory nominally, at least, subject to the authority of Koetei: in this way I calmed my own apprehensions as philosophically as I could; but

I had more difficulty in assuring my followers, and especially the two Chinese, that they would find their heads and pigtails quite safe in the morning.

Nothing, in fact, happened to disturb our night's rest; and next day I made overtures to these Forest People, speaking to them through an interpreter, and was surprised to find that they seemed to possess equal, if not superior, intelligence to their neighbours. They seemed willing to oblige, and I easily induced them, by promises of beads and tobacco, to undertake to go into the forest daily, collecting animals, birds, and insects for me. They shook their heads at the mention of birds, saying that in consequence of the failure of the wild fruit crop, through the drought, the birds had died in great numbers, and were very scarce.

I laid out before their admiring eyes my whole stock of merchandise—beads of various colours, buttons of brass, silver, or glass, ribbon edged with gold lace, small knives, shilling razors, toy balloons, Japanese knives, gay-coloured prints, and above all a good stock of strong Java tobacco, and finally money. The cash they showed no appreciation of; but for all the other articles, with the partial exception of the beads, which were unfortunately not all of the proper pattern to suit the Dyak taste, they found some strange use. The large glass beads they would stick in the holes in their ears; the ribbon was used for making ornaments of various kinds; the prints were also useful, while the whistling balloons excited universal delight.

The Orang Poonan, with their dogs at their heels, would start every morning at sunrise on their collecting trips, with a *lebét* (bag) on their backs, their quiver of poisoned arrows hung at their left side, their blowing-tube in one hand, and a paddle in the other. No Dyak, either man or woman, ever goes out without a paddle, which is to a Dyak what a walking-stick or an umbrella is to an Englishman, only even more indispensable. Arrived at the riverside they would always bathe before embarking in their praus, but never partook of any food before starting. I also made several excursions up some small creeks, starting at daylight and returning at noon. I was generally accompanied either by some of the Orang Poonan or by the Modang Dyaks, who all seemed anxious to help me, and would go ashore and penetrate into the dense bamboo thickets whenever they heard the note of a bird. The result was, however, on the whole, poor; and it generally ended in hearing the birds only, and not in seeing them. The foliage was so thick that it was impossible to see more than a few feet, and if a bird was shot there was little chance of recovering it. One afternoon, however, when I was staying "at home," suffering from an attack of fever, a Poonan brought me a beautiful bird, the sight of which was so gratifying that I forgot all about my illness, and made a sketch of it and skinned it. It was a species of flycatcher; the body and tail were white—a very unusual colour for the tropics—the tail and wings edged with black, as if in mourning; the head and throat of a dark blue metallic lustre; the eyes dark brown, and encircled by a band of naked wrinkled skin, which, like the beak, was of a sky-blue colour. The most striking feature was the tail, the two middle feathers of which were of extraordinary length. The Poonans and Dyaks all assured me it was a very rare bird; I afterwards found it was common in Bali and Malacca.

Tan Bon, whom I had engaged for sixty florins a month, with an advance of three months' wages, which he asked under the pretence that he understood the skinning and preparing of birds, proved an utter impostor. He had not the least idea where or how to begin; but the birds brought to me were unfortunately mostly common, and I could therefore afford to let him have a number of them to practise upon, so that he eventually became more efficient. Chinamen, as a rule, are handy and skilful at this work, and my ill luck in getting one so unskilled as Tan Bon was all the more annoying. The Dyaks and Poonans used to watch us with great interest, and were sorely puzzled to know of what use the skins could be. I explained that the white men were anxious to see what kinds of birds there were in Koetei, and whether they were the same as those in the adjoining islands; and, as they got more at ease, and saw that I was in earnest in what I said, they displayed considerable interest in my operations.

At times their curiosity was excited to an inconvenient pitch.

The women at first used, at the most, to peep into my room when they thought I was not looking, and would run away when I went towards them or spoke. By degrees, however, they got bolder, and neither children nor women showed the slightest hesitation in asking for "presents." One wanted beads, another cloth, and a third buttons; sometimes offering in exchange fowls, fish, or fruit. But they tried to drive most terribly hard bargains, and would consult with each other whether what I offered them was equivalent in value to their own goods, even in some cases coming back, after making a bargain, and asking for their fruits and fowls to be returned.

The Poonans, finding their daily excursions into the forest did not produce any valuable results, offered to go on a week's expedition, and return with all the specimens they could collect. In the meantime my two Chinamen got on the sick-list—one with fever and the other with dysentery, and were soon followed by Sariman and Laban. My time was pretty fully occupied in seeing that they were properly attended to, and in improving my acquaintance with the village of Long Wai and its inhabitants.

The village of Long Wai is the largest Modang Dyak settlement I have seen in Koetei, and the tribe inhabiting it has the reputation of being the most powerful. Though the Rajah pays a yearly tribute to the Sultan, he does not allow himself and his people to be trampled upon by his Malay suzerain and his Pangerans; and, though on perfectly good terms with him, he does not always display the most implicit obedience to his orders.

The population of Long Wai is over 1000. The people are of superior build and physique to the other tribes in Koetei, and belong to what may be called the rich Dyaks.

The houses are built in the ordinary style of Dyak architecture,[1] mounted on poles, and connected with each other by boards laid on posts a foot or two from the ground, forming a regular labyrinth of wooden roads or platforms. This does not appear to have been the case when Von Dewall was in Long Wai in 1849, as he says, "There exists no mutual communication; each house has its own ladder;" though later on he writes, "By means of wooden

[1] See p. 195.

planks one can come from one house to another,"—a qualification, if not a contradiction, of the former statement.

For the first few days of my stay here I found it rather difficult to converse with the people, as Ké Patti was often away cultivating a rice patch a short distance from the village, and there was only one Dyak in the place who could speak more than a few words of Malay. However, I succeeded in making myself understood by signs and ejaculations, and occupied myself in making a short vocabulary of Dyak words, which proved very useful. This will be found in the Appendix. It will be observed the language has the peculiarity that it possesses no R.

In about a week, however, Rajah Dinda and his brother Sinen returned home, and received me very kindly when I called to see them immediately after their arrival. They both spoke Malay, and I was able to converse pretty freely with them.

Rajah Dinda is a powerfully-built man, standing 5ft. 9in., very muscular, and with limbs of Herculean dimensions. His face is rather small, with delicate features, giving him a feminine appearance, which the total absence of beard increases, and which contrasts strangely with the vigour of his prodigious frame. He is descended from an old dynasty which has held authority in Long Wai from *tempo doelo* (olden times), as the Malays say of anything that dates back more than two generations.

He has a quiet and rather hesitating manner in conversation, which suggests the idea that he is anxious to conceal something; but, from my experience, I believe him to be fairly straightforward, and as good as his word. I never saw him excited, but always dignified, though genial, in his bearing. This is no doubt partly attributable to his sense of power, while at the same time it enhances the respect with which he is regarded by his people and neighbours.

Dinda has been converted, nominally, to Mohammedanism, chiefly through the influence of the Sultan of Koetei. But his conversion was, I believe, rather a matter of personal convenience or gratification, than of conviction. He had, at the time of my visit, five wives, four of whom were almost as tall and muscularly built as himself. He gained the affection of two of his wives while on a head-hunting excursion at Long Wahou, during which he boasts of having killed five Dyaks with his own hand, and from which he returned bearing in triumph, in addition to his spoils of war, two tall young girls, who had admired his courage and fallen easy victims to the shafts of Cupid, and allowed themselves to be brought to Long Wai, the joint captives of Love and War! Perhaps the reputed wealth of the Rajah had something to do with the willingness with which these muscular damsels submitted to be taken prisoners. Dinda is said to have 50,000 guilders in hard cash, besides quantities of gold dust, and much wealth in the shape of sacred jars (*gudji blanga*), stores of merchandise, and other property. The Rajah has no Civil List from which he draws his wealth; it is all acquired by trade, and by the results of the labour of his people, who are obliged to render certain services, such as attending to agricultural duties on his private reserves, building houses or praus, &c.

Rajah Dinda seemed very proud of his children, of whom he had a numerous and increasing family. Almost every day at noon he would take his youngest daughter, a fair and really beautiful infant, into the river, and give her a bath, while a Dyak girl held an umbrella over her head as a protection from the sun. One day one of the Rajah's daughters gave me one of the huge straw hats worn by the Dyak women when out at work in the fields. The rim was no less than two feet seven inches in diameter, and served the double purpose of umbrella and sunshade.[2] To complete the favour, I begged Rajah Dinda to get one of his wives to make me a bark jacket,[3] for which I promised that she should be handsomely rewarded; and a few days afterwards he came over to ask me to go with him to the palace, and see how the work was getting on.

Two of his wives were busy making a little fancy braiding round the top of the garment; but what attracted my attention more than the needlework were the hands of the dusky sempstresses. The whole of the backs of their hands were decorated in a most elaborate and artistic manner with tattoo marks, the symmetrical pattern of which was exceedingly remarkable. I asked

[2] See Plate 26.

[3] See p. 185.

permission to make a drawing of the tattoo marks; but the ladies were coy and would not decide, leaving it for Rajah Dinda to say whether I might do so or not. With his usual willingness to oblige me, Dinda smiled and nodded his head, saying, *Boele* (must). So I ran back for my sketch-book and was soon engaged in making the drawings, which are reproduced in Plate 20, Fig. 1.

The ice being once broken, the ladies were good enough to let me sketch their feet, which were also elaborately tattooed; and I have consequently the pleasure of introducing my readers, in Plate 20, Fig. 2, to the feet as well as the hands of one of Rajah Dinda's wives. All the married women here are tattooed on the hands and feet, and sometimes on the thighs, as in Plate 6. The decoration is one of the privileges of matrimony, and is not permitted to unmarried girls.

Having succeeded so far in obtaining the goodwill of the ladies of the Rajah's family, I endeavoured to buy a pair of their large, heavy tin earrings, which hung from the loops in the lobes of the ears; but they were unwilling to sell any. I succeeded, however, in purchasing a small piece of tin, with which Rajah Dinda showed me the whole process of the manufacture of these precious ornaments. Taking a long, straight piece of bamboo, the hollow of which was the same diameter as it was intended that the earrings should be, he fixed on the top of it the half of a cocoa-nut shell, with a hole bored through, in which the upper end of the cane was inserted, the whole forming a tube, with a cup at the top. Wrapping the tube in a cloth, he melted the tin in a small ladle, and poured it into the cocoa-nut cup, till the tube was filled. When the tin was cool, he opened the bamboo tube, and took out a long, straight, round rod of tin; which he then bent round a thick, but smooth, piece of wood, forming a ring, with the ends not quite meeting.

CHAPTER VI.

An important bitchara—Warlike preparations—A visit to the Orang Poonan—The Forest People at home—Roast monkey for dinner—White-skinned Dyaks—Their habits and customs—Preparing the arrow poison—A surgical operation—A banquet to the wild people of the woods—The aborigines of Borneo.

On the 12th September there was unusual commotion in Long Wai, which seemed to betoken a sudden termination to my friendly relations with the Rajah and his people. From early morning till late in the afternoon armed Dyaks from other kampongs came pouring into the village, and Rajah Dinda held a long bitchara, or council, with the various chiefs on the platform under his house. Not only men, but, much to my surprise, the women too, were admitted to this council; and presently two of the Sultan's confidential wives came up from Tangaroeng. The length and apparent importance of the conference, and the large gathering of chiefs and armed men, indicated that something serious was amiss. Could it be that the Rajah had taken sudden offence at my intrusion? or could the coming of the Sultan's wives be regarded as a proof that the Sultan himself was meditating some unfriendly action towards me? All that I could gather from casual inquiries, was that the Rajah was full of *soesa* (trouble.) All day long in my room a Dyak was busily engaged in making bullets—pieces of stone covered with lead—and cleaning the guns belonging to the Rajah. My men were anxious, and feared treachery; and the openness of the preparations seemed to increase, instead of disarming, their suspicions. At last I sent Tan Bon to ascertain what was the meaning of the commotion in the village; and he returned stating that all the fuss was owing to the Sultan's desire to increase, and not diminish by hostilities, the population of the country! He had heard that several Dyaks had left Long Wai, and gone to another *negorei*, or county, beyond the limits of Koetei; and he had sent up to say that no Dyaks were to leave his territory on any pretence. He wanted his kingdom to become thickly populated, and those that had left were to come back, or be fetched back by force if necessary.

It was a relief to know that the alarm was not caused by any jealousy of my own proceedings; but it was particularly unfortunate that the minds of the people should be unsettled in this way, just at this time, as I was intending to penetrate into the forest, and endeavour if possible to solve for myself the mystery of the Orang Poonan, or Wild People of the Woods.

My hunting party had not yet returned, but there were still two or three of these people passing to and from Long Wai. Never could I see or hear that they were accompanied by women, but the reports which I heard in the village represented the women being white (*poeti*). This I interpreted to mean "fair;" but there seemed much mystery about them, and all my cross-questionings resulted in eliciting very little information as to the whereabouts of their homes; all the answer I could get was that it was "far away." I made many attempts to induce one of the chiefs who visited Long Wai to let me accompany him on his return, but he refused for a long time. At last he said he would take me one day to their hunting-ground, but he must first return himself and prepare his people for my coming, as they would be afraid if I were to go suddenly among them. They would not even see a Malay, and always remained in the densest part of the forest, where it was impossible to track them without a guide.

To make a good impression I gave the Poonan some rice and beads to take as a present for the women, and told him, through a Dyak interpreter, that the interest should be mutual—that they ought to be as anxious to see me as I was to see them. I promised more presents if he was successful in his mission of paving the way for my visit. In a couple of days he returned, and in a very off-hand way told me I could go with him to-morrow.

We started at sunrise, taking a small prau up the river—the Poonan chief, myself, Sariman, and four of the tribe. After paddling some twenty miles up the stream, the canoe was turned to the left into a narrow creek, up which we proceeded for a couple of hours. Suddenly the prau was stopped, and the Poonan made signs that we must land and go through the forest. I could see no trace of a landing-place; and, though I had kept an anxious look-out for any indications of human habitation, I had seen none. There was nothing to show that the spot at which we had stopped was different from any other point throughout the whole distance we had travelled—no trace of a path, not even a broken branch or other indication of traffic could I see, as a sign that human foot had ever trodden there before. I was afterwards told that the Poonans make marks on trees to show their movements and resting places to each other. After struggling through a bamboo thicket, which, to all appearance, had never before been disturbed by human hand or foot, we found ourselves in the dense forest. The chief made a curious cry, *Hio! hio!* which was answered by another voice in the distance; and a few moments later I was led up to a tall tree, where, sitting under an awning of attap, supported by four bamboo sticks, were three young women, one of them with a baby in a sort of cradle slung on her back; while a fourth woman, much older, was roasting the thick hide of a long-nosed monkey (*nasalis larvatus*) before a fire. Just beyond were two men, who came forward as we approached.

The women were all very small in stature, dirty, and scurvy. The dirt was the more visible on them on account of their light yellowish skin. They were naked, except for a narrow cloth round the loins; in the case of two of the younger women it was barely a foot wide, while the others had a long blue open sarong, such as the Dyak women wear.

They did not seem the least afraid of me, but soon began to ask for beads, &c. Most of the conversation was carried on by means of signs, one woman pointing to her own necklace, for instance, and holding out her hand. Another asked for tobacco, showing a sample in her hand, and saying "Bacco, bacco," which was unmistakable.

I gave them to understand that after I had made sketches of them I would give them presents, and three of the women stood very quiet while I took their portraits. The name of the one in the blue sarong (Plate 16) I ascertained to be Song, while the other woman, carrying the baby, is Mrs. Lūn. On the arm of the younger girl will be seen the marks of a kind of vaccination practised by these people (see p. 213).

By the time I had made the drawings their dinner was cooked. They hospitably asked me to partake of their fare—roast monkey—which I politely declined, though I have heard it is very good eating. The meat was simply roasted over the fire, suspended from sticks stuck in the ground; and the only cooking utensils to be seen were bamboo cylinders used for boiling rice. There was not even a clay pot. I once saw the chief use the shoulder-blade of the monkey as a spoon; but they have no manufactured "cutlery," making use only of the forks which were in use in the time of Adam.

I believe the fairness of skin among the women to be the effect of their perfect seclusion in the dark forest, where the sun's rays penetrate scarcely ever, if at all. The men, though not so dark as other Dyaks, are much darker than the women, owing to the fact that they spend much of their time on the rivers, where the sky is open, and that they frequently visit Long Wai, where they are more or less exposed to the rays of the sun. Individuals of both sexes, however, differ much both in physical build and in colour of skin, as will be seen by a comparison of the different plates. The woman represented in Plate 17 was much darker-skinned than the other two, and of heavier build. Plate 24 represents the chief under whose guidance I visited the Forest People "at home." He was not nearly so dark nor so heavily built as an Orang Poonan who hailed from a district to the north of Long Wahou—considerably further north than the district through which the other roamed—and whose head is shown in Plate 22. The swarthy skin and the loftier forehead of the Long Wahou Poonan contrast strongly with the colour and physiognomy of the others.

My stay among these primitive wild people of the woods was limited to a single afternoon; but I had ample opportunity of observing the customs of the men during my stay at Long Wai, as I made several hunting excursions with different parties of them from time to time.

In Plate 15 I have represented a group of three young Poonans, sketched as they lay asleep in their natural characteristic attitudes during one of our hunting expeditions. These people live day and night in the open air, almost entirely naked, with no more shelter in showery weather than that afforded by an attap mat (*kajang*), which they then place over instead of under them when they lie down on the ground to sleep, as seen in the left-hand figure in Plate 15. They always, however, keep a fire burning at night. In the bag or basket (*lebét*) near the centre of the group is one of these kajangs rolled up ready for carrying, and attached to it are a quiver of arrows, and a gourd containing the little balls of pith which are placed at the end of the arrows to enable them to be blown through the tube. Hung on the branch of the tree overhead are another quiver of arrows, a gourd containing the pith balls, and a mandau, while to the right is a shield.

The men are all armed with mandaus, obtained from the Dyaks by exchange. Their aboriginal weapons are the *sumpitan* (blowing-tube) and poisoned arrows (see Plate 18, Figs. 9, 10), in the manufacture and use of which they are all expert. These are similar to the ordinary Dyak weapons of the same kind described at p. 193, and figured in Plate 18.

I was fortunate enough to obtain by exchange specimens of most of their very scanty stock of personal goods. In Plate 14, Fig. 12 is represented a comb, made of bamboo, split into ten teeth. This is frequently used by them, though I am forced to say not often enough. Fig. 13 represents the poison-plate, on which they prepare the arrow-poison.

I once, quite by accident, had an opportunity of seeing the manner in which the poison is placed on the arrows. When sitting in the house one evening I noticed a smell as of gutta-percha boiling, and seeing the Poonans very busy with their arrows I went up to them, and by signs asked them what they were doing. One of the men replied by pointing to the arrow-head. "*Radjun?*" (poison), I inquired in Malay; to which he replied by nodding his head. I then watched their proceedings. They had a bundle of arrows by their side, and as soon as the poisonous matter was hot they took a small quantity and smeared over a wooden plate (see Plate 19, Fig. 13) by means of a wooden instrument resembling a pestle, till the plate was covered with a thick layer. Then taking an arrow they rolled the head across the plate, so that it became coated with the pasty matter. Next they made a spiral incision in the arrow-head and again rolled it over the plate. The arrow was then ready for use. And terribly poisonous these arrows undoubtedly are. A bird, or an animal as large as a monkey, if hit with one of these weapons will immediately fall with convulsive movements, and a few seconds afterwards life is extinct.

Birds and animals thus killed are eaten by the Poonans, and indeed by Dyaks all over Borneo, without any ill effect. As soon as they have secured their quarry, they remove the arrow by cutting out the piece of flesh into which it has penetrated, to the distance of an inch or so all round.

What this arrow-poison is made of I could never ascertain, notwithstanding all my inquiries on the spot. It certainly contained nicotine—which the Dyaks collect from their pipes when they get foul after smoking. I brought home a specimen, which I submitted to Sir Robert Christison, Bart., for analysis and experiment. Sir Robert not having, since his well-earned retirement from public life, the necessary facilities for an investigation of this nature,[1] very kindly handed the poison to Dr. Rutherford,

[1] I am indebted to Sir Robert Christison for the following observations:—"It is a good many years since I applied myself to the study of the Borneo poison. At that time, however, the imperfect and discrepant accounts of its source, action, and even name, as given by such authors as I could consult, left me quite at a loss regarding every point in its history. The works I refer to are chiefly Leschenhault, the experiments of Magendie, Orfile, and Delisle, the notices by Mérat in his 'Dict. de Matière Medicale,' and some brief references to the subject in the narratives of our naval adventures with the pirates of Borneo and its neighbourhood. There is great confusion from mixing up with one another the Java *Tschettik* (*Tieuté* of the French), the Java *Antiar* or *Upas Antiar*, and the *Ipo*, then stated as the name, or one of the names, of the Borneo poison. Consequently one authority speaks of the poison causing death by coma with convulsions; another by paralysis; another by arresting the action of the heart. In short, you will not wonder that, with such materials, I gave up my work in that direction with despair. *Tschettik*, however, is well known to be got from a species of *Strychnos*, the *S. Tieuté*; and *Antiar* has been referred to

Professor of Physiology at Edinburgh University. Here, however, a fresh obstacle presented itself. Parliament having in its wisdom, and at the instigation of an unscientific agitation, passed a law known as the Anti-Vivisection Act, which places serious restrictions on any scientific investigation necessitating experiments on living animals, Dr. Rutherford has been unable [2] to make any attempt to ascertain the nature, action, and effects of the poison, and to find a cure for it. Our seamen have already been at close quarters with Dyak pirates, and the occasion may easily arise when they shall be so again; and there can scarcely be a question whether the lives of a few rabbits can be placed in the scale against the life of a single sailor who may fall a victim to one of their deadly darts. We can ill afford to lose a second Commander Goodenough at the hands either of South Sea Islanders, of Borneo pirates, or of South American Indians; and the discovery of the nature of the various arrow-poisons used in different parts of the world would be the first step towards the discovery of an antidote. If the anti-vivisectionists object to the immolation of a few rabbits in such a cause, will they submit one of their own bodies for experiment?

The use of the poisoned arrow is a great advantage to the collector of natural history specimens, as no injury is caused to the skin of the animal or bird, the hole caused by the arrow point being so minute as to be quite imperceptible.

When shooting with me the Poonans always begged me for the empty cartridge-cases, and it was some time before I could discover for what purpose they wanted them; but at last I found that they put them as ornaments in the ears.

It is curious that in their intercourse with the Long Wai Dyaks these Orang Poonan do not appear to have adopted any of the customs of the latter. The only thing in which they seem to have profited by their acquaintance with their neighbours is in arming themselves with mandaus, and in a few instances in procuring by exchange a small quantity of cloth, with which they make the

a peculiar species, *Antiaris tonicaria* (Leschenhault), belonging to the family *Artocarpaceæ.* But, so far as I am aware, nothing is yet known of the botanical source of the Borneo *Ipo*—if that be its right name."

[2] See Appendix.

head gear and tjawat which constitute their sole clothing. Although, for instance, they seem to appreciate the advantage of a house to sleep in, they have not introduced into their home in the wild woods the custom of building any kind of habitation.

Even in the case of illness they rely upon their own skill rather than adopt the remedies employed by their neighbours—though in this respect, perhaps, the Dyaks could teach them little that is worth learning. One day one of the Poonans staying at Long Wai fell ill, and complained of a pain in his back. Without hesitation the chief took his small knife from his mandau sheath, and taking a piece of flesh firmly between his fingers made three incisions in the lower part of the back, in the region of the kidneys. In each slit he inserted a bamboo cylinder, two inches long, which he first made very hot, pressing them down firmly, and afterwards applying a little hot water to the wounds. I felt this novel kind of seton, and found the three pieces of bamboo were fastened very securely into the flesh.

Another day the chief himself was laid down with fever, but he would accept no assistance from the Dyaks; and, as he showed no signs of improvement after several days, he was removed by his men to his home in the forest. I never heard whether he recovered.

My visit to the Poonans had the effect of bringing some of the ladies out of their retirement; for a few days afterwards several of the women, accompanied by men who had not hitherto ventured into Long Wai, came to the village and stayed with me for a couple of hours. This was quite an event in the annals of the village, and I told my men to give my visitors a good meal of rice; which they enjoyed heartily as a pleasant change from their daily bill of fare of monkeys, wild boars, serpents, birds, and wild fruits. I found afterwards that the real object of their visit was to beg some salt. They said their friends who had been staying at Long Wai had told them I had been very liberal in distributing salt and other presents; and so, on the strength of this compliment, as well as out of pity for their scorbutic condition, I gave them a plentiful supply of salt, to which I added a few handfuls of "bacco."

I believe these savages to be the true aborigines of Borneo.

They live in utter wildness in the central forests of Borneo, almost entirely isolated from all communication with the rest of the world. A few of the men occasionally visit Long Wai, and are on friendly terms with the Dyaks, but they will not hold communication with a Malay. Their existence has long been known, but no European before myself ever saw one of the women of the race; and it is some compensation to me for all the difficulties and dangers of my journey across Borneo that I am able to lay before the public faithful likenesses of these people, and a correct, if somewhat brief and imperfect, description of their habits and customs.

CHAPTER VII.

Dyak amusements—Musical instruments—A birthday festival—The cemetery—Royal tombs—Buried treasures—The evil spirits angered—Hunting parties—Dividing the spoil—A conflagration averted—A boar-hunt—A swimming boar—An *al fresco* feast—A mountain on fire—Death-posts and human skulls—A mysterious trophy—Forcible ablutions—The Rajah in full state—Boegis robbers—A saw-fish—Down the river—An unexpected meeting.

In the evenings there were always some amusements while the Poonans were at Long Wai. One of them would play on a bamboo flute with his left nostril, while a few Dyaks would sit round the dim and smoky *damar* torch, made from the resin of a forest-tree, and enjoy a cigarette or pipe.

Sometimes they would give a war-dance at my request, on the great floor under Rajah Dinda's house, where a couple of Dyaks, each with a shield (*kliau*) and sword (*mandau*), would face each other in all sorts of attitudes, changing them with a remarkable rapidity to the accompaniment of a two-stringed fiddle (djimpai) or a "kleddi"—the latter a curious instrument,[1] with organ-like tones, rather pleasing to the ear. The music, however, would be drowned by an endless shouting and yelling, proceeding from the audience as well as the performers.

One evening, a little past nine, I had just closed my eyes to enjoy a night's rest when I was awakened by a great noise of singing and stamping. I listened for some time, but still the sounds did not cease, but rather increased. All my men were asleep except Sariman, who said the Dyaks were dancing at some feast. I went out to see what the performance was like, and saw on the same platform under Rajah Dinda's house, quite in the dark, thirteen Dyaks, all men, singing, and walking round in a

[1] See Plate 19, Figs. 1 and 3; also p. 217.

circle, first turning their feet to the right and stamping on the floor, then pausing a moment, and turning to the left, still stamping. Occasionally another recruit joined the company. What was all this about? I kept asking. A woman had given birth to a child! was the answer. And so this jollification was kept up half the night in honour of the little stranger.

The Dyak tombs which I had seen along the river-banks on my way up to Long Wai had keenly excited my curiosity, which was increased by the frequent rumours of the grandeur of the burial-places of the Rajahs of Long Wai. Ké Patti described them to me as large carved structures, which no stranger was ever allowed to visit. His stories of the extreme privacy with which they were guarded only made me the more anxious to see them. But he said he dared not ask Rajah Dinda; nor would Rajah Sinen ask his brother. Dinda had always been very willing to grant my requests, but when I told him I wished to see his fathers' graves he thought I had asked too much. Besides, he added, it was against his *adat*. Time after time I persecuted him for permission to visit the forbidden ground, telling him to leave *adat* a little on one side; still he hesitated, and I found out he was under the influence of the women, who thought I should steal one of the bodies, and prophesied bad luck if a stranger were allowed to go to the sacred place. I reminded Dinda of the Sultan's instructions, that "what I wished to see, I must see" (*Apo soeka liat—moesti liat*). If he preferred, he might himself go with me, and be witness that I had no other motive for going there than to see how his fathers were buried, and make drawings of the tombs. At last the Rajah gave an unwilling consent, and, accompanied by Sariman and five Dyaks, I started one day for the forbidden ground. We paddled down the river for a couple of miles till we came to a side stream on the right, which we ascended for another mile, the banks being lined with bamboo. Landing at a small opening through the thicket, we walked along a narrow path till we came to a small clearing, which was the cemetery of Long Wai. Here, surrounded by the graves of a number of his subjects, lay the bones of Rajah Dinda's fathers, and other members of his family. There were two forms of graves generally adopted by the common people; one a small chamber, raised on posts from ten to twenty feet high, in which the corpse was placed; the other a somewhat similar structure built into a hole in the ground. The latter form was the commonest.

The tombs of the Rajahs were most substantially-built and elaborately-decorated structures of ironwood, with every crack and crevice carefully filled in with putty made of damar resin and chalk[2] to prevent the inroads of insects. The roofs were of laths of ironwood, imbricated. The walls were carved, and rudely painted with representations of birds or quadrupeds, the favourite crocodile of course not being omitted, and the gables at each end were elaborately carved.

Plate 8 shows the "house" in which Rajah Dinda's father and family are laid; while Plate 9 represents the mausoleum of Rajah Sinen's family.

Rajah Dinda's father was buried with all his clothes, his sword, shield, and paddle—with which he is supposed to paddle himself to heaven in his coffin, which represents a prau. In his hands he is said to have had a quantity of gold dust.

Mr. Von. Dewall[3] mentions that the Rajahs and the rich Dyaks do not let the bodies of their deceased relatives remain in these burial-places; but gather the bones, after all the impurities have disappeared, place them in jars, and hide them up far in the mountains—in caves. I never heard that this was the case with the Dyaks of Long Wai, but I was told that the Dyaks on the banks of the Teweh, in the Doesoen district, used to adopt this practice, though they have abandoned it of late years, since the supremacy of the Dutch.

I stayed at the cemetery till noon, making sketches, and taking notes of the features of the place; but was unable to finish my drawings, and left with the intention of returning another day. Just as we landed at Long Wai a most terrific thunderstorm burst over the village, the rain fell in torrents, and the wind was so high that I was afraid our house would fall to pieces. As it was, the attap roof was partly blown away, and in order to keep out the rain and wind the Dyaks, who always have a reserve of these

[2] See p. 202.

[3] "*Overzigt van het Rijk van Koetei.*"

roof-coverings, had to set to work at once to repair the damage. In an hour or two the river rose several feet, and the Dyaks, fearing that the current would carry their praus down the river, hastened down to the beach, which was all under water, and dragged them far up on dry land, and made them fast. In the evening Rajah Dinda came in to see me, calm and stern-looking. He said the women of the palace all blamed him for giving me permission to go to the burial-place, and all this rain and hurricane had occurred in consequence of my intrusion. I said to Dinda that I hoped the rain was wanted for the crops; but the Modangs all answered that, on the contrary, just now, while they were preparing the rice-fields, fine weather was wanted. Fortunately no harm came of the ire of the evil spirits which I had so innocently conjured up; and three days later I went back to the cemetery to complete my sketches. As luck would have it, the women were fated to have their revenge, for on my return in the afternoon another tempest, not quite so violent as the last, but still unusual at that time of year, swept over the village; and I doubt not Rajah Dinda regretted for once in his life that he had not been content with one wife to scold him, instead of being blessed with four.

The Dyaks would go out in parties, once or twice a week hunting the deer and wild boar, both of which are plentiful in all parts of Koetei. Although the thick tangled undergrowth in the forests renders it impossible to penetrate far from the riverside in order to reach the game, and equally difficult to get within range of the animals, the well-trained dogs rarely fail to drive a deer or two and a few boars within reach of the sportsmen, who remain within a short distance of the river. During the first week of my stay at Long Wai a large party, headed by Rajah Sinen, went away hunting early in the morning; before noon I heard a great shouting on the shore under my window, and presently a swarm of Dyaks crowded up the ladder into my room, bearing with them one of the trophies of the chase in the shape of a fine deer. This was followed by three wild boars, for nothing would please Rajah Sinen but that all the game should be brought to me, and that I should select what portion I preferred. I bargained, in the first place, that I should have the skulls of the animals—as a gentle hint to the human head-hunters that my taste for such spoils did not extend beyond wild beasts. Next, I directed "Baba," one of my Chinese servants, and Laban, the cook, to cut some joints or slices for my men, who had had to put up with rather a scanty bill of fare at Long Wai, and subsist chiefly on rice and fruits, fish being scarce and other provisions dear. The prospect of a treat of venison was therefore very welcome to them all, and my two Chinamen especially revelled in the idea of pork for dinner. The fact that the religious scruples of the Malay cook, who professed the Mohammedan belief, prevented him from either cutting up the boar, or cooking any of the meat, did not disconcert them in the least, and it was not long before my larder was plentifully stocked with prime cuts of venison and boar's flesh. Then the animals were removed, and, after Rajah Sinen had taken his share, the remains were divided among the whole village, and the rest of the day was devoted to preparations for the feast in the evening. The meat was cut up into innumerable slices, a dozen or more of which were stuck at a time on a piece of bamboo, and roasted, or rather smoked, over the fire.

I had no sooner congratulated myself on having got rid of my hunting friends than I found blue wreaths of smoke penetrating the cracks in the floor of my room, entering at the door and window, and gradually filling the place. Thinking that in the excitement the house had been accidentally set on fire, I hastened below, and found four or five fires lighted on the platform immediately underneath. Not relishing the idea of being turned into smoked bacon myself, I ordered the fires to be extinguished. To my surprise I found that not merely the flesh, but also the thick hide of the wild boars, was cut into pieces, smoked, and eaten. This *bonne bouche* was mostly reserved for the Poonans. The tusks of the boars were always carefully preserved, and worn as charms, attached to the girdle of the mandau, together with the canine teeth of monkeys, bears, &c.

Von Dewall says "the Modangs of Long Wai do not eat venison." But this statement is erroneous, for, on the contrary, they are very fond of the meat; and whenever a deer is killed every iuhabitant of the village gets a share. The native who actually shoots the animal has the right to the horns, which are much sought after, the bases being used to make the handles of the mandaus.

A hunting day is always an event of interest to the dogs, as well as their masters, for they get a good supply of bones and refuse meat as a reward for the part they have borne in the day's proceedings.

During an excursion of thirty miles beyond Long Wai I had a grand day's sport with Rajahs Dinda and Sinen and a number of Poonans. Our intended quarry was deer, but failing that we were sure to get wild boars. There was also a chance, the Rajah hinted, that we might come across some other tribes, with whom the Long Wai Dyaks were not on the best of terms; and, as he could not answer for the consequences if such were the case, he determined to take three praus and a good following. The largest prau was allotted to me, manned by fourteen Poonans, while Rajah Dinda and his brother Sinen had seven and six men respectively in their boats. Before starting I gave them two picols of rice and a quantity of tobacco, with which, it is needless to say, they were greatly pleased, flattering me with the oft-repeated remark that I had a "good heart."

We paddled up the river from six o'clock in the morning till four o'clock in the afternoon, stopping once to pick up a reinforcement of four Poonans, whom we met watching us from the bank. Beyond this we saw no sign of human existence. All was solemn silence, broken only by the plash of the paddles as the three praus, closely following each other, pursued their course up the winding river.

Presently Rajah Dinda selected a spot for landing; the vessels were made fast to the bank, and the whole party were soon on shore. Rajah Dinda, a head taller than the rest, carrying his spear in his left hand, with massive gold bangles jingling on his Herculean legs, gave his orders in a very quiet and dignified manner, dividing the party into three groups. He, with fifteen men and dogs, was to advance and drive the game towards the second line, behind which, again, the third group was to be stationed, at a distance of some 300 yards. I belonged to the third section. We were all in line, twenty or twenty-five feet distant from each other, and stood thus, patiently, for about an hour, during which we heard no sounds to indicate the progress of the beaters in the first line. Suddenly, however, the dogs began barking, and a general wild chorus of men's voices arose in all directions. All order was now abandoned. Some ran further into the forest, others back towards the river. I could see no sign of deer or boar, but as there seemed to be a general concentration of forces to the water's edge I ran down, and saw a large boar rapidly swimming across the stream —and he swam with the greatest ease—followed, and spurred to increased efforts, by the dogs; but before he could reach the opposite bank a bullet put an end to his efforts, and his body was soon secured, and brought ashore amid general cries of delight.

After this little excitement was over we returned to our posts in the forest, and had not long to wait before a general barking, with which a few short sharp grunts mingled, indicated another successful drive. This time there were several pigs, which were quickly driven through the second line; and suddenly there rushed at me, through the thick undergrowth, a great tusker, not three feet distant, closely followed by a barking and excited dog. It was a moment's work to level my rifle and fire, and the bullet went through the boar and lodged in the lower jaw of the unfortunate dog. I begged the owner of the dog, a Dyak, to let me extract the bullet, but he would not allow me to do so, and the poor animal has since gone about unable to shut its mouth properly.

The result of the day's sport was six wild boars, over which, in the evening, a general jollification took place on the pebbly beach by the riverside, before we returned home. Some of the animals were cut up and divided amongst the party; and fires were lighted, whose lurid glare was reflected in the water, and gave a weird charm to the whole scene, as the blue smoke was carried across the water by the evening breeze, and filtered through the dense foliage on the opposite shore; while the dark forms of the naked savages stood out in bold relief, some flitting around the fires busily engaged in cooking operations, others lying resting at full length on the ground, or sitting, pipe in mouth, calmly surveying the scene.

In the distance, at a place the Modangs called "Woo-ohalla," could be seen a burning hill, from the summit and sides of which dense smoke issued. It was a coal formation on fire, and had been burning since the memory of man.

During my stay I looked anxiously for skulls, of which, according to the custom of the Dyaks, and the reputation which the Long Wai tribe had for bravery, there ought to be a large collection somewhere, especially Long Wahou crania, taken from the neighbouring tribe further north, who are the greatest enemies of the Long Wai people. A leaning post[4] standing alone on the shore, which is shown in my sketch of the village (Plate 7), is the only visible indication that the Long Wai people have been successful head-hunters. For some reason or other Rajah Dinda, and all the people, avoided the subject whenever I spoke of it—an indication, perhaps, that their intercourse with the outer world was having some influence on their barbarous customs.

Mr. Van Dewall, who spent three or four days at Long Wai, in April, 1847, says in his "*Overzigt van het Rijk van Koetei*," that "near the burial-place of the last Rajah of Long Wai, on the right bank of the river, stand upon posts nine human skulls, which the people had secured on their murderous excursion to Wahou, after the decease of the Rajah." On my way up the river I had seen one bleached skull, stuck up on the top of a tree; but this was all the outward and visible sign I could find of the head-hunting practices of the people. One day, however, I was looking round Dinda's house, in company with Ké Patti, when I observed something strange hanging under the roof, wrapped in a dried old banana leaf. I was going to examine the contents, when both Ké Patti and Rajah Sinen shouted to me *Tida boele, tida boele* (must not, must not). I asked if it was a skull, but they did not answer. Sinen was very angry, because he thought I was going to take the mysterious object down; and from this fact, as well as from the evasive answers they gave to my questions, I strongly suspected the innocent-looking banana leaf did contain a human skull. This

[4] Van Dewall says that "before the house of the *Kapoeie* (Rajah) of Long Wai stand seventeen rough posts, fifteen to twenty feet long. These are monuments that a party has been out head-hunting, and returned with one or more heads."

suspicion was afterwards confirmed, for when at Long Puti, some months later, I saw several human crania thus preserved in a dried leaf.

I was very desirous of going to Long Wahou, to visit the great rivals and enemies of the Long Wai people who live there; but I could neither get a canoe for the journey—the Sultan's praus, which had brought me up, having returned to Tangaroeng—nor induce any one to accompany me. The Long Wai Dyaks of course gave a very shocking account of their neighbours; but from what I have seen and heard I should imagine it is "six of one and half a dozen of the other," and that the Long Wahou people are neither better nor worse than the rest of their race.

In Plate 10 I am enabled to give a likeness of a Long Wahou warrior whom I subsequently met at Tangaroeng. His bulky form, contrasting with his thin and comparatively small face, put me in mind of Rajah Dinda.

My stay at Long Wai lasted over a period of seven weeks, during which time I had ample opportunities of making myself acquainted with the Dyak character, and studying their manners and customs.[5] They frequently told me very plainly that they did not care to have strangers amongst them, and they displayed an unwillingness to answer inquiries about their customs, and a superstitious reserve in their communications if they thought they were being watched.

Still I managed to establish friendly intercourse with them, and fortunately they maintained peaceful relations with the neighbouring tribes during my stay among them. Peace is not usually of long duration. There are births, "namings," marriages, burials, always occurring; and, on every such occasion an incursion into the adjoining territory is necessary, and a state of war prevails for a time. As the result proved, my departure was coincident with an event which was the signal for a general preparation for war. One of Rajah Dinda's wives presented him with a child—a son, much to his delight—a few days before my departure, and I left Long Wai in a state of general excitement in consequence. Already mandaus were being sharpened, and shields furbished up,

[5] The result of my observations here and in other parts of Borneo is embodied in separate chapters, pp. 182-232.

in readiness for a head-hunting expedition. The child could not be named unless the head of some luckless neighbour was duly cut off, and brought home in triumph.

My peaceful relations with the tribe were only marred by the quarrelsome nature of my cook, a fair specimen of a Boegis. The Dyaks were very willing to cut wood for me, and render various services, assisting my other servants in many ways. But this Boegis was both cowardly and lazy, and made himself so obnoxious that he was literally Boycotted. The only service that was willingly rendered to him by the Dyaks was one day, when they had complained that this Boegis never bathed, and I ordered him to be marched down to the river, and induced him to submit to have his head shaved. Both Dyaks and Malays are very scrupulous about bathing, even if the operation does not always have the desired effect. They have not yet been taught the use of soap, and bathing does not necessarily mean absolute cleanliness. Still they bathed, and that was something; but the Boegis refused even that tribute to the god of cleanliness; and when I gave directions that he should be ducked by force, if he did not bathe willingly, and that he must lose his hair as a penalty for the—even for a Malay—unconscionably large number of lodgers that found cover there, there were plenty of willing arms to assist him in his ablutions, and plenty of hands, skilled in cutting off heads as well as hair, ready to perform the necessary tonsorial duty.

The last few days of September were occupied in packing up my natural history collection, and other goods and chattels. The Dyaks watched my proceedings with the keenest interest; and when I had nearly finished packing they came and offered for sale or exchange any number of plates, mats, baskets, and other articles of native manufacture. The Poonans, who had rendered me throughout the greatest assistance, helped me carry my baggage down to the prau which the Sultan had sent up to fetch me; and on the morning of the 26th I left, to return to Tangaroeng. A young Dyak came down to me at the last moment, and, whispering, said in a few broken words of Malay that he belonged to the southern part of Koetei, and begged to be allowed to accompany me. He was a servant of Rajah Dinda, so

I dared not take him without permission, and the lad himself was afraid to ask.

The Rajah himself came down to the shore to bid me good-bye, and a *slaamat jallan.* He probably wanted to impress me with the importance of a Rajah of Long Wai when in full state, for he was dressed in a black satin jacket, with six heavy large gold buttons, something similar in workmanship to the silver buttons worn by the peasants in the interior of Norway; a crimson Boegis sarong cloth was slung across his broad shoulders, in Andalusian fashion; and round his legs he had a series of heavy gold bangles. Thus arrayed, he certainly presented a very striking and commanding appearance as he walked slowly down the beach.

Then, with unfeigned pleasure at their return home, with a merry song, my crew plied their paddles vigorously, and the prau floated rapidly down the swift stream.

At Moeara Tjaloeng we found a disturbance in the village. A party of Boegis, who had come on a trading journey, had been stealing *engros* (money), rattans, and wax, and had gone off with the booty, and the inhabitants were at their wits' end to know what to do. So Ké Patti suggested that we should stay a day here, and try and settle the matter. A bitchara was held accordingly in one of the largest houses, and all the facts laid before us amid a Babel of tongues. In the midst of the consultation a boat-load of Boegis landed at the village, appeared on the scene, well armed as they always are, and were denounced by the inhabitants as the culprits. After two hours' deliberation they agreed to return part of the spoil, and were let off without further punishment.

As we were leaving in the afternoon, two Koetei Malays in a boat came alongside, and offered me a quantity of fish, mostly a species of *silurus*, common in all the rivers of Borneo. Among them I noticed a small saw-fish, the beak of which was about eighteen inches in length. I had bought a similar one in Celebes, with a curved handle fixed to it, which was said to have come from New Guinea, and to have been used there as a weapon.

Tangaroeng was reached on the 3rd October. Here the Sultan told me the Assistant Resident was at Pelaroeng; and, as I had received an invitation from Mr. Seitz to visit him there, I went down the next day, and reached Pelaroeng about four p.m. I was somewhat surprised to meet a strange European face on the shore, and still more so when the stranger addressed me by name. It was a pleasure to see a white face, and to hear my native tongue after being so many weeks among a semi-barbarous people. An explanation was soon forthcoming. It was Captain Andresen, the commander of the Sultan's steam yacht "Tiger," a Scandinavian by birth, who, leaving his father's house in Apenrade as a sailor many years ago, had become captain of a vessel trading along the Chinese coast, and had made several voyages to Koetei. Here he met the Sultan, and was eventually appointed commander of his yacht. He had been told of my visit to Koetei, and having heard that I also was a Scandinavian he established my identity by addressing me in Danish. A few minutes sufficed for mutual congratulations; and, as we were talking, we were joined by Mr. Seitz, the Assistant Resident, who said he was starting to-morrow in the Sultan's steam yacht for the northern coast, and invited me to join him.

COLOUR PLATES

PALACE OF THE SULTAN OF KOETEI.

CARL BOCK, DEL.

C.F. Kell Lith. Castle St. Holborn, London.

DWELLING AMONG TOMBS.

CARL BOCK, DEL.

C.F. Kell Lith Castle St. Holborn, London.

ARCHITECTURE AT TANGAROENG.

CARL BOCK, DEL.

C. F. Kell, Litho. Castle St. Holborn, E. C.

DYAK BOY AT HOME

CARL BOCK, DEL.

C. F. Kell, Lith. Castle St. Holborn, W.C.

LONG-WAI DYAK IN WAR COSTUME.

CARL BOCK, DEL.

C. F. Kell, Lith. Castle St. Holborn. E. C.

THE BELLE OF LONG-WAI.

CARL BOCK, DEL.

C. F. Kell, Litho. Castle St. Holborn, E. C.

CARL BOCK, DEL.

C.F. Kell Lith. Castle St. Holborn, London.

THE VILLAGE OF LONG-WAI.

CARL BOCK, DEL.

RAJAH DINDA'S FAMILY SEPULCHRE.

C. F. Kell, Litho. Castle St. Holborn, E.C.

CARL BOCK, DEL.

C.F. Kell Lith. Castle St. Holborn, London.

MAUSOLEUM OF RAJAH SINEN'S FAMILY.

CARL BOCK, DEL.

C. F. Kell. Lithr. Castle St. Holborn. E.C.

A LONG WAHOU WARRIOR.

CARL BOCK, DEL.

C. F. Kell, Lith. Castle St. Holborn. E. C.

TRING DYAK'S WAR DANCE.

CARL BOCK, DEL.

C. F. Kell, Litho. Castle St. Holborn. E. C.

SIBAU MOBANG, CHIEF OF THE CANNIBALS.

CARL BOCK, DEL.

G.F. Hall, Lith. Castle St. Holborn, E.C.

SULAU LANDANG; A FULL-DRESS PORTRAIT.

14.

C. F. Kell, Litho. Castle St. Holborn, E.C.

CARL BOCK, DEL.

WILD PEOPLE AT HOME.

CARL BOCK, DEL.

THE FOREST PEOPLE: MOTHER & MAID.

G. F. Kell, Litho. Castle St. Holborn, E. C.

CARL BOCK DEL

POONAN WOMAN

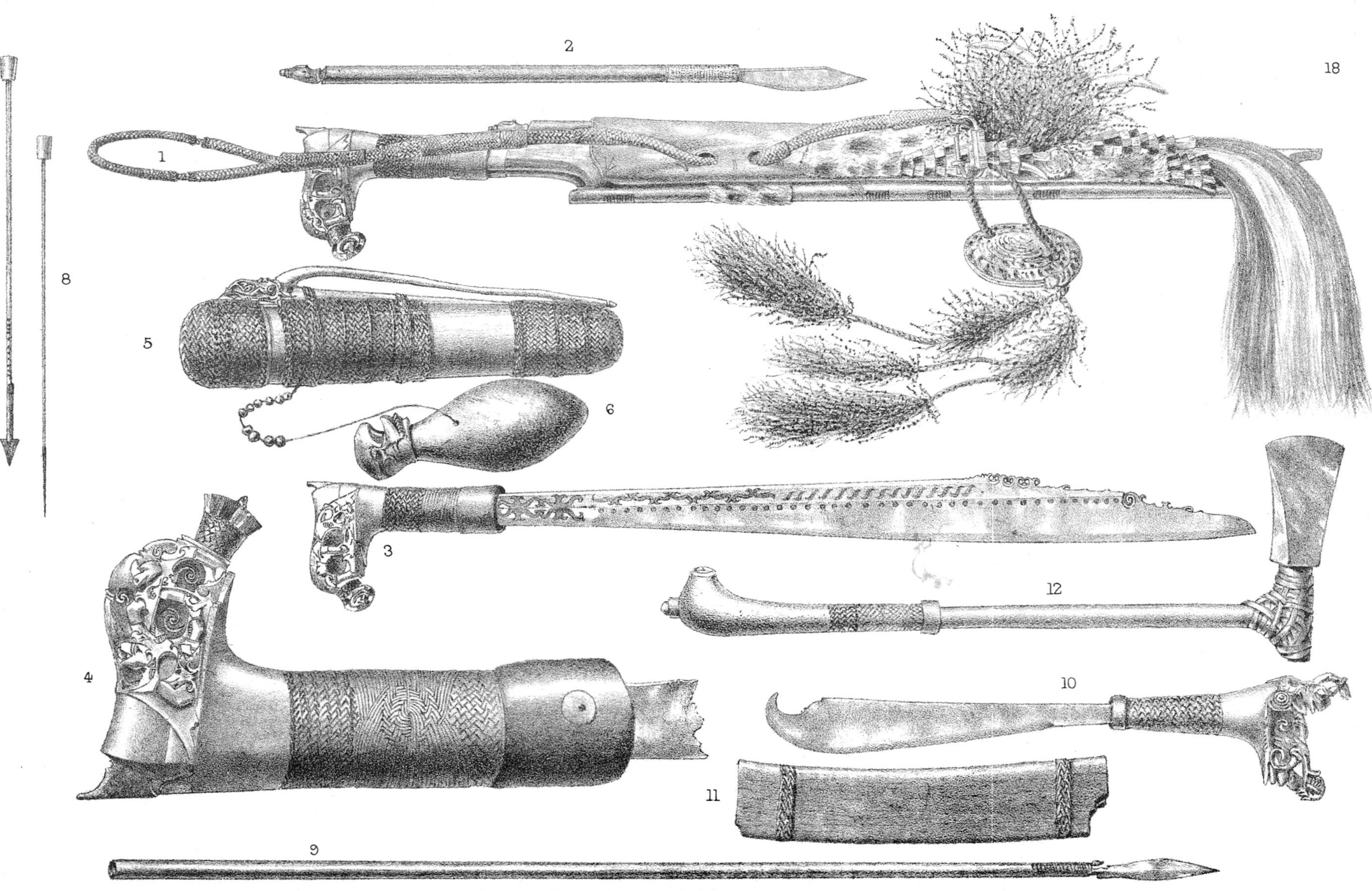
18
2
1
7
8
5
6
3
12
4
10
11
9

19

1 2 3 4 5 6 7 7a 8 9 10 11 12 13 14 15

CARL BOCK DEL.

DYAK UTENSILS CANOE &c.

C. F. Kell, Litho. Castle St. Holborn, E. C.

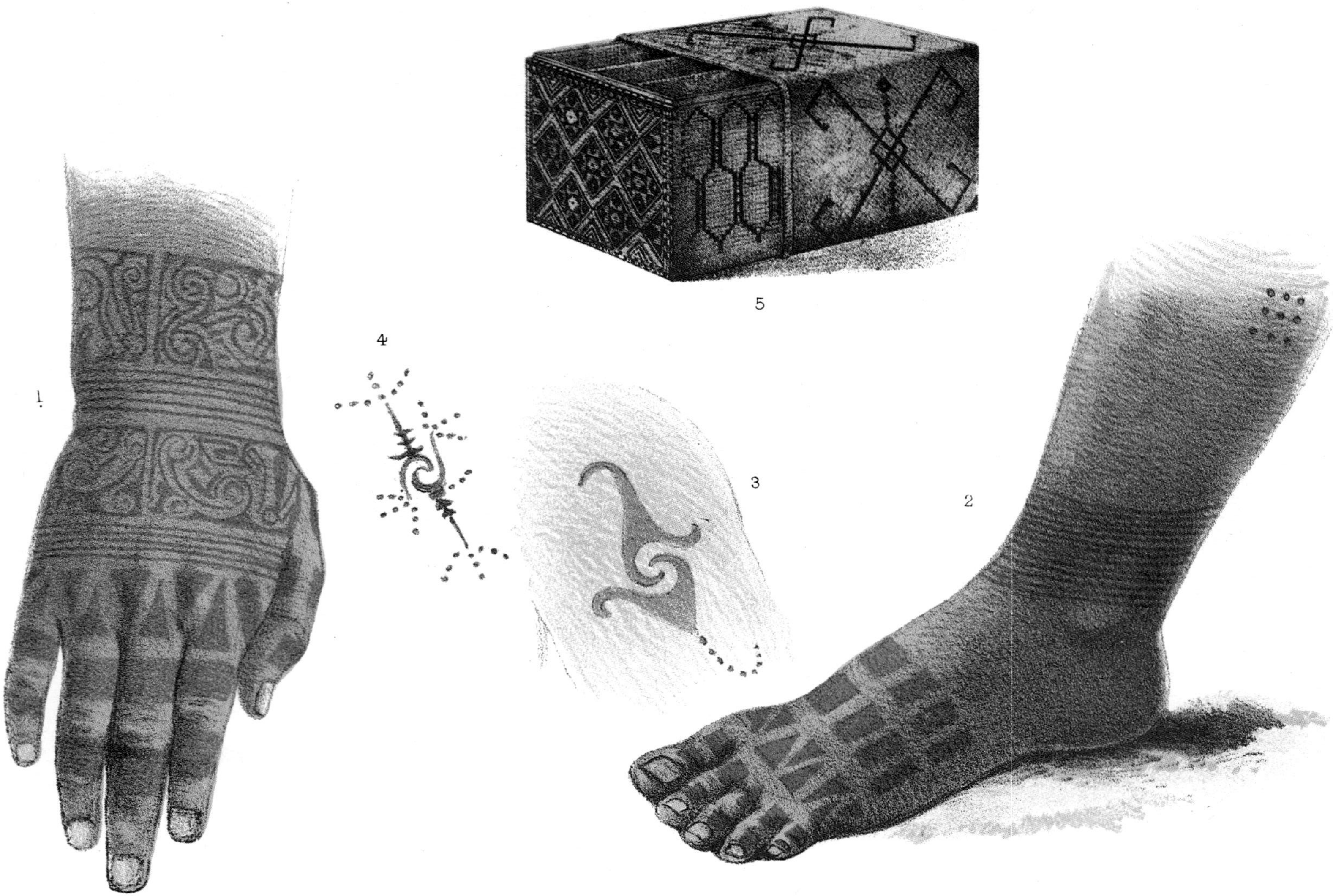

5

4

1

3

2

CARL BOCK, DEL.

(1 to 4) TATTOO MARKS (5) SIRIH BASKET.

C.F. Kell Lith. Castle St. Holborn. London.

21

1

2

3

CARL BOCK, DEL.

(1 & 2) TWO OF MY FOLLOWERS. (3) MANS COIFFURE OF LONGBLEH.

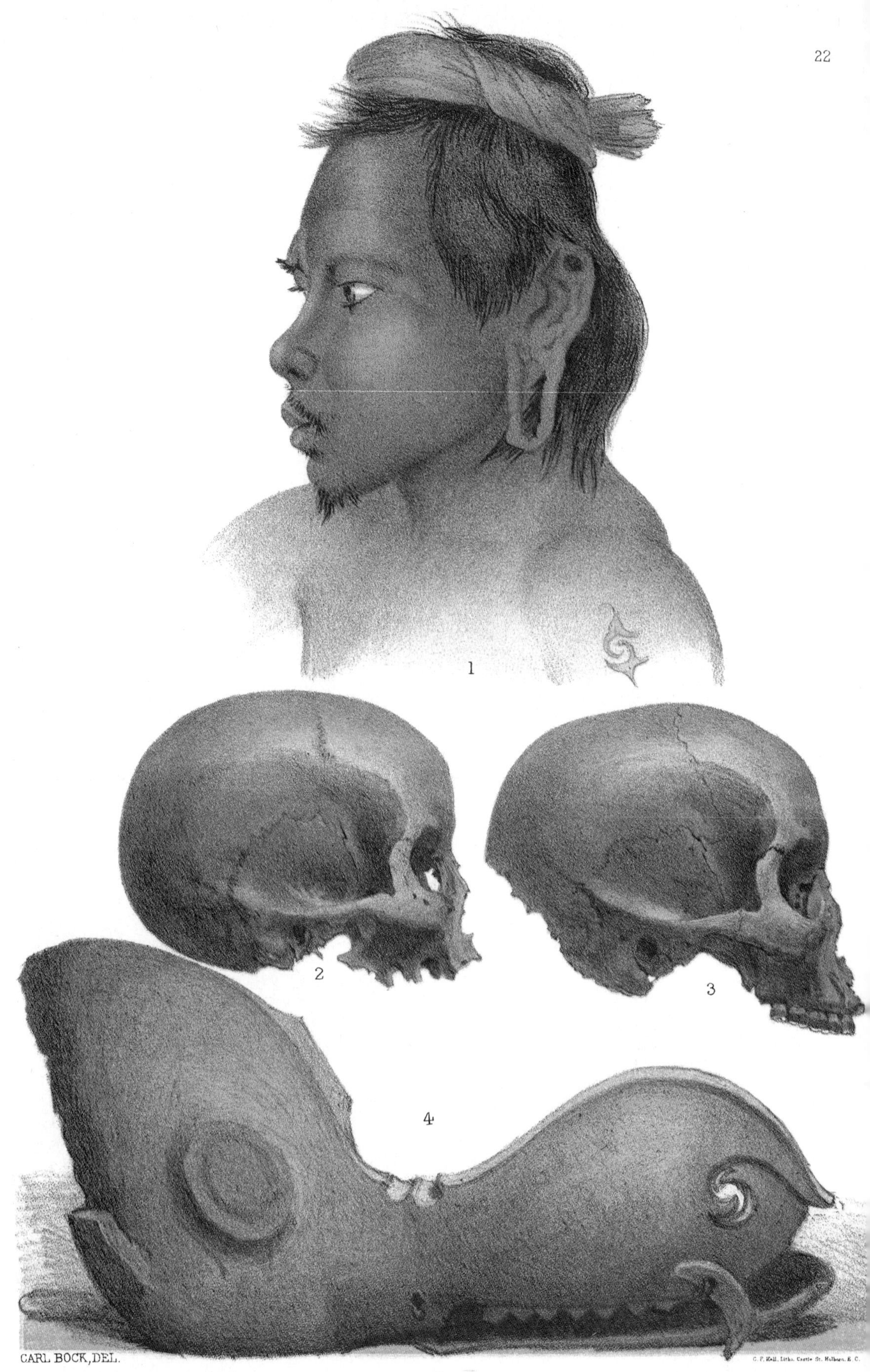

CARL BOCK, DEL.

C. F. Kell, Litho. Castle St. Holborn, E. C.

(1) Poonan from N. of Long Wahou. (2-3) Human Trophies. (4) Festive Mask.

CARL BOCK, DEL.

C. F. Kell, Lithr. Castle St. Holborn, E.C.

HETDUNG, MY FAVORITE DYAK BOY.

CARL BOCK, DEL.

C. F. Kell, Lith. Cast'e St. Holborn, E. C.

A CHIEF OF THE FOREST PEOPLE.

CARL BOCK, DEL.

C.F. Kell, Lith. Castle St. Holborn, London.

DYAK CHIEF LYING IN STATE.

CARL BOCK, DEL.

C. F. Kell, Litho. Castle St. Holborn, E. C.

ORANG-BUKKIT FROM AMONTAI

LONG-WAI WOMAN RETURNING HOME

2 4 1 9 7

3 6 8

5

CARL BOCK, DEL.

DYAK IDOLS & CHARMS.

C.F. Kell Lith. Castle St. Holborn, London.

CARL BOCK, DEL.

C. F. Kell, Litho. Castle St. Holborn, E.C.

ON A HEAD HUNTING TOUR.

CARL BOCK DEL.

CROSSING THE RIVER BENANGAN.

C. F. Kell, Litho. Castle St. Holborn, E. C.

CARL BOCK, DEL.

G. F. Kell, Lith. Castle St. Holborn, E.C.

A MALAY BRIDE — THE HONEYMOON

CHAPTER VIII.

The Sultan's steam yacht—Captive pirates and slave-dealers—A sea trip—A night scene—Phosphorescent creatures—Flying fish—A waterspout—"Pirates"—A false alarm—Tarakan island—A marine forest—A coal bed—Negotiations with the natives—Ugly customers—The Crown Prince of Boelongan—A coral bank—Stung by sea anemones—The east coast of Borneo—A pirate prau and no mistake!—More captive pirates—On board the war-steamer "Riouw."

THE "Tiger," so named from the royal emblem of Koetei, was a fine steam yacht of about 120 tons, built in Glasgow, very long for her breadth, and capable of steaming at a very high rate of speed.

We went on board about midday on October 5th, but just as we were about to start the war-steamer "Salak" came in, having a large prau in tow.

"Another pirate business," said Mr. Seitz, rubbing his hands. "The commander of the 'Salak,' Captain Van Heerwarden, is a lucky fellow. He is always getting some prize."

"How is that?" I interrupted.

"His vessel only draws six feet," replied Seitz, "and he can pursue the pirates into most of the creeks that they can take refuge in. Besides, the pirate praus are the objects of his most particular attention. Once you draw blood, you know, or in other words take a prize, and pirate-hunting, like most other sports, improves upon acquaintance."

So we went ashore to hear results, and presently the commander came, and reported that he had twenty Solok slaves on board, with four pirates, the latter safe in irons, while in the prau were twelve other slaves and the dealers. The last-named were, however, only "suspected," as they were furnished with papers from the Sultan of Boelongan.

This interlude, and an accident the "Tiger" had meanwhile met with—breaking an anchor-chain and losing an anchor, and consequently getting fast on a mud-bank—caused us to postpone our departure till the next day. At seven a.m. we were under steam, and by noon we were out of the delta of the river, with its seventeen arms.

Besides the Assistant Resident, the company consisted of the Pangeran Bandahara, who knows all the people along the coast, with his *djoroe tjoelis*, or secretary; Rajah Dadu of Tidoen, who lives at Sanga Sanga, not far from Pelaroeng; and Mr. Seitz's *précis* writer, a young Chinaman.

It was a treat to see the sea again and watch the changing panorama on shore—a relief from the everlasting forest of the interior to be able to gaze into the depths of the ocean,

"Deeply, darkly, beautifully blue,"

and peer speculatingly at the hidden things of beauty that lay beneath its surface. Some of these would reveal themselves as the darkness came on. Then could be seen myriads of medusæ, discharging flashes of light like meteors in the ocean; or a train of dim white phosphorescence—a luminous glow—gliding in serpentine movements along the surface of the dark water, indicating the presence of incalculable hosts of infusoria, too minute for human eye to detect. The gorgeous effects of sunrise and sunset, when ocean and sky were painted in manifold delicate tints; the paler and calmer glory of the moon, casting her silvery light over the dancing waters; followed by the heavenly host of stars, shining like little suns in another ocean of blue, and illumining with their brilliant rays the dark waves beneath,—these afforded such scenes as, once viewed amid the surroundings of a tropical panorama of sea and land, could never be forgotten.

Once a flying fish fell on board, but was devoured by the agile and ubiquitous cat before it could be subjected to more scientific dissection. On the 7th October we saw a large waterspout, several miles off, going towards Celebes, in the direction of which heavy rain was falling, and the sky was very hazy, though it was quite fine and clear where we were.

At ten a.m. on the 8th October, the weather fine, and no land in sight, the man on the look-out suddenly cried,—

"Badjaks!" (Pirates).

The possibility of encountering pirates had never entered our heads, and Mr. Seitz at once inquired if the captain had arms on board. The latter in reply pointed to four brass cannons, of last century pattern,—

"All in disorder, except one, which is used for saluting," said he.

We went into the cabin, and found half a dozen Snider rifles: but where were the cartridges?

"I left them at Samarinda," said the Pangeran Bandahara, with a rueful expression of countenance and an expletive that will not bear translating.

Mr. Seitz began to be uneasy, and we were discussing whether we should show fight, firing the saluting cannon to prove that we had heavy guns on board, or display that "better part of valour" called "discretion," by returning, when the captain carefully scrutinized the *badjaks* through his telescope, and they turned out to be two harmless nipa palms, floating on the water.

After the excitement had passed off, some of the crew amused themselves with fishing: there was not much sport, but expectation was aroused presently when one of them called out "*Dappat ikkam!*" (Caught a fish). He hauled in his copper line with care, but pleased anticipation gave way to disappointment when he found his "fish" was nothing but a piece of nipa stem. After these experiences the word nipa came to be regarded as synonymous with deception.

At six p.m. we anchored a quarter of a mile off Pulo Tarakan, or Tarakan Island, in seven fathoms of water; and lay there for the night.

The next day the captain, engineer, and I went ashore, and found, skirting the coast for a depth of 100 feet, a thick belt of casuarinas, behind which was dense forest. The roots of the casuarinas were partly uncovered, and often formed curiously tangled masses, more or less covered with *nerita*, while in the crevices were numerous *murices*, *cerithium*, and *nassæ*. The shore here is a tertiary coal formation, and the Dutch war steamers have occasionally had recourse to the tertiary deposits at Tarakan Island when short of coal, paying the Sultan of Boelongan a royalty of eight guilders a ton. Mr. Seitz, however, was anxious to form a regular station here, to be supplied with coal from the mines of the Sultan of Koetei at Pelaroeng, and his object in coming to the island was to arrange if possible with the natives for the establishment of such a depôt. He accordingly summoned a meeting of the chiefs on board the "Tiger" to discuss the subject.

The inhabitants are chiefly natives of Solok, and Boegis from Celebes, some 300 in number, whose sole pretence at legitimate trade is the collection of a small quantity of gutta percha of inferior quality. About twelve o'clock two praus came alongside, containing fifty or sixty rough-looking savages, armed to the teeth with all manner of weapons—mandaus, lances, flint-lock guns, blowpipes, and arrows. Had they had any evil design they could have overpowered us, and murdered us one and all. Mr. Seitz, however, took the precaution not to allow more than twenty to come on board at a time.

The chiefs, termed by courtesy Pangerans and Rajahs, were dressed in sleeveless jackets of gay-coloured silk or cotton, fastened with gold or gilt buttons, and with another dark-coloured cotton jacket underneath. After hearing the Assistant Resident's proposition, they said they were willing, on condition of receiving a fixed annual payment, to sign an agreement with the Resident to assist in the erection of a coal store, and whenever a gunboat called to help load her with the necessary supply of coal; but after a couple of hours' talk they said they could not decide at once, and would come again to-morrow and finally settle matters. When they were fairly away from the vessel, Mr. Seitz relieved his feelings by taking, in good old Dutch fashion, a glass of gin-and-bitters, saying, "I am glad the rogues have gone!"

In the evening, before sunset, we made a short excursion up the river; but it looked very uninviting, both banks being lined with aquatic trees, and as darkness was rapidly setting in the engineer suggested a strategic movement to the rear, in case we might encounter a pirate's nest by going further.

The next day Mr. Seitz awaited with some impatience the promised visit of the Pangerans and Rajahs, and as they did not put in appearance by eleven o'clock he sent for them. An hour later they came, forty-two in all, still very suspicious, and better armed, I thought, than on the previous day; for, in addition to the native weapons, several of them had revolvers stuck in their waists. They accounted for their suspicion by saying that the Commander of the "Salak" had captured one of their praus, sunk it, and taken the people on board to carry them before the Court of Justice at Bandjermasin, because their "pass" from the Sultan of Boelongan was not exactly clear. Mr. Seitz promised them that he would make inquiry, and, if their statement was correct, that their people should immediately be restored to them.

Still, no satisfactory arrangement could be come to with the chiefs on the all-important matter of the coal depôt, and Mr. Seitz was obliged to send for the Sultan of Boelongan himself to come and decide the question. The Rajah of Tidoen volunteered to fetch his Highness from Boelongan, a six hours' journey by prau; and early on the morning of the 12th October he returned, saying that the Sultan was not at home, having gone up country to attend to his rice-fields, but his eldest son was following, and would be on board in a couple of hours. Indeed, three praus could already be seen in the distance, lightly skimming the waves, and preparations were at once made to receive the distinguished savage. Decks were cleaned, the cabin put in order, bunting displayed, the Dutch flag hoisted over that of Koetei, and soon after breakfast the Crown Prince of Boelongan was on board, accompanied by his younger brother and a numerous suite of over sixty people, among whom were two Hadjis, whose presence was indispensable at any important meeting. I am bound to admit, in simple truth, that the whole party presented a very unprepossessing appearance. The Crown Prince, a man of between thirty and thirty-five years of age, would have passed muster in any collection of coolies in Sunday costume. With one eye he looked in the direction of Boelongan, and with the other he gazed towards Celebes. Of course he could not help it; but the absence of all amicable relations between his two eyes certainly detracted from any dignity with which his rank might otherwise have invested him.

He was barefooted, but dressed in black satin jacket and trousers, with gold buttons. His followers had rags of all colours on them, consisting mostly of a pair of short Boegis "trousers." One individual had a cotton jacket, with English sovereigns for buttons. The exchange per pound sterling, especially for coins of the "Sydney Mint," was very high at Boelongan, fourteen and sometimes as much as fifteen florins being given for a sovereign, which is equal to 23*s.* 4*d.* to 25*s.* The coins are melted for manufacturing purposes.

No sooner had the Boelongan people come on board than the Tarakan folks followed, so the little steamer was overcrowded. Mr. Seitz had an hour's conversation with them, but nothing could be arranged. They were still embittered over the captured prau affair, and no document was signed to-day, the natives asking time again to "consider."

At low water I went out amongst the coral reefs to collect shells, taking half a dozen men with me; but found few beyond the common but beautiful *Cypræa tigris.* The sea-bottom is one vast irregular mass of coral, comprising many varieties.

The coral masses presented a very beautiful appearance, their varied colours being rendered doubly brilliant by the few inches of water, as clear as crystal, which covered them. Here and there were fissures and crevices holding deep pools, where scores of small fishes, crustaceans, and greedy sea-anemones, sought shelter. The zoophytes were of brilliant colour and enormous size, and woe betide the luckless shrimp that ventured within reach of their long tentacles, which they spread out and waved unceasingly, ready to close upon their heedless prey. I put my finger several times in the centre of the larger *actiniæ,* which grasped it firmly with their tentacles, leaving a stinging sensation like that produced by the touch of a nettle.

The third day of the negotiations on the coal depôt business resulted in a satisfactory arrangement being made with the Crown Prince of Boelongan, who paid us another visit with his suite on the 13th October, and informed Mr. Seitz that the people were ready to accede to his terms. So the agreement was drawn up, and duly signed by the Crown Prince and the Pangerans, and formally attested by the *djoroe tjoelis.*

The next day we left Tarakan for Batoe Tanagat, the boundary-line claimed by the Dutch Government between their territory and that of the Sultan of Solok and Brunei. Soon after mid-day we came in sight of the coast of Borneo, the natural features of which are here in striking contrast to the formation further south. Instead of undulating country or low hills, high mountains rise abruptly from the shore, covered from head to foot with grand primæval forest; while further inland is a chain of still loftier mountains, whose blue peaks are lost in the mist and clouds.

Suddenly, again rang out the cry,—

"Badjaks ahead!"

This time it was an unmistakable pirate prau—no innocent nipa palm—rowing rapidly towards us and in the direction of Boelongan. The captain slackened speed, to give her the chance of altering her course; but she put a bold face on the matter, and hoisted the Dutch flag as she neared us, as a sign of her injured innocence. We were not in a position to pursue her, being without arms or ammunition, or she might have fallen an easy prey to the superior speed of steam.

"Besides," said my jovial friend Mr. Seitz, "she will be something for the captain of the 'Salak' by-and-by. The badjaks don't trouble us, so why should we disturb them?"

At four p.m. we arrived at Batoe Tanagat, where the Dutch war-vessel "Riouw" was lying at anchor, being stationed here to guard the interests of the Dutch Government, who had a dispute with the Sultan of Solok and Brunei as to the boundaries of their respective territories. The Sultan had lately made a concession of part of his territory to Messrs. Dent, Overbeck, and Co., and the Dutch Government protested against the boundary-line of the ceded district as having included some of their own territory.

As we approached we saluted the "Riouw," whose commander sent us a cordial invitation to dine with him, and sleep on board that night.

A curious spectacle presented itself as we reached the deck of the "Riouw." There were no less than forty-seven slaves, most of them women and children from Solok, besides twenty-two slave-dealers and pirates from the same locality, all of whom had been captured during the past fortnight. Most of the pirates were in irons; and the captain showed us in his cabin a motley array of arms and ammunition, including guns, spears, and some splendid krisses or swords, many of them inlaid with gold, which had been taken from them.

"So," said Seitz, "you don't leave all the prizes to be picked up by the 'Salak.'"

"No," replied the captain, "there are enough and to spare, without our being jealous of each other. We can afford, even, to give the 'Tiger' a chance now and then, though she belies her name in the adroit manner in which she avoids a badjak when she meets one."

Many were the anecdotes told that night of the incidents of every-day life among the pirate nests of the Celebes Sea. A glance at the deck of the "Riouw," and the thoughts which the villainous gang and their victims huddled together there conjured up, contrasted strangely with the beauty of the natural scenery of which the vessel was the centre, and showed how the fair face of Nature was marred and blurred by the hideousness of the deeds of darkness performed by the miserable off-scourings of humanity, to whom the light of civilization and Christianity had not yet penetrated.

No pirate prau crossed our path as we steamed back on our return to Koetei across the blue Celebes Sea, and we reached Tangaroeng without adventure on the evening of the 19th October.

CHAPTER IX.

The Sultan's birthday—Great preparations—Fetching the guests—An Oriental luncheon *recipe*—Triumphal arches—The Sultan's throne—Betel-chewing women—Contrast of European and Oriental customs—A royal banquet—A ballet dancer—War-dances—A royal reception—The ladies of the hareem.

THE last ten days of October were devoted to great preparations for the festivities that were to take place on the 28th of that month, in honour of the Sultan's *harie toewan besar*,[1] or birthday, when his Highness would complete his forty-third year. I was staying at the time on board the "Tiger," which lay moored off the quay, opposite the Kraton, or palace, and had ample opportunity of observing that preparations were being made upon a large scale for the great day. The whole population, not merely Malays, but a few Dyaks as well, seemed to be occupied in carrying up to the palace great quantities of planks, rattan, attap, and other materials for the purpose of constructing a spacious covered place which would serve as a "crush-room." I had received, through Pangeran Bandahara, a special invitation to be present at the festivities; and the day before Captain Andresen received orders to go down to Pelaroeng and fetch the Assistant Resident. Head winds and heavy rain—regular "Tiger" weather, as Captain Andresen called it—accompanied us; but we ran down in three and a half hours, and duly delivered our message to Mr. Seitz. On the way back next morning we stopped at Samarinda, and picked up the family of Mr. Moore, the only English merchant there, besides sixty or seventy sons of the Celestial empire, and a number of the Boegis subjects of the Sultan.

Here, too, we had to replenish our commissariat. It is a custom that all passengers by the "Tiger" provide their own food,

[1] *Harie* = day; *toewan* = year; *besar* = great.

whether specially invited or not. Fortunately we had an excellent caterer in Mr. Seitz, whose inclination towards good feeding was well known, while Mr. and Mrs. Moore added to our table. The indispensable Dutch "gin-and-bitters" was served at eleven, which, like the Swedish "smörgosbord," acts as a stimulus to a good luncheon. Luncheon, or rice table, was ready at twelve, served in the excellent style for which the Dutch are so noted. Here is the receipt: first, take on your plate a portion of boiled rice; this is dry enough in itself, but add to it the numerous odds and ends which are indispensable adjuncts to the table, such as a leg or piece of breast of a fowl, fried in cocoa-nut oil and cocoa-nut crumbs, a boiled egg or two, a piece of fried pisang, a bit of beefsteak, a little fried fish, or some of the stinking dried ones if you prefer them, a couple of the tiny red anchovies from Macassar, a gherkin or two, not omitting a couple of the splendid fried prawns: mix the whole composition together, and you have a dish which cannot be excelled for the tropics. After luncheon, as a matter of digestion, you make yourself *lekker*, to use a Dutch expression, or comfortable; that is, exchange your ordinary dress for a cotton jacket, and a pair of wide, gaily-printed cotton trousers, and enjoy a siesta, for the extreme heat during the middle of the day does not allow of any exercise.

About three o'clock we arrived in sight of Tangaroeng. The town was evidently *en fête*. Flags were flying in all directions, and the people showed by their dress, as well as their movements, that they were taking a "holiday." Not that the mode of life among the Malays necessitates any such recreation. Their daily habits are those of a people to whom the idea of work is utterly distasteful, and it is difficult to say in what consists their ordinary "business." Still, to-day, there was no mistake about the suspension of all labour. Pleasure was to reign supreme, and these naturally indolent people were evidently bent on making the best of the opportunity for indolence which the occasion presented.

Not long after our arrival, Pangeran Bandahara came on board, and informed us in the name of the Sultan that his Highness would receive us at five o'clock. Mr. Seitz attired himself in his uniform, but I had unfortunately left my dress clothes at Macassar, and had to appear in my ordinary blue serge travelling-suit. In order, however, to put on a little "gloss," I wore the ribbon of the order of St. Anna.

Precisely at five we left the yacht and went to the palace. The whole place was transformed. The path to the palace was entirely covered with white calico; on all sides were poles, with banners and streamers flying in the wind; at the foot of the pier or landing-place, and again opposite the entrance to the palace, was a "gate of honour," built of bamboo, covered with red cloth, and decked with flags, and bearing numbers of lamps which were to be lighted up at night. The display of flags was confined to the Dutch and Koetei colours; but so numerous were these emblems that the whole stock of red, blue, yellow bunting and cloth in the stores of the merchants at Samarinda was exhausted in order to supply them. I could hardly believe that this was the dirty "street" through which I had so often passed ankle deep in mud. Over the inhabitants a similar change had come. Instead of half-naked, dirty, brown-skinned beings, there were numbers of men, and women, and children, all decently arrayed in their best clothes, of all colours, some of cotton, some of silk, and often enriched with gold thread.

Inside the palace the change from the every-day appearance of the place was no less remarkable. At the entrance we were received by eight Pangerans, all attired in richly embroidered uniforms not unlike those of the Dutch residents in Java. The native carpenters, whom I had been accustomed to see there, busy carving monuments of ironwood for the graves of the Sultan's family and household—the fat-tailed sheep running about at their sweet will—the old men and women slumbering in odd corners—the little girls selling kwé-kwé, a sort of native pastry—the groups of people playing heads and tails, or discussing the virtues of their fighting cocks,—these were all gone, replaced by an orderly crowd of really well-dressed people, who had come to pay respect to the Sultan and witness the "reception" of the various deputations that were to come to congratulate his Highness. The heavy iron-wood pillars supporting the roof were entirely concealed in flags, while from the ceiling hung flags again. On the gallery facing the entrance to the Pandoppo was written in large red letters in Malay the motto, "Many happy returns of the day to the Sultan of Koetei." Under this gallery was a raised platform, in the centre of which was a seat, overshadowed with a gilt canopy borne on pillars, which latter again were folded round with gay-coloured flags. This was the Sultan's "throne," on which the Sultan himself sat, ready to receive his subjects and visitors. He was dressed in hussar uniform—dark blue cloth with gold lace, exactly copied from the one worn by his Majesty the King of the Netherlands; and his breast was adorned with the great gold Medal of Merit, suspended from a heavy chain, and with the Dutch Order of the Lion. On his head he wore a shako or helmet of the old pattern, with a great plume of the tail feathers of the bird of Paradise.

This uniform might have given a stranger the idea that the Sultan commanded a cavalry regiment: whereas the only horse in the whole of Koetei was a small pony, the property of the Sultan, but certainly not a weight-carrier, and not yet broken in. The idea of such a hussar, mounted on such a steed, was intensely ludicrous. For the rest, the uniform suited him admirably.

As we approached the daïs the Javanese gamallang, or band, played a characteristic tune, and we were conducted by the Sultan to seats on either side of him, whence we had a good view of the whole scene. The concourse gradually but quietly increased, till there could not have been less than a thousand people present. Suddenly there was a dead silence, broken a few seconds later by the noise of a salute of thirteen guns, fired on board the "Tiger."

I was struck by the fact that women were the predominating element in the multitude assembled inside the Pandoppo, and that they were mostly old. They were generally dressed in rich-coloured silk sarongs and jackets, the hair neatly tied up behind in a knot and fastened with a diamond pin, or at least with a bunch of fragrant flowers, chiefly the unopened buds of boenga melur (*jasminum sambac*) and boenga kananga (*uvaria*), very much like the English jasmine. Many of the women had other strong-scented flowers in wreaths round the head, or woven into the hair.

Most of them wore diamond buttons in the ears. They all sat quiet as stone images, without moving or speaking, but all the time chewing betel-nut and sirih, each with her sirih box before her, as well as a spitting-box! In order to be well provided with these most necessary utensils for this event, the Sultan's jewellers and plumbers had been busy all through the month, making an additional stock of spittoons, both of silver and brass. I had some time before had the pleasure of being shown by the Sultan the process of moulding them, and wondered to what practical use he could put such a number as I saw in all stages of manufacture. Now it was clear to me why such a quantity was wanted.

These people filled the body of the hall. Immediately below the platform stood or sat all the officials of Koetei, in their respective uniforms—an endless number of mantries, secretaries, harbour-masters, inspectors of mines, receivers and controllers of taxes, &c. All these wore uniforms laced with silver, to distinguish them from the princes, who had gold.

Presently the tedium of sitting, staring and being stared at, was relieved by a couple of servants, dressed in black with gold lace, and wearing a rosette of red or yellow silk, bringing in lemonade, coffee, tea, and biscuits. The ladies preferred tea, and the Sultan, with his usual politeness, himself supplied their wants, with the preliminary question in broken English, "Mevrouw, you take sugar and milk—milk sappie?"—"sappie" meaning cow, to distinguish the milk from the tinned milk usually supplied.

Some of the Sultan's plate, from his stock in his warehouses, had evidently been brought out for this occasion. The tea and coffee services were entirely of silver, and there were three splendid biscuit boxes filled with cakes and other unconsidered trifles. The Sultan preferred lemonade, and would insist on opening the bottles himself, much to the detriment of his white kid gloves. By-and-by the heat began to tell on those condemned, for ceremony's sake, to sit in heavy uniforms and clothes unsuited to the climate. Great beads of perspiration formed on the brows of ladies and men alike. The Sultan, galantuomo as he was—his natural politeness having gained considerably during a recent visit to

Java—ordered *ajer wangie,* or eau de Cologne (*ajer* = water and *wangie* = scented), and handed it round to the ladies.

This contrast, or rather commingling, of the refined habits of Western civilization with the ruder Oriental customs afforded a very striking picture. After sitting there one hour in state—ruler and honoured guests partaking of European refreshments in presence of the people, and his subjects meanwhile indulging in the, to European eyes, revolting practice of betel chewing—the assembly broke up. Our party returned to the "Tiger," whither half an hour later the Sultan followed us, to personally invite us to dine with him at eight o'clock.

What a pity the Sultan has no European steward, who could arrange his magnificent silver service to advantage, and lay a table properly, with taste and symmetry; and half-a-dozen well-trained waiters to serve during dinner! On Pangeran Sosro devolved the duty of seeing to the proper conduct of the banquet. With a golden rosette on his breast and stick in hand he acted as master of the ceremonies, and gave the waiters instructions with the stick right and left how to serve.

The bill of fare opened with a strong soup, followed by meat, pastry, and then the Sultan's favourite dish, beefsteak—very tough! and asparagus with sour sauce. The Sultan was particularly partial to this vegetable—which was not freshly grown in the country, by the way, but the tinned article—and carefully served the sticks himself by twos and threes. Bordeaux was provided, and the Sultan requested that we should command any other beverage. I suggested that champagne was the most suitable drink for such an occasion.

"It is true, it is true," said the Sultan. "I had quite forgotten it. I have abundance of chests; many dozens." Whereupon his servants climbed quickly up a ladder and brought down a chest, and in a few minutes the wine was foaming in our glasses. It was certainly, if truth be told, not of the best quality, but the necessary toasts were duly honoured in it, when, the more important business of the dinner being over, the dessert was brought in.

Later in the evening, to the noise of the incessant gamallang, the Sultan's *première danseuse,* a Javanese beauty, performed a few characteristic dances, or *pas seuls*—rather, a succession of *poses*—accompanying them with a song, after which the Sultan retired.

Outside, a few Dyaks were indulging in their dances and mimic combats, amid the applause of the assembled Chinamen and Malays. These were kept up, with other amusements, till two o'clock in the morning, the whole population making a night of it in a remarkably decorous manner. The usual gambling and cock-fighting were omitted to-night, for a wonder, and the people seemed to be on the tiptoe of expectation for the final act of the day's drama.

Suddenly there was a general hush as the Sultan was seen to enter the audience-chamber again, and take his seat on the throne. This time he was dressed in a Governor-General's uniform, and wore on his head the massive gold crown, weighing something like four pounds, and in shape not unlike the Papal mitre. Suspended round his neck glistened a huge diamond, as large as a pigeon's egg—the same perhaps which had been the innocent cause of so much difficulty on its first acquisition by the Sultan. With great dignity he seated himself under the canopy on the throne. Immediately following him was his brother, the Pangeran Rato, who, this time acting as master of the ceremonies or marshal of the procession, carried a thick bamboo cane mounted with gold as a sign of authority. Bowing to the Sultan he made a short speech offering his congratulations; to which the Sultan replied. Then all the other Pangerans separately addressed their ruler, who again responded to each personally. Then the deputation of Chinese merchants, with a few Klings, arrayed in their picturesque garments of many colours; and after them the representatives of the Boegis, headed by their chief from Samarinda. These were followed by a number of Hadjis, headed by a handsome Herculean Sheik, who acted as spokesman and in a clear voice made a long speech invoking the blessings of Allah and the Prophet on the head of the Ruler of Koetei, and wishing him many happy years of life and power.

Last, but not least, amid the miniature thunder of saluting guns, came the ladies of the hareem, headed by the Sultan's sister: all unveiled, and gorgeously arrayed in rich apparel of silk and satin, and cloth of gold; with arms and necks laden with bracelets and necklets studded with magnificent diamonds and other gems. They numbered between forty and fifty altogether, and were of various ages; some of the younger ladies were beauties whose presence would have graced any European assembly. With timid steps and downcast eyes, glancing neither to the right nor to the left, they approached the throne, bowed slowly, and passed out of sight to return once more to their seclusion.

Thus ended the eventful day. The orderliness of the whole proceedings and the manner in which the festivities were conducted reflected the greatest credit on all concerned; the evidences of wealth which were produced by the people, as well as the Sultan and his court, were such as to excite the surprise not only of myself but of the other European visitors. No one who has seen Tangaroeng in its every-day aspect could believe that such a feast could be celebrated in such a manner in so miserable a place.

CHAPTER X.

Financial arrangements—More delays— Illness of Sariman—Kichil—The commissariat—The Sultan's hesitation—Inspecting the big prau—The feast in honour of the walking baby—A visit from Rajah Sinen—Head-hunters fraternizing—Driving Satan away—Procrastinations—At last—Porpoises in the river—Pulo Juboe—Plague of mosquitoes—A bee colony—Moeara Kaman—Medicine for the rice—Blood-thirsty visitors—Kotta Bangoen.

It was not till Sunday, the 2nd November, 1879, that I was furnished with the "sinews of war" for my overland journey. On that day Mr. Seitz, the Assistant Resident at Pelaroeng, with whom I was staying, received a communication opening the credit I had asked for; and I at once sent a messenger to the Sultan, who had so often told me that he would be ready whenever I was, saying that I should be prepared to start in seven days, and asking to be provided with one of his large praus, as these vessels were difficult to hire, either at Pelaroeng or at Tangaroeng, being generally used by their owners for trading purposes.

On the 7th November the Pangeran Bandahara came and told me that his royal master had sent his prau to fetch me, and was really going to accompany me on the journey. But Bandahara brought no written letter as I had asked, and I consequently felt doubtful whether the Sultan really knew his own mind in the matter. Besides, the Pangeran politely hinted that there was no hurry, as the servants of the Sultan's household were preparing for another *slaamat* or feast, this time in honour of the fact that the Pangeran Praboe's child had learnt to walk! Such an event could not be permitted to pass unnoticed.

Meanwhile I informed my Java boys, Ali, Sariman, and Siden, that I had definitely resŏlved to travel overland to Bandjermasin. They had already heard of my intention, but the Malays had been playing upon their fears and exaggerating the dangers of the journey, and now they coolly asked permission to return to Soerabaija at the first opportunity. I replied that they must stay with me and fulfil their contract, especially as I could get no men here in their place; besides, they were all in my debt. But they complained of illness, and said they were not strong enough to stand the fatigues of the journey. Siden, it is true, had had occasional attacks of fever, but was easily put right with a few doses of quinine and castor oil, but the principal ailment from which both he and Ali were suffering was "home-sickness." Sariman had often told me what a "jolly place" Soerabaija was—*banja rami rami* (plenty of pleasures)—and his companions were of the same opinion. Still Sariman was really very ill, having been reduced to skin and bone in the unhealthy climate of Long Wai, and my conscience told me I ought not to take him with me, as I might lose him on the road; so I promised to let him go home. He could not sufficiently express his delight, and came forward to thank me, lying, Javanese fashion, flat on his stomach, and crawling towards me, saying, *Tarima cassi banja, Toewan* (very many thanks, sir). He was still more pleased when I paid his passage to Java, and gave him a gratuity of thirteen guilders for his good conduct.

Ali and Siden were inclined to desert. The former, a big lazy fellow, complained to the Assistant Resident, who simply referred him back to me; and after a *bitchara* he and Siden consented to keep to their bargain, on the condition that I would let them return home immediately on their arrival at Bandjermasin. This I naturally readily agreed to do.

As for my two Chinamen, they were courageous enough with their tongues, but that was all. Tan Bon Hijok, who was really a first-rate mandoer (foreman), said he had had enough of Dyak adventures, and was going to begin trading at Bandjer. But Tan He Wat offered to re-engage himself upon condition of receiving an advance in his wages, from twenty to twenty-five florins a month; and, as I had taught him to skin birds properly, and he was accustomed to my ways and was useful to me in various things, I agreed to his terms.

In Sariman's place I managed to engage a Java lad, Kichil by name, who had lived many years in Koetei, and had before travelled in the interior, as servant to Mr. Dahmen, late Resident at Pelaroeng, who unfortunately died just beyond the borders of Koetei, in an attempt to make the overland journey. Kichil said they had had *banja soesa* on the road, although Dahmen had a force of 1500 men with him; and he represented the Teweh district as being especially dangerous.

When I first asked him if he would go with me he did not think he was strong enough to undergo the hardships of the journey again. He afterwards agreed to go, but asked higher wages than I had intended giving. Knowing, however, that he was an honest lad, and was acquainted with the country, I agreed to his terms, and so completed the list of my personal attendants.

The next thing to engage my attention was the provision question. At Samarinda I bought a large quantity of rice, enough, in case of emergency, to last three months for twenty-five men, also dried fish and *lombock*, the humble daily fare of the natives. For my personal use I bought some tins of oxtail soup, salmon, preserved peas, jams, and Huntley and Palmer's biscuits, the average price asked for all the tinned provisions being two shillings and sixpence per pound.

Besides the provisions, I purchased a quantity of different sorts of calico, braids, and tobacco, for presentation to my native friends, or enemies, in the interior.

Thus provisioned, I took leave of Mr. Seitz on the morning of Sunday, November 9th. He shook me warmly by the hand, wishing me *goede reis*, but strongly urged, as a sort of encouragement, I suppose, that I should give up the expedition if the Sultan did not accompany me. I had, however, fully made up my mind to undertake the journey, Sultan or no Sultan; but, as the general feeling seemed to be that the Sultan's presence would afford a certain *prestige* and protection, I had requested Mr. Seitz to furnish me with a letter to his Highness, reminding him of his promise to the Government that he would accompany the expedition. The impression that he would not go with me was strengthened when I reached Samarinda, where my kind friend

Mr. Moore told me his Highness had held several councils at Tangaroeng, at which all the Pangerans and Mantries were present, and that the question of his journey had been decided in the negative. Instead of his company I was to have a chief as an escort.

Amid all these doubts and hesitations it was refreshing to hear the cheery tones in which Mr. and Mrs. Moore welcomed me to their house, where they insisted on drinking "Success to the Expedition" in good clicquot, and afterwards speeding me on my way with a genuine English "Good-bye." I did not reach Tangaroeng till midnight, so stayed on board the prau all night. Next morning, early, I landed, and met the Sultan on the rickety structure that did duty for a pier or landing-stage, and immediately put the question whether he really meant to go, at the same time handing him Mr. Seitz' letter, which he read carefully.

"*Belun tau ; bran kali*" ("I don't know yet; perhaps"), was all the reply I could elicit. But, when I urged that he had had long enough to make up his mind, he proposed that we should go and look at the big prau which he was having constructed specially for the journey.

It was a fine boat, nearly seventy feet long, hewn out of a single ironwood-tree, and fitted with raised bulwarks all round to increase its carrying capacity and stability. But neither cabin, nor seats for the crew, nor internal fittings of any kind, were yet visible. Still, this was an earnest of what the Sultan intended doing, and I plied him vigorously with flattering remarks on his courage and power, told him how favourably the Dyaks at Long Wai had spoken of him, how proud Rajah Dinda had been to receive the mission about the emigrant Dyaks, and how anxious he was to promote the greatness and wealth of his master the Sultan. Whether as the result of these soft words or not I cannot say, but towards noon he had another great gathering of all his councillors and nobles, to discuss the knotty point; and a little later he came to me, and said he had decided to go, fixing Wednesday, the 19th November, for our departure. He added that he was sending men in advance to have people ready in the Interior, and let the natives know that we were coming.

In the meantime the Pangeran Sosro had kindly invited me to take up my quarters again in his house; and on entering I found great preparations going on for some important ceremony or feast, and discovered that the celebration of the slaamat in honour of the Pangeran Praboe's child, who had just learnt to "run on its legs," was still going on. The next three days and nights were devoted to a succession of festivities and semi-religious ceremonies. Cock-fighting occupied the early part of the day. At ten o'clock numbers of Boegis came to the open yard adjoining the palace, bringing their pets with them. The Sultan's birds were ranged in rows in their conical baskets, preparatory to taking part in the combats, and an open crowing competition began. Then came the battles and the betting, the Sultan carefully examining his own birds, fitting on their spurs, and betting freely on the result. The first day over twenty-five birds were killed. On one occasion the proceedings were varied by a duel between two Dyaks, armed with sticks of rattan; each was provided with a wooden shield wrapped in *tappa*, and padded on the head, shoulders, and left arm with thick mats of bark; the hands were also similarly protected. The contest was continued at intervals throughout the day, and carried on with vigour and good temper, and afforded a good idea of the skill with which these savages use the mandau and shield in actual war.

At six o'clock all play would cease, and the Sultan, like a good Moslem, would array himself in a long white gown and go to prayer. Then came the dinner-hour, to be followed again by the usual cock-fighting tournaments and gambling.

Occasionally the proceedings were enlivened by an "amok" Boegis, spreading dismay through the usually quiet town. One night one of these excitable gentry killed no less than three men, and wounded five others, before he himself fell a victim to a well-directed blow from a mandau. The only information elicited by inquiry as to the cause of the riot was that, as usual, a woman dispute (*prampuan prekara*) was at the bottom of it.

One morning I was agreeably surprised to see my old friend Rajah Sinen suddenly appear at the Palace: and still more so to find that he was soon afterwards joined by a chief of the Long

Wahou tribe, the great rivals of the Long Wai people. There was some slight awkwardness between these representatives of so many slumbering and smouldering tribal animosities; but, like well-bred chiefs whose enmity was rather political than personal, they displayed no signs of the animosity which might be supposed to have animated their swarthy breasts. A battle royal between two such combatants would have been a sight to see! Rajah Sinen was certainly not so big as his brother Dinda, but he was a well-proportioned specimen of humanity; while his rival of Long Wahou would have turned the scale at sixteen stone at the very least—see his portrait in Plate 10—and no superfluous fat! all solid muscle!

I took the opportunity of bringing the two men together as often as I could, and spoke to them of the advantage of throwing open their country to trade, instead of keeping it closed by tribal animosities and head-hunting customs. Taking Sinen's hand, I placed it in that of the other.

"You must make friends!" I said (*moesti bikkin sobat*).

They looked awkwardly at each other, not knowing how to act, then silently dropped each other's hands.

"You must not get heads," I continued (*tida boele dappat kapala*); but a doubtful smile was all the reply I could get to my proposition.

The nights of the 17th, 18th and 19th of November were devoted to "rami rami" of more than ordinary significance, of which the covered court outside the Sultan's private room was the scene. From the middle of the attap roof was suspended a huge bundle of long grass, reaching to the ground, round which danced four Dyaks, arrayed, as actors, in a special sarong made of blue cloth, upon which were sewn stars, and figures of deer, made of white and red cloth; on their heads they wore a sort of coronet, made of red cloth, with strings of beads and bells hanging down. As they danced round this bundle of grass they sang to a musical accompaniment performed by a group of Malays sitting on the ground. After dancing a little while the four actors turned round and round a great number of times, enough to make any ordinary mortal giddy. When tired of this gyratory movement they sat down on a swinging seat—a long flat board with the ends carved to represent the head and tail of a crocodile —that hung from the roof. Having rested here for a time, they walked up to a sort of altar erected near the centre of the ground, on which were placed banana and maize leaves and grass, laid in different patterns, and ornamented with a few Chinese vases. After walking round this structure several times they went down on hands and knees, making a grunting noise, and crept around it as if seeking for something. On inquiring what this something was I was told it was Satan that the men were looking for. Needless to say they caught him, or at least found him and drove him away to their complete satisfaction.

This episode satisfactorily terminated, three hideous old women, dressed in red cloth sarongs, faded from frequent use, were brought in with great pomp, carried on the shoulders of Malays, and took their seats amidst great silence on the large swinging bench in front of the altar. Not a sound escaped the great crowd, who regarded the business as most serious. The old women then began to swing themselves, and, whether owing to the heat or to give themselves an air of affectation, they kept fanning themselves with a Chinese paper fan. At midnight shots were fired from a number of guns, amid the shouts and cries of the population.

This ceremony was repeated on three nights, with a slight addition to the programme on the second evening. Besides the three old women there were three younger ones, and all the six were furnished with a bow and arrow, at the end of which were fastened from one to six wax lights. These fiery arrows were each shot several times against the altar, the lights of course being extinguished each time. The object of this was to drive Satan away. One of the young damsels was particularly bashful, and amused the crowd very much, creating roars of laughter and some hissing by running past each time her turn came to shoot without trying to drive the devil away.

The entertainment was sufficiently diverting for one night, but the proceedings after midnight, when the "rami rami" consisted chiefly of shouting and firing of guns, were of little interest; and, if

Satan was frightened away as effectually as sleep during those three nights, the people of Tangaroeng had no cause to complain of the success of their religious exercises.

The Sultan and all his court tried to deceive me into the idea that the proceedings were merely a token of respect to their ruler (*kapunan* or *hormat*, *i. e.* respect or homage). But from various sources I gathered that the business was really the remnant of the pagan practice of "driving Satan away"—a practice which the Sultan was ashamed to admit was countenanced in his own palace, and which he made believe to be merely a popular demonstration of respect to himself.

The third day of these ceremonies was the appointed day for my departure from Tangaroeng, and I called upon his Highness in the morning to again point out to him the necessity for starting without further delay, or at least giving me a prau and letting me proceed alone. He listened to me attentively, and, again repeating his regular promise that he would be ready in a day or two, said he was really speaking in earnest this time. As he uttered these words the Pangeran Kartasari came in, and received his master's orders to proceed at once in advance as far as Moeara Pahou to make preparations for our journey, and have praus ready on the Lawa, and make a path in the forest. This was only a minute's conversation. Kartasari kissed the Sultan's hand, and, with a *slaamat jallan* from his Highness' lips, was off.

In the evening, after the performance of the two previous nights had been repeated, the ceremony of sprinkling the old women who had acted, with the sacred water from a small river near Sanga Sanga, the former capital of Koetei, took place. All sorts of healing properties were attributed to this water. By noon on the following day Satan had been satisfactorily driven away, and the slaamat was finished with two salutes of seven guns each, and a public dinner of rice and sugar-water.

Now that this feast was over I was determined to brook no further delay, lest another slaamat should intervene and postpone our departure again. The Sultan this time promised to start on Sunday, the 23rd November, but I said I could wait no longer: I must go to-morrow.

"Sikamandrie cannot start for three days," replied the Sultan, "as he is putting in order the graves of my family." Now Sika mandrie was the very Pangeran whom I wished above all others to accompany me, as I had been informed that he had great influence on the Teweh and in the Doesoen district. The Sultan tried to induce me to give up the plan of the overland journey, pointing out its dangers, with the oft-repeated story of the treachery of the Dyaks, who even in his own country were addicted to poisoning strangers. I told his Highness however many dangers there were, an attempt at least must be made, even if a retreat were the result; and he finally consented to my leaving to-morrow with Pangeran Sokmaviro, adding that he would himself follow in a few days.

At last the day arrived for leaving Tangaroeng—promises turned into reality. On going down to the river early on the morning of the 21st November, I saw a large white painted canoe lying in the water, the crew busy making a thatch roof as a protection against the glaring heat of the sun. In the middle was a little cabin, nine feet long, with just room enough for my mattress and one trunk. On the sides of this little cabin were pegs, upon which three of my guns were laid, while my revolver and the splendid mandau (sword) presented to me by the Sultan hung on either side. Another prau was also in readiness for Sokmaviro, and a third to store the provisions in. The Sultan came down to the river and saw me off, and with his usual attention asked me if I was well stocked with preserves, giving me, among other things, four loaves made by one of his wives. Among other presents I received was a plate of cakes from the Radenajo (wife of Pangeran Sosro), each in the shape of a letter, and forming the word "Slaamat" (success). At noon I took leave of the Sultan and his sons, and the word was given to start:—

"*Souda klar.*"—"Ada," replied the crew, and we were off, my prau leading, with a crew of nine men in charge of Mantrie Anga; then came the prau laden with provisions; and Sokmaviro brought up the rear. Our praus kept close in shore, to avoid the current; and occasionally a native would quietly ask *Di mana* (where or whither)? to which the crew, especially my Chinese servant, took delight in answering *Commissie piggie di Bandjer.*

About sunset we arrived at Pulo Juboe, where we stayed the night; but the mosquitoes were too ready for a change of diet, and scared sleep away as successfully as the Satan hunters at Tangaroeng. When daylight appeared I saw four porpoises playing round the prau, swimming in a circle one behind the other. They were about seven or eight feet long, and played about for nearly half an hour, occasionally jumping out of the water, and squirting a little water from the blow-hole. The Malays said these animals were very common here.

Amid heavy rain we resumed our journey, and nothing of note occurred all day. Later we stopped for the night, and my crew begged to be allowed to light a fire on board the prau to keep the mosquitoes away; although we had fifty pounds of powder on board, I could not deny their request. It rained hard all night, and the fire went out before morning, so that the men had no means of cooking their breakfast, and had to wait till the sun appeared before they could get any dry sticks for the purpose.

Presently, as I was reading, Kichil shouted loud to me, "*Madoe toewan; moesti liat*" (Bees, sir; you must look). Opening the little skylight in the roof of the cabin I stood up, and saw a lofty tree close to the river, not five yards from the banks, covered with bees'-nests. I had never before seen such a congregation of nests. My men counted over fifty of them, all of an oblong shape, but of various sizes, as every one was in course of construction. The smallest was little less than two feet in length. The stem and branches of the tree, the trunk of which rose sixty or seventy feet from the ground before sending out a single branch, were covered; and as the bark of the tree was of an ash-grey colour, while the nests were dark brown, the latter were very conspicuous. I saw many bees'-nests later on in the course of my journey, and they were all attached to trees of an ash-grey colour, and apparently belonging to the same species. While on this subject I may mention, that the honey from the wild bees (*Apis dorsata*) is by no means so sweet in flavour as that from the honey-bees of Europe, and the wax seems to be of an inferior quality.

Presently we passed several rice-fields, in which were a number of bamboo sticks stuck at irregular intervals over the cultivated ground. On these sticks were tied bundles of rice, or leaves, or strips of cloth. On inquiring what these sticks meant, I was told they were *obat di paddi* (medicine for the rice)—a charm, hung there to ensure the success of the crop.[1] At one p.m. we arrived at Moeara Kaman; Pangeran Sokmaviro, whom I had not seen since we left Tangaroeng, and the other prau, soon followed. Our boats were fastened to a floating house, where the Mantrie (or commander of the place) lived. He asked me to enter his dwelling, meanwhile sending one of his boys to the other huts in search of a chair for me. To my surprise he brought one—certainly a wreck of a chair, but it was a change after the necessity of sitting so long cross-legged in native fashion, or lying full length in the canoe. A couple of the Mantrie's wives were in the room; one of them was lying on the bamboo floor giving her little infant breast, while a dozen other children divided themselves into groups and stared at me. In a corner of the room sat an old woman, probably the grandmamma, busy making one of the huge circular straw hats, ornamented on the top with a star pattern in bead-work. A few mats, two mattresses, half a dozen brass rice trays, and four or five spittoons, formed all the furniture that the place could boast.

All night long were we tormented by mosquitoes. This time I had two fires lighted on board my canoe, but, though there was smoke enough and to spare, the mosquitoes heeded it not; they did not get a feast of white man's blood every day. The more I fought against the enemy the more reinforcements did he bring up. The incessant cries of my men, *Allah njamok! Allah njamok!* were kept up all through the night in a sort of subdued chorus, accompanied at frequent intervals by a slap, as in desperation the hand was brought vigorously down, first on one part of the body then on another, in the hope of thinning the ranks of the blood-thirsty insects, and alleviating the pain by setting up a counter-irritation. If these bloodsuckers, I thought, are going to pursue us in this manner night after night, it will be best to give up all thoughts of the overland journey. How people would laugh to think that the expedition had been turned back, not by head-

[1] See *Pomali*, p. 230.

hunting Dyaks, but by mosquitoes! It rained heavily again all night, and the covered canoe seemed to give shelter to the insects; and I was not sorry to see the first streaks of light breaking through the dark sky, and to give the order to leave Moeara Kaman, and, I fervently hoped, its plague of mosquitoes.

For a long distance the banks of the river were quite uninhabited. A few white herons might be seen on the banks, and small troops of sandpipers skimming along wherever there was a sandy plot of ground, over which they could with difficulty be traced owing to the similarity of colour; while in the trees we often saw monkeys (*Semnopithecus cristatus*), which the Dyaks call Boehis, disturbed by the paddling of the canoes, and rushing down to seek cover in the thicket. My mantrie said there would be no houses before we got near Kotta Bangoen, so at nine a.m. I told my men to fasten the canoe to the shore in order to get our breakfast, and they soon made a couple of fires in the forest and boiled their bamboo kettles of rice. So far my second journey up the Mahakkam had been over familiar ground. Soon after leaving Moeara Kaman we passed through the strong eddy caused by the inflow of the Telén, and then leaving that river to the right, and continuing a westerly course up the main stream, entered a district which was new to me. At two in the afternoon we arrived at Kotta Bangoen, a large village, with more than 1000 inhabitants, all Malays and Boegis. Many of the former are from Bandjermasin. These I class as "labouring" Malays.

CHAPTER XI.

A dead forest—Collecting gutta-percha—Votive lamps—An ancient Hindoo idol—Arrival of the Sultan—A monkeys' paradise—A hunt in an aquatic forest—A remarkable bird—Unwilling recruits—Through the lake region—Allo—Swallowed by a crocodile—Native fruit gardens—Moeara Pahou—Curious mode of fishing—Cooking the fish—Trade with the Dyaks.

The aspect of the country here is all flat forest. The late drought had roasted the trees to such an extent that, although this was the rainy season, the forest in many parts, especially on the right bank of the Mahakkam, consisted of trees with bare trunks and branches, more like an English landscape in early winter than the everlasting summer to which the eye is accustomed in the tropics.

Another result of the severe drought was seen in the scarcity of animal life. I made several trips into the forest, accompanied by Kichil and two native lads who knew the neighbourhood, but scarcely saw either feather or fur. Everything seemed to have been killed or driven away by the drought.

The houses are nearly all on the right bank of the river, built at long distances apart from each other. I only saw three floating houses. These latter are very convenient, for if the owner, who is generally a trader, wants to remove, he only unfastens the stout rattan rope by which his house is anchored to *terra firma*, and glides down with his home, wives, children, fowls, and other pets, to any place he may select further down the stream. Such a house is seen in Plate 2. There was a trader here who had come down from the interior in this way. For going up the river these floating structures are of no use, the current being too strong.

More than a dozen trading praus from Samarinda were lying here, exchanging or selling their goods.

A little rice is cultivated here, besides pisangs, sugar-cane, and maize. Still the natives, as in all parts of the interior, have barely food enough for their own consumption, and hardly anything could be bought save rice. Though the river swarms with fish, none could be purchased here; but some of my men at once began to amuse themselves with angling. On the banks of the small rivers or streams falling here into the Mahakkam, there is abundance of rattan, which the natives cut. They also collect beeswax and honey, as well as gutta-percha, or, as they call it here, "mallau." At Tangaroeng and Samarinda it is called gutta, whereas all over the interior it is known by the name of mallau.

When collecting gutta, the Malays take a two or three days' journey into the forest. For fear of being murdered by the Dyaks, they go in parties, from twenty to thirty, for mutual protection, and very often are accompanied or joined by friendly Dyaks. On two successive evenings after my arrival at Kotta Bangoen, I noticed after sunset a number of lights floating down the river. Each lamp was made of half a cocoa-nut shell, containing some oil and a cane wick. I at first thought they were set afloat by boys playing; but seeing these tiny lights again on the third evening, I inquired what they were, and it was explained to me that they were a sort of vestal lamp, set burning and floating down the river by the wives of those Malays who were out collecting mallau—a sort of charm to keep them safe and ensure success in their search.

During my stay here, the Pangeran Sokmaviro found a decent house for me, where I could sleep untroubled by mosquitoes. It belonged to an elderly Malay from Bandjermasin—a "hadji," who had performed the stipulated journey to Mecca, to worship at Mohammed's tomb. He had prepared a comfortable bed for me, consisting of a mattress laid on a low seat in the corner of the room, enclosed by a gaudy-coloured mosquito curtain, under which I could enjoy a night's rest, free from all insect plagues. In Plate 30 will be seen just such a bedstead.

Here I heard of the existence of a very fine bronze figure, representing a Hindoo goddess, known by the name of "Dingaugi,"[1] which was in the possession of a Dyak at Keham. I wanted to buy the idol, but the owner, who brought it most carefully wrapped up in a cloth, would not sell it, and charged me ten florins for the privilege of making a sketch of it. The ears of the goddess were pierced with large holes, the lobes hanging down like those of the Dyaks. The owner said the idol was made of stone, and I at first took it to be so, but on scratching it with a knife I found it was bronze. At the capture of Kotta Bangoen by the Bahou and Modang Dyaks, nearly 100 years ago, one foot of this image was broken by some of the chiefs—wilfully, as is alleged—and the tradition runs that the same people who were guilty of this act of sacrilege died shortly afterwards.

But Brahma and Vishnu are no longer known in Borneo. The religion of the Dyaks perhaps savours somewhat of the superstitions of Brahminism; but among the Malays, Allah is the only true God, and his Prophet is Mohammed.

The 25th November was a great holiday amongst the followers of Islam. My host—dressed in a long red silk robe reaching to the ground, with countless small buttons to match, an embroidered turban on his head, and holding in his left hand a kris and a string of beads—went at eight in the morning, followed by a couple of slave boys, to the mosque to pray.

Towards noon on the 28th November I was surprised to see the Pangeran Bandahara come up the river with a crew of fifteen men; and still more surprised when he told me that the Sultan himself was following. A few hours later his Highness' prau came in sight, flying the standard fore and aft, and followed by six other canoes, containing altogether some 150 men. The Sultan had with him no less than six wives, a number of fighting cocks, and other impedimenta, showing that he, at least, did not intend to suffer *ennui* on the journey. He soon came to me, and

[1] Since my return home I have found in "Overzigt van het Rijk van Koetei," a description of an ancient idol, said to be of stone, and called "Gendawagie," which exactly corresponds with the one above referred to, and is evidently the same thing, with the name spelt somewhat differently.

said that he would not have been happy if he had left me to go alone, relating over again all his former accounts of the ferocity of the Dyaks, and the necessity for adequate protection. He expected another 350 men to follow, as his present escort of 150 was not sufficient, and until they arrived he would stay here and take me shooting and fishing.

The Sultan's arrival gave an unwonted appearance of animation to the village. The crews from the praus all came ashore—an unprepossessing lot of Boegis and Malays—and for the rest of that day busied themselves in cooking their meals, washing their scanty garments, and fishing—for they had to eke out their frugal ration of rice and salt with whatever their luck or skill in fishing might bring them. Just before sunset the Sultan himself had a large net cast into the river, but caught nothing.

The next day was devoted to a great hunt. Precisely at six o'clock, as the sun appeared above the horizon, we started up the river—five canoes and over sixty men. Our course lay up a narrow stream, called the Soengei, or River. Gadang, which was overshadowed by lofty trees, whose thick foliage completely excluded the sun's rays. It was long before we saw bird or animal, and no sound of animal life struck the ear; but I was lost in admiration over the magnificent trees, and their beautiful variety of foliage, and the orchids and creepers with which they were covered, regretting all the time that I was no botanist, and that the true meaning of much that I saw was lost upon me.

Lofty trees were common, with a straight stem from sixty to eighty feet high before throwing out a single branch or showing any sign of foliage. Endless climbers, twisted like a rope, hung from tree to tree, very often reaching the ground in confused and tangled masses. These climbers form a striking feature all over the tropics, hanging and seeming to creep and cluster together in snake-like forms, resembling serpents all the more from the fact that often for many yards together no leaf or bud can be seen on the shining smooth brown surface. Up in the forks of the trees were numerous orchids; but, though this was the flowering season, of the thousands of orchids I saw as we rowed up the little river only one appeared with flowers, and those were so minute as hardly to be noticed. Great ferns in profusion spread out their large and variegated leaves, growing high up in the deeply-furrowed stems or branches of the trees.

At last the Sultan saw some birds in a lofty tree, and asked me to shoot at the same time as himself. We both fired, and—missed! The Sultan said his brother Pangeran Mankoe was a good shot, and had excellent eyesight, and he invited him to come in our canoe. He has a great respect for his brother, and I believe to a certain extent fears him; but, though he asked him several times to a seat beside him, Mankoe declined each time, bowing and putting the palms of his hands together; he would not feel comfortable to sit on a level with his royal master and brother, and preferred sitting cross-legged on the bottom of his own canoe. Our unsuccessful shots had frightened away the birds, and, as we saw no more for some time, breakfast was proposed as an agreeable change.

We had now paddled three miles up the river, and were entering the lake Gadang Morong, four miles long by two and a half miles wide. In the distance, in a south-westerly direction, could be seen Mount Tinjavan, said to be 1500 feet high. We paddled along the shores of the lake—or as near to the edge as possible, for the lake may almost be said to have no shores. All round the trees stand out in the water more than a hundred feet from *terra firma*, sending down long aërial roots resembling mangroves. Paddling in this aquatic forest was out of the question; the Malays took hold of the roots and branches of the trees, and pulled or pushed the canoes through them. Here we expected to get birds. Several snake-darters and herons were seen, but the birds were shy; and the noise of the Malays, shouting and splashing as they hauled the five canoes through the watery maze, frightened them out of range. Our next move was up a small creek, where Pangerans Mankoe and Praboe were so fortunate as to shoot a couple of birds for me. They were sitting in a high tree, and as they fell several of the Sultan's men at once jumped in the water and made their way into the dense forest, cutting the thick vegetation with their mandaus. One bird was recovered at once, but for a long time the men searched for the other in the direction in which it had fallen, when one of them called out "*Tida ada.*" (Have not got it). To this the Sultan at once replied in a loud voice, "*Dappat moesti itoe boeroeng*" (You must find this bird). This had a startling effect on the men, and in a few minutes the bird was happily found, still alive, and given up to me.

The body of the bird was of a green-black, or "invisible green," colour; the head was covered by a sort of hood—not of feathers, but of fleshy tentacles, of an orange-yellow hue; while just behind the eye was a round patch, a little larger than the eye itself, of dark olive-green stiff feathers, which the bird could erect and depress at pleasure. These formed a protection to the ear, at the same time enabling the bird to employ to the fullest extent its powers of hearing—a beautiful provision of nature, fitting the bird to live in the dark and thick forests, where the sense of hearing would be much more useful to it than that of sight, and where the chance of injury to the ear would be far greater than in the open air. Round the throat was a broad ring of brilliant vermillion, and the thighs were of a similar hue.

As we were returning home down the Soengei Gadang our attention was suddenly arrested by a large black snake with yellow spots, lying twisted round one of the overhanging branches, with his head downwards as if watching for prey in the water. Pangeran Mankoe brought the animal down with my twenty-bore gun as dead as a log.

Near the mouth of the river we saw a large *bjawa* (crocodile) basking himself in the sun; several guns were aimed at him, and the monster retired into the water.

The next day or two were devoted to buying and preparing canoes for the expected contingent of Dyaks and Boegis who were to complete our force. On the 1st December two praus arrived from Tangaroeng with Boegis soldiers, under the command of four kapitans or captains, wearing as a sign of authority a detta, or head-dress, of red Boegis cloth interwoven with silver, and armed with a very handsome kris. Still the Dyaks of Long Wai and Long Wahou, who had been summoned to meet the Sultan, failed to put in an appearance; and none of the Malays in the village seemed any more willing to obey orders to provide a number of followers to accompany the Sultan to the frontier, although outwardly professing the greatest obedience. They complained that not only would they not be paid for their services, but they would also have to provide themselves with food and all necessaries. It is hardly to be wondered at that they objected to such terms, especially as they did not pretend to conceal their fear of the Dyaks. One morning the Sultan and Crown Prince went away in two praus "recruiting" in the neighbourhood, but the people somehow heard of their intentions, and all—men, women, and children—ran away from their houses into the forest, where of course it would be useless to hunt after them.

Finding that my departure from Tangaroeng had been followed by such good results in the speedy determination of the Sultan to follow me, I resolved to leave Kotta Bangoen, and trust to the Sultan's coming after me in the same way. Besides his trouble with his recalcitrant subjects, the Sultan had so many occupations —cock-fighting, entertaining his ladies, holding *bitcharas*, and getting an occasional *pitcha*, or rubbing down—an operation which was performed by an old woman, said to be very clever in her profession—that the chances were he might remain at Kotta Bangoen for another month. So in company with Sokmaviro, Tomongoeng, and Bandahara, I determined to leave him, and try to take a short cut to Moeara Montai. Instead of following the ever-winding ways of the Mahakkam, with its strong current against us, we pulled up a side stream called the Ajoeboenga, which flows through a large lake, Semajang. Emerging from the comparatively narrow stream into this large sheet of water seemed like entering the ocean, so vast by comparison did the expanse of water look. The heat here was intense, owing to the absence of the friendly shelter of the trees. Lake Semajang is about fifteen miles long, and is connected by a narrow channel or creek with another lake, Malintang, about five miles in length, into which another creek flows called Sambiliong, full of weeds and grass, and buried in a gloomy forest. This channel has only a foot or eighteen inches of water in it, and is so narrow and so overgrown with trees that there is barely room for a canoe to pass through, and not the slightest chance of turning. My canoe grounded twice, though drawing only a foot of water, and some of the crew had to get out, scramble through the wilderness of wood, and drag her off again.

The scenery here was very picturesque, though "scenery" is perhaps hardly the word to use, for you can only see a few feet in front of you; the winding stream turns and twists in all directions —here so narrow as hardly to be navigable, there opening out as it sweeps to the left or the right, and giving a glimpse into the heart of the forest—now overgrown with a mass of grass and reeds, now comparatively deep and clear, affording with the varied vegetation a succession of changing views, limited in extent, but each a picture in itself.

Here I heard the voices of birds singing and whistling in greater numbers than I had heard them in any part of Borneo, but not a feather could be seen. All around us were the melodious and strange voices, but no songster came in sight. The branches of the trees, which overhung the water like a rich canopy, were covered with orchids, the colours of which were in splendid contrast with the dim religious light which pervaded the place. For two or three hours we struggled through this gloomy tangle of forest growth, till at last we again emerged on to the Mahakkam itself, and ascended the main stream till we came to the village of Moeara Montai, where a small stream of the same name enters the Mahakkam. Passing up this tributary we came to Lake Tambatoeng, whence our course lay up another small river called the Allo, on which is a village of the same name. Here Tomongoeng landed and went in search of "lodgings to let." The best accommodation to be found was in a large house occupied by three or four families, with a swarm of children. One of these was only seven days old, and was as red as a boiled lobster, with abundance of hair on its head. The good people here were Malays, and had heard of the approach of the Sultan and the "Commissie," but did not expect us so soon; but the women and children soon stowed themselves away in the smaller rooms, while the men set to work to make the larger apartment habitable for their guests. A petroleum case covered with a mat had to serve as a table and seat; but I had the unwonted luxury of a mosquito curtain.

To my surprise the Sultan and suite reached the village an hour or two after my arrival. In the evening we went out to shoot deer, which were said to be plentiful in the neighbourhood. The country was, however, too full of water, and all the successful hunting that took place was on the part of a crocodile, which took a fancy to one of the Sultan's dogs and devoured it.

The inhabitants of the village get their living by fishing. The lakes and streams adjoining swarm with fish; and on the platform under every house was a quantity of fish, dried and drying, and not particularly savoury, reminding me somewhat of the great fishing stations at the Lofoten Islands in Norway. In a southerly direction could be distinctly seen the blue peak of Goenong (Mount) Bratus, said to be the highest mountain in Koetei. At the foot of the mountain live a tribe of Dyaks, who, the Sultan told me, eat the excrement of animals, especially of the wild bull.

At eight a.m. on the following morning I left Allo, descending the river, crossing Lake Tambatoeng, and entering Lake Djempang, which is connected with the former by a narrow channel. There are evident signs that these two lakes have, within a very recent period, been one. The water is gradually drying out, the shores being covered by vegetation and successive deposits of alluvial mud, till, at no distant date, the water will be replaced by dry land. At present, the Lake Djempang is about eighteen English miles in length, and six miles broad. I took a series of soundings, and found its depth varied greatly, from one to fifteen fathoms. Among the high grass on the banks wandered numbers of white and grey herons, searching for frogs or insects, while on the tree-tops sat adjutants and snake-darters, that flew away at our approach.

Seven hours after leaving Allo I reached the extremity of the lake, and entered the small river Baroe, which eventually again connects the string of lakes with the Mahakkam. Passing rapidly along this narrow shallow stream, my canoe had a narrow escape of being capsized, the keel touching the submerged trunk of a tree, and half filling with water. Fortunately no real harm was done, and, after stopping to clear away the hidden danger from the path of those who were following us, we proceeded on our way. Here the banks showed signs of cultivation—first a rice-field or two, then large gardens of pine-apples (*nas*), succeeded by sugar plantations and banana grounds. The pine-apples were especially delicious, and nowhere have I tasted sweeter and more juicy than those procured later at Moeara Pahou, a village situated at the point where the river of the same name joins the Mahakkam, where we arrived about five p.m. This is the furthest advanced Malay settlement in Koetei. Beyond it is Dyak country, pure and simple.

The houses at Moeara Pahou over a hundred in number, are plaited bamboo structures, mostly built on rafts in the river, which is both wide and deep. On shore is a large *misigit*, or mosque, to which the few faithful are summoned to prayer every morning by a large wooden drum, made of the broken stem of a tree, with a hide stretched over one end, giving a deep sonorous boom when struck. Sokmaviro found me a house on the river close to this mosque, so I had the full benefit of the solemn booming every morning. The Malays here farm large gardens of pisangs, cocoa-nuts, sugar-cane, and maize; and the rivers yield abundance of fish, chief among which are the silurus, so common everywhere, and a flat fish exactly like a sole, very plentiful, and good eating. Many of the inhabitants get their living by fishing, the produce being sold here dried and smoked. A common way of preparing the fish is to scrape off the scales, cut the fish open along the back, remove the intestines, put a bamboo through the mouth and down the whole length of the fish, then tie a rattan round to keep it together, and roast it over a fire. The natives have various ways of fishing—with nets, baskets, or hook and line; while for very large fish they have a very curious device. They make a roughly-carved wooden model of a bird, to the underpart of which is fastened a piece of thick string, about two inches long, with a hook attached; this bird is secured by a line round the neck and allowed to float on the water, the hook suspended beneath. It seems a very impracticable means of catching fish, but the natives told me that they only use it when the water is thick, and that then they rarely set this odd kind of "night line" without hooking a fish. The river here is more than ten feet deep.

The inhabitants do a large trade with the Dyaks, who come down with their produce—rattan, gutta, and edible birds'-nests, and occasionally a couple of the precious bezoar stones—to exchange or sell, for the Dyaks are beginning to fancy the Dutch silver *ringits* (dollars).

CHAPTER XII.

A fishing and hunting party—Dyaks from Long Bléh—A deputation from the Tandjoeng Dyaks—Men's chignons—A cannibal scare—Wild war-dances—Elaborately tattooed women—A cannibal priestess—Tid-bits of human flesh—Taking the portrait of the cannibal chief—An unprepossessing physiognomy—A ghastly gift—Raden Mas, the gold noble.

On the day after my arrival I was surprised by Kichil suddenly coming into my room and announcing the coming of the Sultan, who had informed us of his intention to stay a few days at Allo. On my asking the reason for the sudden change of mind, he made an expressive grimace, and said the smell of the fish there was intolerable. He was immediately visited by deputations of the various *kapalas* and *mantries* in the neighbourhood, who brought with them every afternoon presents of fruit, eggs, &c. One fine afternoon a dozen of the principal ladies came to pay *hormat*, and it was rumoured that his Highness was to select an addition to his hareem. Each one carried a brass plate or bowl, covered with a white cloth, the contents of which they seemed to guard jealously from public gaze, though on inquiry I was informed they contained nothing but rice, eggs, or honey.

Early in the afternoon of the 9th November the Sultan and I went fishing and shooting up a small tributary of the Mahakkam called the Djintang, which flows from a lake of the same name. The stream, like all the rivers in Koetei, goes in ever-winding ways, and the banks are lined with magnificent forest vegetation, which prevented our shooting either birds or animals. It is easy to shoot, but not so easy to recover the game. The Sultan's hunter wounded a long-nosed monkey, which fell with a crash from the tree; three or four of our men hurried up to secure it, but the beast had strength enough to get away and disappear. When we came to the lake the Sultan proposed to try our luck at fishing. As the sun with fiery colours gradually sank below the horizon, the Sultan directed all the boats to form a circle, and at a given signal from his Highness, who stood in the bow of his canoe holding a net in his hands, all the nets were thrown out simultaneously. This was repeated three or four times, but without any success. It was too late in the day for fishing, as the fishes in these lake regions retire before sunset to the shore, remaining all night amongst the great masses of high aquatic grass. The Sultan then ordered an immensely long but narrow net, several hundred feet in length, to be set some twenty feet from the shore, and a canoe with a crew remained all night to keep watch, returning the following morning with a rich harvest of fish.

On our return from fishing we found a great number of Longbléh Dyaks of the Modang tribe had arrived to escort us over the frontier, and were moored on the opposite side of the river to that on which our praus lay. Their chief came at once to the Sultan to ask for some rice, which was given to them, and in a few minutes their fires were blazing on the bank. I went across the river the next day to converse with them. The canoes were apparently very old and in want of repair, and the general appearance of the people, and all their accoutrements, indicated a state of poverty compared with that of other tribes. The chief's prau had a square bow, with a painted figure-head of a death's head. The chief himself wore a jacket of leopard-skin, or rather the simple skin of the leopard, with a hole cut in the neck, through which he passed his head, while the head of the skin hung over his chest and the main portion of the skin covered the shoulders and back, the tail almost touching the ground. On the head of the skin, round the edge and inside, were fastened a few conical shells and a large shell of mother-o'-pearl (*Meleagrina.*) His head-dress was equally characteristic; it was a conical cap, made from a monkey-skin, with a piece of metal sheathing fastened on the front, and a few rhinoceros feathers stuck in the top. Round his neck he wore several strings of beads. A portable seat of plaited rattan, fastened behind to a tjawat, completed his outfit.

The chief spoke a little Malay, and asked me a number of questions. Why did I want to go this long way to Bandjermasin, when there was a *jallan apie* (a "fire-road," *i. e.* a steamship)? What was I going to do with the drawings I made? Why did I ask so many questions about his people and other tribes? I explained to him, by means of an illustrated book I happened to have by me, that I was writing about the natives of Koetei, and so on; and he seemed quite ready to answer my questions, provided I gave satisfactory replies to his, which was not always a very easy task.

His people seemed a fine, well-built, muscular lot of men. Very few of them had any tattoo marks, and the holes in their ears were much smaller than those cultivated by their neighbours of Long Wai. The only ornaments they wore were bead necklaces; but they all carried a number of *tambatongs* attached to the mandau girdle. The mandaus were in all cases perfectly plain, without ornamentation of any kind, either on blade, handle, or sheath.

In the cabins of all the canoes were strewn a number of caps and jackets of various materials. The jackets were mostly sleeveless, made of very thick cloth, and padded with cotton wool, as a protection against sword-cuts and poisoned arrows; others were of bear-skin, or monkey-skin (*Nasalis larvatus*), or goat-skin, while a few were made of the bark of a tree, with a little embroidery stitched on.

Detachments from another tribe, the Tandjoeng Dyaks, also came to pay their respects to the Sultan. There were representatives of two branches of this tribe, from Bantang and from Boenjoet. They are not so muscular and tall as the Dyaks in the north of Koetei, but rather slightly built. They do not tattoo as a rule. I only found one with a + on his arm. They make only small holes in their ears, very often wearing no ornaments in them (see Plate 21, Fig. 3), but they all wear necklaces, mostly a string of beans, called *Boa kalong*. I observed one with a curious necklace composed of red beads and the teeth of a species of bat, set alternately, and producing a pretty effect, the white teeth contrasting well with the vermilion beads. From the necklace, wrapped in a piece of dirty red flannel, hung a talisman. I was very anxious to purchase this necklace. I could not make my wishes understood by signs, or else the man was perverse and would not part with it, and none of my men could understand the dialect, so I took him to the Sultan—who by the way seems to be acquainted with all the languages and dialects spoken in Koetei, and they are numerous enough, except that of the Orang Poonan—and explained what I wanted. His Highness spoke a few words to the Dyak, who agreed to let me have the necklace, but only on the condition that he kept the talisman; he could on no account part with that. He took the necklace off and began to unfold the little piece of flannel, handling his charm as carefully as if it was a precious stone, or at least a bezoar. When he at last hesitatingly held it in his hand for me to see, it proved to be only a tiny piece of yellow wood. I gave in exchange for the necklace three yards of blue cloth.

All these Dyaks wore their hair in a very becoming fashion, reminding me much of some of the so-called chignons in fashion among the ladies some years ago in Europe. The hair is cut short below the occiput, while on the crown it is allowed to grow to a great length, sometimes reaching to the knees. This long hair is rolled up in chignon fashion (see Plate 21, Fig. 3) and fastened by a sort of head-covering made of bark, resembling the New Zealand tappa. This is the only instance in which I saw this material dyed—coloured red, blue, or yellow. The *tjantjoet* or *tjawat* is mostly of the same material, being preferred to cloth, as being more durable.

I was struck by the fact that none of the mandaus worn by these men, again, were ornamented, all being perfectly plain. They often begged for tobacco, and one day I let them taste a drop of brandy, which they did not like. I was told that among the Tandjoeng Dyaks there are only a couple of houses in each village, but so large as to contain between them the whole population of 400 to 500.

At Moeara Pahou I had expected to meet a party of the much-dreaded Tring Dyaks, a branch of the Bahou tribe, having sent a messenger from Kotta Bangoen with a request that the Rajah would meet me here with a number of men and women of his tribe. I had taken the precaution to send a present of a picol of rice and some fish in proof of my friendly intentions, and promised that, if the chief would allow me to make a few sketches of his people, he and they should be liberally rewarded. It was four days' journey from Kotta Bangoen to the Tring settlement, and I was not surprised to find on reaching Moeara Pahou that none of them had arrived. But when two or three days had elapsed and still no Trings appeared on the scene, I determined to go myself to their kampong; but the Sultan and all the people said it would not be safe to do so: the people were cannibals, and were hated as well as feared by all their neighbours, and they might possibly think that the large force which the Sultan had collected here was brought together for the purpose of attacking them, especially as some of the assembled tribes were unfriendly to the Trings. I explained that I must see them, having heard so much about their atrocities and cannibalism. The Government would expect me to report upon these savages; and I should be to blame if I did not see them, both men and women. So the Sultan sent a canoe, with a reliable man in charge, to request the Trings to put in an appearance. Four, five, six days passed, and still no Trings came, and, more strange, no canoe returned. Were the crew killed and eaten? The Sultan could not sit still under such a possibility, and sent another large canoe, well armed, and in command of a Kapitan, who came back in three days, bringing the first envoy with him, and some forty Trings besides, including four women.

The men seemed to exhibit in their bearing a strange mixture of shyness and suspicion. They wore a tjawat, or waist-cloth, of bark, and a head-covering of the same material. They were slightly tattooed—a small scroll on the arm or calf of the leg; and they all had their ears pierced, and the holes enlarged, though only a few of them wore any ornament, generally a wooden cylinder, in the ears. I sketched one of the men in war-costume, bribing him with a couple of dollars to go through the war-dance. Running round and round, stamping his feet heavily on the ground, shouting at the top of his voice, flourishing his mandau as if striking an imaginary foe, and then guarding himself with his shield, he gradually became so excited and furious in his movements, cheered on by the cries of his companions, that I was not sorry to think that I was not witnessing a *pas de deux*. (See Plate 11.)

The women were much more elaborately tattooed than the men, the whole of the thighs and the hands and feet being covered with blue patterns. Their dress consisted of a sort of petticoat, either of a blue or neutral tint, fastened round the hips and reaching to the ankles, bordered at each end with a red piece of cloth. Many of them wore round the waist several strings of large beads of a turquoise, dark blue, or yellow colour. These I found were highly prized, being very old (from *tempo doelo*), and no longer procurable. Round their necks was also a profusion of beads. Of head-coverings they wore two sorts, both of which are figured on Plates 13 and 14; the one a conical hat, without a crown, covered with fine bead-work, and bound round the edges with a strip of red flannel; the other, merely a narrow band of red flannel, beaded at intervals in regular patterns, and fastened with a button behind.

The lobes of the ears were pierced, sometimes in no less than three places in addition to the large central slit (see Plate 13), the principal holes being enormously enlarged by the weighty tin rings hanging in them. The kapitan told me that these people live in large houses several hundred feet long, but extremely dirty inside, and of a wretched appearance outside. The houses, he said, were literally full of skulls taken by the tribes in their head-hunting expeditions. I noticed that the other Dyak tribes did not go near the Trings during their stay at Moeara Pahou, not disguising their fear of them, and their disgust at their cannibal practices.

These people speak quite a distinct language, and none of the Tangaroeng Malays could understand a word that they said; fortunately the old Boegis kapitan who brought them could converse fluently with them, having lived some years amongst them as a sort of tax-officer for the Sultan, and with his assistance I was enabled to obtain much information. Among the visitors was an old priestess, who gave full details concerning the religious beliefs, &c., of the tribe. This information was elicited by the kapitan, and interpreted by him to a Malay writer, who took down the statements on the spot. These statements have since been translated for me, and are embodied in the chapter on the religious rites of the Dyaks.[1]

[1] See p. 220.

This priestess allowed me to take her portrait, which is reproduced in Plate 14. The most striking feature is the enormous length of the loops formed in the lobes of the ears, from which heavy tin rings were suspended. She allowed me to accurately measure this monstrous deformity; and the exact measurements are given in p. 187.

Next, the absence of eyebrows will be noticed. The eyebrows are either entirely wanting or very scanty in all the members of the tribe, who pull them out, considering their absence a mark of beauty.

The elaborate tattooing on the thighs is also a striking feature.

The shortness of the hair, again, is in contrast to the length to which the women of all the other tribes allow their hair to grow; and the colour of the skin is slightly lighter than that prevailing among the Dyaks, the Orang Poonan alone excepted.

This priestess in the course of conversation told me—holding out her hand—that the palms are considered the best eating. Then she pointed to the knee, and again to the forehead, using the Malay word *bai, bai* (good, good), each time, to indicate that the brains, and the flesh on the knees of a human being, are also considered delicacies by the members of her tribe.

Having interviewed this priestess, I had the honour of an introduction to the famous, or infamous, chief of the cannibal Dyaks, Sibau Mobang, whose portrait is given in Plate 12. He came into my house one day, accompanied by his suite of two women and three men, and I hardly know whether host or visitor felt the more uncomfortable. His personal appearance bore out the idea I had formed of him by the reports I had heard of his ferocity and the depravity of his nature; but I was hardly prepared to see such an utter incarnation of all that is most repulsive and horrible in the human form.

As he entered my floating habitation he assumed a sort of air of hesitation, almost amounting to trembling fear, which added to, rather than detracted from, the feelings of repulsion with which I viewed him. He stood for a moment or two, neither moving nor speaking, watched me narrowly when I pretended not to be looking at him, and then sat down quietly a couple of yards from my feet. He is a man apparently about fifty years of age, of yellowish-brown colour, and a rather sickly complexion. His eyes have a wild animal expression, and around them are dark lines, like shadows of crime. He is continually blinking his eyes, never letting them meet those of his interlocutor, as if his conscience did not allow him to look any one straight in the face. His face is perfectly emaciated, every feature shrunken and distorted. The absence of teeth in the gums gives the bones an extra prominence. A few stiff black hairs for a moustache, and a few straggling ones on his chin, add to the weird look; his ears hang down low, pierced with large holes two inches in length. His right arm, on which he wears a tin bracelet, is paralyzed, and he is unable to open the right hand without the assistance of his left, lifting each finger separately, and closing them again with little less difficulty. For this reason he wears his mandau on his right side, and the many victims that have fallen to this bloodthirsty wretch during the last few years he has decapitated left-handed. At that very time, as he sat conversing with me through my interpreter, and I sketched his portrait, he had fresh upon his head the blood of no less than seventy victims, men women and children, whom he and his followers had just slaughtered, and whose hands and brains he had eaten.

He told me his people did not eat human meat every day—that was a feast reserved for head-hunting expeditions; at other times their food consisted of the flesh of various animals and birds, rice, and wild fruits. For a whole year, however, they had had no rice, owing to the failure of the crops. When I heard this I told Kichil to bring forward a large kettle of rice which was boiling, and to place it before my guests, together with some salt. The eagerness with which they ate the rice, rolling it first between their hands so as to form solid rolls, bore out the statement that they had lately been kept on very "short commons" indeed.

The whole time he sat in my room Sibau Mobang seemed very grave, and kept incessantly turning his head away from me, so that it was not difficult to get a portrait of him in profile. His grim visage, his still more grim manner, made me wonder whether he could ever laugh. The idea seemed horribly ludicrous; I tried however to get a smile on his countenance, but without success, until, when I had finished my sketch, I handed it to him to examine. He scrutinized it closely, then looked at me for the first time full in the face, and actually smiled, a ghastly grim smile, horribly suggestive of nightmare. He made signs that he wished to keep the sketch, but I made him understand that I could not let him have it. I gave him, however, various presents, and two dollars to each member of the party whom I had had the privilege of sketching, besides a picol of rice, some strings of beads, and twenty-four yards of calico to divide between them. Sibau Mobang gave me in return two human crania, trophies of his head-hunting excursions—one that of a male, the other of a female, but both, as usual, wanting the lower jaw; they were wrapped up in pisang leaves, and are figured in Plate 22. He also with some reluctance gave me a *kliau* (shield), of the ordinary soft wood, painted in grotesque patterns, and ornamented with tufts of human hair most ingeniously stuck on, similar to the one shown in Plate 11. Such a shield is considered a great treasure, being decorated with hair taken from human victims.

This cannibal, however, is not the chief Rajah of the Tring Dyaks. Their nominal ruler is Raden Mas, a chief who, at the instance of the Sultan, his suzerain, gave up cannibalism in order to embrace the Mohammedan religion, and enjoy the advantage of a plurality of wives. He is very rich, very powerful, and very independent of the Sultan, who is obliged to humour him very much to keep him on good terms, and who, on the occasion of his supposed conversion to Islam, gave him the title he now holds of Raden Mas: *Raden* = noble; *Mas* = gold. The latter term refers to the stores of gold-dust which he is reputed to possess, hidden away in his village.

The Raden was invited to join the Sultan's suite and accompany him to Bandjermasin. He has large eyes and prominent cheek-bones, and the unsightly long holes in the lobes of the ears; but his general appearance is by no means repulsive. Dressed in a neat cotton or silk jacket, with gold buttons, and a pair of short Boegis trousers, he was, compared with his second in command, Sibau Mobang, quite a gentleman.

CHAPTER XIII.

Leaving Moeara Pahou—The village of Dassa—Native sculpture—Domesticated buffaloes—Scarcity of animal life—Ladies at the bath—Stemming the rapids—A lofty village—Long Puti—A Dyak Rajah lying in state—The country of the men with tails—An inconvenient tail—An expedition in search of the missing link—More rapids—A deserted country—Landing at Moeara Anan—On the look-out for a night attack.

Early in the morning of Monday, 15th December, my fleet of five praus left Moeara Pahou, my boat leading, and the rest paddling in single file at short intervals behind. Shortly after noon I saw projecting beyond the line of trees on the beach, at a curve in the river, a tall post surmounted by a rudely carved figure—a sign that we were near a village which had distinguished itself in head-hunting. I expected to find a large settlement, but was surprised to see only three houses. As we approached, some women and children "scuttled" up the ladders, while others peeped at us through the openings in the walls, as though they took us for enemies. This was the village of Dassa, inhabited by a settlement of the Benoa Dyaks, as those tribes are called who dwell on the banks of the Moeara Pahou and its tributaries. I landed with Kichil, and at once went into one of the houses, which were of the ordinary Dyak design. The inner walls were ornamented outside with grotesque figures—some representing the inevitable alligator, in various positions; another a man being swallowed by an alligator—a very common scene in real life in Koetei, and one which would seem rather to encourage a hatred than a reverence for these saurians among the inhabitants. I also noticed hanging on one of the walls three compressed balls of hair, of a brownish colour, which the chief told me had come from alligators—the indigestible remains of some prey, perhaps human!

Another of the carvings represented a Dyak riding on an animal meant for a boar; while on a third wall was depicted a Dyak returning from a head-hunting tour, with a head in his left hand. Further down the room was hanging suspended against the wall a small model of a house, somewhat resembling a Noah's ark, from the door of which protruded a carved serpent, which was represented to me as being a valuable medicine for the stomach.

Round the houses was a cleared space, where for the first time in Koetei I saw several *karbaus* (buffaloes) grazing ; surrounded, of course, by numberless litters of black pigs.

Having rested here and taken our meals, we continued our cruise, till we came about sunset to a solitary house, containing twenty inhabitants. Fastening our praus to the shore, we remained here for the night, the Dyaks bringing out some rice and eggs on a tray, as a present for the Pangeran Sokmaviro. Sunrise again saw us paddling onward, the boats starting, as usual, with a spurt, or race, which died away five minutes afterwards, to be renewed at intervals of two or three hours. There was nothing to relieve the monotony of the day's proceedings; a long-nosed monkey or two sitting on the top of a lofty tree were the only signs of animal life to be seen,[1] until at one p.m. we came to the junction with the long looked-for stream the Lawa. Here there was a miserable settlement where two Malay traders had collected a great quantity of rattan on rafts.

Here the Pangeran Sokmaviro said he would stay a day to get a smaller prau, more suitable for ascending the small river with its many rapids; and fortunately he succeeded in bargaining with one of the Malay traders for a prau which, with a little repair, could enable him to continue. Still I decided to proceed, accompanied by the Pangeran Tomongoeng, and followed by one of the Sultan's kapitans and twelve Boegis soldiers. For four hours we went up the gradually narrowing River Lawa without seeing a hut, when at five p.m. one of my men noticed a Dyak standing on

[1] The Dyaks living on the Moeara Pahou river told me they never came across any animals in the forest except monkeys and bats, which were abundant. The former are eagerly hunted, both for their flesh and skin, as also for the *galiga*, or bezoar stones, found occasionally inside; while the teeth of the latter are worn as talismans, and made into necklaces.

a small ladder, and two praus drawn up on the bank. My crew were anxious to stay here for the night, giving the usual excuse that there were no more huts for many miles to come; so I gave the order to make fast to the shore. This done, the men as usual immediately jumped with one accord into the river for a swim.

There was no appearance of a habitation, but I landed, and found standing in a maize-field, and hidden from the river, a house containing four families, with nine children. The people said they had not been settled here long; but they had already a fine field of maize, some sugar-cane, and melons, growing a short distance from the house. The men were all tattooed with a small mark , either on the forehead, the arm, or the leg.

On returning to the boat I was followed by three of the men with their wives and six children. It was past six, their usual time for bathing and filling their bamboo-cane water-carriers. Pangeran Tomongoeng, like a good Mussulman, had spread his little carpet in the prau, and was engaged in prayer, stooping every now and then to kiss the mat on which he knelt. The native women, without taking the slightest notice of our presence, walked straight down to the river, and removing their scanty clothing descended into the water, the two young wives first, then an older woman, with a one-year-old baby on her back, and behind them the children and men. Each carried a long piece of bamboo, and after filling these with water, and performing their ablutions, they returned as they had come, quietly and unconcernedly, to their home.

Next morning we proceeded on our journey. The Lawa here was not more than seventy feet wide; and, as the country was hilly on all sides, we looked forward to some difficult work pulling up stream. Shortly after eight we overtook three small praus, each with four men of the Tandjoeng Boenjoet tribe, all dressed in war costume, of sleeveless jackets either of padded cloth or of bearskin, ornamented with several rows of beads or pebbles; the chief wearing a cap of monkey-skin bearing a brass plate in front, the rest having rattan hats decked with a quantity of hornbill and Argus-pheasant feathers. In the middle of each prau were heaped up shields, lances, and baskets. Towards noon we passed the small settlement of Mallar, where the women all wore wooden cylinders in their ears instead of rings, a pair of which I procured in exchange for some beads. They are figured in Plate 19, Figs. 4 and 5.

Soon afterwards we came to a series of rapids and falls known as Keham[2] Tring, of which the Sultan had often spoken to me as being very dangerous and difficult to pass, with the water falling fifty or sixty feet. The rapids proved, however, to be much less formidable, the total fall not being more than five or six feet. There was a good volume of water flowing down, and we feared that we might have to carry the praus, as well as the luggage, overland. After indulging in the luxury of a bath in the freshening waters, we consulted as to the best means of surmounting the obstacle; a couple of long-nosed monkeys assisted, at a respectful distance on the top of a neighbouring tree, at the consultation, and solemnly watched all our proceedings without stirring from their lofty position. It was decided to wait till the morning before attempting to pass the rapids; and meanwhile Tomongoeng fixed an upright pole in the water and marked it, and also made a notch in an adjoining rock, to gauge the rise or fall of the river. In the meanwhile two of the crew went into the woods to cut some strong poles for "poling" the praus in the narrower and more rapid parts of the river; while the rest of the crew made long ropes of twisted rattan for towing with.

By next morning the water had fallen more than a foot, and was running with much less violence, so we determined to unload only the heavier luggage, and haul the canoes through the boiling water. Tomongoeng's prau was first dragged over, as being the smallest of the three, some of the men, who were all excellent swimmers, getting into the water and pushing it up, while others hauled at the rattan ropes; next came the kapitan's boat, in similar fashion. When my turn came I determined to remain in the boat with the steersman; and twenty pair of strong arms hauled at the ropes, while twenty pair of lungs frightened the monkeys with a loud "Ya! Ya! Ya!"—"Aio! Aio! Aio!"

Then came the task of carrying up all the luggage, and re-

[2] *Keham* = rapid.

stowing it on board; and not half an hour after the whole process had to be gone through again at another rapid, more powerful than the last. Here more yelling occurred; and it struck me more forcibly than ever how universal is the habit of shouting when a number of men, especially sailors or "watermen," unite their forces in any hauling or pushing operations.

Still two more small rapids had to be surmounted, fortunately not sufficiently strong to necessitate unloading; and at nine o'clock we came to the village of Langla, strangely situated, for a Dyak settlement, on a hill, on the left bank of the river, and surrounded with plantations of *nangka*—a large green, juicy, melon-like fruit—cocoa-nuts, and sugar-cane.

Three hours later we came to Long Puti, the largest and neatest Dyak village I had yet seen, containing no less than 1800 inhabitants. Our advent caused an excited multitude of people to rush down to the shore; but they permitted us to land quietly, and I made straight for the nearest large house. In the central part of the village was an extensive open space or field, in which stood the symbol of renown in head-hunting excursions, a tall pole in a slanting position, surmounted by a carved figure representing a crowned Rajah, in the very un-Rajah-like act of holding out his tongue as far as he could reach (see Plate 27, Fig. 2). This was really the coat of arms, or rather crest, of the community, whose prowess was acknowledged by all the surrounding tribes, and who had probably chosen their crest as an emblem of defiance.

It so chanced that the first house I entered was that of a chief just deceased, whose remains were lying in state in the large room of the place. In the centre of one side of the room, which was no less than 120 feet in length, stood, raised on four posts, a coffin, in the shape of a prau, with the sides painted in red, black, and white scrolls. On the lid of the coffin was spread the *tjawat*, or waist garment, which had been worn daily by the deceased chief. Above the coffin was an attap roof, from which hung a cup, formed of part of a cocoa-nut shell, filled with water, while food was also daily placed on the coffin—so the guard who was watching over the corpse informed me—in case the dead warrior should feel hungry or thirsty in his long journey to heaven.[3] His best clothes and weapons were deposited inside the coffin.

From one end of the coffin was suspended a wooden model of an animal, supposed to be a bear, which was expected to act as a charm to protect the dead from all possible dangers on his last journey; and at either extremity hung a bamboo candlestick holding damar torches. These were renewed from day to day, and kept always burning. An exact representation of the coffin is given in Plate 25. The woman and child in the doorway are the widow and child of the dead chief. All the time I was examining and sketching the coffin they stood at the entrance to the bedroom, which led out of the principal room. They were in "deep mourning"—not clothed in black as in Europe, or in white as in China, but with the hair closely shaven off the head, presenting a most ghastly sight.

Although the body had been dead fifteen days there was not the slightest smell in the room, the coffin being hermetically closed with a sort of putty made of gutta-percha mixed with fine fibres obtained from the bark or leaves of a tree.

I asked when the burial was likely to take place; but the attendants answered that they did not know; the time was uncertain; they must first have "luck" in some way or other, either a good rice harvest, or, what was most probable, a successful head-hunting expedition. A head or two must be secured somehow, since it was a chief who was dead.

I looked into two or three of their houses, but found the general arrangement very similar to that prevailing in other Dyak settlements. The only remarkable circumstance was the manner in which the graves were scattered, irregularly, over the muddy ground amongst the houses, each with a carved wooden board[4] to mark the spot.

The usual hordes of pigs were disporting themselves in the congenial mud, while a few buffaloes wandered about, looking very uncomfortable, searching in vain for a blade of grass in the reeking filth around.

[3] For a description of the route supposed to be travelled by the departed spirit on its way to the Dyak heaven, see p. 224.

[4] See p. 220.

On my return to my prau I found the Sultan, with his numerous fleet, had followed me. The Dyak praus were all moored on the opposite side of the river, keeping apart from the Malays. The Sultan's large prau, flying the yellow standard with the tiger *rampant*, was fastened close to mine; and in the evening we dined together on a raft in the river, on which a table and two seats were hurriedly constructed. We were now on the confines of the territory of the Sultan, who was anxious to make as large a display of force as possible. He had recently, he told me, lodged a complaint to the Dutch Government against the Doesoen tribes, whose territory we should now enter, and who were the great rivals of the Long Puti Dyaks, making frequent incursions into their territory.

More interesting, perhaps, was his statement that we were now within a short distance of the country in which the tailed race of men lived. The existence of these people was the common talk, not only here, but all the way down to Tangaroeng, and they were variously stated to dwell in Passir, and on the Teweh river. We "discussed" these people over a basket of durian. This was the first time I had tasted this celebrated fruit. The smell of the fruit was not very appetizing, and the flavour—to my taste—resembled that of bad onions mixed with cream.

The Sultan's men were short of provisions, but their commissariat was replenished by a heavy requisition which the Sultan made on the people of this the largest settlement at the furthest extremity of his dominions. So there was great feasting, not only on board the praus, but on shore, where the people killed goats and buffaloes, and distributed a slice to every person in the village. In the evening the hill was ablaze with innumerable fires, round which gambling and card-playing, smoking and sirih-chewing, alternated with the operation of cooking and eating the meal; while the dogs kept up a continual barking and fighting over the bones that were thrown to them as the feast proceeded.

The conversation about the tailed race brought back to my mind various rumours of the existence of this "missing link" in the Darwinian chain which had reached me at different times during my travels in Borneo, and I determined if possible to settle the point one way or the other. The question has often occurred to me whether Mr. Darwin received the first suggestion of his theory of man's simian descent from the fables concerning the existence of tailed men which obtain credence among so many uncivilized people; or whether the natives of the Malay Archipelago and the South Sea Islands, having read the "Descent of Man," have conspired together to hoax the white man with well-concocted stories of people possessed of tails, living in inaccessible districts, and maintaining but slight intercourse with the outer world. It is certainly a curious fact that similar stories exist, not only in Borneo, but in other islands in the South Pacific—New Britain for instance, where missionaries have more than once been tempted into hazardous expeditions in search of the great physiological prize, the missing link in the chain of evidence proving the descent of man from monkey.

I made inquiries in the village, and found a strong general belief in the existence of people with tails in a country only a few days' journey from Long Puti. Such definite statements were made to me on the subject that I could hardly resist the temptation to penetrate myself into the stronghold of my ancestral representatives. Tjiropon, an old and faithful servant of the Sultan, assured me, in the presence of his Highness and of several Pangerans, that he had himself some years ago seen the people in Passir. He called them "Orang-boentoet"—literally, tail-people. The chief of the tribe, he said, presented a very remarkable appearance, having white hair and white eyes—a description which exactly agreed with one I had received some time previously from a young Boegis, when travelling by steamer to Samarinda from Paré Paré in Celebes. As to the all-important item of the tail, Tjiropon declared with a grave face that the caudal appendage of these people was from two to four inches long; and that in their homes they had little holes cut or dug in the floor on purpose to receive the tail, so that they might sit down in comfort. This ludicrous anti-climax to the narrative of the trusty Tjiropon almost induced me to discredit the whole story. At any rate, I thought, the Orang-boentoet must be in a very high state of development—or rather, perhaps, in the last stages of retrogression—

if the extremely sensitive prehensile tail of the spider-monkey has so lost its elasticity in these people as to incommode its wearer to such a degree. The Sultan, however, was highly impressed with the truth of Tjiropon's story. He had often heard that there were among his neighbours, if not even among his own subjects, a tribe with tails; but he had hitherto discredited the rumours. "Now," he said, "I do believe there are such people, because Tjiropon has told us. I have known him for twenty years, and he dare not tell a lie in my face, in presence of us all."

So we asked Tjiropon if he would go and pay another visit to his former friends, and bring one or two of them to introduce to us. He was at first unwilling to go, on account of the disorder existing in Passir, and of a predilection which the inhabitants were alleged to have for poisoning strangers. But a present of 600 florins and of a suit of clothes, and the promise of a reward of 500 florins if he brought a pair—or couple, should I rather say—of tailed people safely to Dutch territory, overcame his scruples. The Sultan decorated the clothes I gave him with a set of silver buttons, adorned with his coat of arms, so that he might present a respectable appearance before the Sultan of Passir, to whom he was furnished with letters of introduction. Thus armed with authority, and with an escort of fifteen men, Tjiropon set out on his expedition, with orders to *rendezvous* at Bandjermasin.

Having despatched Tjiropon on his important mission, we continued our journey up the stream, leaving Long Puti at six a.m. on the 20th December; but we had not gone far before the river became very narrow and shallow, and the current so strong that we proceeded with difficulty. Having stemmed two rapids, we were confronted by a series of falls, which necessitated our unloading the canoes, and carrying the luggage about a mile through the forest, the river meanwhile taking a long sweep of two or three miles to the right. Unfortunately, I was myself added to the list of *impedimenta*, being seized with a sudden attack of fever, and had to be carried in my hammock through the forest by four Dyaks. In the meantime our canoes had been safely hauled over the falls, and through the rapids above, and were in readiness to take us on to Moeara Anan, which we reached in the evening.

Between Long Puti and this place we had not met with a single human being, the whole country being uninhabited, and none of the villages marked in Dr. Schwaner's chart now existing. This may be accounted for by the fact that the Dyaks often remove their settlements when the rice-fields in the neighbourhood become exhausted.

Here the River Anan flows in a north-westerly direction into the Moeara Lawa, which at this point takes a northerly course.

The scene at the riverside, as our party of amok-loving Boegis, and of savage Dyaks clad in war-costume of skins and feathers, landed at Moeara Anan, was weird in the extreme. The darkness of a tropical night, which the moon in her first quarter did little to relieve, was rapidly setting in, and torches were lighted to enable us to get our goods safely ashore. The place was quite deserted by its original inhabitants; but on a sort of natural quay which served as a landing-place we found our advance party—whom the Sultan had sent forward from Long Puti under the Pangeran Sikamandrie, to make arrangements for crossing the watershed of the Lawa and the Benangan—awaiting us. Bamboo ladders were brought into requisition to assist in the debarkation, but they proved ill-constructed and rotten, and were rendered slippery by the recent heavy rains; and many were the stumblings and jostlings among the Dyak porters as they carried their burdens across the slippery mud to dry land. Sikamandrie conducted us to some temporary houses which he had had constructed for our use. There were three principal buildings, connected together by a bamboo floor, for the use of the Sultan, the Pangerans, and myself; and surrounding these were rows of sheds for the men, large enough to accommodate 500. The houses were cleverly constructed of plaited bamboo and bark. In each room was a circular table, the top being made of plaited bamboo, and the stem of a stout cane, split at the bottom into sixteen parts.

The Dyaks of the surrounding district are noted, even among Dyaks, for their ferocity, and Sikamandrie informed us that one of his party had been killed by natives just before our arrival; fearing a night attack from some of the tribes—who because they were not at war among themselves were the more likely to attack strangers—he had taken the precaution to erect outside our encampment, and facing the forest, four look-outs, or guard-houses, mounted on high posts, and commanding an extensive view of the country on all sides. The one Dyak reported by Sikamandrie as having been murdered was multiplied that night a hundredfold in conversation among our followers. My two Javanese lads were more really frightened than the rest; but the fate of the dead man served to keep the whole party on the alert, and we had little fear that the sentries stationed in the look-outs would sleep at their posts. One reason for these precautions was found in the fact that the people had a strong objection to being governed by, and taxed for the benefit of, a Malay ruler; and the visit of the Sultan might be construed by them into an attempt to impose his authority upon them, which they would possibly immediately resent.

His Highness, taking no heed of these considerations, was so pleased with the arrangements made for his visit that he expressed his intention of remaining here a week. I was anxious for many reasons to continue my journey without delay. Urging that I was getting short of provisions for my men, I asked what I should do to get a fresh supply; to which he replied, with the indolence so characteristic of all Orientals, "You are always in such a hurry, and go full speed. My men have been on half-rations for more than a week—only rice once a day; for the rest, they must look out for themselves, and find wild fruits or fish."

CHAPTER XIV.

A forced march through the forest—Spider-thread bridges—A frugal meal of fruit—A forest picture—Curious growth of roots—Extracting gutta-percha—A Dyak camp—Bargaining with the natives—A rainy night in the forest—Rough walking—A wilderness of stones—Absence of volcanic phenomena in Borneo—The denuding force of tropical rains—An appeal to arms—Chilly nights—A night in the forest—Fire-flies and glow-worms—Midnight noises—Poisoned fruit—A rough road—Ruins of a Dyak fortress—Arrival on Dutch territory—Down the Benangan—Scylla and Charybdis—The River Teweh.

THE night passed without any adventure, and next morning found me up early, making arrangements for my march through the forest towards Moeara Benangan. The fever had left me, and the only drawback was the Sultan's unwillingness to start himself or let me go. During our conversation he told me he had dreamt of the tailed people, and of the success of Tjiropon's mission; and I urged that this was an omen in favour of my starting at once. Sikamandrie was to have accompanied me; but at the last moment there was so much shilly-shally and vacillation on the Sultan's part, that I decided to go on without him. My force consisted of fifty-two Dyaks as coolies, and twenty-two men under the command of two Boegis Kapitans, lent me by the Sultan as an escort; and with my trusty Kichil at my side, or rather at my heels—for we had to march in single file through the dense forest—I advanced to the west, announcing my intention of pushing on to Moeara Benangan by forced marches, walking from sunrise to sunset, with an hour's rest in the middle of the day. To this the men all readily assented, as they felt the end of their journey was approaching, although the coolies had to carry from forty to sixty pounds each. They bore their burdens on their back, refusing to carry a double weight slung on bamboo poles between two men, in the fashion so common in other parts of the East.

For a portion of the distance we were able to take advantage of a road or path, which had been made through this part of the forest especially for the Sultan's convenience, and which, though rude and wretched to a degree, was better than the untrodden soil. The country was peculiarly undulating, being a succession of knolls or small hills, about fifty or sixty feet in height, all closely covered with timber. At frequent intervals creeks and deep ravines, rivulets, and even considerable streams, occurred to break the monotony of the scene, and on the first day's march no less than twenty of these had to be crossed. The deepest and widest were spanned by Dyak "bridges," consisting sometimes merely of the trunk of a tree which, growing conveniently on the bank, had been cut down and allowed to fall over the chasm; sometimes of a single bamboo, or two bamboos joined together, with a slender rattan railing three feet above to serve as a balance. Some of the latter bridges were as much as 110 feet in length, and it required no slight skill to traverse them in safety. The solid stems of the trees did not always afford very firm foothold; but the bamboo bridges would yield under the weight of the "passenger," and sway to and fro in the centre in such a manner as to induce sea-sickness and giddiness in those who, like myself, were inexperienced in the art of crossing them. I frequently had to avail myself of the assistance of two Dyaks, one on each side of me, before I could accomplish the passage; and when, safe on the other shore, I sat down and watched the speed and agility with which my coolies not walked, but "trotted," across the slender thread, carrying a burden of half a hundredweight on their shoulders, or with a still heavier load suspended by bamboo poles between two of them, I could not help comparing the lissome actions of these barefooted savages with the awkwardness of civilized man in boots.

The first day's march was accomplished without any notable incident, but it terminated in a very uncomfortable manner, for I had outmarched the greater part of my followers, and found to my dismay on camping for the night that none of the carriers bearing my tinned provisions was within reach. Some of the Dyaks offered to cook me some rice; but this I declined, having fresh in my memory the warning of the Sultan not to accept food from any of them, for fear of poison. The natives are very fond of fruit, which is not surprising, as the water in the rivers is very unpalatable, being thick with mud and decayed vegetation, and swarming with infusoria. I had started with a supply of filtered water, but before the first day was over my men had discovered its virtues, and drunk it all. Luckily there was still one remaining link between myself and civilization in the shape of a few bottles of seltzer-water, kindly given to me by the Sultan. But I could not live on seltzer-water, and when I saw some of the men collecting fruit from the neighbouring trees, and eating it with evident relish, I was tempted to taste some. They called it rawa-rawa. In appearance it resembled a head of burdock, inside which was a fruit like a small plum, with a flavour similar to that of the red currant, but slightly more acid. Meanwhile some of the party set about collecting wood for making fires, a task of no little difficulty, owing to the recent heavy rains; but some dry twigs were found, and the click of flint and steel was soon afterwards followed by the cheerful crackling of the blazing wood from six large fires. Then came the native cooking operations: small clay pots, and, failing them, large hollow pieces of bamboo, were filled with water, and in these primitive utensils the rice was boiled.

Grouped round the blazing fires, some busily attending to the preparations for supper, others as busily occupied in smoking, others again already seeking in sleep the necessary rest for the duties of the morrow, my little company of half-tamed savages presented a picturesque appearance in this fitful light, and, having made arrangements for a proper watch to be kept, I wrapped myself closely in my rug and fell asleep, tired and hungry, watching their movements, and wondering how many miles behind were my lagging companions and my tinned provisions.

Next morning we started early, trusting that our rear-guard would overtake us before the evening. The earth was covered with a thick mist, which rose steaming from the masses of leaves that lay rotting beneath the trees. Walking on, I was struck by the great variety and beauty of the foliage. Hardly two trees seemed alike; the colours—ranging from brilliant green, through the darker shades to olive, and then graduating off to browns, reds, and yellows—now harmonized, now contrasted with each other in effects which, if reproduced on the walls of Burlington House, would be called untrue to nature.

Many of the forest-trees assumed most fantastic shapes, the growth of the roots especially being often extremely curious. The roots of a tree, instead of converging underground at the trunk, would grow upwards above the surface of the ground, and meet in mid air, the trunk proper springing from them at a distance of ten, twelve, or fifteen feet from the earth. Sometimes two, or more often three, principal roots would thus emerge from three almost equidistant points in the dense layer of leaves and tangled undergrowth, and approaching each other at an acute angle would unite into a single stem, giving the tree the appearance of a gigantic three-legged stool. Sometimes the number of roots and rootlets thus growing above ground and meeting in the air was beyond calculation. It is difficult to say whether this, to English eyes, abnormal growth was the more remarkable on account of its curious appearance, or from the persistence with which it repeated itself throughout the forest. It appeared as if the soil was so rich that the trees were forced into the air before the ordinary operations of nature had had time to complete their course, or that the trees had dragged their roots after them in their anxiety to push their heads above the level of their neighbours that crowded them in on all sides.

Some of the trunks rose to the height of twenty or thirty feet from their roots before sending out a single branch; but in the forks of the branches, and from cracks and crannies in the rough barks of many of them, grew ferns in infinite variety, with noble leaves, now of a deep dark green, now so pale as to be almost white; sometimes the dark leaves were flecked with silver or golden spots, and those of more delicate tint would be similarly dotted with dark markings. Climbers and creepers of all kinds and colours clung to the stems and overran the branches of the trees, from which they hung downwards in tangled clusters, or pendulous festoons.

Many of the trees, including several distinct varieties, were pointed out to me by the Dyaks as yielding gutta-percha; and I asked them to show me the manner of extracting the juice. The method was extremely simple. With two sharp strokes of a mandau a deep notch was cut in the bark, from which the juice slowly oozed, forming a milky-looking mucilage, which gradually hardened and became darker in colour as it ran down the tree. The native collectors of gutta-percha make a track through the forest, nicking the trees in two or three places as they go, and collect the hardened sap on their return a few days afterwards.

About five p.m. we came to an encampment where a number of Dyaks were assembled, under two chiefs, anxious to see the Sultan and the "white man," of whose approach they had heard. After a few words of greeting, I determined to rest here and await the arrival of the remainder of my party, of whom I had heard nothing since my departure from Moeara Anan. I was famished after my two days' walk, without other food than that supplied by the rawa-rawa, and another kind of wild fruit called "cho," resembling a small apple, and tasting like a cranberry, which we had gathered on the road; and I was not unwilling to take this opportunity, while resting for a time, of conciliating the new people among whom we had arrived, and rewarding those members of my own party who had kept up with me. On inquiring if they were tired they made no complaint, except that I had walked very fast, and that the road was "*koetoer*" (dirt or mud). Fortunately some twenty of the porters, with a stock of calico, beads, buttons, and other articles, had followed close to their leader, and I distributed the greater portion of the goods, giving the two chiefs and my two Boegis Kapitans sixteen yards of black calico apiece, and to each of the others a few yards of print, with an assortment of beads and buttons adorned with the Dutch arms. Some of the men asked for gunpowder, but I had made a rule not to give powder unless I got birds or animals in return; and, though I was able to make one or two exchanges, I did not obtain anything very valuable here. One swarthy warrior offered me a leopard-skin, the *felis macrocelis*. The head and part of the feet were wanting, but in other respects it was a nice skin. I offered him three dollars for it, which he readily accepted. These skins are very much sought after by the Dyaks, who make of them their war-costume, by simply cutting a round hole below the neck, through which the warrior passes his head, leaving the skin to hang loosely down his back, and the tail trailing on the ground after him. Sometimes a skin is cut into small pieces, and made into round caps, or into mats, which the Dyak when not on the war-path hangs conveniently behind him, so as to form a sort of cushion when sitting down. The teeth and claws are worn as talismans and ear ornaments.

My attention was arrested by a fine necklace of four rows of large oblong red and white agates, called lameangs, worn by one of the Dyaks, who from his demeanour and general appearance seemed to have no slight idea of his importance, and who was regarded with some respect by his neighbours. The stones were very fine specimens, some of them measuring two or three inches in length. They were so nearly transparent that the string on which they were threaded was easily discernible. As I walked up to the man to examine his necklace he withdrew a step backward, looked fiercely at me, and put his hand menacingly to his mandau. My men saw the mistake, and explained to him that I merely wished to look at his lameangs, when he quietly allowed me to handle them. I made the wearer of this ornament several tempting offers for his gems, but could not prevail upon him to part with a single stone. "Nda! nda!" he said, shaking his head; they were talismans, and would protect him against all manner of ills. If he sold the white man his charm, how would he be able to drive away evil spirits?

By the time the bargainings and questionings were over, I heard the welcome news of the arrival of the remainder of my escort, who pleaded the badness of the roads and the weight of their burdens as an excuse for their delay. But worse was in store for them, for after midnight the rain came down in torrents: even the thick trees under which we bivouacked afforded no shelter against a tropical storm, and sleep was impossible. We started at sunrise, to find ourselves walking in mud nearly knee deep. My strong boots were worn to pieces, and worse than useless, since they allowed the small stones—to say nothing of the water and mud—to penetrate, and my feet were sadly galled. Like Achilles, I was forced to admit that my heel was my most vulnerable point: for with one of them cut to the bone and bleeding, I was obliged to discard my boots, and wrap my wounded foot in a towel. Here, again, I thought, was an instance of the disadvantages under which civilized man labours when compared with the savage. I dared not halt, with only three days' supply of rice left; but limped along as best I could, thankful that nothing worse had befallen me. Before noon we reached the river Benangan—not navigable here, on account of several strong rapids—and crossed the stream by means of a bridge formed of the trunk of an enormous tree recently felled for the purpose, and lying as it fell, straight across the river.

The walking got worse and worse, and two hours later we reached the edge of the much-talked of "Field of Stones." I had heard much about this *Jallan Batoe* from the Sultan, who had told me of its caverns and subterranean passages, of its stones a hundred feet in height, thrown together side by side with a narrow passage hardly wide enough for a man to creep between. Various legends were current concerning this wilderness of stones in the middle of the forest. It was the haunt of evil spirits, who had thrown a spell on the ground, turning trees into stone. Here, surrounded by the eternal forest, and hidden from human gaze, the spirits were believed to hold high revel beneath the wooded shade, preparing their enchantments for the confusion of man. Covering an area of several square miles, and cropping up as it were in the centre of a vast forest, this Field of Stones is well calculated to arouse the superstitious dread of a savage people. Its appearance may be likened to that of a flower-garden over which a heavy hailstorm has swept—only that the hailstones were stones and rocks, ranging from small pebbles to huge boulders and angular masses many hundred tons in weight, while the plants were mighty giants of the forest towering a hundred and fifty feet above the surface of the ground. Imagine such a scene, over which the repairing hand of time has thrown its veil in the growth of fresh vegetation which has shrouded the ruins beneath a mantle of green, and you can form an idea of the general effect of the *Jallan Batoe.*

There scattered in wonderful confusion like the remains of a ruined castle: here standing erect and orderly as if carved by chisel and levelled by plumb-line and square: some in ponderous masses as "large as a house," fifty or sixty feet in height, and of still greater width and thickness: others heaped like so many petrified cocoa-nuts, or like a pile of forty-pounder cannon-balls: here bare and gaunt like the pillars of Stonehenge: there moss-covered and decked with ferns or gorgeous flowers: in all directions for miles and miles the stones lie scattered. Some of them have assumed fantastic shapes, in which the imagination can easily picture a travesty of the human form, or of other familiar objects: others again are marked with quaint devices, where wind and rain have put the finishing touches to natural cracks and crevices, and made them assume the appearance of deliberately carved inscriptions, like those seen on ancient weatherbeaten tombstones—or rather, like the curious "picture writings" found on scattered stones and rocks in British Guiana and other parts of South America. A valley of stones is not often marked with such a variety of features as that possessed by this *Jallan Batoe.* Scarcely two stones or groups of stones are alike: if a Titanic battle-field or playground, with its living host of occupants and all their equipment, had been suddenly petrified, the result could hardly have been more striking than the scene presented by this wilderness.

And side by side with the grey immovable stones wherever they can find a foothold spring up giant trees, the gorgeousness of their foliage, the graceful movements of their boughs, and the cheery rustling of their leaves, contrasting strangely with the still silence of the rocks far above which they tower. From a crevice in some of the larger stones springs here and there a stunted iron-tree, which, starved on the uncongenial soil, seems in its gnarled and knotted outline to have partaken of the nature of the sterile rocks on which its roots are forced to feed. On the summit of another rock, again, covered with the rich vegetable mould, the collection perhaps of centuries, grows a magnificent acacia, whose roots, bursting beyond the limits of their narrow cradle, are protected from the heat of the sun by its far-spreading branches.

For miles our route lay through this wilderness of sterility and fertility combined—sometimes creeping between two parallel walls of stone, thrown so closely together that there was barely room to squeeze the body sideways; sometimes making a considerable détour to avoid a more than usually rough spot. In some places the earth was covered with small loose stones, most difficult and painful to walk over; in others, the ground seemed to be of solid rock, and great care was necessary in walking to prevent one's feet being fixed in one of the innumerable crevices, which were the more dangerous from being partially covered by vegetation. I spent a considerable time in searching for subterranean passages or caverns, which are reported to exist here, but was unable to find more than one small cave of no special character, although prolonged search might possibly reveal many such features. Many of the large stones were so lightly balanced on a small foundation that it seemed as if the exercise of a moderate force would be sufficient to overturn them; but, though I tested many, I could find none so evenly hung as to rock to and fro like the celebrated Logan Rocks of Cornwall and the Scilly Islands.

This phenomenal region is situated almost exactly beneath the equator. I was at first inclined to attribute its existence to volcanic agency, although, unlike its neighbours Java and Sumatra, and the Philippines, and, indeed, nearly all the islands of the Malay archipelago, Borneo has no active volcano, and is not now subject to earthquakes or other volcanic phenomena. None of the violent earthquakes or volcanic eruptions, which have been frequent of late years in the surrounding islands, seems to have caused the slightest disturbance in Borneo. This is, indeed, a very remarkable circumstance when the position of Borneo is taken into consideration. In 1852, for instance, Manilla was almost destroyed; in 1856, Great Sanger Island was the centre of a wide-spread disturbance; in 1863, Manilla was again thrown into ruins and 10,000 persons lost their lives; in 1879 and 1880, Java on the one side, and the Philippines on the other, suffered terrible visitations: but in none of these cases were similar phenomena observed in any part of Borneo. Indeed, there is no actual record, or even tradition, of any such event in the island.

The nature of the stones, however, which are of a rubbly limestone formation, precludes the possibility of their volcanic origin. On the other hand, the Field of Stones bears no trace of glacial origin; and the only hypothesis on which its existence can be satisfactorily accounted for is the denuding force of the torrential tropical rains, which have gradually bared the limestone deposit.

We reached the Bumbangan, a branch of the Benangan river, at sunset, and found, in burning fires and recently occupied sheds, traces that the spot had not long been evacuated by a party of Dyaks. My men were soon disporting themselves in the cool waters; but, tempting as the opportunity was, I was warned by lingering traces of fever to deny myself the luxury of a bath.

As the expiring fires were fed with fresh fuel and new ones lighted, numbers of natives were attracted to the spot, armed all of them with the inevitable mandau. Their intentions were fortunately pacific; and, although an appeal to arms took place during the evening, it was of a bloodless nature. Like their more civilized fellow-creatures of the West, these children of the forest were fond of displaying their worldly wealth, and a general comparison of the relative merits and value of their mandaus ensued. The conversation turned on heads and head-hunting, and many a tale was told of personal adventures and death-struggles, in which the superior strength, size, or keenness of blade of his mandau had won the victory, and the head of his victim, for the narrator. Various expedients were resorted to in order to test the sharpness of edge of a particular weapon; but the favourite mode of proving the edge of the blade was to shave the hairs from the shin of the leg. The possession of a highly-decorated and well-finished mandau is looked upon as a sign of authority, or at least of precedence; and, being appealed to on a question of the relative value of different specimens, I took occasion to exhibit the weapon which the Sultan had presented to me. It was carefully handed round and closely scrutinized, the carving of the handle, and especially the inlaid work in the blade, exciting general admiration. After this I had the satisfaction of seeing the other weapons put aside—a tacit admission of their inferiority.

As the evening drew on, the cold became very intense; and, although I felt that the sensation was partly due to my feverish state, I could not help wondering how the Dyaks, naked save for a "tjawat" round their loins, could endure with so little discomfort the extreme changes from the heat of the day to the cold of the night. Some of them lay full length on the ground, without any extra covering; others threw over them a thin mat; while others again would coil themselves up, the knees brought close to the chest, and the chin resting on them. The Malays, on the contrary, seemed to feel the cold almost as much as myself, and covered themselves, head and all, with calico wraps.

As our fires, though tended by three watchmen, got low from time to time, the air became illumined with the intermittent light of numerous fireflies, whose tiny torches seemed to be answered again by the less intense, but more steady, spark emitted by glow-worms, which were swarming on the damp ground. I captured several fireflies, and always found the brilliant light change to a dull opalescent green hue, only faintly discernible, but still quite distinct.

The long night-watches are kept by these fairy-like insects dancing to the strange midnight music of the forest. Over and above the monotonous hum caused by myriads of insect wings beating the still air, resound the hoarse croaking of frogs and the livelier staccato notes of nimble crickets. Now and again a falling nut or branch startles some of the feathered tribe, and a hurried flapping of wings seems to silence all minor sounds. As the darkness—which seems all the more intense on account of the brilliancy of the stars peeping through the curtain of foliage overhead, and the dazzling movements of the fireflies close around one—rapidly gives way to the light of day, the lamps of the firefly are extinguished, the crickets and frogs are hushed, the birds break out into joyous song, or loud shrieks and childlike screams, and the intermittent "bark" of the kijang,[1] with the occasional howling and chattering of monkeys as they chase

[1] *Cervus muntjac*, a species of antelope, whose cry resembles the bark of a dog.

each other along the boughs overhead, renders rest and sleep impossible.

The solitude of a night in a forest is a myth conjured from the brains of poets. Not a moment passes but some sound—strange in itself, or seeming strange, even if familiar, because heard amid unaccustomed surroundings—falls on the ear. The rustling of the leaves during the silence of the night, "when the sweet wind does gently kiss the trees," causes a soft whisper, which appears distinct from the same sound heard under similar circumstances by daylight. The pitter-patter of the rain, bringing down numberless leaves during a sudden shower, produces an entirely novel impression on the ear; and a tropical thunderstorm at night in a forest, when the rain falls as if it would sweep every tree bare of its foliage: when each flash of lightning seems to single out a forest giant on which to expend its force, and to set the whole forest ablaze: when the deafening reverberations of the thunder-clap roll through and through the mighty aisles of nature's own many-columned cathedral—such a scene is beyond the power of pen to describe or pencil to picture.

We left Bumbangan at six a.m. on the 24th December, on the last stage of our journey to the watershed of the River Barito. Owing to the incessant rains the road was worse than ever, being often two feet deep in muddy water. We were still traversing a portion of the Field of Stones, and the walking here was what might be expected on a newly macadamized street in London before the steam roller had been set to work, and after a gas explosion and the bursting of the main water-pipes had torn great chasms in the road and flooded it.

Soon after leaving the Field of Stones we met a party of Dyaks, who, with great hospitality, offered us fruit; but we were suspicious about it, and declined the gift. It afterwards appeared that the same party offered some fruit to the Sultan of Koetei when he passed the locality some days afterwards, and some black dots with which some of the fruit was marked were regarded as proof that it had been poisoned.

After this the country began to get less timbered and very hilly, some points rising some 400 or 450 feet above the general level. Creeks and small streams abounded, all of which tended to the south-west, in the direction of the Barito. In this broken country we came to the ruins of a Dyak fort, formerly the stronghold of the insurrectionary chief Soro Patti, who, with a small band of Dyaks, managed for two years to hold out in this fastness, and to defy the whole power of the Dutch. His defence of the Field of Stones cost Holland more in men and money than all the rest of her war operations against the Dyaks. All that now remains of the fort is a number of great baulks of ironwood, with stone boulders, lying scattered in all directions down the hillside.

Still numerous creeks and streams had to be crossed by means of the spider-web-like bridges, at one of which we had to pause while a party of Dyaks came over in the opposite direction. It turned out to be Pangeran Kartasari, with a body of men who had been constructing rafts on the Benangan for the Sultan, whom they were now going to meet. Kartasari told us we were not far from the Dutch boundary; and great was the joy when at 12.30 we reached Tico, a "village" consisting of two small Dyak houses situated on the banks of the Benangan, and in Dutch territory. Here two praus had been prepared, through the kind orders of the Resident of Bandjermasin, by Raden Kasoema, the native chief appointed to administer the affairs of the Doesoen district. Kasoema himself had gone to meet the Sultan, and the people were surprised that I had not met him on the road. Having no reason, therefore, to stay at Tico, I gave my men an hour's rest, and, having seen what remained of my baggage safely embarked, was not sorry to start on my cruise down the river.

The river was very full and a strong current running, so that I hoped to reach Benangan that night. But great caution had to be exercised in shooting several small rapids, where the river, largely increased in volume by the rains, whirled in strong eddies over the rocky bottom. Large trunks of trees, carried down by the flood, were tossed about like corks on the boiling water, and were often more dangerous to our small craft than the legitimate Scyllæ and Charybdes that we had to avoid on the way. The river was about one hundred yards wide, but the overhanging branches of the giant trees often met midway over the water, and formed a grateful shelter from the rays of the afternoon sun. Occasionally a break in the stretch of woods revealed rice-fields recently planted; and other signs of increasing population and industry among the inhabitants met our view in quick succession, to be as rapidly lost to sight as our little vessels, urged still faster in their downward course by paddles wielded by strong and willing arms, rushed onward towards the sea. Between Tico and Benangan we passed about a dozen Dyak settlements; one of the larger houses, surrounded by a high fence of sharply-pointed plants, was the residence of Pangeran Tomongoeng.

The village of Benangan is situated at the confluence of the river of that name and the Teweh. We rested here only long enough to obtain a larger and more convenient prau; and then my crew willingly agreed to row all night, in order to reach the town of Fort Teweh, some few miles further down, on the following morning.

The night was gloriously fine, and there was no difficulty in keeping our course along the centre of the eddying stream. It could indeed have been easily distinguished by the keen eyes of the look-out stationed in the prow had the weather been much less favourable, for the limits of the dark stream flecked with spots of white foam were clearly defined against the more sombre shadows on the wooded banks.

This was Christmas Eve! I was anxious if possible to spend the following day somewhere within the confines of civilization, and the town of Teweh, or Lotoentoer, was my only chance of such sanctuary—a poor substitute, at best, for the places with which my memory of past Christmas Days was associated; still it was better than the habitations of Head-Hunters, with the risk of being poisoned by a savage proffering his dainty fruits.

CHAPTER XV.

Christmas Day—An unexpected rencontre—Civilization at last—Fort Teweh—"Absent friends"—The yellow Barito—A highway of commerce—Bekompai—The final stage—Arrival at Bandjermasin—The Sultan's reception—An oriental Venice—Scene on the river—The European quarter—Chinese settlement—The diamond mines—Historical review—English and Dutch enterprise—Mild dissipation.

CHRISTMAS DAY! The message of "Peace on earth, goodwill toward men," was little known to these barbarians among whom my lot was temporarily cast. Early in the morning of this day we encountered two praus full of Dyaks, all armed, and in complete war-costume, paddling laboriously against the swift current. Orders were given to slacken speed as we approached them, and my guide, Sahadan, inquired their errand.

"The Dyaks of Koetei are coming to take heads from among our friends in Doesoen, and we are going to fight them," was the reply.

Sahadan assured them that we had just come from Doesoen, and that all was peace; explaining that the Dyaks of Koetei were only coming to Doesoen to escort the Sultan and the "Commissie." But the chief in the foremost prau doubted his words, and looked at us with suspicion.

"We will not rest till we see with our own eyes, though the river fights against us," he answered, and ordered his rowers to ply their paddles again with all speed against the stream.

We reached Fort Teweh at noon. Our arrival was not unexpected, for a large and motley crowd of Dyaks and Malays—men, women, and children—had gathered in front of Raden Kasoema's house. What a contrast did the village present to the scenes to which I had become accustomed in Koetei! There, no law was observed save that of self-will and indulgence—no order maintained except where it could be said to be secured by the extermination of the weak by the strong. The rights of property were not respected, simply because they were not known to exist. Every one helped himself to what he could, where he could, when he could, and how he could. Each party, each individual, was an object of suspicion on the part of his neighbour. Trade in its most embryonic state hardly existed, for no man would think of giving anything in exchange for an article that he coveted; sufficient for him that he was strong enough to gain it by force, by murder if need be, and to keep it by virtue of his reputation as a Head-Hunter. But here, almost at the confines of Dutch territory, law and order were respected and observed; on all sides were signs of a flourishing trade; crime met with its retribution at the hands of justice; labour was respected and paid for; and Malays and Dyaks, only occasionally in communication with the white man, worked harmoniously together for their mutual welfare and the good of the State.

The population of Fort Teweh, or Lotoentoer, is about 2500, nearly 1000 being pure Dyaks, who live on the right bank of the Barito; and the rest a mixed race of Dyaks, Malays, and Boegis, professing a religion of which Mohammedanism is the basis, with a superstructure of Dyak superstitions, who keep together on the left bank of the river Barito, where it is joined by the Teweh, holding themselves aloof from the Dyaks.

All the inhabitants of the town are keen traders. Agriculture is little practised, only a little rice being grown, not nearly sufficient for local consumption. At the time of my arrival, several cargoes of rice from Bandjermasin were waiting to be landed. The staple production of the district is rattan, of which large quantities are conveyed to Bandjermasin in rafts, of great length and height, which, as they glide down the river, resemble floating fortresses. A great deal of excellent timber is cut for boat-building and house-building purposes. Wax and gutta-percha and edible birds'-nests are also collected in the neighbouring forest, and sent down the river to Bandjermasin. Both Dyaks and Malays, and the mixed races as well, are well advanced on the path of civilization. The Dutch character has impressed itself strongly on the habits and morals of all classes. The Dutch dress is largely adopted, and a *pâtois* of the language is current among the people. Fort Teweh was for many years the farthest advanced military post of the Dutch in the interior of the Island of Borneo; and, only a few days before my arrival, the garrison had been recalled to Fort Boentoek some sixty miles nearer Bandjermasin. This fact is evidence enough of the stability of the sovereignty of the Netherlands Government in this quarter, but the former name of the settlement—Lotoentoer—is significant of a grave disaster to the Dutch army during the war of 1859-64, when a party of Dyaks boarded the war-steamer "Onrust"—a name of ill-omen, signifying "trouble"—and killed the whole crew, officers and men, save one native sailor who escaped by swimming ashore. The Dyaks scuttled the ship, which still lies deep below the muddy waters of the Barito.

Here I spent Christmas Day in the year 1879. I celebrated the occasion after the European fashion by having cooked a large plum-pudding, which I had carried across Borneo, preserved in a tin, and by drinking the health of distant friends in a glass of champagne. As I "drained the flowing bowl," I was struck with the reflection that, frightful as are the crimes for which the abuse of intoxicating liquors is responsible, it is not always the case that "teetotalism" and virtue, or "drink" and crime go hand in hand. The bloodthirsty, cowardly savages of the centre of Borneo are mostly water-drinkers; the only native substitute for alcoholic liquors is the well-known toewak, made from honey and rice. Whether they would be better or worse if "fire-water" were introduced into their midst, and they developed a liking for it, I will not venture to say; but it is at least a fact that human nature in its lowest form, unredeemed by a single ray of religion or of civilization, has not in this case, at least, been helped on the backward path by the curse of "drink."

On the 28th December, the Sultan and suite arrived at the fort, and was received with demonstrations of respect by the people. I tried to obtain news about the war-praus that we had met, but could get no particulars. All that I heard was that his Highness was very footsore, and that he had run the risk of being poisoned by, probably, the same Dyaks who had offered my party some fruit near Tico.

Raden Kasoema, in whose house I had been staying, and who had now returned with the Sultan of Koetei, was exceedingly kind, and helped me hire a large prau and crew to take me and my men to Bandjermasin, for which I started on the 29th December. I was to pay 10*s.* sterling for the hire of the boat, and 7*l.* as wages, besides provisions to the crew of seven men. At five p.m. we passed Fort Boentoek, but having the current in our favour, we determined to continue our journey all night, and arrived at eight o'clock on the following morning at the large village of Binkoewang, where we stopped to buy some fruit. Three hours later, we passed Mankatip, another Malay settlement, and towards sunset arrived at Pamingir, a village situated at the mouth of a river of that name, flowing into the Barito, where we rested for the night. The river here was quite yellow with the mud which it brought down from the country above, to deposit it by and by on its low-lying banks, or on the fast-increasing delta at its mouth. The stream was flowing fast, but we were still a long distance from Bandjermasin, and this was the last day but one of the year. I had wished, if possible, to reach the port to-morrow, or at latest by New Year's Day, and asked Kichil if he thought it possible to get to Bandjermasin by the following evening. The crew had all paddled bravely, and were worn out with their long row; but with a bathe in the muddy water, and the promise of an extra rupee a-piece if they reached the town by to-morrow night, they agreed to row all night and all day, and undertook to be at Bandjermasin in the afternoon of the 31st.

At sunrise, we arrived at Moeara Bahan, or Bekompai, on the right bank of the Barito, by far the largest and most important place we had yet seen. For more than two miles, the houses built on posts extended along the river side, surrounded by plantations of bananas, penang, and cocoa-palms, while not a few lay in the river itself, built on rafts, called *rakits*. Many of them were decorated with tasteful carvings on the roofs and sides of the walls. Hundreds of praus were moored to the banks, forming shops, where rice, salt, calico, and prints of all sorts were offered for sale; and numerous *djoekangs* (small praus), with a solitary individual in each—generally a woman, wearing an immense hat, that concealed her entire face from an inquisitive gaze, and protected her at the same time from the rays of the burning sun—were moving simply along from *rakit* to *rakit*, from house to house, offering for sale a great assortment of fruits, and dried or fresh fish, &c.

"Bekompai," says Schwaner, "is the key to the commerce of about 2300 geographical square miles of Borneo. The produce of Nagara and Barito, also a great deal of merchandise from the Kapoeas and Kahaijan, find their way to the world's commerce by way of this village."

The people are a mixture of Malay and Dyak blood, intermingled occasionally with Boegis and Chinese. This mixture has been going on for more than two centuries, according to Dr. Schwaner ever since the Mohammedan religion was introduced, in 1688. It is not of rare occurrence that Bekompai men marry Dyak women. I am not at all acquainted with their language, but it is far from pure Malay; and I was told they have many Dyak words in their vocabulary.

Here is a fort, with a garrison, admirably situated from a strategical point of view, commanding the Barito and the Nagara river opposite, and entirely closing the entrance to the interior of the country.

The nearer we came to Bandjermasin the greater became the traffic. The river as it got gradually wider and wider seemed to be still more and more crowded with craft, proceeding both upwards and downwards, and at five o'clock we reached the capital of Southern Borneo.

I jumped ashore with a sense of relief and thankfulness that the last stage in the journey of over 700 miles was at length successfully completed, and took up my quarters at the only hotel in the place, called the Pasengerahan, kept by a pensioned Javanese officer, Mr. Maska, under whose excellent care I was not sorry to have the prospect of a few days' rest. My health was somewhat shaken by the fatigues of the journey, and the necessarily unhealthy conditions under which a great part of it had been performed.

The following day the thunder of the guns on board the "Riouw," which had temporarily exchanged stations with the "Salak," and in the forts ashore announced the arrival of my friend and fellow traveller, the Sultan. I was too unwell to go and meet his Highness, who in the afternoon sent the Pangeran Praboe to offer his congratulations on the successful accomplishment of our journey.

Bandjermasin, or Bandjer, as it is commonly called, for the sake of brevity, the capital of Southern Borneo, is situated in latitude 3° 22′ S., and longitude 114° 38′ E. It has, according to Mr. Meijer, the late Resident, a thrifty and prosperous population of 38,000, living in houses either floating on the water or built on the banks of the Barito and on the island of Tattas, formed by the two arms into which the tributary stream Riam-Kina divides at its mouth, known as the Kween and the Kajoe Tangi.

The low-lying shores being covered with water at every flood tide the houses that are not floating are raised on piles. All communication is by water, and the scene presented every morning in this oriental Venice is very picturesque, as hundreds of tambangans—small canoes, with prow and stern peaked high in the air, and a small covered seat in the centre—move ceaselessly from house to house, laden with fruits, vegetables, and sweet-scented flowers; or with dried fish, rice, cocoa-nuts, and other provisions. Moored to the shore, or to the larger structures which serve as warehouses, are numbers of large covered boats, built of ironwood, called sampangs, for the construction of which the Bandjer people are celebrated; while others are just returning from a trading expedition, laden with the brittle pottery-ware from Amontai, or with pisangs and sugar-canes, cocoa-nuts and durians, the produce of the interior or of the neighbouring islands.

To take a canoe and join the busy throng, paddling about from stall to stall in this floating market—a sort of Covent Garden and Billingsgate combined—is a pleasant way of spending the cooler hours of the morning in Bandjermasin, and affords ample opportunity of studying the various nationalities represented there.

Here, sitting beneath the little awning in the centre of her canoe, her head half hidden under a huge palm-leaf hat, is a Dyak woman, offering pisangs and durians, piled in heaps at either end of the little vessel. Ugh! the odour of the great prickly balls so highly esteemed in the East! How can any one relish a fruit which nauseates with such a vile smell? There, is another floating costermonger's barrow laden with cocoa-nuts, piled up like cannon-balls high above the gunwale. At the next turn you get to the lee side of a Chinaman's stock of stinking fish, and hasten to windward, till the odious odour is replaced by the sweet perfume of the mass of flowers which lie so lightly on the floor of a canoe paddled swiftly along by the strong arms of a Malay belle, whose black hair is decked with one of the choicest of the flowers from her lovely stock of wares: never, you think, did camellia look so fair as that white flower against the dusky skin and still darker hair of the Malay flower-seller. It is a treat to stop a minute or two and linger over the fairy cargo, which before many hours will be withered in the hot sun. Here comes a larger sampang, with a crew of unlovely Boegis, and a cargo of the famous Boegis sarong cloths and dettas, floating lazily up with the tide; and no sooner have you made way for this than you narrowly escape collision with a coasting vessel, manned by Klings, singing their monotonous song as they haul at the ropes and make ready to sail away again on another trading trip. And so, amid a confusion of voices, and in an atmosphere alternating between the perfumes of Eden and the most sickening fumes of putrifying animal and vegetable matter, you may pass the early morning. As the sun rises towards the zenith the multitude of boats gradually disperse, and before noon the turmoil gives way to a scene of listless repose.

On the point where the Kween leaves the main stream is a small island called Pulo Kambang, literally "Flower Island"—a forest-covered swamp, swarming with monkeys. This is a favourite resort of the people of Bandjermasin, forming as it were a natural "monkey-house," the inmates of which, though dwelling in their native freedom, are quite tame, and will take food readily from the hands of visitors. The long-nose variety are especially numerous. I made an excursion to this place one day, together with the Sultan and a large party, accompanied by a band of music and quite a fleet of canoes. Notwithstanding the unwonted noise and excitement, the monkeys seemed, after the first few minutes, quite unconcerned, and swarmed down to the water's edge close to the boats.

The town of Bandjermasin is divided into several kampongs, in which the different races form separate communities.

The official Dutch part of the town is on the so-called island of Tattas, at the mouth of the Riam-Kina. This island is really little more than a mudbank, being nearly covered at high water, and only wholly exposed at low water. The houses are arranged in narrow streets, which at high water are a series of miniature canals, through which the small native tambangans can just pass; while at low water they are nothing more than a series of mud ditches, from which a most unwholesome effluvium arises. About one hundred European officials, civil and military, live here. The houses are all built of wood, of only ordinary appearance; and there are, besides, a club, or *roema bolla*, a hospital and commodious barracks for the troops.

The natives of Bandjermasin and district are under a chief bearing the title of *Ronggo*, who is appointed by the Government, and receives a salary. The Chinese, Arabs, and Boegis, are also governed by their own chiefs, each of whom is appointed by the Resident. These chiefs, or lieutenants, are unpaid, a rich and influential personage being always selected to fill the post.

Just opposite the European settlement, on the left bank of the Kween, is the Chinese kampong. Here Lee Boon Kim, the Chinese Lieutenant, received me most kindly, and under his guidance I was enabled to visit the establishments of many of the leading traders. Lee Boon Kim sets a good example to his fellow-countrymen, being noted for his integrity and business-like habits. Would that as much could be said for all his neighbours!

Nearly every house in the Chinese quarter is a shop or bank (*bank van leening*). John sits in the doorway or under the verandah, with his long opium pipe in his hand, and dressed neatly in a clean white tunic ornamented with filagree buttons of gold or silver, wide black cotton trousers, and a pair of soft felt shoes. His motto in trading is "small profits and quick returns," and goods of every kind can be bought cheaper here than in the European quarter. But in money-lending transactions John Chinaman never charges less than twenty-four per cent. interest, and always insists on good security. He is polite to a degree. If a chance customer, or any one merely "looking about," enters the shop, John asks him to sit down, and offers him a cup of tea, or, if a European, a glass of beer. He is open to barter, and if you don't open your eyes you must open your purse, for the sole aim of the Chinese is to accumulate a fortune.

The Chinese traders are, however, a good pattern for the Malays, who have been greatly influenced by them. Besides being good shopkeepers they are very industrious: many are artisans, excellent carpenters, good tailors, shoemakers, and jewellers. But their curse is their taste for gambling. In the evening, when business is over, they will sit with a friend or two under the verandah, lighted up with a grotesque Chinese lantern suspended from the ceiling, smoke the indispensable opium pipe, and have a game of cards, over which the betting is fast and furious. When it happens that John is entirely ruined by card-playing, his gold buttons and everything conceivable gone, he will proceed to Martapoera, to the gold and diamond-mines, and try to repair his lost fortune.

Bandjermasin was formerly famous as a diamond-market, and supplied the great dealers and cutters in Amsterdam with gems from the mines of Martapoera. But since the South African diamond-fields were discovered the diamond-mines in Borneo have been almost at a standstill, and stones there are now no cheaper than they can be bought in Europe. The Malays assert that the Martapoera diamond is purer than any other kind, and does not lose its brilliancy. A few dealers still go round the houses and offer them for sale. Intending purchasers, if they have any experience of the cheating habits of the Malay, always take the native with his diamonds before the Assistant Resident. Most of the officials know the value and genuineness of the stones, and the Malay has too much respect and fear to take any undue advantage before *Toewan besar* (the great man) as they call the Resident.

Although the mines of Martapoera have scarcely been worked of late years, the cunning Chinamen, in order to keep the reputation of Bandjer as a diamond-market, import every year over 10,000*l.* worth of Cape diamonds, which find their way to China, and to the numerous princes and nobles all over the Archipelago who buy them for real Martapoera stones. Considerable value is attached to one particular sort of diamond, called the *inten boentoet* (tail of the diamond). Dr. Schwaner says the natives call it the "soul of the diamond" (*diamantziel*), but I never heard it mentioned by that name. It is generally of a round form, with a granulated surface, semi-transparent, of a greyish-black or greyish-brown colour. The people all say it is so much harder than the ordinary diamond that they are unable to cut or polish it. These *inten boentoet* are in demand amongst the Chinese, who set them in rings, believing them to prevent certain diseases. Soon after my arrival at Bandjermasin a Frenchman and his son came to stay there for a few days, having received permission from the Dutch Government to dig for diamonds at Martapoera. They were lucky in securing the services of a pensioned soldier who could speak French, for *Messieurs les Francais* could converse neither in Malay nor in Dutch, and it is very difficult to make a Malay understand you by merely nodding the head or shrugging the shoulders.

Many of the Chinese here are half-castes, born of Malay or Javanese women; and though always conversing among themselves in the Chinese language they all speak Malay.

The Malay part of the town lies distinct from the Chinese kampong, at the point where the Kween leaves the Barito.

Bandjermasin is one of the oldest trading-ports in Borneo. As long ago as the seventeenth century the Dutch East India Company made commercial treaties with the natives, but owing to the deceitful and treacherous character of the people the trade had to be abandoned. In the eighteenth century relations with them were renewed, but were frequently interrupted from the same cause. According to Mr. Hugh Low, the English in 1706 attempted to establish a factory at Bandjer, but before their forts were finished their haughty and insolent behaviour brought down upon them the vengeance of the Sultan, who attacked their settlement in the night with 3000 men and burnt it; but as the Europeans had received notice of his intention they had retired to their ships, which to the number of four were in the harbour. These also were attacked by the infuriated Sultan and his injured subjects, and, though the two largest escaped, the two smaller ones were burnt, together with the greater part of their crews. Soon after, the Sultan, finding the loss of trade affected his revenues, informed the English that a free trade might be carried on with his dominions, but that he would never suffer them, or any other nation, to fortify themselves in his country.

In 1711, according to Dr. Hollander, the first Dutch factory was established in Bandjer, and in 1747 the Dutch succeeded in establishing a settlement and a fort on the island of Tattas. Forty years later the Sultan made a treaty, whereby he handed over the whole of his territory to the Dutch East India Company.

The Dutch, at the time when Marshal Daendels was Governor-General (1810), formally abandoned their settlement; and in 1811, when Lord Minto happened to be in Malacca, the Sultan requested the English to reoccupy the place instead of the Dutch, and Mr. Alexander Hare was commissioned to make an arrangement with the Sultan to check the pirates.

Notwithstanding his official position, Mr. Hare formed a plan, so says Dr. Hollander, to found for himself a principality in the interior of Bandjermasin, on the same plan as that later adopted by James Brooke in Sarawak. He received for that purpose from the Sultan a piece of territory which was very sparsely inhabited, and got many inhabitants of Java transported as colonists to this locality, where they were employed to lay out coffee and pepper plantations; and here he reigned over them as an autocrat.

On the restitution of Borneo to the Netherlands, after the general peace in 1816, Hare was obliged to leave his country, and most of the Javanese whom he had decoyed thither were sent back to their own land. He ultimately established himself with some slaves in the Kokos Islands, where he again played the *rôle* of an independent prince, till 1827, when another Englishman, J. Ross, came and settled in one of these islands. Owing to disputes that arose between Ross and Hare, the latter left the Kokos Islands, while Ross remained, and eventually became chief of a thriving mercantile colony.

The family of Ross is quite well known all over the East; I often heard the name mentioned by merchants as that of the king of the Kokos Islands. The present "king" is the son of the Ross whose advent caused Hare to quit the place.

Since then trade has rapidly increased, and Bandjermasin is at present the largest trading-port in Borneo, and is annually visited by a great number of ships, many of them of large size. The principal exports are rattan, gutta-percha, edible birds'-nests, resin, wax, dried fish, various sorts of timber, and gold dust. Very fine plaited mats of rattan, in various coloured patterns, made by the Dyaks of Kapoeas and Kahaijan, worth from six to eight florins each, are also exported.

The imports into Bandjermasin are coloured prints, white and black cotton cloth, gambier, tobacco, salt, opium, Chinese earthenware, copper wire, beads, &c.

During his stay here the Sultan was the lion of the place, and expressed the greatest satisfaction with the warmth of his reception. He spent much of his time purchasing presents to take home to his wives. Among other things some sewing machines took his fancy, and a couple of perambulators, which he expected might shortly prove useful. I suggested that he should give me a commission to send him out a gross of these useful little carriages on my return to England.

Before his departure the Resident gave a ball in his honour; and when the "Tiger" came to convey him back to Tangaroeng he carried away with him most pleasant recollections of his visit to Bandjer. On leaving, his Highness presented me with a magnificent brilliant ring, as a mark of friendship and a *souvenir* of our long journey together.

While indulging in the mild dissipations of the place, and recruiting my health for a trip into the Mindai and Amontai districts, I had time to arrange more carefully the results of my observations of the country through which I had passed, and of the people inhabiting it.

To these details the next two or three chapters will be devoted —the only introductory remark being that the notes are confined to a description of what I saw of the territory of the Sultan of Koetei, and of the Dyak races inhabiting that territory.

CHAPTER XVI.

Geographical sketch of Koetei—Position and area—Physical aspect—The River Mahakkam—Principal mountains—A hill reaching to heaven—A white mountain—The formation of lakes—Geology—Climate—Seasons—Flora—Useful plants—Population—Different races inhabiting Koetei—Restrictions on trade.

KOETEI, or Coti, is the largest and most important of the semi-independent states in Borneo, extending from latitude 1° 30′ S. to 1° 40′ N., and from longitude 114° 15′ to 119° E. at its broadest part. On the west it is bounded by the range of mountains of the Doesoen district and Passir; on the north, by the mountain chains of Boelangan and Berouw; on the south, by the district of Passir and the sea; and on the east by the Celebes Sea and the Straits of Macassar.

It covers an area of about 37,000 square miles, or nearly one-fifth of the whole of Borneo.

The general aspect from the sea is that of an immense alluvial undulating plain of mangroves, backed by low mountains in the distance. The north-eastern shores are lined with casuarinas, whose drooping branches give them a very picturesque appearance. The greater part of Koetei, especially near the coast, consists of alluvial soil, raised but little above the sea-level, and of the greatest fertility, brought down by the River Mahakkam and its numerous tributaries. Rising in the mountain chain in the north-west corner of Koetei, this river takes a winding course to the sea at Pelaroeng, where it is over a mile wide, forming a delta, with seventeen arms and embracing fifty miles of coast. This delta is one of the most difficult to navigate in the Indian Archipelago, but the river is navigable as far as Moera Pahou for steamers drawing not more than ten feet of water.

An oblique line drawn across Koetei from the source of the Mahakkam to the sea is over 300 miles; and the river, taking into account its winding course, cannot very well be less than double that length. Beyond Moeara Pahou, however, nothing is known of the Mahakkam. Major Müller is the only European who ever passed beyond Moeara Pahou; and the gallant Major and his party were murdered by the Dyaks, at the instigation of the then Sultan of Koetei, in 1825, a short distance beyond that place.

Both the main stream, however, and its tributaries—the Moeara Pahou, the Telén, and the Moeara Kaman—are accessible to native canoes, affording great facilities for internal communication. At the village of Moeara Kaman, where the Mahakkam bends south and takes up the river of that name, as well as at the entrance of the Telén, there is a very strong current.

For miles of its lower course the banks of the Mahakkam are nothing but muddy swamps, lined with mangroves and nipa palms; higher up, the country is dense low-lying forest; but above the Dyak settlement of Long Wai the country becomes hilly, though there is no regular range of mountains. South-west from Kotta Bangoen is the Goenong (mount) Tinjavan, which I think is about 1000 feet high. From the village of Allo I saw, quite in a southerly direction, a large mountain, which could not be far short of 5000 feet high, called the Goenong Bratus; the Sultan assured me it was the highest in Koetei. On the frontier between Koetei and Passir is the Goenong Balik Pappau, another mountain of note.

According to the Dyaks, there is in the extreme north-west corner of Koetei one great central chain of mountains, called Teebang, where are the sources of the great rivers of Borneo—the Kapoeas, the Mahakkam, and others.

Other rumours say that the sources of the Mahakkam are in the mountain Tepoe-Poerau. This mountain is so high that it is said to be within a trifle of reaching heaven. The Bahou Dyaks told Dr. Schwaner that the top of this mountain was always "white"—an expression which has been supposed to signify that it is a snow-clad peak. I am, however, inclined to think that the white appearance is due rather to the existence of thick mists, which are frequently so opaque and white as to look like snow. I have myself often been struck with the resemblance which the hillsides in Sumatra, enveloped in these thick morning mists, bear to a snow-covered range of mountains.

Borneo is rich in lakes, or Danaus, as they are called; and in Koetei I passed through a regular chain of them. The distinguished traveller, Dr. Schwaner, tells us in his "Borneo" how these danaus are formed:—

"By danau must be understood an inland mass of water in the deepest part of a swampy district. They are only to be met in the low-lying countries and in the immediate vicinity of rivers. Their mode of formation is often very similar to that of the Antassans or Troesans (passages or canals), such as those in the Martapoera and other rivers of Borneo, which are channels used for the purpose of shortening the water route. Some of these channels are dug by hand, but most of them have formed themselves by the force of the water in times of flood. A channel thus formed eventually enlarges to a danau, or lake. At every flood the water in the river flows into the danau and enlarges it; the swampy formation extends further and further, and the exposed surface, owing to the inundation, gets larger and larger. This explanation of the formation of the danaus, and the extensive morasses which one meets in the neighbourhood of rivers, rests on some accurate observations, and entirely supersedes the theory of volcanic action, to which the occasional depth of some of these lakes has been attributed. The presence of baulks of timber and foundations on the bottom of some danaus, and of the channels connecting them with the main stream, is a proof that in former times the districts have been peopled which now, owing to the gradual sinking of the surrounding country, have changed into morass.

"The danaus have no determined shores; the ground sinks imperceptibly to its greatest depth; and the continued changes of the land surface cause just as numerous enlargements or diminutions of the area of the lakes or danaus."

The principal danaus of the Mahakkam are the Djempang, Semajang, Gadang Morong, and Malintang. The two first are more than fifteen miles in length.

Coals I have found very abundant in Koetei near the banks of the rivers; the Sultan works a couple of mines very profitably, his best customer being the Dutch Government. Iron is also found in the interior; and I have been shown samples of gold by the Dyaks, who, however, keep the places where it is found secret, as they have no desire that Europeans should come into their territory.

The climate near the coast, that is, as far as Tangaroeng, may be looked upon as healthy, considering the position immediately beneath the Equator. The heat is certainly very trying from noon to three p.m.; the average temperature is from 90° to 92° Fahr., while at Long Wai it often was as high as 95° in the shade. The early mornings are the most agreeable part of the day in the tropics. At sunrise the thermometer generally showed 72°, while in the evenings I found it to be 82°.

Considering the country is traversed by the Equator, one would expect a greater heat; but the combined influence of the prevailing humidity and of the luxuriant vegetation with which the country is covered, and of the frequent sea breezes, tends to lessen the heat. I must say I never felt the heat so trying in any part of Koetei as in the Red Sea, along the sandy, dreary Arabian coast. The few Europeans accustomed to live in this part of Borneo agree with me that many worse climates might be found in the Archipelago. The nights are exceedingly damp, owing to the condensation during the cool night of the vapours raised during the day from the extensive swampy ground.

In the Interior I do not think the climate at all healthy. I had proof of this in the fact that all my men were often attacked with violent fevers and dysentery, partly owing, no doubt, to the badness of the water from the rivers which they had to drink.

The rainy season in Koetei begins in November, and lasts till March, when, with the south-east monsoon, the "dry season" approaches. This is called the dry time of the year, because it does not rain so regularly, and in such torrents, as in the wet season; but hardly a day passes without slight showers. During the rainy period the banks of the rivers are flooded, and for miles inland the country is under water. This was the case when I crossed from Koetei to Bandjermasin. Near Allo I saw the natives propelling small canoes into the forest, along channels which were perfectly dry for the rest of the year.

The flora is represented in endless forms—trees of gigantic dimensions and great value, while orchids and palms teem in the dense forests, and the banks of the rivers and creeks are clothed with bamboo and several species of the valuable rattan, the most important article of commerce in the island.

I will only just enumerate those trees and plants which struck me as common and useful. For miles the nipa palms (*Nipa fruticans*) and the mangroves cover the banks of the rivers. The former grow to the salt-water line, and are invaluable to the natives as roof covering for their houses, the leaves being split and made into attap. The fruits are eaten by the natives, and the nectar of their scented flowers is food for the great swarms of bees, and other less valuable insects.

The nibong, a palm that grows in great abundance near the mouths of the rivers, furnishes the natives with a vegetable. I cannot say much for the excellency of its flavour, as it is very tasteless. A more important part of the tree is perhaps the stem, which is made into posts to support the houses, or split to make flooring.

In the interior the bamboo takes the place of the nibong for an endless variety of purposes, too well known to require a detailed account here.

Another palm that grows in swampy places is the sago. The natives make attap from the leaves; but they do not understand how to extract the sago of commerce—the most nourishing of its products.

The cocoa-nut, also so well known, is highly esteemed by the Malays, as well as Dyaks. It grows in abundance, but the production of cocoa-nuts does not equal the consumption; and great quantities are imported in small vessels, of from ten to twenty-five tons burden, from Celebes. Paré Paré is a great place for cocoa-nuts and oil. The husk is commonly used for scrubbing purposes.

The stately areca palm (*Areca alba*), with a stem fifty feet in height, and not more than twenty inches in circumference, is farmed everywhere for the sake of the nut, called penang, which is one of the ingredients used in betel or sirih chewing—a disgusting habit universal all over the East. The Malay damsels are very fond of the flowers, which are sweetly perfumed.

Sugar-cane (*Sacharum officinale*) is also grown in small quantities for home consumption, and the soil is admirably adapted for it, as well as for the growth of tobacco.

The forests are full of trees, producing splendid timber, both hard and soft. Foremost perhaps ranks the *kajoe besir* or *tebelian*, the ironwood, which is one of the few trees that are too hard for the white ant to destroy. It is much used by the natives, who can afford the labour, for building purposes. *Kajoe bintangor* is a wood chosen for building boats or canoes, while the *Kajoe bawan* is much used by carpenters. More choice woods are the ebony, and the scented *Kajoe rawali;* the latter is very expensive. It is difficult to get large planks from this tree, but it is much in demand by the natives for making trunks or boxes. The wood smells like aniseed, and this is one of the few woods that insects do not touch.

In the neighbourhood of the villages the Dyaks generally also cultivate limau (*Tetranthera citrata*), cladie (*Colocasia antiquorum*), obi (*Dioscorea alata*), and maize (*Zea mais*).

The population is estimated at from 150,000 to 180,000. The Sultan gave me both these numbers; but I am inclined to think the first is the most correct, as the different Pangerans variously reckoned the population at about 150,000 in the whole of Koetei.

Dr. Hollander, in his "Land en Volkenkunde," puts the population down, according to Melville, at 60,000; and Gallois and Weddik estimated it at 100,000. Since their works were written, immigration from Celebes has been going on at no small rate; and the Sultan, anxious to make Koetei a "large country," and develope its resources, despatches his steamer frequently to Bandjermasin, to fetch emigrants to settle in Koetei. His agents go up the Barito, and especially to the thickly inhabited Amontai districts, where they manage to attract a number of emigrants by paying whatever debts they may have incurred, and promising them large plots of free land. In October, 1879, the little steamer succeeded in getting no less than 414 immigrants from Amontai.

The country is inhabited by Malays, Boegis, a couple of hundred Chinamen, and a few Klings; and, in the interior, by Dyaks.

The Dyaks belong to different tribes, and inhabit the banks of the Mahakkam, and all the small rivers flowing into that river beyond Moeara Pahou.

The most powerful of these tribes are those of Long Wai, on the Moeara Klintjouw river; next in power come their neighbours at Long Wahou, on the river of the same name; and then the Trings, the only cannibals in Koetei, inhabiting the banks of the Mahakkam near its source. In the interior wander about the *Orang Poonan*, or Forest People. The Koetei Malays are confined to the coast region, and to the low parts of the Mahakkam, below Moeara Pahou. They are the "sovereign people" of the principality. The Boegis are natives of the southern part of Celebes, who have settled in Koetei, where they are getting numerous and very powerful, especially at Samarinda. They are active, and carry on a good trade. Dr. Hollander says that "they may not go further up the river than Tangaroeng, where they carry on their commerce with the natives from the interior, who may not descend the river farther than to Tangaroeng." If this was the case in Dr. Hollander's time it is not so now. I have met large Boegis trading praus far up the Mahakkam. At Moeara Kaman, an important village, I saw more than a dozen Boegis, selling their famous cloth, English prints, rice, and cocoa-nuts, with which their sampangs were laden.

The Chinese, however, by order of the Sultan, and at the request of the Dutch Government, are not allowed to go into the interior. They are settled chiefly at Samarinda, though there are a few stray Celestials at Tangaroeng and Sankolirang.

CHAPTER XVII.

The Dyak tribes—Personal characteristics—Albinos—Their clothing—A hint to travellers—Bark fabrics—The Dyak at home—War-costume—The ladies' wardrobe—Mutilating the ears—Earrings and other ornaments—"There's luck in odd numbers"—Heirlooms—Ten pounds' weight of jewellery—Charms—"For external application only"—Professional tattooers—Privileges of manhood and matrimony.

The Dyaks of Koetei inhabiting the banks of the Mahakkam and its tributaries above Moeara Pahou, which is the farthest inland Malay village, are closely allied to the Malay races. Their average stature is short, although taller than that of the Malays. They have strongly-built, well-developed fleshy bodies, and muscular and well-proportioned limbs. The Dyaks of Long Wai and Long Wahou and the central and northern parts of Koetei are above the average height. Such bulky forms as are common among the Zulus are never seen among the Dyaks. Only once did I see Dyak or Malay in Koetei, either man or woman, whose size seemed too great to be comfortable; and that was a Malay woman in Tangaroeng, who was, I believe, chief cook to the Sultan, and no doubt reserved a few chickens' legs for her curried rice every day. Dwarfs I never came across. I particularly asked for cripples or monstrosities, but only saw *one*—unless I include a couple of Albinos, who were light in colour, the skin being rather reddish and very scurvy, peeling off in scales. Their hair was light brown, and the eyes grey. I was told that such Albinos were not uncommon in Koetei. Wens are, however, very common, nearly every third woman being troubled with such a protuberance, often as large as a child's head.

The natural tint of the skin of the Dyaks is a yellowish brown copper colour, slightly paler than that of the Malays. The women as a rule are lighter in complexion than the men. The hair is glossy black, or black-brown, coarse, and straight; it is worn long behind, hanging sometimes to the waist, but trimmed short over the forehead. Among the old folks I noticed the hair turned grey, but never saw a bald-headed Dyak.

It is seldom one meets a Dyak with hairs on the face. If they are present it is only a few straggling ones as a moustache, or on the chin. I do not say they are unable to obtain that facial ornament; but the women abhor a beard, and the men, to please them, pluck out with a pair of pincers the few hairs that grow on the face, as soon as they appear.

The eyes are dark brown, or black, and generally very bright; the principal facial characteristics are the broad nostrils and the prominent cheek bones. A light skin is much admired by the Dyaks, who often pointed out to me a woman with a skin rather paler than usual, whom they called *poeti* (white).

Mr. Perelaer writes: "Parisian fashions have not yet penetrated to Borneo's primitive inhabitants. . . . . The Dyak knows far too well the climate in which he moves." What was true in 1867 remains equally true to this day. Some of the tribes do not adopt any more extensive wardrobe than was considered necessary by Adam and Eve in Paradise before the well-known apple dispute took place; but Malay influence, in the shape of a spangled jacket or a finely-woven Boegis sarong, is certainly making progress amongst some of the tribes. In the scanty clothing that they do in a few instances adopt, the Dyaks are certainly practical. The dress of the men when at home consists only of a tjawat or waist-cloth—a long scarf which is passed round the waist half a dozen times, and the ends left hanging loosely, one in front, one behind. This serves the important part of keeping the abdomen warm.

All travellers in tropical climates know, or ought to know, the necessity of preventing chill in this part of the body. A thick flannel band or belt should be always worn, night and day, moving or stationary, if the traveller would avoid the serious danger of dysentery. This tjawat is either made of white cotton, or, if the wearer affects to be in the height of fashion, of the favourite blue cloth. If the Dyak has not the means of obtaining a piece of cloth, he makes a tjawat by taking a piece of the bark of a tree, beating it until the softer portions of the wood are destroyed, and the fibrous portions remain in the shape of a rough fabric somewhat resembling the *tappa* of the Fiji islanders. This material is very durable, and almost waterproof, and is used for many purposes where protection from the rain is required.

The head covering is formed of the same materials and in a similar manner, the crown of the head being left entirely uncovered, as the natives do not seem to have any fear, or even knowledge, of sunstroke. Sometimes, instead of the plain blue or white turban, the well-to-do Dyak buys a printed handkerchief of many colours, with which he adorns his head. These two articles form the only clothing, properly so called, of the Dyak at home. Sometimes, instead of a detta or turban, a cap, made of rattan, is worn.[1]

The indispensable mandau, however, suspended by a cord or belt from the left side, and a small sirih basket for carrying tobacco and the ingredients for betel-chewing, are always carried. To the tjawat is sometimes attached a roll of matting folded or fastened into a rectangular form, which hangs behind, and serves as a cushion or chair when sitting down; and generally a few ornaments, which I shall presently describe more particularly, complete what I may call his "mufti." In Plate 3 is represented a Dyak lad "at home."

A Dyak in war-costume is quite another figure. He is then a savage in every sense of the term, his extensive equipment enhancing the appearance of barbarism suggested by "Nature unadorned." On his head he wears either a plaited rattan helmet of conical shape, into the top and sides of which are stuck the long tail feathers of the Argus pheasant and hornbill;[2] or a rough cap of monkey skin or bear skin. His body is covered by a jacket—often sleeveless—of different coloured cloths, padded with cotton wool to keep off the poisoned arrows; or, more often, a kind of shawl is made from the skin of a leopard (*Felis macrocelis*) or bear, through the upper part of which a hole is cut so that the head

[1] See Plate 19, Fig. 9.   [2] See Plate 19, Fig. 10.

may pass through, and the skin allowed to fall over the chest and behind the back. The fore part of this covering is ornamented with feathers, beads, or shells of the large pearl-oyster (*Meleagrina margaritifera*), and the sides are trimmed with pieces of red cloth. (A picture of a warrior in such a costume is given in Plate 28.) Under this the tjawat is always worn. On the left side is hung the mandau, and behind this are the quiver of arrows and a similar but smaller case containing the pith pellets. In the right hand is held the blowing-tube (sumpitan), from which the tiny poisoned arrows are blown, and which also serves as a spear; while the left hand grasps a shield (kliau). The neck, arms, and legs are decked with various ornaments, among which one or more of the indispensable tambatongs or charms (see p. 189) are sure to figure.

The ladies' wardrobe is not much more elaborate than that of the men at home. The upper part of the body is usually uncovered; but a sarong, or petticoat, of some bright-coloured cloth is hung round the waist, sometimes barely reaching to the knee, sometimes nearly touching the ground. The ordinary head-dress is either a tall conical hat[3]—the appearance of which is very becoming—without a crown, embroidered with beads; or else a small piece of ribbon similarly trimmed.[4] Sometimes a jacket is worn. Of this there are two prevailing types; one, the common kind, is a short loose jacket[5] made of beaten bark, the edges being bound with coloured cloth, and the sides sometimes ornamented with rough embroidery; the other kind of jacket resembles in shape the "ladies' jersey" lately so fashionable in this country, but does not fit so tight, and is not quite so long, only slightly covering the sarong.

When working in the fields the women wear a large but light hat, made of straw, or leaves, the brim of which has a diameter of from two to four feet. This hat is exceedingly "practical," serving the double purpose of umbrella and sunshade.

One of these hats was given me by Rajah Dinda's sister, and is figured in Plate 26. It is made of nipa leaves, the crown being ornamented with beadwork. These hats have evidently been adopted from the Malays, by whom they are commonly worn in Sumatra

[3] See Plates 5 and 14. [4] See Plate 13. [5] As in Plate 26.

as well as in Borneo. Among the Javanese they are also very generally worn.

Dyak children usually go naked till they are seven or eight years old.

Ornaments are worn in great profusion among the Dyaks by men and women alike; and, to load the person with them, they will undergo the most painful tortures. The lobes of the ears, for instance, are pierced, and gradually enlarged by the insertion of various large and heavy objects. A child's ears are perforated when it is only six months old, and from that day the hole is forcibly increased in size, till the lobe of the ear forms a loop from one to four inches or more long. At first wooden pegs are placed in the hole. These are afterwards replaced by a couple of tin or brass rings. If a Dyak belle cannot afford such luxuries, she will take a leaf and roll it up and insert it in the ear. Gradually the weight is increased by the addition of other larger rings, till the lobe of the ear often gives way under the strain and splits. I have counted as many as sixteen rings in a single ear, each of them the size of a dollar. The rings are generally made of tin, and cut so that they can be removed and replaced at pleasure, care being taken that the divided part shall hang lowermost. I have weighed several of these rings in use among the Tring and Long Wai Dyaks, and I find they average 3 oz. 330 grains troy.

Sometimes discs of wood, often coloured or otherwise ornamented, and varying from one to one and a half inches in diameter, are inserted into the opening thus made in the ear. (See Plate 19, Figs. 4 and 5.) In addition to this mutilation of the lobe, the helix of the ear is pierced or slit in several places, and in these holes pieces of red or blue ribbon or cord are tied, or buttons, pieces of wood, and feathers inserted. (See Plates 5 and 13.)

The elongation of the lobe of the ear attains its greatest development among the Tring Dyaks. A Tring woman is figured in Plate 14, the length of whose ears is represented by the lines A. B. C. These are from accurate measurements taken by me; and show:—A. the total length of the ear, 7·1 inches; B. the length of the gash in the lobe, 4·75 inches; C. the distance between the level of the chin and the bottom of the ear, 2·85 inches. Among the Long Bléh Dyaks, on the other hand, who live only four days' journey from the Trings, the fashion is adopted in its least exaggerated form.

A. B. C.

This horrible mutilation of the ear is practised by the men also. They do not, however, carry it to the same extreme as the women.

Besides this central slit in the lobe of the ear, the Tring women pierce one or two additional holes in the loop of flesh on either side. In Plate 13 is the portrait of a Tring woman who had three of these subsidiary gashes.

Whenever a man has distinguished himself in securing heads, he is entitled to decorate the upper part of his ears with a pair of the canine teeth of the Borneo leopard. This decoration is greatly coveted among the Dyaks in Koetei, where it is the exception to meet with a man who is not so ornamented. As I have every reason to believe that the rule is strictly enforced that no man shall enjoy, unauthorized, any of the privileges appertaining to successful "head-hunters," I can only come to the conclusion that the slaughter of human beings there must largely exceed the slaughter of leopards.

I am inclined to think that the elongation of the ear-lobes among the Dyaks is handed down from the Hindoos; for on examining the very beautiful ancient bronze Hindoo idol, already referred to as having been found in Koetei many years ago, I was particularly struck by the large holes in the lobes of the ears of the goddess.

Earrings, however, are not the sole ornaments affected by the Dyaks. The women load themselves with necklets, bracelets, and anklets of various kinds, for the sake of attracting the favour of the men. Round the neck are suspended several strings of beads—those known as "Venetian" being most highly prized—or wild beans (*Boa kalong*), or stones, or the canine teeth of bats. A variety of agate stones, called *lameangs*, brought to the coast by Malay traders from Singapore, are highly prized for making necklaces, a medicinal or prophylactic power being attributed to the almost worthless stones, in exchange for one of which the natives will willingly give a few cattis of gutta percha or other produce. These are much worn in the south of Koetei, near the frontier of the Doesoen district.

Several rows of bracelets, ivory rings, coils of thick brass or copper wire, or strings of shells, load the arm and wrist. The bracelets and armlets are always worn in uneven numbers, the Dyaks in this, as in many other customs, such as in designing tattoo marks, &c., being very partial to the numbers 7, 9, 11, and 13. Few silver, and still fewer gold, ornaments of any kind are possessed by the natives. Finger-rings are seldom worn. At Long Puti I exchanged a few strings of beads for one which was made of horn, and rudely carved with a wavy pattern.

Round the waist the women wear four or five coils of large stone beads—red, blue, and yellow—which form a support to the sarong, or petticoat.

Curiously enough, while various miraculous and valuable qualities are attributed to most of their personal ornaments, these waist-bands seem to be the only articles valued as heirlooms. The women attach great value to these rows of beads, especially if they are not new: and when I wanted to buy a set, the answer was that it had been in the family so long, and dated back to so remote a date (*tempo doelo*), that they could not part with it. Sometimes they tried to recount the pedigree of the article, but could never get further back than their great-grandmother.

The legs are adorned with heavy brass and tin rings, and a Dyak "swell"—if the term be applicable to the female sex—will often carry—and rejoice in the burden—a load of ornaments of base metal and stones beads, and bones, weighing altogether some ten pounds.

The men are not proof against this particular vanity; and often rival the ladies in the profusion of their ornaments. Their leglets are made of ivory wings, or of rattan cords, wound round with silver wire. The agate necklaces are also prized by them. I have already mentioned (at p. 153), an unsuccessful attempt which I made to bargain with a Doesoen native for his agate.

These stones, however, are worn more as charms than as ornaments pure and simple. The charms, or *tambatongs,* deserve separate mention.

They consist of various natural objects, or rudely carved representations of human figures, and other articles. In Plate 27, Figs. 3 to 8, are drawings of different tambatongs; these I may call the "artificial" charms, among which ought to be included a miniature porcelain pot, containing some stinking stuff which the Dyaks call "obat" (medicine). I am inclined to believe that this "obat" is "medicine," intended for "external application only," and in other words consists of poison for their enemies. Among the natural objects which do duty for charms, to which a preternatural power is attributed, suspended on the mandau belt may be seen pieces of wood, or rattan, of abnormal growth, pebbles carefully sewn up in pieces of flannel, and the canine teeth of the leopard and bear, the latter occasionally so fashioned as to form a whistle, as in Fig. 5.

The custom of ornamenting the body with tattoo marks is adopted by all the Dyaks of Koetei, with the exception of those in the Long Bléh district; and, as will be seen from the specimens given in Plates 14 and 20, some of the designs have very great artistic merit. The marks are either on the arms, hands, feet, thighs, chest, or temple. The women are more elaborately "got up" than the men, and seemed proud of displaying their skin-deep beauty. The more intricate patterns are executed by professionals, who first cut out the outlines in wood, and then trace the design on the part of the body to be decorated, filling it in with a sharp-pointed piece of bamboo, or a needle dipped into a pigment prepared for the purpose from vegetable dyes. The operation is very painful, and often takes a long time to execute, and the marks are absolutely indelible. The tattooing takes place, in the case of men, when they attain to manhood; and, in the case of the women, when they are about to be married. In Plate 6 is a portrait of an old woman of sixty, the marks on whose thighs were as distinct and bright as when they were first executed, perhaps forty or forty-five years previously. Different tribes, and different individuals of the same tribe, have different methods of tattooing. In some it is the forehead or chest; in others, the hands or feet; in others, the thighs that are tattooed. The greatest slaves to this fashion are perhaps the damsels of the Long Wai and Tring tribes, who unite in themselves the fashions of nearly all the other tribes. Whereas the others are content with ornamenting only one part of the body at a time, a Long Wai or Tring lady must be tattooed in various parts of the body.

CHAPTER XVIII.

Dyak weapons—The mandau, or sword—Skilled workmanship—The shield, or kliau —The blowing tube—Natural scouring-paper—Poisoned arrows.

THE Dyak armoury is neither extensive nor costly. Neither breechloaders nor Gatling guns find a place in the list of native weapons. In nearly every village may be found, it is true, some old-fashioned guns—more dangerous to those who use them than to those at whom they are fired—in which the natives are very fond of wasting powder: while, at Long Wai, Rajah Dinda is protected by—or, rather, has under his protection—three brass cannon, a present from the Sultan. But fire-arms do not suit the genius of the Dyak or his style of warfare. What his arms, however, lack in the application of modern science, they make up in their suitability to the nature of the country in which they are used, and the skill with which they are handled. Every Dyak is a born warrior. From his earliest youth he is trained to the use of arms, and to take his part in the defence of his native home, and in raids on those of his neighbours. Not that "military service" is compulsory. The love of war, the desire to emulate his neighbour in deeds of valour, the anxiety to gain a reputation as a head-hunter, is innate, and the Dyak needs no other incentive to his murderous work than the example of his fellows. His father found his weapons enough for his purpose, and he has no desire and no need to attempt to improve upon them, so long as he has the opportunity of proving their temper and quality, and of making the most of their excellence by his own skill.

The principal weapon is the *mandau*, literally "head-hunter," of which each Dyak has from four to six. These are placed in a rack hung against the wall in his room, the weapon being always kept out of its sheath with the blade greased to prevent rust. The blade—concave on one side, and convex on the other—is about twenty-one inches long, nearly straight, one and a half inches broad in the middle, and tapering towards the end to a sharp point. It has only one cutting edge, the back being a quarter of an inch thick. The blade is made of steel or fine iron, which is abundant in Borneo. Although I have often seen the blade in the rough, in process of being sharpened and properly shaped, I have never seen either mine or smelting furnace, and could not ascertain where the raw material really came from.

The process of grinding and sharpening is very slow, and to polish and put a proper edge on a plain blade occupies more than a fortnight. Many of the blades are beautifully inlaid with brass along the sides near the back, while others have open scroll patterns cut right through the blade (see Plate 18, Fig. 3). How this work is done I could not ascertain, as both Dyaks and Malays were very chary of giving any information, and very unwilling to show me any of their tools. Regular workshops do not seem to exist, each man being apparently, to a great extent at least, his own cutler.

The handle or hilt is generally made of deer-horn, sometimes of ironwood, and is highly ornamented with scrolls and ingenious and symmetrical designs of animals, trees, monsters, &c. The only instrument used for the purpose is a broad sharp-pointed knife—means which seem quite inadequate to the end attained, for many of these carvings would do credit to a skilled English workman (Plate 18, Figs. 1, 2, 3, 4).

A thick rim of gutta-percha marks the point where the handle is fitted to the blade. Here are hung tassels of horse-hair, dyed various colours, or more often of human hair taken from victims.

The sheath is made of soft wood, the two sides being separately cut, and joined securely together at three or four points by coils of beautifully plaited rattan. The end of the sheath is guarded by an ivory ferule; and about two inches from its extremity depends a tassel of hair, the length of which increases according to the higher rank of the owner of the mandau.

On the under side of the sheath is a receptacle made of bark, carrying a small knife (see Plate 18, Fig. 2), the blade of which is three and a half inches, and the handle twelve inches, in length. This knife is used by the Dyak for severing the heads of the victims that fall to his mandau, and removing from them the fleshy parts; also for skinning animals killed in the chase; and in the more peaceful work of carving the ornaments which adorn his mandau, &c.

The sheath is carried by a belt made of very finely plaited rattan; the "buckle" or fastening consists of a loop at one end of the belt, through which is passed a piece of shell, or the upper mandible of the hornbill, or, as I saw among the Tring Dyaks, the kneecap of a human being, fastened at the other end of the belt.

Round the belt hang a numerous array of beaded tassels, and the idols or charms (*tambatongs*) described on a former page.

The next article in the armoury of the Dyaks is the *kliau*, a wooden shield, from three feet to three feet four inches long, and fifteen to sixteen inches broad, convex towards the outer centre, and with the ends cut to form an obtuse angle. Both sides are covered with red paint, or ornamented with red scrolls and figures (see Plate 15). Among the Trings and one or two other tribes, it is the fashion to adorn the outer side of the shield with tufts of human hair (see Plate 11). The inner side is furnished with a convenient handle, which is easily gripped by the hand. This shield forms a valuable weapon of defence against blows from the mandau, while it is perfectly proof against the poisoned puff-arrows. The Dyaks even believe it to be proof against bullets; but Mr. Perelaer proved this not to be the case by firing at a shield with an ordinary smooth-bore gun at 200 paces.

The *sumpitan*, or blowing-tube, from six to seven feet long, and about one and a half inches in diameter, with a bore of half an inch (see Plate 18, Fig. 9), is made of ironwood, the bore being drilled by means of a long sharp-pointed piece of iron while the wood is in the rough: the polish, both inside and outside, is obtained by the use of the dried leaves of a tree (*Daun Amplas* of the Malays), which are used as a substitute for sand-paper in Sumatra as well as Borneo. The under side of these leaves when dry is rough, resembling very fine sand-paper. At the upper end the sumpitan is furnished with a short spear and a small iron hook, which are strongly fastened to the tube with plaited rattans. I never could ascertain the use of this iron hook, but I find that Mr. Hugh Low, in his "Sarawak," p. 330, says it is used as a "sight," by which the aim is regulated: I have no doubt that this is correct.

Through this sumpitan the Dyak blows his poisoned arrows (*langá*), light thin darts (see Plate 18, Fig. 8), made of bamboo, nine and a half to ten inches long, two or two and a half millimètres thick. The point, which is very fine, is dipped into poison in the manner already described on p. 73.

For killing large animals the arrows are furnished with a barbed iron blade (see Plate 18, Fig. 7).

At the upper end the arrow is furnished with a piece of pith (*buà*) to fit the bore of the tube, by means of which it is blown through the tube. This takes the place of the "nock" and "shaftment" of ordinary arrows and also serves as a balance. These tiny darts the Dyak blows with unerring aim to a distance of forty or fifty yards, bringing down the smallest bird without difficulty.

The quiver (*tolór*) wherein the arrows are kept (see Plate 18, Fig. 5), is made of a section of bamboo, about thirteen inches in length and two inches in diameter, bound with ornamental rings of plaited rattan, fitted with a bamboo lid, and often ornamented on the top with a shell (*Helix Brookeana*).

The quiver is suspended to the mandau belt by means of a wooden hook, and to it is attached a small gourd (*hung*) (see Plate 18, Fig. 6), containing the pieces of pith, which are fitted to the end of the arrows when blown from the tube. The wooden stopper of this gourd is often carved to represent a monster's head.

This completes the war-equipment of a Dyak: but to the list of his weapons should also be added a long lance, used chiefly in wild boar hunting.

CHAPTER XIX.

Dyak architecture—A domestic menagerie—Wooden pathways—Wooden tiles—Internal arrangements of the houses—The furniture—A Dyak æsthetic school—Blue china mania—Relations of the sun and moon—Forged marks—Culinary utensils—Lares et Penates—Produce warehouses.

In a country overgrown with timber trees, both hard and soft, with bamboo, and with palms, a house is easily constructed with a small amount of labour, and little or no expense. These materials exclusively are employed in the construction of Dyak houses.

The villages are mostly built along the banks of rivers, though here and there are solitary houses, hidden from view among the forests, at a short distance from a stream or creek.

The houses are from eighty to 160 feet in length, twenty to thirty feet in width, and with walls about ten feet high, the ridge of the roof rising another five or six feet. The house proper has only one floor, raised about fifteen to twenty feet from the ground, on posts of iron-wood, or other hard timber, soft wood being unable to withstand the humidity of the air and ground. Under the actual habitation is a raised floor or platform of boards and bamboo poles, about four or six feet from the level of the ground, and open on all sides, which serves many purposes. Here the women pound their rice; here the men hold bitcharas, or councils; here the infants are nursed; and here the rising generation play, or practise war-dances, or take lessons from their elders in the use of the mandau and shield.

The ground under and around these platforms, however, is always in a filthy state—a mud pool in fact, in which the pigs, which are always in force in a Dyak settlement, root about in the garbage thrown from the houses, adding to the general filth. Besides the pigs, cats with short knobbed tails, something like the Manx breed, semi-starved dogs, used for deer-hunting or boar-hunting, and fowls roam about at their sweet will, on terms of equality with each other and their masters, forming altogether a most "happy family."

I only twice saw buffaloes (*karbaus*) among the domesticated animals in a Dyak settlement, and that was in the village of Dassa and again at Long Puti.

In some villages each house is joined to its neighbour by a series of planks, also raised on posts, by means of which it is possible to walk from house to house without touching the ground (see sketch of Long Puti, Plate 7). The natives could not give me any particular reason for the adoption of this custom, but I can testify to the advantage which these pathways offered, in my eyes at least, in keeping the pedestrian out of the filth and mud with which the ground is nearly always covered.

The floor of the house proper is reached by a ladder, consisting of a block of timber or thick board, in which deep notches are cut to form steps. I found it very difficult to mount these primitive ladders, especially when booted; but the barefooted and practised natives ascended them with the greatest facility.

The floor of the habitation is composed of bamboo, and the walls of mixed bamboo and timber boards. The roof is covered either with wooden tiles or with *attap*, i. e. split leaves of the nipa palm, which grows abundantly in the island. The palm leaves are collected into bundles about four feet long, three feet wide, and a foot thick, which are laid closely together on the beams of the roof, and form a cheap and durable covering, that will withstand the torrential rains of the tropics for six or eight years together. The wooden "tiles" are merely pieces of soft wood, half an inch thick and six inches wide, by thirty inches long.

I noticed a Dyak near Long Wai who had felled a tree of some soft wood in the forest, and was busy cutting the stem into small logs, which he afterwards brought to the village on a raft. He told me he would get from this one stem perhaps 600 tiles, the current price for which was fifty cents per hundred. He could cut 200 tiles in a day, working almost without interruption from sunrise to sunset, and the only implement he used was his mandau.

These wooden slabs are laid on the roof much in the same fashion as slates or tiles at home, overlapping each other, but tied on with rattan instead of being nailed. The gables of every house that has any pretension to "style" are ornamented with a large carved scroll. When I inquired the origin or meaning of this ornamentation all the answer I could get was "It is our custom."

As a rule the houses are provided with a couple of sliding doors, and they seldom have more than two openings which serve as windows, whatever the number of occupants. Three or four families, or more, reside together in the same habitation.

Internally, the house is divided longitudinally by a bamboo partition. One of the long compartments so formed serves as a sleeping place for the unmarried youths and men, and as a general living-room for all the occupants; while the other compartment is subdivided into a series of smaller rooms for the married members of the family, and the women. In front of the door of the long room, adjoining the ladder, is often an open platform or balcony of bamboo or wood, which is used for various domestic purposes—drying rice, or laying "the clothes to dry."

Chairs and tables form no part of the furniture of an ordinary Dyak's house; mats, made of fine plaited rattan, either plain or stained different colours, and worked into various patterns, form the Dyak's seat. In a corner, near the fireplace, will generally be found stored a collection of crockery-ware, for the Dyak is something of a china-maniac, and belongs to the modern æsthetic school, setting great store by the china vessels which he procures in exchange for the various products of the country from the Malay merchants, who again have purchased them from the Chinese traders at Singapore or Macassar.

The Dyak representative of the blue-china school, however, goes beyond the European devotee in his veneration for old crockery. Among his greatest treasures are a series of *gudji blanga*, a sort of glazed jar imported from China, in green, blue, or brown, ornamented with figures of lizards and serpents in relief. These pots are valued at from 100 florins to as much as 3000 florins (8*l.* to 240*l.*) each, according to size, pattern, and, above all, old age combined with good condition. According to the native legend, these precious vases are made of the remnants of the same clay from which "Mahatara" (the Almighty) made first the sun, and then the moon. Medicinal virtues are attributed to these urns, and they are regarded as affording complete protection from evil spirits to the house in which they are stored. A very full account of the various legends connected with these gudji blanga is given in Mr. W. T. H. Perelaer's most interesting work, "Ethnographische Beschrijving der Dajaks," pp. 112—120. That author, however, gives them different names, the nearest of approach to that by which I have always heard them called being *Balanga*.

This china craze among the Dyaks has proved, as in England, an excellent opportunity for the exercise of John Chinaman's skill; and very clever imitations of old vases, with cracks, chips, age-stains, and other indications of antiquity, most exactly reproduced by them, are offered for sale at Samarinda at five florins each; but, unlike many London connoisseurs, your Dyak is never taken in by these spurious gudji blangas, preferring to give hundreds of guilders for a real specimen. Each true plastic relative of the sun and moon has its pedigree, which is passed down from generation to generation.

The "indigenous" household utensils consist of a number of bamboo joints, of various lengths and sizes, which are used as water-bottles, replenished twice a day from the river, or, suspended longitudinally over the fire, do good service as pots for boiling rice; plates made of iron-wood, in the shape of a large spoon or bowl with a very short handle, often carved to represent the head of a crocodile or a fabulous beast (see Plate 19, Figs. 7, 7a); spoons made of a piece of bamboo (see Plate 19, Fig. 14); spoons or ladles ingeniously manufactured out of a gourd, a portion of which is cut away, and the pulp removed, while the stalk is left for a handle (see Plate 19, Fig. 11); and bowls or saucers made out of cocoanut-shells, the edges of which are often carved and ornamented with fret work (see Plate 19, Fig. 6). Very serviceable bottles made of plaited rattan are used for storing rice (see Plate 19, Fig. 8).

On the walls are hung the mandaus (more particularly described on another page), with sometimes an old flint-lock gun or two, nearly always bearing the George IV. mark; while the lances, blowing-tubes, and other weapons are stowed away in a corner, together with perhaps a heap of fishing-nets, some brass trays and gongs, musical instruments,[1] &c.

Among the articles which may be regarded more as household ornaments than as furniture are the dried human skulls, which are to be found wrapped in banana leaves, in the habitation of nearly every well-regulated Dyak family. These are hung up on the wall, or depend from the roof. The lower jaw is always wanting, as the Dyak finds it more convenient to decapitate his victim below the occiput, leaving the lower jaw attached to the body.

Every house also contains a number of tambatongs or charms, in addition to those carried on the body. Some of these household gods are of considerable size, and all of them of extreme ugliness. In Plate 27, Fig. 1, is shown the style generally prevailing among the Long Wahou tribe.

Besides their large dwelling-houses, the Dyaks have small out-houses, where they store their produce, such as rattan, bees'-wax, gutta, &c.

The Dyaks in the valley of the Moeara Anan and Benangan live in small communities of between twenty and thirty souls, including children, and do not build such large houses as those just described, dwelling in huts erected 200 or 300 yards away from the banks of the river, and hidden from view—the only indication of their existence being a prau here and there, fastened to the trees on the banks, or partly drawn ashore.

[1] For description of musical instruments, see p. 217.

CHAPTER XX.

Daily occupations of the Dyaks—Agricultural operations—Sowing the rice—Plagues of rats—Wild boars—A terrible famine—Agricultural implements—Damar resin—A useful cement—Smoky torches—An invaluable plant—Floating fortresses—Waterproof baskets—Collecting gutta-percha—Bees'-wax and honey—Curious bees'-nests—Edible birds'-nests—Bezoar stones—Hunting and shooting—A curious bait—Canoe-building—Fancy work for the ladies—A substitute for soap.

At about seven every morning most of the natives are in commotion. Men and women, also young boys able to work, all get ready to go to their accustomed work. They all take a basket on their backs, and paddle in their hand, the men carrying also a blowing tube and arrows, &c., and go down to the river to embark in the praus—from eight to ten persons in each. As a rule a dog or two will accompany them, taking their place in the middle of the prau, where the "odds and ends" necessary for the day's work are heaped up. From Long Wai fifteen or twenty praus used to start every morning, their crews going hunting, farming, fishing, or what not. At sunset the Dyaks would return from their day's hard work, the men bringing firewood, the women generally some fruit, such as pisangs, water-melons, and obi.

First among the industrial occupations of the Dyak is agriculture. Every Dyak has his rice-field, on which he grows sufficient rice for his own consumption. He selects a piece of forest-land—often a mile or two from the village—and begins, with the assistance of his family, to clear the ground. The large trees are cut down, and either made into tiles or hewn into boards, or used as firewood. As soon as the ground is pretty well cleared of the large timber, the Dyak sets fire to the undergrowth, the ashes of which act as a manure. All this is done in the months of March and

April, or, as they would call it, at the beginning of the "dry season"—for they have no idea of the division of the year into months. From August to the middle of September they are engaged in making—just as the Malays do—small rafts, from three to six feet long, which they cover with a thin layer of earth, on which they sow, very thickly, the rice seed. These rafts are then placed in the river, so that they are always moist, and in a very short time they are covered with a mantle of young plants of a most exquisite light-green colour. Having sown their rice, the Dyaks build small huts in the fields, remaining there till the miniature plants are transplanted out into the newly-cleared field, on which the women all the time have been busily engaged in removing the weeds, which grow almost as fast as they are destroyed.

The Dyaks have also to guard their plantations from the wild boars, which are very numerous in Borneo, and also against those great enemies to the rice-fields, the swarms of rats and mice. These pests, however, it is impossible to keep down, and in four or five years' time they utterly destroy the rice-fields, so that the Dyaks are continually forced to select new grounds. The Borneo rice is inferior to that grown in Java, where the "sawah" or terrace cultivation is adopted, which is so fully described in Mr. Wallace's admirable work "The Malay Archipelago."

Besides their rice-fields, the people have near their houses plantations of maize (*djagong*) the grains of which they are fond of eating roasted, bananas or pisangs, a sort of turnip called *koedjang*, sugar-cane (*taboo*), penang, and a few cocoa-nut palms.

The produce of these gardens and fields is only sufficient for the immediate wants of the people; and when a drought occurs, as it did in 1878, a famine is the result. Many of the Dyaks told me of the privations they had endured owing to the long dry season which had occurred just previously to my visit. Numbers of them had subsisted for more than a year on roots and wild fruits; and even these would have failed had the drought lasted much longer. The worst effects of the famine were averted by the aid of the Sultan of Koetei, who sent large supplies of food to his starving subjects in the forests; but even when I was at Long Wai, in

1879, the rice crop was so small, owing to the drought, that the people had to get rice from Tangaroeng.

Their agricultural implements are few. I know of no more than two—the mandau, with the little knife attached, and a peculiar axe, or rather adze (see Plate 18, Fig. 12), the iron of which is fastened with cords, made from the sinews of deer, plaited in chequer-fashion, to a shaft made of a piece of hard wood. This again is stuck into a long handle, to which it is firmly fastened by means of gutta-percha. The instrument has a fine balance, and the Dyaks handle it with great skill, especially in bringing down large timber. The underwood and creepers are cleared with the mandau. The women rarely use the mandau, but employ for their work, such as cutting the paddy, a small knife, which is carried in a sheath (Plate 18, Figs. 10 and 11).

During the dry season the Dyaks, especially the women, go out in numbers and collect *damar*, a sort of resin, which is produced in abundance by certain kinds of trees, three different kinds being recognized, viz. dark brown, yellow, and nearly white and transparent. The "damar" runs from the trees to the ground, and is often mixed with earth and very dirty. When this is the case the natives make a sort of putty which they call *doempoel*, first pounding the resin, then adding to it a little chalk and cocoa-nut oil. When packing up my collections of birds, &c., I found that the wood was split in several places, leaving cracks sufficiently wide to admit ants and other destructive insects. Observing this, a Dyak made me some "doempoel," and filled up the crevices, making the case perfectly tight. This putty hardens quickly after it is applied, and is very durable. The damar is also used in the manufacture of torches, which are made of bundles of leaves mixed with powdered resin. When burning these torches emit a very feeble light, but a very strong smoke and smell. The superior advantages of petroleum will no doubt soon be appreciated among the Dyaks, as they already are among the Malays, who have for some years burnt this oil, which they call *minia tana* (earth oil).

The cutting of rattan is, however, the chief occupation of the Dyaks. This is carried on in the rainy season, when they make excursions to the very numerous rivers and creeks, on whose banks the several species of this valuable prickly climbing plant are found growing in great abundance. There are three sorts in special demand in trade—the *Rotan irit* which is the best, the *Sankolirang*, and an inferior variety. The price at Samarinda varies from ninety-five florins to twenty-five florins for 100 *ikkat* or bundles—each bundle containing forty rattans. The apparent difference in quality is so slight that it requires an experienced eye to detect it. The rattan is sold to Malay traders and by them brought down to the shipping ports on immense rafts—those on the Barito river sometimes measuring 300 or 400 feet long and 60 or 70 feet wide, made of a number of large trees tied firmly together by means of rattan rope. Upon this raft a floor of split bamboos is laid, on which the cargo is piled, a space, with a passage leading to it, being left in the centre, where the owner and his wives, and slave debtors [1] (*pandelinge*) live during the journey, which often lasts many weeks, no means of propulsion being used, and the raft merely gliding down with the current. A space three or four feet in width is left all round the edge of the raft, along which the crew can walk, keeping watch in all directions. The navigation consists merely of steering, which is effected by means of a long pole, lashed astern, to act as a rudder. Thus gliding slowly down the stream the lofty pile of rattan looks like a floating fortress.

At Samarinda and Bandjermasin the rattan is sold to the Chinese, who often have advanced a large sum of money to the Malay, previous to his departure for the purpose of collecting the produce in the interior. Neither Malay nor Chinese will do the least work till he has received "*vorschott*," *Anglicè* "an advance." The merchant gets, of course, no security for his

[1] Slave debtor is the term applied to a servant who has got into his master's debt. If he cannot pay the debt the master may hand him over to another master, who pays the debt for him, and the servant then becomes indebted to his new master in the amount so paid, and is called a "slave debtor," giving his services until the debt is worked off. This very rarely happens; on the contrary the servant generally contrives to add to the amount of his indebtedness, and lives in a perpetual state of semi-bondage, with which his indolent nature fully harmonizes. I have seldom seen a slave debtor discontented with his lot.

vorschott, but has a lien on the rattan when it arrives, and gets it a little below the market-price. The raft is sold together with its cargo, and the wood, being sawn into planks, is exported.

Besides forming the chief article of trade in its raw state, rattan furnishes the material for the manufacture of an endless variety of useful objects. Take away his bamboo, and you take away the Dyak's house. Take away his rattan, and you deprive the Dyak of half the articles indispensable to his existence. What crochet-work is to the European lady, rattan plaiting is to the Dyak housewife. She is always manufacturing either sleeping-mats, sitting-mats, sirih boxes, baskets of all shapes and sizes, and for all kinds of uses, besides long pieces of plait to be used as cords, ropes, or threads, in dressmaking, house-building, raft construction, and the hundred-and-one other purposes of daily life in the forest.

In some parts of the interior I have seen baskets made from the bark of the trees, which are perfectly watertight.

The next produce which claims the Dyak's attention, and is largely exported, is gutta-percha (*mallau*), which is yielded by many different species of trees. The tree yielding the best gutta-percha is called by the natives *Komallau Durian* from the resemblance of its leaves to those of the Durian. Another variety is known as the *Komallau Ramas*. The natives eat the fruit, which is somewhat sweet in flavour. The juice when first extracted is of a milky-white colour; but it turns chocolate-brown as it hardens by exposure to the air. The Dyaks have not yet graduated in the science of forest conservation. Instead of making incisions at regular intervals in the bark of a tree, and extracting a portion of the juice at different periods, by which its further growth would not be prevented, they usually adopt the radical expedient of cutting the whole tree down. The consequence is that the material is becoming more and more difficult to procure, and will eventually become scarce, if not extinct, in the island. The price at Samarinda of the best gutta-percha, known as *isonandra*, is 130 florins per picol of 120 katties, the katti being equal to one and a quarter pounds avoirdupois.

Another occupation is gathering wax (*liling*) from the nests of the indigenous bees. Along the banks of the rivers may be seen hundreds of high straight trees, covered with from twenty to sixty nests. It is a curious fact—at variance with the almost universal habit among all animals to conceal their nests as much as possible —that the bees always select for their nests a tree with a light grey bark, against which their dark-coloured homes stand out very conspicuously. These wonderful architectural structures, again, are always placed near the river, never in the interior of the forests. If this is done by an instinctive desire to protect the nests from the ravages of monkeys and other animals inhabiting the woods, it is strange that the insects should defeat this object in the colour of the nests. I was told by the Dyaks that the Orang Poonan (the forest people) are the chief collectors of wax, pulling down the nests in the night, when it is very dark, and driving away or suffocating the insect communities by means of their smoke-producing damar torches. They often get stung during the operation, but bear the pain with indifference. The honey (*madoe*) is nearly all kept by the natives for home consumption, and the wax exported, the price, uncleaned, being 80 florins per picol of 120 katties.

The natives, and especially the Orang Poonan, also make it a regular industry twice a year to visit the caves in which a species of swallow, the *Hirundo esculenta*, breed, and to collect their nests, which form the basis of the celebrated Chinese dish of birds'-nest soup. These edible birds'-nests (*sarong boeroeng*) are of two varieties, and fetch high prices, the whiter kind realizing from 160 to 180 florins per six katties, and the coloured or inferior quality selling for from 110 to 115 florins per six katties.

A curious industry is the collection of *galiga*, or bezoar stones, which are also mostly secured by the Orang Poonan. These *galiga* are highly prized for medicinal purposes, and are sold at fabulous prices to the Boegis, who re-sell them to the Chinese. There are two sorts, the *galiga landak* and *G. boehis*. The former, the more expensive of the two, are derived from an external wound on the porcupine. They are very light in weight, and of a brown colour. They taste exactly like quinine; and so strong is this property that when a piece is held inside the hand, and the tongue applied outside, the bitter taste can be detected. It appears to me that these galiga are composed of bits of leaves, &c., gradually collected on the wound, and formed into a ball by the congealed blood. The other sort, the *G. boehis*, are found at times, the Dyaks tell me, in different parts of the body of the boehis monkey (*Semnopithecus cristatus*), called in the interior *boehis*. They are of a greenish-brown colour, often beautifully polished, and are mostly kidney-shaped, though varying in colour. They are nothing else than gallstones, similar to those found in human bodies. The Chinese grind the galiga to a powder, and take a little of it in a tumbler of water. The curative properties attributed to this draught are legion; there is not an ailment that it is not able to cure. It may, indeed, be called the "Holloway's Pills and Ointment" of the Chinese, rolled all into one.

Bezoar stones have been known in Europe for centuries; the oldest European work published on bezoar stones is, I believe, "I. Wittich, von den wunderbaren Bezoardischen Steinen," &c. Leipzig, 1592. The Sultan of Koetei has a very fine collection of these stones, of various shapes, sizes, and colours, valued at many thousand guilders. Amongst them were several objects certainly not galiga, but simply the spines of a species of *echinus*, which he told me were of great value as a cure for stricture. One very beautiful specimen of *G. boehis*, which he presented to me, was valued at sixty guilders; it measures forty-four millimètres in length, and twenty-nine in breadth (see Plate 27, Fig. 9).[2]

[2] Since the above was written, I have found an article in the *Colonies and India*, giving an abstract of a paper on Bezoar, read before the Straits branch of the Royal Asiatic Society by Mr. A. Hart Everett, who, speaking of the *G. boehis*, says :—"The part of Borneo which produces these stones in the greatest abundance seems to be, according to native reports, the district about the upper waters of the Balungar (Batang Kayan). The story is that the head waters of this river are cut off from its lower course by an extensive tract of hills, beneath which the river disappears—a report by no means unlikely, if the country be, as is probable, limestone. The people of the district have no communication with the lower course of the river, and are thus without any supply of salt. They use instead the waters of certain springs, which are probably saline mineral springs, and which are also frequented by troops of red monkeys. The Bezoars are most commonly found in the stomachs of these animals, through their drinking the saline water." This theory of the formation of *G. boehis* cannot be reconciled with the conditions existing in Koetei. Of the *G. landak* the paper goes on to say :—"The 'Guliga Landak' is obtained from the porcupine, but is compara-

The Dyaks are keen sportsmen, spending much time in hunting and fishing, to which they are passionately addicted, not merely for purposes of food supply, but for the sake of sport. Of fishing they are especially fond. The numerous lakes, rivers, and creeks teem with fish, which furnish a large portion of their daily food. They generally capture their finny prey by means of a net, but often use a hook and line baited with a flower or a worm. At p. 126 I have already described a curious mode of setting night-lines adopted by the Dyaks at Moeara Pahou.

Several species of *silurus* are common in all the rivers of Borneo. There is also a species of flat fish resembling a sole, which is found in the fresh water as much as 200 miles away from the sea. Saw-fishes are often captured, but are not used as food.

While fishing is thus easy, hunting is, on the other hand, very difficult in Koetei, owing to the thick impenetrable forest, and to the fact that during the rainy season the soil is very muddy, and often, near the rivers especially, quite under water. Deer and wild boars are however regularly hunted, the latter being especially numerous, and attracting the Dyaks' attention not merely for the sake of the flesh, of which they are very fond, but also because of the damage they do to the-rice fields. The Dyaks hunt with dogs and lances. Sometimes may be seen the strange sight of an old warrior sallying forth in search of game armed with an old-fashioned flint gun—the only occasion on which I ever saw a Dyak attempt to use fire-arms for any other purpose than for the sake of making a noise.

We have seen the Dyaks are by no means idle; they have plenty of occupations, differing according to the time of year. When not engaged in any of their daily pursuits, they busy them-

tively rare; this, we believe, is the only description which is believed by the native physicians in India to possess any value as an antidote for the poison of snakes, &c., and in the treatment of fevers, asthmatic complaints, &c. The usual test for a good Guliga is to place a little lime on the hand and to rub the Guliga against it, when, if it be genuine, the lime becomes yellow. Imitations are by no means rare; and on one occasion some Bakatans succeeded in deceiving the Chinamen, who trade in these articles, by carefully moulding some fine light clay into the form of a Bezoar, and then rubbing it well all over with a genuine one. The extreme lightness of a real Guliga and the lime test are, however, generally sufficient to expose a counterfeit."

selves in building a new prau or canoe (*halok*); for, as already stated, they invariably settle on the banks of a stream, and all communication is by water. Their praus are serviceable vessels, hewn out of a single large tree. A drawing of one is given in Plate 19, Fig. 15.

They are altogether good workmen, expert in the use of the mandau, which is their axe as well as their sword, skilled in forging their arms, and very clever at carving in ivory and wood. Their taste for the fine arts certainly ranks above that of the Malays, at least in Koetei.

The women make from the fibre of a plant the thread with which the bark fabrics forming their home-made garments are sewn together, bound, or embroidered; and some of them can weave. They also make their own vegetable dyes, the favourite colours being blue, red, and yellow, and are very clever at bead work. The tops and sides of their hats and other headgear, and other garments, are often ornamented with exquisite specimens of bead work, always in scrolls or geometrical patterns, and displaying great skill and taste, both in design and in arrangement of colour. The women also perform the necessary household duties of washing, pounding the rice, cooking, &c., and fetching water from the river.

The women and children bathe three times daily—morning, noon, and evening. Morning and evening each woman and child takes to the river a number of bamboo canes, which serve as water-bottles, which they fill with water, carrying them up in a basket on their back. Soap has not been introduced among the Dyaks, but they wash themselves with lemon instead. A performance of daily occurrence among both sexes is to look after any intruders in the hair, for in spite of all their bathing I found the people very dirty.

CHAPTER XXI.

Moral character and mental capacity of the Dyaks—Honesty and truthfulness—Loyalty to the chiefs—Taxation by the Sultan—Slavery and cannibalism—Husbands and wives—Tribal affection—The rising generation—Tobacco and opium smoking—Betel-chewing—Time reckoning—Abstemiousness—Diseases—Vaccination—Snake-fat as an ointment—Materia Medica—Superstitious rites—Indifference to heat and cold.

In mental capacity the Dyaks are on a footing with the Malays, but are not so slovenly and lazy as the latter, and have more inclination for work. They are not so reserved as the Malays, being fond of talking and amusements, though calm and not easily excited. Like all savages, they are very inquisitive and superstitious. While I stayed at Long Wai they were continually consulting the flight of birds. I could see they were concerned about me; and, when I asked them if they had any objection to my remaining amongst them a little while, they said they would rather be without visitors. As regards morality, I am bound to give the Dyaks a high place in the scale of civilization. The question may be put, how can morality be attributed to a Head-Hunter? I am going to point out their good qualities first, and shall later deal with the head-hunting customs and their origin.

The divine command "Thou shalt not steal" is strictly observed by the Dyaks; robberies and theft are entirely unknown among them. They would never touch any of my articles, however trifling, without first asking permission. They made up for this, however, by begging with the greatest importunity for anything that took their fancy. They are also very truthful. If they could not satisfactorily reply to my questions they hesitated to answer at all; but if I did not always get the "whole truth," I always got at least "nothing but the truth" from them. I wish I could say as much for the Malays and Boegis, who, from the crowned head downwards to the humblest soul, are reputed tellers of falsehoods. I said to the Sultan one day, while he was swaggering in his usual way about his principality, "I think you are copying modern diplomatists;" he laughed, and replied "*Joesta allus*" (to lie fine).

Slavery does not exist among the Dyaks, with the single exception of the Bahou Tring tribe, who not merely practise slavery, but put their slaves to torture and death. Slave debtors (*pandelinge*), however, are common in all parts of Koetei, and seem usually well satisfied with their lot.

The Bahou Trings, again, are the only cannibals in Koetei.[1] Their cannibal customs are more fully described at pp. 134, 218.

Notwithstanding the practice of head-hunting carried on by every tribe at the expense of its neighbour, the members of each community live in harmony together, and the word of their chief is their law. The Dyaks, however, are not at all on intimate terms with the Malays, who often cheat them · so they, in return, do not mind chopping a head off when a favourable opportunity presents itself.

The Sultan is respected by nearly all the tribes, but he does not exercise any real power over the people in the interior, only troubling himself, through his nobles, to collect the poll-tax of a dollar a head, which is leviable on all except children.

The people assert, no doubt with much truth, that though they only have one head each they are taxed as if they possessed several of those most necessary adjuncts to the human body; but they pay the "ringit" (dollar) two or three times over, consoling themselves probably with the idea that, if they only have one head of their own, they have several of their enemies' heads strung up in the bedroom.

The Dyaks show great respect for their wives, and are very fond of their children, whom they take it in turn to nurse. While the

[1] According to Dr. Hollander's work "Land en Volkenkünde," there is another cannibal tribe in Borneo, the Djangkangs, in Sanggouw, in the Sintang district.

Other tribes have human sacrifices on the occasion of their Tiwa feast; not from mere bloodthirstiness, but from the superstition that the sacrificed serve the departed as slaves in their future abode.

able-bodied people are away attending to their daily occupations, the aged, both men and women, remain at home and look after the rising generation. The women, who are the beasts of burden, as in Sumatra and Java, are soon worn down by age and the heavy labour they have to perform in farming the land. The man always asks the woman's opinion, and *vice versâ;* for instance, a woman does not like to part with anything without having first the consent of her husband: at Long Puti a woman had a pair of carved wooden cylinders for the ears, in exchange for which I offered her some tempting beads, but, as her husband was away at the time of my visit, she would not part with them. Members of the same family or tribe have strong feelings of sympathy for each other. When a Dyak is ill at home the women nurse the patient in turn. During my journey through the forest, across the watershed from Moeara Anan to Moeara Benangan, a Dyak suddenly got a severe attack of fever and had to be left behind; but four of his tribe volunteered to remain by him, and at once began to erect a little hut for the invalid near a stream of water.

The Dyaks marry early, but have only one wife. Rajah Dinda and his brother are exceptions, but they are supposed to be "verts;" these two stalwart Dyaks, on the advice of the Sultan, embraced the Mohammedan religion, so that they could indulge in the doubtful luxury of several wives. To judge by the appearance of some of the youngest couples I saw—for the Dyaks have no idea of their own age—the girls marry from the age of fifteen, and the men at about twenty.

A Dyak family seldom consists of more than three or four children. When an interesting event is about to happen, the lady is secluded in a small house, where she remains for several months, during which no stranger is allowed to enter the hut. The mother carries the infant in a curious portable cradle, a semi-circular contrivance slung behind the shoulder, in which the infant sits erect with the legs hanging (see Plate 16).

The little brown bundle of humanity is subject to all the ordinary wants of human nature, and when it utters the universally recognized warning cry, as a protest against the pangs of hunger or thirst, the mother simply brings the chair forward, without in any way interfering with her regular occupation. Babies are nursed for a couple of years, and even longer. They are usually laden with silver bangles, strings of coins, shells, beads, small bells, and other rattling ornaments.

The children are always full of life and play, ever ready for a game, and, as they begin to feel their growing strength, for trials of endurance and skill. It is a phenomenon to see a Dyak child who is not running, jumping, fighting or wrestling, either with one of its companions, or, failing that, carrying the war among the pigs or the poultry. In the evenings they practise dancing, or playing a kind of flute, through which they blow from the nostril.

By and by the "young ideas" begin to smoke, following the example set them by their papa and mamma. The Dyak pipe is a very peculiarly constructed instrument, consisting of a stout bamboo cylinder, about twenty-two inches long and one and a half inches in diameter, which contains water to cool the smoke; inside this tube is placed a piece of split rattan filled with fibre, which absorbs the nicotine; about one inch from the end of this tube is inserted, at right-angles, a slender carved piece of ironwood, about eight inches in length, and bored with a hole rather more than a quarter of an inch in diameter; this constitutes the bowl, which contains only a very small quantity of tobacco. The Dyak, however, never takes more than half a dozen puffs at a time, as the Java tobacco which is generally used is very strong, and the smoke is always swallowed.

Cigarettes, made of a little tobacco rolled up in a small piece of banana leaf, are largely used. The use of opium is, in some districts, rapidly extending among the "rich" Dyaks. The habit of sirih and betel chewing, probably introduced by the Malays, is also universal, and is the only habit the Dyaks carry to excess.

The Dyaks reckon their periods of time by the full moon, half moon, and new moon.

They have no fixed hour for their meals, and are very temperate, both in eating and in drinking, confining themselves to water, except on the occasion of their feasts, when toewak, a drink made from honey, is indulged in. I have sometimes offered the Dyaks a glass of brandy or a cup of chocolate, which they would look at, or smell, and then decline, saying in Malay, "*Tida bissa*" (don't understand) or "*tida soeka*" (don't wish).

Notwithstanding the out-door life of the Dyaks, and their moderation in eating and drinking, it is not surprising that, in the malarious climate, and the unsanitary state of their houses, they are subject to fevers and dysentery. Skin diseases are common, owing no doubt to the scarcity of salt.

The Orang Poonan are especially subject to skin diseases of both scaly and ulcerative form. I have already referred to the frequent occurrence of wens among both Dyaks and Malays. It is no exaggeration to say that every third woman is afflicted with a protuberance in the throat, varying from the size of an apple to that of a child's head.

Smallpox occasionally makes serious ravages among the people. As a safeguard against this disease they have a sort of vaccination system, wherein faith or belief plays a greater part than medical science. I have on more than one occasion seen the native place a piece of tinder on his arm or thigh, burn it, and let it burn a wound. This they believe to be an infallible preventive. In Plate 16 may be seen the row of spots on the arm of a girl, the result of this operation.

That the Dyaks are not as a rule unhealthy is proved by the rapidity with which wounds and fractures heal. They, and the Malays also, are very fond of the fat from the boa constrictor as an ointment, and apply it to all kinds of external wounds. As an instance of the efficacy of the ointment, I may mention the case of a Malay from Amontai, who had received an ugly wound in his head from an *Amok* Boegis, part of the skull being removed, and the brain laid bare. The only means he adopted was to apply serpent's fat to the wound, and bind it up. In less than three weeks the wound was closed. I am not prepared to attribute the whole of this rapid recovery to the virtues of serpent's fat. It may perhaps be taken as an illustration of the happy dispensation of providence, which has given the native constitution an aptitude for quickly repairing skulls in a country where they are so easily broken. Certain it is, however, that such a hole in a European's skull would not have been mended in a tropical climate in thirty times three weeks, if ever.

The Dyaks have also certain plants from which drugs are made. It struck me that the women are best up in the *Materia Medica*, as they generally prepare the roots or leaves, and also administer the doses to the patients and act as nurses; but they are very unwilling to give any information about their medicines.

Superstitious rites play a more important part in the physician's art among the Dyaks than medical or surgical skill. The *tambatongs* or charms are regarded as more potent instruments of good than all the poultices or ointments, plaisters or medicines in the world. When these have been tried without avail, in any serious case of illness, recourse is had to *pomali*. The door of the house is shut, and outside it a bunch of leaves is hung, to show that the place is what would be called in the South Seas *tabu*, sacred, or set apart. Nobody is allowed to enter. The patient is left to himself until *Satan* is driven away.

In different diseases different tambatongs are looked to for aid. In Plate 27 are shown several typical charms, each of which is regarded as proof against, or a cure for, certain specific ills. The Tring Dyaks, and those of Long Bléh and Long Puti, have no end of these charms, in infinite variety of well-conceived ugliness, hung round their necks or waists.

I could not find that the Dyaks attribute any virtue to the galiga or bezoar stone, which they collect and sell at such fabulous prices to the Malay traders for the Chinese.

The Dyaks can endure without apparent discomfort considerable extremes of heat and cold. At night, when the sensation of cold is frequently very great, owing to the rapid radiation of heat and the resulting moisture, the natives often sleep with nothing more over than they have worn during the heat of the day. Sometimes they cover themselves with a long piece of thin cotton cloth, or with a mat of rattan, but this is the exception rather than the rule. During my travels in Borneo I was very glad to have a thick blanket to cover me at night, and even then never felt too warm; but the natives did not seem to mind the cold.

CHAPTER XXII.

The head-hunting rites—A problem in white administration—Cause of the extinction of the Dyak race—War-dances—Native musical instruments—Cannibalism—Human sacrifices—A penitential performance—Murdering the victims—Drying the skulls—A death feast—Torturing the doomed—Monuments of bloodthirstiness—Courting among the cannibals—Marriage ceremonies—Omens—The penalties of paternity—Coming of age—The "last scene of all"—The road to the cannibal's heaven—Signs of mourning—Funeral rites among the cannibals—A funeral dance at Long Wai—The Long Wai Dyak's journey to heaven—Burial of a Rajah at Long Wahou—Collecting skulls—Another Paradise—Witchcraft among the Dyaks—Dyak divinities—Fate of a Mohammedan missionary.

THE barbarous practice of Head-Hunting, as carried on by all the Dyak tribes, not only in the independent territories, but also in some parts of the tributary states, is part and parcel of their religious rites. Births and "namings," marriages and burials, not to mention less important events, cannot be properly celebrated unless the heads of a few enemies, more or less, have been secured to grace the festivities or solemnities. Head-hunting is consequently the most difficult feature in the relationship of the subject races to their white masters, and the most delicate problem which civilization has to solve in the future administration of the as yet independent tribes of the interior of Borneo. The Dutch have already done much by the double agency of their arms and their trade to remove this plague-spot from the character of the tribes more immediately under their control; and the Sultan of Koetei does all he can to discountenance it. Still, as has been seen, even he is not altogether free from the superstitious weaknesses which beset Malays and Dyaks alike, and while *pomali* is practised in Tangaroeng it is difficult to see how head-hunting can be altogether abolished in Long Wahou. In the more inaccessible regions of the interior, therefore, the practice has full sway; and the natives everywhere, when the question is discussed with them, are shrewd enough to bring forward arguments from the practices of the whites in favour of their own acts.

"The *Orang blonda* (white men)," said Rajah Dinda of Long Wai to me one day, while speaking on this very point, "have been killing the Dyaks and Malays on the Tewéh by hundreds,"—referring to the Dutch war in the Doesoen district in 1859-64,—"because they want to take their country and collect more rice and gutta; and why should they object to our killing a few people now and then when our *adat* (custom) requires it? We do not care for the instructions of the white men, and do not see why they should come into our country at all." After this blunt reply I observed as much reticence on this subject as Rajah Dinda himself displayed.

Head-hunting, or, as the Dutch call it, *Koppensnellen*, is the keystone, so to speak, in the edifice of Dyak religion and character. Its perpetual practice is no doubt one great cause of the rapid extinction of the race; and it is possible that before the custom can be entirely abolished the people themselves will have improved each other off the face of the earth.

In all great events of their lives the Dyaks require that human heads shall be procured. When a Dyak wants to marry he must show himself a hero (or, as the Malays term it, an *Orang brani*) before he can gain favour with his intended; and the more heads he can obtain the greater the pride and admiration with which he is regarded, not only by his bride, but by the whole tribe. When a Rajah is dead, heads must be secured; for, according to Dyak belief, the victims serve as slaves to the departed Rajah in heaven. Whenever a child is born to a Rajah—in Long Wai at least—heads must be got before it can be named.

It is a rule among all the tribes that no youth can regularly wear a mandau, or be married, or associate with the opposite sex, till he has been on one or more head-hunting expeditions. A mandau is presented to him, probably, at his birth, or when he receives a name; but not till he has washed it in the blood of an enemy can he presume to carry it as part of his every-day equipment.

Before venturing on a head-hunting excursion, Dyaks have war-dances or games, completely arrayed in war-costume. At my request some Dyaks at Long Wai gave specimens of these performances. When I first requested one of their number to let me see how they looked when they went out head-hunting they laughed, and hesitated, asking among themselves whether they should show themselves or not. But the almighty dollar, as the Yankees term it, proved its power even here. No sooner had I said I would make a present of a couple of dollars (*ringits*) to any one who would attire himself in full war apparel, and permit me to make a sketch, than half a dozen were anxious to earn the gratuity. On Plates 4 and 28 will be found the sketches which I made at Long Wai of Dyaks in full war-costume. Plate 11 represents a Tring Dyak, in undress, performing the war-dance.

The "war-dance" in each case was very similar. Two men, with mandau and kliau in their hands, begin first slowly walking round and round some distance apart, taking long strides, and stamping the feet with great force to the ground, uttering savage yells the while, gradually getting nearer to each other. A sort of sham fight ensues with the blunt side of the mandau. In "undress rehearsals" sticks of rattan are used instead of swords, and the arms and backs are padded with bark. The shouting increases as the fight gets hot; the bystanders join in; and a wild yelling takes place, which indicates pretty fairly the soundness of Dyak lungs.

Sometimes the performers wear a great wooden mask—a rude representation of the head of the alligator, a reptile for which the Dyaks show the greatest veneration and fear. A drawing of such a mask is shown in Plate 22, Fig. 4.

Music is never wanting. Besides the monotonous gongs and discordant tomtoms introduced by the Hindoos, various instruments of native manufacture are played. One is a two-stringed fiddle, called a djimpai (see Plate 19, Fig. 1), played with the fingers like a banjo. It is open at the back, and the strings are made of fine split rattan. A still more curious instrument, producing a pleasing organ-like tone, is called the kleddi (Plate 19, Fig. 3). It is composed of six tubes or pipes of bamboo stuck in a cluster into a gourd, the stalk of which forms the mouthpiece. The pipes are from twelve to nineteen inches long, each having a hole on which the fingers act like keys. At the top of the longest pipe is placed a short jointed piece of bamboo, which has no doubt something to do with regulating the tone. Mr. Augustus Franks, of the British Museum, has a Chinese book in which there is figured an instrument made in a very similar manner, but a much finer work of art. A third native instrument is a flute (Plate 19, Fig. 2), which is played through the nostril.

To the ordinary horrors of head-hunting—the simple murder of their victims for the sake of their heads as trophies, practised by all the Dyaks—the Bahou Tring tribe add the tenfold worse practices of cannibalism and offering of human sacrifices; not only killing their enemies according to the Dyak reading of the maxim "Live and let live,"—"Kill, or be killed,"—but taking captive those that they do not put to death and eat on the spot, and reserving them for slavery and ultimate death by torture.

When the chief of this tribe has decided to go out kidnapping and head-hunting, the people, women as well as men, are called together to confess. Should it appear that some youthful members have infringed the recognized laws of the tribe as regards marriage, or that the sanctity of the marriage vow has been violated, certain penalties are inflicted on the offending parties, such as a fine of a fowl or a pig; and when the offence is purged, and the moral character of the tribe is, according to their opinion, re-established, a prophet is sent out with twenty or thirty "penitents," to observe omens either in the air or in the woods. These penitents are youths who appear at birth to have had certain marks, signs of misfortune, on them, and who, in order to get the marks to disappear and to prevent the evil which their presence forebodes, must atone, or go through penitential performances, such as depriving themselves during a certain portion of their lives of salt or fish, or of every kind of clothing. This party of omen observers proceed a day's march into the depth of the forest, and regular communication is maintained between them and the rest of the village, so that they can be informed of anything that happens while they are away from home. Should any one die in the tribe they must return to the village, taking up their dwelling in a shed specially built for them. As soon as the funeral is over they resume their journey, not returning until they have satisfied themselves that the omens are favourable for the expedition about to be despatched.

Then the chief summons all the male members of the tribe, and when the preparations are complete—perhaps two or three months may elapse before this is the case—the armed party sets out to attack a neighbouring village belonging to another tribe. The attack is generally made in the early morning, after the people have taken breakfast, and a signal is given on a drum. The heads of the slain are taken off, and dried over a fire; these trophies are reserved for the chief, while the people must be satisfied with the meat of the bodies. The captives are made slaves, and also serve as sacrifices on certain occasions.

On the return of the party it is the custom to have a feast, called the *tiwah* feast, or death *fête*, which lasts ten days. These feasts are also held in celebration of various events, such as on the occasion of the death of a chief, and at them not only are the captives who have been taken prisoners in the marauding expeditions sacrificed, but the richer members of the community give a number of "slave debtors" to be put to death.

Mr. Perelaer describes a tiwah held in 1863 on the Upper Kahajan River, at the funeral of Tomongoeng Toendan, which lasted eight days, and at which forty slave debtors were slaughtered.

When the fatal day has arrived, a pole is fixed in the ground, having at its upper end a rudely-carved human head, with the tongue stretched at full length out of the mouth. This pole, usually made of ironwood, is called *sapoendoe*, and stands out of the ground a little more than the height of a man. At this post is the slave doomed to suffer martyrdom. Opposite him the youths and able-bodied men are drawn up in a row, armed with their lances and in full war attire, and step forward one after another to wound the wretched man, while the *balians* and *bassirs*[1] (priests and priestesses) howl a dismal song. When

[1] Dr. Schwaner and Mr. Perelaer both refer to these functionaries as being employed

many slaves are offered, their sufferings are relatively short, though never lasting less than one hour. If, however, the giver of the feast is not rich, and only a few slave debtors are killed, each unfortunate victim may stand three, four, or even six hours chained against this fatal pole. His tormentors purposely wound him but slightly, in order to satisfy to the utmost their thirst for blood; and the suffering wretch dies a lingering death, succumbing simply from loss of blood.

Nearly every village has its special symbol, in recognition of the distinction which its inhabitants have gained in successful head-hunting, consisting generally of a large wooden post placed in a conspicuous position in front of the village, ornamented with some local device or crest. At Long Wai this crest is merely a ball, with a spike on the top. At Dassa and Langla it was a monstrous head; at Long Puti, a figure representing a crowned Rajah in a very inelegant attitude. These posts are shown in Plates 7 and 27.

At Long Puti there were also a number of smaller posts, of all shapes and sizes, which I at first took for ordinary grave-stones; but which were also used, I have little doubt, as "death posts" at the Tiwah feasts.

Although an eye-witness of many of the incidents of Dyak life, I was not fortunate enough to be present at the various solemnities customary at a Dyak wedding or funeral. I obtained, however, much information through repeated inquiries among individuals of the various tribes through which I passed; and especially at several councils of Dyaks, held at different places at which I stopped for the special purpose of supplying me with authentic particulars. At these meetings I was accompanied by two Malays, who were fully acquainted with the Dyak language, and who wrote

in different parts of Borneo to act as mediators between the gods and the people, and on the occasion of a funeral to recite the virtues of the dead and make a request that he may be received into heaven. There are two classes of them, the Bassirs, who are men dressed as women, and the Bilians or Balians, who are women, the last named being the more influential of the two. Their chief functions are to make as much noise as possible. Dr. Schwaner and Mr. Perelaer state that these people, both men and women, are ordinarily occupied in various disgusting and immoral practices when not specially engaged at feasts, funerals, &c.

down the particulars in the Malay tongue. These records were afterwards translated for me by Mr. Seitz, late Assistant Resident at Koetei, and Mr. Emann, head clerk to the Resident at Bandjermasin, who was recommended to me as the best Malay scholar in Borneo.

The information thus obtained is given in the following notes on the ceremonies attending the marriage and death of a Rajah, and the birth of his children, and the feasts given when they receive their names and on their coming of age.

When a Rajah of the Tring Dyaks—the cannibal tribe—solicits the hand of a young girl in matrimony, he sends through a friend, never venturing on such a mission himself, to the object of his admiration a number of a certain kind of beads, named *loekot*, a brass basin, and some clothes; if the lady accepts these presents, the engagement is regarded as being formally contracted—much in the same way as the acceptance of the "engaged" ring completes the first formal stage in the marriage negotiations in England. After the expiration of one or two months, the bridegroom goes on a visit to the parents of the girl, remaining with them some time, and helping them in their daily occupations. This visit is of no specified duration, provided it does not last a year. At the close of the visit the bridegroom makes his bride a present of two slaves, and the marriage can then take place at any time. Still there are a few matters of etiquette to be observed. The bridegroom elect is strictly forbidden to eat off the same plate as his bride, nor must he partake of betel and sirih from the same box. As the time for the celebration of the nuptial ceremonies approaches, he gives the bridegroom's mother a quantity of rice, *ketan* (a sort of rice), some fowls and pigs; and the relations of both families are invited to participate in the marriage festivities.

The "order of matrimony" is celebrated in the following manner:—

The bride and bridegroom, who before have not enjoyed the privilege of sitting *vis à vis*, are on this occasion placed face to face on a copper tray, on which they sit holding one another by the hand. And now, during the thunder from small cannon, called *lilas*, one of the eldest male members of the assembled party steps forward, holding in his hand a mandau, which is dipped in the blood of a pig and a fowl. Smearing first the hand of the bridegroom, and then that of the bride, with the blood, he cries out the names of the male spirit "*Baak*," and the female spirit "*Hiroeh Bakak*," implores their protection, and recommends the married couple to their care, wishing them all sorts of earthly blessings. During this ceremony the guests give vent to their feelings by yelling and laughing.

This ceremony over, the members of the family set to work killing pigs, and making preparations for the feast, which, with music and dancing, lasts the rest of the day.

The following morning the bride and bridegroom are allowed to bathe together; and while they are going to the bathing-place, carrying their own clothes with them, noises are made on the gongs, while the wedding guests are witnesses to this other episode in the marriage vows. The fourth day after the marriage is a very important one, for on that day the married couple must observe omens, in which all Dyaks are great believers. For that purpose they go out of the house, and, taking with them a piece of rattan (the emblem of life), begin to look for something eatable from the vegetable kingdom—it may be either a fruit or a root, which afterwards serves as a dish in which they read their future.

The flight of birds is keenly watched by the Dyaks in all parts of Borneo, the movements of the hornbill and hawk, and the manner and direction of their flight, being especially regarded as emblematic of future events.

When the bridegroom perceives his wife to be in interesting circumstances he goes out head-hunting, and he is not allowed to return before he can bring one or more people's heads to lay at his wife's feet, or one or more captives to testify to his prowess. The more skulls he can bring, the more is he admired and loved by his wife, and the more feared and respected among his own tribe. On his return he is always entertained at a feast in celebration of his bravery. After the departure of her husband, the woman must go with the upper part of her body naked; but on his return she is allowed to put on a jacket. If the marriage is blessed with the birth of a son, the infant receives a mandau (sword), a kliau (shield), and a cap, as presents from the father. If it is a daughter, she receives as presents a short sarong, and a jacket made of the bark of a tree. The birth of the child is celebrated by the usual sounding of gongs throughout the village.

Then follows the ceremony of giving the child a name or names. On such an occasion the grand-parents on both sides give a feast, at which the baby is present, covered with a pisang or banana leaf, and the names are selected in accordance with the signs observed in the leaf.

The marriage rites observed by a Rajah of Long Wai or Long Wahou do not differ materially from those performed among the Trings. The bridegroom, however, instead of sending presents of beads to his chosen bride, sends his mandau to her father, and three days later the wedding presents are despatched, consisting of a couple of flags, some sarongs and mats, guns to be used for firing salutes, some pigs, and a special bed for the bride's use.

At Long Wahou the birth of a son is welcomed by the beating of drums, and the firing of guns; and these sounds are the signal for the infliction of a series of penalties on the father, who is forbidden for three days to drink water—he probably makes up for the deprivation by imbibing a large quantity of toewak—and who for five months must sleep and eat in solitude, and neither take salt with his food, chew sirih, nor smoke.

When the child is five months old the Rajah is at liberty to live as before, and commemorate his return to a rational existence by giving a great feast, at which pigs and fowls are the principal dishes in the bill of fare. After the feast is over the infant gets a name, and a month later another *slaamat* (feast) on a large scale follows. From 200 to 300 people from the Rajah's own country are invited; and friends are asked from other *negoreis* (districts). Wild boars and fowls are again killed, and on this occasion the *jambattan*, or bridges (I believe by this are meant the boards or gangways connecting all the houses, see view of Long Wai, (Plate 7), must be rebuilt, and the houses are palisaded with ironwood.

When the boy is "of age," say about fifteen years, he goes with other Dyaks to get *mengajoe* (heads). One trip is not deemed enough, but he makes four different excursions; and as soon as he has obtained one or more heads he is allowed to chew sirih and smoke, to wear a tassel of hair on his mandau, and ornament his ears with weighty rings and teeth, and last, but not least, to marry.

A Long Wai Rajah is not obliged to pay the same penalties of paternity as are exacted from a Long Wahou Rajah, but similar customs prevail as to the coming of age of the son.

Among the Tandjoengs a marriage cannot be celebrated until the sanction of the parents of the girl has been obtained. They also fix a certain number of household and other utensils to be given to their daughter. If the man cannot give the required goods from his own means, or through the help of others, the marriage cannot be concluded; but when he has brought what is required to the house of his future mother-in-law, the indispensable Balians are called, who for three days perform certain secret and mysterious acts, in which banana blossoms play a great part. When they have terminated their witchcraft, they bless the happy pair, and the marriage ceremony takes place.

Polygamy is not forbidden among the Dyaks, though only practised by the chiefs.

The "last scene of all" in the "strange eventful history" of a Dyak Rajah is an elaborate performance, occupying several days, and varying very much in detail in different districts.

Among the Bahou Tring Dyaks, the cannibals of Borneo, the following rites are observed on the death of a chief: The death of the Rajah is announced by the beating of a gong, on hearing which the people at once proceed to the house of the deceased. Whilst they are gathered there the chief's body is washed and afterwards rubbed in with salt, and dressed in his best apparel, and placed in a sitting posture; in his hands are placed his shield and mandau. After some time, the arms are taken away, the body is undressed, wrapped in a piece of cloth, and placed carefully on the ground. Whilst the garments are being removed, a singer stands close by and chants a hymn, in which he describes the road which the departed must travel, in order to come to his tribe in the other world.

The dead wanders first, according to the singer, to a river named *Biraie tanggalan*, to cross which he has to make or get made a canoe and paddles. He then turns his steps to the mountain *Toekoeng Daijang*, and goes on till he comes to another river called *Loeng*, afterwards climbing the mountain *Piloeng*, where he meets one man of his tribe. The journey is continued to the river *Danoemlang* (valley of tears), where the wandering spirit encounters several men, women, and children, to whom he must give clothes. Leaving this Valley of Tears, he comes to a great caterpillar, to which he must give some *kladi* (a certain plant), and then he goes up the mountain *Limatak*, where he sees a lot of flies and also a big bear: to the bear he must make a present of a pig. Going further, he meets a man who holds an iron weir (bow net), to whom he must offer pisangs and sugar-cane, so that he can proceed unmolested on his way. Further on he comes to a river, which is watched by a man named *Tamai Patakloeng*, to whom he must give the barbules which grow round the mouth of a certain species of fish (sp. of *Silurus*). After this he meets a woman, *Hadau Daliau* by name, who is busy stamping rice; as she is anxious to persuade him to help her, he must avoid her and pursue his journey quickly: proceeding further he comes to a fire in the middle of the road, which he has no sooner passed than he encounters a woman with a pair of ears large enough for him to take shelter under from the rain. The next objects that meet his eye are the stems of two trees, over one of which he must jump, while the other he must cut in two with his mandau. If the deceased is a woman she must cut this tree over with her knife. On going further the spirit comes to the mountain *Goelhoeli*, and as soon as he has begun to ascend the mountain he feels that he does not belong any more to this world. Presently a very narrow road leads to a forest called *Noea pirau*, where the deceased meets his parents and a woman named *Alanpatai*. Next, the river *Soengei Tali Barouw* has to be passed, in which he takes a bath, and another mountain has to be surmounted. After all these fatigues, the spirit is refreshed by eating some fruit, and at last he is safely landed in the heaven of his tribe.

As a reward for instructing the spirit in the details of the long and intricate journey it has to perform, the singer receives the clothes, mandau, and shield of the deceased. The following day, the members of the tribe are again gathered together, and as a sign of mourning shave off the hair from the head,[2] and also tear off either their sarong or their jacket, and run about with the upper or lower part of the body naked; this mourning lasts until they have had a "good harvest," by which is generally meant a few heads. When the people are all assembled, and have all adopted these signs of mourning, the body is placed in the coffin and brought to a chapel, those who are carrying the body, and the clothes which have to be deposited with the dead, taking great care that they do not stumble or fall, as such an occurrence is considered an omen that the fallen will not live long. At the tomb are generally placed four wooden idols, representing tigers, whose souls—for the Dyaks believe that every object has a soul—are to act as servants for the good Rajah in the other world. As soon as the coffin is deposited in the chapel, the people return home and have a funeral feast, which lasts one month.

At Long Wai the following is the ceremonial observed on the occasion of a Rajah's death and burial. As soon as the Rajah has breathed his last the drums and gongs are set going to a particular beat or tune, called *tomoeng*, a sort of "Dead March," on hearing which the people gather together without delay at the place where their dead ruler lies. Here the various duties connected with the funeral solemnities are assigned to different persons; some have to make bridges, others to cut the prau-shaped coffin, which is hewn bodily out of the trunk of a tree; others, again, to carve idols of wood—hideous representations of bears (*thoeng*) and leopards (*lahdjio*) or men. When these are all ready, the body is brought to a place where it is washed; and then, covered with a piece of white calico, it is brought back to the house and placed on a great wooden plank, and attired in the costume ordinarily worn by the Rajah when alive. Over the body is then erected an attap roof, which is, however, afterwards removed; then the

[2] This method of showing mourning is also practised in Africa by the Wanyóro people. (See "Journal einer Reise von Mrúli," &c., by Dr. Ermin Bey. "Petermann's Mittheilungen." May 8, 1879.

people present call on the Rajah's predecessors, and sing, or rather shout, till they are exhausted. After this the Rajah's body is undressed, his mandau and blowing tube are fixed in his right hand, and his shield in his left. A woman (probably a professional, belonging to the order Dr. Schwaner calls *Bilians*) takes her seat next to the deceased, and begins to speak to him, telling him what to do—that he must go straight ahead, neither turning to the right nor to the left, and that he must not be afraid should he meet any one howling or crying. When this woman has uttered the necessary admonitions, the body is placed in the coffin, being laid on a nice cushion, under which is a mat of the best quality; while between the cushion and the mat money is deposited, and the hands of the dead man are filled with gold. At his head, and also at his feet, is placed copper *traij* (a sort of gong), as well as his different costumes of any value.

For three days the people are praying and dancing round the coffin, and a special dance is performed by five women and two men. Fashion evidently alters even among the Dyaks, for it is a *sine quâ non* that these people must be dressed in costumes from *tempo doelo* (times gone by). The women hold in their hand a mandau, and on their head is fastened a living red fowl. One of the men has only a mandau; while the other has a drum. The drummer runs eight times round the coffin; then he rests a little. Presently he trots again, but only seven times. When this is finished the coffin is placed under the house, where the praying is continued, and again the drummer performs the circuit of the coffin, first eight and then seven times. The poor Rajah's bones are not yet fairly at rest; he is carried in his coffin to a small house specially built for the purpose, whither also the idols (*tambatongs*) are taken, as well as the skulls of the various people the Rajah has murdered. After six days are over the minor people are permitted to pay their last respects to the departed chief. The coffin is now brought to its final resting-place—the "mausoleum"—with a procession arranged in the following order: Before the coffin proceed the two men who had taken part in the dancing round the coffin, both now armed with a mandau, and one of them playing a drum. Behind the corpse come the five women, one holding a mandau, and another a red fowl. When the procession is close to the graveyard the coffin is placed in a small enclosure or shed without a roof, and the two men take lances and throw them against the coffin, which is now placed in the mausoleum, while a number of idols are left outside, either stuck in the ground or hung on the posts supporting the building.

Among the Long Wai Dyaks the following is the journey which each departed spirit is supposed to perform. Immediately after death the spirit goes to a certain tree called *Patoeng*, or *Wateng Ladji*, resembling a carved idol, which lies across his path. Going on further, the spirit comes to a kampong (village), the head of which is a woman named *Dijon Ladji*. Proceeding still further, the departed comes to another village, where the chief is also a woman, named *Dikat Toewan Ballang*. Still wandering, the dead arrives at the third village, the name of whose chief, also a female, is *Longding Dakka Patai*. On the spirit goes to another kampong, whose chief is named *Kapung Lunding Dakago*; and again to a fifth village, where another female chief is met, by name *Longding Dahak*.

We have followed the departed through no less than five villages or kampongs. The scene now changes to a river running from a mountain called *Lung Mandin*; this stream is of course sacred, and is guarded by two women, one named *Talik Bong Daong*, the other *Sasong Luing Daong*. The country where the river runs, and wherein all these kampongs are situated, is known by the general name of *Long Luing*. As the confused story here ends, I presume the dead is now lodged in Paradise.

The funeral obsequies of a Rajah of Long Wahou again are different. The body is first washed—not by ordinary members of Dyak society, but by those who are of rajah descent—and dressed in the every-day clothes of the deceased, whose mortal remains are then deposited on the floor under the house, where he usually sat during life. One of the principal chiefs must accompany the body

* In the translation of the narrative the expression "across the road" is used, but, unless the Dyak spirit land is much better organized than the Dyak earth, the term cannot be taken literally, as I never saw a track worthy to be called a path, much less a road, in any part of the interior of Borneo.

below; and meanwhile the carpenters are set to work to get the coffin made, being paid for their services with the Rajah's money. As soon as the coffin is ready, the body is placed in it, and two gongs, one at the head and one at the feet, as well as all the clothes worn by the Rajah, especially his war costumes, are also deposited in the coffin. After the expiration of six days the population come, men, women, and children, and wish the deceased a happy journey. The coffin is now placed in a small house, where the people again assemble, to repeat their good wishes for the safe journey of their chief to the Dyak heaven. Here the corpse lies a month, during which time the people must not work, and Dyaks from other districts are not allowed to come near. In the meantime, however, word is sent round in the late Rajah's country to his friends to look for heads; as many as possible of these horrid trophies are desired, for according to Dyak belief the beheaded people will be slaves to the deceased Rajah in heaven. These heads are fixed on the top of posts, which are erected round the Rajah's final resting-place, each head on a separate post, the ceremony of fixing the heads being accompanied by the beating of gongs. The heads are eventually removed from the poles and hung on the trees near the river. All these ceremonies are the occasion for a succession of feasts, during which a great number of pigs and poultry are killed, and plenty of powder wasted, for all Dyaks are very fond of the noise of fire-arms, and burn powder whenever they have an opportunity. And when the feasting is all over, it is time to think of erecting a monument to the Rajah's memory; this consists of a large carved wooden figure, intended to represent the dead Rajah, which is honoured by the very name of the deceased, and receives the same marks of honour as the Dyaks accorded to their chief when he was alive.

As to the spirit journey of a Long Wahou Dyak, the following is the legend which obtains credence in that tribe. The Long Wahou Dyak believes that when he dies he will go *back* to heaven, as if he had originally come from thence. This heaven is divided into different sections or apartments, one of which is named Kong-kong. When the dead has been there a little while, he begins to cultivate rice. A Dyak who has been murdered cannot go to the Kong-kong heaven, but remains in another one, and does nothing there but fighting and murdering. Women who have died through illness go to Kong-kong, but those who have died in child-bed are, strange to say, doomed to the heaven where the murdered men are.

Closely connected with the Dyak religious belief is the absurd custom of *pomali*, which is practised also by the Alfuros of Celebes and Timor, and in the Mentawei Islands. It is allied to the *tembu* or *tabu* of the South Sea Islanders.

The only outward indication that pomali is being resorted to is a bundle of maize leaves stuck into the ground, or bushels of rice suspended from a bamboo post, either in a rice-field or under the house of a person who is ill. All strangers are forbidden to cross the threshold of a house where this signal is placed. Twice I was about to enter a Dyak house, when I was forbidden to go further, and the symbol of *pomali* was pointed out to me. On inquiring for what reason I was prohibited from entering, I was told that Satan was in the room with a sick man, and the good spirits were being invoked to drive him away and cure him of his illness.

I could not, however, gain much information on the subject, as the natives were very unwilling to give me any details. All I can state with certainty is that three sorts of pomali are practised among both Dyaks and Malays in Koetei, the latter still adhering to many heathen customs. The first is for a good harvest, and is commonly practised for almost every crop; the second is for the sick; and the third for the dead.[4]

[4] Mr. Hugh Low in his "Sarawak" also mentions three kinds of *Pomali*, or as he calls it *Pamali*. The following is his interpretation :—" The first, *Pamali Mati*, is on a house, and on everything in it, for twelve days after the decease of any person belonging to it. During this time no one who is not an inhabitant of the dwelling can enter it, nor are the persons usually residing in it allowed to speak to such, nor can anything, on any pretence whatever, be removed from it until the twelve days of the prohibition be expired. Its conclusion is marked by the death of a fowl or pig, according to the circumstances of the family.

" The *Pamali Peniakit* is undertaken by a whole village during any sickness which prevails generally amongst the members of the tribe. It is marked by a pig slain, and a feast being made in order to propitiate the divinity who has sent the malady among them. In its severest form it is of eight days' continuance, and during this

Although the Dyaks place such faith in their *tambatongs*, or charms, attributing wonderful virtues and power over evil spirits to them, they are not idolaters in the sense of kneeling down and praying to these objects. They all believe in an Almighty Being, known as Mahatara, Hatalla, or Allah (from the Arabic), and they believe that every organic being is endowed with a soul.

At Moeara Pahou I met a number of Tandjoeng Bantang Dyaks, who believe in two gods, one a male, the other a female, besides spirits, which are lodged in certain species of trees. The members of this tribe do not make charms, either of wood or of stone. They differ also from the other tribes in the fact that they do not as a rule tattoo : I saw one with an ordinary cross tattooed on his arm. Neither do they all wear earrings; and those that do are content women as well as men, with very small holes in the ears.

Weddik's "Overzigt van Het Rijk van Koetei," in *Indisch. Archief*,

period everything in the village is at a standstill, the inhabitants shutting themselves up from all intercourse with strangers. This form of Pamali prevented my personally visiting the *Brâng* and *Sipanjang* tribes, as they were under the taboo when I was in their vicinity for a kind of dysentery which was prevalent among them.

"The *Pamali Peniakit* is also undertaken by individuals when any member of the family is sick; thus, parents often put themselves under its regulations, fondly hoping that by denying themselves for a time the pleasures of intercoursé with their fellow-creatures, they will prevail upon the malignant spirit, which is supposed to have shed its withering influence over their offspring to restore it to its wonted health and strength. *Bye Ringate*, the chief of the Sennah Dyaks, was dying from a severe dysentery. His children told me, sorrowing, when I visited their village, that pigs had been killed, and the great Pamali had been tried in vain, and that a person who had come from a distant tribe had also failed to effect a cure, and as a last resource they wished to have some medicine from the Europeans. On returning I sent some pills to him, which Dr. Treacher, the clever surgeon at Sarawak, had given me for the purpose; and though, when he found himself get better from their effects, he took more of them than he should have done, we had the satisfaction of hearing that he had perfectly recovered. I never visited the tribe after this occurrence, but should suppose that it must have shaken their belief in the Pamali, and established the reputation of the European doctor in its place.

"The *Pamali Omar*, or taboo on the farms, occurs immediately after the whole of the seed is sown. It lasts four days, and during that period no person of the tribe enters any of the plantations on any account; a pig and feast are, according to their practice, also necessary.

"The proper observance of these various forms of Pamali is probably amongst the most ancient of their customs, and was practised by their tribes previously to the introduction of the Hindu religion."

for 1849, pp. 136, 137, gives more details about the Tandjoengs than I was able to ascertain. According to him they believe in a Supreme Being, to whom they give the name of *Naijoekh Seniejoeng*. He is the fountain of all good—rich harvests, success in their undertakings, a numerous offspring, &c. All misfortunes they attribute to evil spirits, to drive which away is only in the power of *Naijoekh Seniejoeng*, whose assistance they therefore implore.

Near the village of Radjoèkh stands a solitary Niboeng tree, planted by an evil spirit (*hantoe*) and no Tandjoeng dare approach it, much less touch it.

As already stated, the Sultan of Koetei tried some years ago to convert the Long Wai Dyaks to Islam. He sent a head priest among them for the purpose, but hardly had the missionary begun by telling the Dyaks of the extreme sensual enjoyment in the Mohammedan Paradise, and of the earthly privileges of being allowed four wives, instead of one, when he was assassinated—and here ended the missionary labours. The Sultan has nominally converted the two Rajahs at Long Wai, who embraced Mohammedanism for the fascination of being allowed several wives. For the rest, they adhere strongly to all the rites of their tribes handed down to them from generation to generation.

CHAPTER XXIII.

Up the Barito again—Nagara—Amontai—A fertile district—Barabai—An equine apparition—Result of the search for the men with tails—The tail-people of the Sultan of Passir—The journey to Mindai—Destructive squirrels—A hunter at home—Mindai—Collecting specimens—A novel mode of burglary—A visit from the chief of the hillmen or Orang Bukkit—Chopping up an idol—Characteristics of the Orang Bukkit—Their dress and ornaments—A hot mineral spring—A counterfeit coiner—The scaly ant-eater—The säät or gobang—Tiger-cats and leopards—The binturong—The long-nosed and other monkeys—Remarkable vitality of the kukang—The rhinoceros—Crocodiles and other reptiles—Back to Bandjermasin—Mosquitoes—Fishing with poison—A storm in the Barito—Packing up—Von Gaffron—Good-bye—Homeward-bound.

After I had sufficiently recovered in health I left Bandjermasin on the 26th of January, accompanied by Kichil and Tan He Wat, who had both proved themselves faithful servants, for the Amontai district. Mr. Meijer kindly placed at my disposal the small Government steamer "Ceylus." This mode of transport was vastly superior to the native vessels, here called *djoekongs* or *sampangs*, in which, "cribbed, cabined, and confined," one has no room to take the slighest exercise. From the loftier deck of the steamer, the Barito seemed now to present an entirely different aspect from its appearance as I had descended it a few weeks previously. The long low flat mud-banks seemed less monotonous than before, with the distant background of hills in sight, and the many aquatic birds disporting themselves on the foreshore.

About five p.m. we arrived at Moeara Bahan or Bekompai. The "Ceylus" took coals in here; and as it was a fine moonlight evening the captain steamed up the Nagara all through the night, in order to reach Amontai by noon on the following day. Soon after four o'clock we came to the large town of Nagara, and for more than two hours we steamed past the long line of houses.

Even at this early hour the inhabitants were on the move, and in front of every habitation stood a group of men, women, and children, watching the "Ceylus" as she passed.

Nagara is a busy place. Its muskets and swords (*klewangs*) are known all over the East, but the Dutch have of late prohibited the manufacture of arms. The iron is got from the Doesoen district. There are also large brickyards and potteries, the pottery ware being noted for its brittleness, the cause of which probably lies in the burning, as the clay is of good quality. There are also a number of boatbuilders here, who make excellent large boats of ironwood. The women make mats and attap roofs from the leaves of the sago palm, of which there are very extensive plantations. The place is unusually well supplied by nature; not only is the land very fertile, but the river and the numerous *danaus* and tributary rivulets swarm with fish and freshwater shrimps, and the banks are frequented by immense flocks of a small species of wild duck, called *belibit*, which is very good eating, and of which large quantities are sent to Bandjermasin, and even to Java; the selling price is about five-pence each. In addition, large herds of semi-domesticated buffaloes roam about the fields in the neighbourhood. Nagara finds a market for all its produce in Bandjermasin.

In no part of Borneo have I seen so thick a population as round Nagara and Amontai, the next village higher up the river. If the population of the whole island bore any proportion to the numbers located in these two districts, it would resemble Java; and I am far from saying that Borneo could not support such a mass of people. On the authority of the Assistant-Resident I give the population of the district of Nagara as over 300,000; still that number I thought below the mark.

The country has flourished wonderfully since it came under Dutch rule. At the time when Dr. Schwaner travelled here he estimated the population at 60,000; Melvill, later, calculated it at 120,000; and Müller again set it down at 100,000. True, these estimates were made more than fifty years ago; but reckoning that the population has increased in that time by 200,000 souls the increase has been at the rate of 4000 people a year.

Amontai was reached on the 27th, at noon. This place is now the peaceful centre of a district which a few years ago was the scene of a lengthened guerilla war. The people, who were of a very unruly nature, are now fairly quiet and contented, and the task of governing them, though still no sinecure, is comparatively easy. The Resident certainly always finds plenty to occupy his attention, and has to display considerable tact in dealing with his somewhat fanatical "subjects." With the assistance of two Controlleurs, one at Barabai, and one at Tandjoeng, and a few native writers to transact all the civil business, and with a couple of hundred soldiers to inspire respect, Mr. Clausz manages to keep in order the most populous district in Borneo. Mr. Clausz kindly offered me hospitality, while my men had no difficulty in finding quarters in the village. Tan He Wat was delighted to see some of his countrymen here, and, as usual, he soon managed to find out some one with whom he could claim relationship. Amontai is the centre of a great fruit-growing district. Numbers of small canoes come down from Tandjoeng laden with unripe fruit, which is reshipped here in larger vessels for the great market at Bandjermasin. Sago is largely cultivated, and thrives wonderfully well in the morasses, which extend for a considerable distance on each side of the river.

The whole country is low and flat, and no place for a naturalist, so I determined to go on to Barabai. With two praus, and still accompanied by Kichil and Tan He Wat, I passed a short distance up the Belangan, and thus into the Krias or Karias, an "antassan" in course of formation, the water coming from the Kambat River, and so narrow that it was with the greatest difficulty that the praus, though little more than three feet wide, could pass up. We met several praus laden with fruit and sago root, and it was only by forcing a passage through the high reeds that lined the banks that we were able to pass each other. Then numbers of herons and snipes were disturbed in their retreat, and, worse still, legions of mosquitoes revenged themselves upon us for intruding on their privacy. After several hours' struggling through the wilderness of reeds we emerged into the Kambat, a wide stream, with a stiff current running down against us. At Batu

Kanga my canoe journey came to an end. Here I was surprised to meet a fellow-countryman, Dr. Michael Cohen, one of the many foreign medical men in the Dutch service, who accompanied me to Barabai. Mr. Dannenbargh, the controller at Barabai, had kindly sent a horse for my use; and, as Dr. Cohen and I rode side by side beneath the shelter of the cocoa-nut palms, many of the women and children would run out of the houses that lined the road at our approach, and retreat again as quickly, half afraid at the unaccustomed sight of a couple of men riding on the backs of two strange animals. Horses have only been introduced into this part of Borneo during the last few years, and their use is still confined to the Dutch officials. The natives, who had never seen a horse before, manifested the greatest curiosity when the first mounted official rode among them; and down to the present day the women and children are very much afraid at the sight of these animals, especially when ridden by a man.

In the distance was the mountain chain dividing the Dutch territory from Passir, where, according to current belief, the race of tailed men dwell, in search of whom I had sent Tjiropon.

One day, while staying in Bandjermasin, I heard that Tjiropon had returned. I was surprised that he did not come to me to announce the results of his search for the tailed race; and when I sent for him his face gave no token either of success or failure as he entered my room. For a long time all the answer I got to my questions was a shake of the head, which, though so far conclusive, did not afford sufficiently detailed information. I questioned him long and vainly as to the why and the wherefore of the failure of his mission. Presently he made a meagre statement, to the effect that he had seen the Sultan of Passir, and had delivered to him the letter from his Highness of Koetei, but he had seen no tailed people. Beyond this I could get no explanation. Somehow old Tjiropon seemed utterly crestfallen. Was he thinking of the 500 guilders which I had promised him if he brought me a pair of the interesting people? I tried to cheer him up, and asked him about the nature of the country and the people through which he had passed, but could get nothing out of him. At last he suddenly exclaimed, "Before Allah! I *have* seen the *Orang boentoet* long ago, and have spoken to them, but I could not see them this time."

I was not satisfied to leave the question thus unsettled, and without saying anything more to Tjiropon I determined to send another party into Passir, and sought the assistance of the Resident of Bandjermasin, who kindly furnished me with a letter to the Sultan of that country, asking him, if a race of tailed men really existed in or near to Passir, to give me full particulars, and if possible to send me two of them. Several obstacles, however, presented themselves. In the first place, it was difficult to get men to go into Passir at all. The people had the reputation of being among the most ferocious in Borneo. At Amontai, however, with the assistance of Mr. Clausz I got four Malays, on the strength of the protection afforded by the Resident's letter, and by the promise of a large gratuity, to undertake the mission. Another difficulty presented itself. I wanted a written reply to my letter, as I gravely doubted whether Tjiropon had ever delivered the former missive; but Mr. Clausz' assistant said the Sultan of Passir could not write a letter, although he was able to write his name. However he engaged for me a Malay writer, who would note down what the Sultan said, and get his Highness to sign the "deposition." After twenty-five days' absence the party returned with an interesting communication from the Sultan of Passir. It appeared that Tjiropon had after all delivered the letter from the Sultan of Koetei, in which the latter potentate asked his royal cousin to send him two of the *Orang boentoet*, or "tail people;" but the letter had been misunderstood by the Sultan of Passir. The suite in attendance upon him were known collectively as the *Orang boentoet di Sultan di Passir*—literally the "tail people of the Sultan of Passir;" and his Highness, taking offence at the supposed request of his brother ruler that two of his personal attendants—in fact, his confidential men—should be sent to him, had waxed exceeding wroth, and, calling Tjiropon before him, had ordered him to depart immediately. "If the Sultan of Koetei wants my *Orang boentoet*," said he, "let him fetch them himself."

And so the Sultan of Passir, expecting an attack from the

Sultan of Koetei in response to this challenge, had been arming himself ever since, erecting fortifications, and preparing for war. The letter from Mr. Meijer had satisfactorily explained matters, and put his Highness at his ease. His mistake was, perhaps, pardonable, for he sent word that the only *Orang boentoet* he had ever heard of were those, so called, forming his suite.

Meanwhile I was advised to go on to Mindai as the most likely district for collecting birds and animals in abundance. So I ordered twenty-four coolies, and on Saturday, the 31st January, we started, the coolies in advance, carrying the boxes, slung—one between two men—on stout bamboo poles. The road lay through a thickly inhabited district, with plantations of the sago-palm and cocoa-nut palm on all sides. The former trees are cultivated here on a scale of magnitude unrivalled anywhere in the south of Borneo, chiefly for the sake of the leaves, which are used for thatching the houses and for making mats. The root is also eaten, but the people do not understand the method of preparing the sago of commerce.

Wherever there are cocoa-nut plantations squirrels are abundant, and it forms one of the chief amusements of the native boys to kill these graceful but destructive creatures, with arrows shot from a blowing tube. By means of their sharp incisors the squirrels gnaw a hole in the top of the cocoa-nuts, through which they drink the milk or juice.

Not only here, but in all parts of south-eastern Borneo, squirrels of many kinds are common. They are shot by the Dyaks for the sake of their flesh, which is said to be excellent.

And now we came to the village of Biraijan, or Greijan, another populous village, with over 2000 Malays, situated on the banks of the Batu-Kijau, which are here from thirty to fifty feet high. The whole village is imbedded in a mass of cocoa-nut palms, which thrive here remarkably well, and attain a great height. Here the Controlleur at Barabai had told me I should find a valuable guide, Lora by name, who knew the country well, and was a good hunter, possessed of great personal courage. It was not long before we succeeded in hunting down this hunter in his home. He was a powerfully built man, with a keen and intelligent look, and an expression which showed that he was not easily to be deceived. A peculiar appearance was given to his face by the fact that he had only one ear. It appeared that some years ago he had had a quarrel with a Dyak, who had cut his right ear clean off. The best surgeon in Europe could not have performed the operation more skilfully. Every particle of the ear was gone, and not a mark to show that any other part of the head had been touched. In return for this delicate attention Lora had paid his adversary the compliment of cutting his head off. Mr. Dannenbargh had warned me to be on the alert, as Lora had not a particularly good character for honesty, or for good temper. The whole population of Biraijan feared and hated him at the same time. He had enjoyed for a time the civic honour of *kapala kampong*, or chief of the village. According to his own account he had begged the Controlleur to relieve him of his duties; but the real fact was that he was short in the cash-box—like his predecessors and successors—after having collected the poll-taxes.

At all events he proved a most useful guide, and was quite aware of the value of his services. We stayed at his house—the best in the village—and were treated to a sumptuous repast of boiled rice, salted eggs, dried fish, and above all the delicious fried prawns so common in most of the rivers. Lora served the feast in quite orthodox style, covering the table with a piece of white calico, and providing an armchair and two plain chairs for his guests. Among other symbols of civilization which his household boasted were a European bedstead, a Swiss clock, and a lithograph portrait of King William of Holland, which he pointed to with pride in proof of his loyalty.

The next stage was Laboehan, a distance of ten miles through fruit plantations, intersected here and there by patches of forest, and with houses at frequent intervals along the road. In some durian trees I saw several loetongs (*Semnopithecus pruniosus*), and Lora shot two; but the skins were spoiled by the large shots going through the head.

When we reached Laboehan, a village peopled by a mixed race of Dyaks and Malays, Lora called a meeting in the evening, and told the men that I would buy all sorts of animals, dead or alive.

There were four animals—met with in great abundance here—which Lora specially told the men to get for me, both alive and dead: the *Tangiling* or scaly ant-eater, the *Săăt* or skunk, the wildcat (*Felis planiceps*), and the civet-cat (*Paradoxura musanga*); the two last-named animals were caught in traps, the others with the hands as towards evening they came out of their retreats in search of food. He then addressed a flock of little boys, telling them to look for insects and shells, and they would get *doits*.[1] They of course were delighted, and promised to look; but when, a fortnight afterwards, we inquired on our return for the results of their search, we found their newly evoked ardour had cooled before the sun had set.

The next day (February 2nd) I left Laboehan by daybreak, after having had some difficulty with the natives, who were unaccustomed to coolie work, and complained of the weight of my boxes. They began quarrelling among themselves who should have the lightest, some of them saying they had sore feet—quite a common complaint amongst any native porters! The road, too, was very bad, they said, along a muddy path in the forest and across two rivers. So I divided the luggage into equal portions, and after some trouble and many exclamations of *Brat, brat, sekali* (Heavy, heavy, to be sure), we managed to get the boxes on their backs and make a start. The road lay through bamboo groves, with an occasional rice-field. The first village we approached was Batu Kijau, situated on the river of the same name, which is navigable as far as Amontai.

After an hour's walk we got into a mountainous district, and made our way through a valley, with lofty mountains rising almost perpendicularly on both sides. One mountain, the Baloe, was almost a perfect cone, sprinkled with trees all over, while round the foot the natives cultivated rice-fields. We had to cross the river Batu Kijau again, and a smaller stream called Loman, the water in both of which was at the time fortunately not much above the knees. Then the country became covered with forest; the path was often knee-deep in mud, with a thick layer of troublesome stones at the bottom.

[1] 5 doits = 1 penny.

At two o'clock we came to Mindai, ten miles from Laboehan, a "village" consisting of but two miserable huts, between which there was not much to choose. I selected the one nearest the river—a bamboo shed sixteen feet long by eight feet wide, and only a foot elevated from the ground. It was occupied by a Malay, his wife, and a baby. I do not think they were much pleased at receiving four more guests, even for the "consideration" of a few dollars as rent for the time being. The roof was not at all waterproof, so Lora and the landlord at once set to work to patch the holes with the aid of some palm-leaves. The furniture was equal to the architecture of the house—a few mats, half-a-dozen thick bamboos for water, and a couple of earthen pots for cooking purposes standing in a small part of the house partitioned off from the rest, and known as the kitchen. The hearth consisted of three stones resting on a heap of ashes. Of *articles de luxe* the family possessed a little basket containing tobacco and sirih, while on the wall hung a very nice two-stringed fiddle. I tried more than once to buy this instrument, and offered at last a sovereign for it, but the woman was quite unwilling to part with it. The couple were not indolent; they had not been long settled here, but had already cleared a considerable patch of forest from the hills behind the hut, and planted there bananas and cocoa-nuts, and were now occupied in making *ladangs* (rice-fields.)

We made ourselves as comfortable as possible under the circumstances, and next morning I was up early, and went into the forest to look for insects and shells. I found a small cyclostoma in great abundance—the *Pterocyclos Loweanus*—on the moist earth and amongst dead leaves. A little boy who had been watching me quietly for some time came up, and showing me a large but dead shell of the *Helix Brookei*—the largest snail species in Borneo—asked if I wanted "*isri bangsa*" (this sort). I offered him twenty-five cents apiece for all that he brought perfect, and with the animal; but the little fellow shook his head, and said they were difficult to procure. In my wanderings I came across a number of huts scattered about here and there on the woody hillside, and the natives gradually became accustomed to me, while a number of lads came and offered to collect on the same terms as I had offered to the other; but during the time I stayed here they only procured four good live specimens of the *Helix Brookei*, proving that this is an exceedingly rare shell in this part of Borneo, though common, I hear, in Sarawak. They also brought me a sinistral Helix of a dark, reddish-brown colour, which I found to be new, and which I propose to call *Helix Mindaiensis*.

I had expected that coleoptera would have been abundant, owing to the fact that the hills had just been cleared for cultivation, but was very much disappointed in this respect. Though I had a number of active little boys, who came every morning anxious to earn a few coppers, I found none.

Two or three days after my arrival here, my Chinaman and Lora came to warn me that they had discovered that the natives meant to rob me. Lora told me he had seen two men from Biraijan, who had nothing whatever to do in this mountain wilderness except to attempt to steal some luggage from me. He explained to me the common way of entering houses and stealing. First, the thief would enter the hut and sit down quietly—never asking permission, of course, as most natives invite themselves—and while talking would take a survey of the room, and see where the boxes or chests were placed. At night he would crawl under the hut, remove a portion of the flooring, and open the boxes from the bottom, and thus extract the contents. Lora asked permission to shoot any one that came near the hut during the night. "Certainly," I replied, "shoot as much you like." Whether the would-be-thieves were deterred by the fact of our being well armed or not, we fortunately escaped their polite attentions. As a safeguard against such depredations by robbers, it is well to change the position of the chests every evening, and to place them at night on trestles or logs of wood, so that when the robber has broken through the floor he can be at once discovered.

In the mountains a few miles off live a race of Dyaks known as Orang Bukkit (hillmen)—a mixed race of Dyaks and Malays, but with more of the Malay blood in them. The prominent cheekbones are the principal feature indicating their Dyak descent.

A few days after my arrival here I received a visit from the chief of the Orang Bukkit, Tomongoeng by name, accompanied by half a dozen of his men. They all wore the ordinary tjawat of dark-blue shirting, but the chief was distinguished from the rest by a short red-and-white-striped flannel jacket. Tomongoeng was very thin; the cheek bones were especially prominent, and the eyes and cheeks deeply sunken; his ears were pierced with small holes, in each of which hung a leaden ring the size of a finger-ring; on his head, the hair of which was getting grey, he wore a blue head-cloth. I took him to be about fifty years of age. He appeared idiotic, looking at me with a vacant expression and a half-look of fear, his mouth half-open all the time. He begged me for a cigar, which he lighted the wrong end; and after smoking a few whiffs he gave it to a younger brother who was with him, and who did the same, returning the remainder to Tomongoeng, who put the stump into his tobacco-box. Tomongoeng had an eye to business, for he offered me a couple of fowls for sale, asking one guilder each for them. When I told him I did not want them, he calmly replaced his fowls under his arm, and at once walked home with them. I wanted to go back with him, or at least to return his call; but Lora told me his brother was very ill, and that he could not receive me; so I was prevented from visiting the chief of the Dyaks of the Mindai district in his own home. However, I saw numbers of his people, and met Tomongoeng himself on two or three subsequent occasions.

These people occupy the whole range of mountains running in a southerly direction, and dividing the Dutch territories from the independent States, beginning with Passir, Tanah Boemboe, and Pagattan; they are heathens, and very superstitious and inquisitive. Like the other Dyaks, they have implicit confidence in their tambatongs, of which they have a considerable number, mostly carved wooden images, very roughly wrought. Tomongoeng gave me one, about four feet long—a rude representation of a crocodile, made of plain wood, with the eyes and teeth of the monster painted black. It was not worth the trouble and expense of transporting, so one day, to the great amusement of my men, I told my cook to use it for firewood. Tomongoeng happened to come by just as the flames were devouring the image, but did not say anything. Like all Dyaks, they dislike anything in the shape of Government authority. Lora told me they are liable to pay poll-tax, but it is often difficult to get anything out of them They are poor and indolent in the extreme, troubling themselves little with the cultivation of their *ladangs* (rice-fields), but preferring to grow djagong (maize), nangka, kladi, katjang, &c.

One remarkable feature in their domestic economy is that they do *not* go head-hunting; and, to my great astonishment, Lora assured me that head-hunting does not even belong to their *adat* (custom). To the best of my knowledge, this is the only tribe of Dyaks who do not practise head-hunting, or who do not include the horrid custom among their statutes or beliefs.

I cannot describe the Bukkits as other than an ugly people; their appearance betokened extreme poverty, and great lack of intelligence. The only dress of the men consisted of a tjawat, some made of stamped bark, others of cloth; and a head-covering composed of a piece of black or blue calico. None that I saw were tattooed. Their weapons consisted of a sumpitan, or blowing-tube, with a spear at the end; and a knife with a short handle terminating in a round knob, and a long, broad blade, flat along the cutting edge, but with the back rounded off towards the extremity. None of them wore the ordinary mandau. The women always carried a basket on their back, containing all their worldly goods —a little tobacco, a flint and steel, and some tinder—and the provisions for the day. On Plate 26 I have figured a young Orang Bukkit. The women were dressed in a blue sarong of homespun material, and a sleeveless jacket of black or blue calico. Both sexes had small holes in the ears, some wearing earrings, others not. The women stuck a bundle of leaves into the hair at the back of the head. All of them, both men and women, were very fond of chewing tobacco as well as betel. Men, as well as women, wore round the arms and neck strings of a kind of bead made of a small marine shell (sp. of *Nassa*), from which they cut the whorl away, leaving only the part round the mouth; the columellar lip is much expanded in these shells. Lora told me that the traders from Passir and Tanah Boemboe get these shells from the coast, and exchange them for gold dust and wax. I tried to buy a string of them, or procure some of them in exchange for other beads, but I could not induce the people to part with any. Nowhere else in Borneo have I noticed these *Nassa* ornaments, though occasionally in other parts I have seen a *Helix Brookei* worn as an ornament, or used for other purposes —as, for instance, to form the tops or lids of the arrow cases.

I was more successful in collecting animals and birds than shells; but owing to the humidity of the climate I was obliged to dry the skins every day, by placing them in the sun, and each morning I found them quite moist again; for the skins of the civet cats, skunks, and other animals to which a mass of fat adhered, I was obliged to have a fire outside the hut, and erect a small bamboo stand on which to dry them. In spite of all my precautions, and the application of turpentine to keep the softer parts, especially the feet of skunks and ant-eaters, from decaying, I lost several good skins.

Not a hundred yards from my hut was a warm spring, the water from which had a strong sulphurous smell and taste. The Orang Bukkit frequently came down to this spring, they, as well as the Malays, having great faith in its healing properties. Near it was the skeleton of a hut, erected by some pilgrim who had paid a visit to this *obat* place. The sick savages would come down to the spot, and, like their betters in Europe, go through a course of "the waters," using them both externally and internally. Nearly every day might be seen either an Orang Bukkit or a Malay carrying away the water, in a bottle or one of their bamboo vessels.

One day a Malay brought me a scaly ant-eater, for which I paid him a rupee. As I handed him the coin he at once pronounced it a counterfeit. Lora, to whom I appealed, said the same, adding that many false coins, both rupees and dollars, were passing current just then in Bandjermasin and district. The imitation was so perfect that I could not detect the baseness of the coin without the closest examination. Lora said he knew the man who made them, and that he had been commissioned to capture him. When I suggested that hunting coiners ought to pay better than hunting animals, he said the man was not so easy to reach, for he lived in the mountains, in the independent parts of Passir or Tanah Boemboe.

This was the only district in those parts of Borneo through which I passed in which I met with the scaly ant-eater (*Manis javanica*). It is, however, very common, not only at Mindai, but at Biraijan and Barabai. The Malays there call it *Tangiling*. Owing to its slothful and inactive habits it is very easily caught. In the daytime it sleeps, rolled up like the common English hedgehog, in the trees, and is especially fond of selecting those trees on the forked and furrowed branches of which there are plenty of the giant ferns and other parasitic vegetation so common in a tropical forest. Towards dusk it comes down from its arboreal retreat, and goes to the ants' nests, or, failing them, digs in the ground for worms. Its powerful claws are admirably adapted for burrowing. I opened the stomach of two scaly ant-eaters, but found nothing but ants—ants by thousands—in them. The easiest way of killing them is to put them in a box and drown them. The flesh is highly esteemed by the sons of the Celestial Empire.

Another animal which I found in great numbers in the Amontai district is the sāăt, or gobang (*Mydaus meliceps*). The natives always knew it by the name of sāăt. It is a stinking badger. The body is short and rounded; the head—especially the nose and mouth—very much resembles that of a pig; the snout, which is of a pinkish flesh colour, and the whole of the face as far back as the ears, is devoid of hair; but the body is covered with a black, bristly hair, with a yellowish-white band running down the back, from the top of the head to the end of the tail, this band being broadest on the head, and gradually tapering backwards. The feet, which are very short, are also bare, and are armed with long and sharp claws. The tail is hardly perceptible, not an inch long. The total length of the body is from one foot to one foot four inches. Under the tail are two small glands containing a fluid, which the animal discharges when irritated and at other times. The odour emitted by this fluid is very pungent and disagreeable, resembling the smell of Peruvian guano when mixed with muriatic acid. When I had two or three of these creatures in captivity I would cause them to discharge the secretion by disturbing them, and found that after several successive emissions both the quantity and the pungency of the matter diminished. Raising their short tail they would eject a small quantity of the fluid, though they have the power of emitting the smell alone. The odour is retained long after death. I have noticed it very strong in animals that have been preserved in spirits for several months.

These animals are never seen in the daytime, when they rest in burrows in the ground; and it was only at night-time that the Bukkits and Malays succeeded in capturing me a specimen or two, by watching the holes of their retreat, and capturing them as they emerged after dusk in search of food. Their food consists of

THE SĀĂT OR GOBANG (*Mydaus meliceps*).

worms and larvæ. They have from three to four young at a time. The saat makes a noise resembling that of a dog just before it begins to bark; and when moving about keeps up a snuffling or low grunting noise, something like a pig.

That the animal only lives in mountains at an elevation of more than 7000 feet, as stated in some works on natural history, is perfectly erroneous. In Amontai, Barabai, and Biraijan, where sāăts are as common as rats, the elevation does not exceed eighty or a hundred feet. In Sumatra, again, the highest elevation at which the sāăt is met with is not 1000 feet, and at that height it is scarce.

The flying lemur, or kubing (*Taleopithecus volans*), is said to be rare; but probably it escapes the notice of the natives on account of the colour of its fur, which closely resembles that of the bark of the trees it inhabits. I saw one, and one only, during my stay at Mindai.

Tiger-cats (*Felis planiceps*) are exceedingly common at Biraijan, and, like the *Viverra zibetha* and the *Paradoxura musanga*, are unwelcome guests in the village, on account of their poultry-killing propensities. But no royal tigers infest the forest wildernesses of Borneo, where they might, perhaps, prove destructive in killing a few head-hunting Dyaks. A harmless species of leopard is found —the *Felis macrocelis*—the skin of which is prized by the Dyaks for making one of their war-costumes. The Dyaks often go in search of it, but it is by no means common anywhere.

Among other animals whose skins are employed by the Dyaks in different parts of Borneo may be mentioned the honey-bear (*Ursus malayanus*), and the rare *Artictis binturong*. The Malays say they are both *jakkit dappat* (difficult to get); but in Koetei I frequently saw their skins used for making the Dyak caps and head-dresses.

The binturong, however, is more seldom met with in Borneo than in Sumatra. It holds a place half way between the civet cat and the bear. It is nocturnal and arboreal in its habits, feeding on fruits and birds—in fact it may be said to be omnivorous. I had a tame binturong in Sumatra, which lived principally on rice and bananas. When eating, it would take its food between its paws like a bear, sitting upright on its hind legs. The binturong has a very intelligent face, with pencil ears which help to give it a very sharp expression. Its body, which is covered with shaggy dark fur, is about three feet in length; and the tail, which is prehensile but covered with long fur tufted at the end with white, even longer. The feet are armed with sharp claws.

The long-nosed or proboscis monkey (*Nasalis larvatus*), which is hunted for the sake of the flesh by the Dyaks, and particularly by the Orang Poonan, who not only eat the flesh, but roast the thick hide and devour it, keeping the skulls as charms, is to be seen here as well as in the interior of Koetei, and also near Bandjermasin, at all hours of the day, inhabiting the thick forests on the banks of the rivers—never in large troops, but always in small groups from two to four, and selecting the very tops of the highest trees. They are very slow in their movements, and not easily disturbed. I remember on one occasion the Dyaks near Long Wai pointed out to me three long-nosed monkeys sitting sunning themselves in a very lofty tree, out of shot range. The savages made loud noises, but the monkeys took no notice, until presently I discharged a shot at them, when they turned their backs upon us, and with two long leaps disappeared amid the thick foliage.

The Dyaks call this monkey *Bakara*, and the Bandjermasin Malays *Bakantan*. I never heard it called *Kahau* or *Kaha*, the name sometimes given to it from its supposed cries. Indeed I have never heard it making any noise, even when shot at. Other monkeys are generally pretty quick in letting their voices re-echo in the forests, as a warning to their fellow-creatures, when wounded or merely startled; but the Bakantan or Bakara quietly disappears when disturbed, with a few well-chosen leaps of at least twenty feet from branch to branch. The remarkable feature in this monkey is the disproportionately long fleshy nose, which gives it its specific name. This nose is quite *sui generis*. It is neither of the Roman nor the Grecian type: neither can it properly be called aquiline: and it is certainly the very opposite of the familiar "snub." It neither stands out nor turns up, but hangs down, projecting from one to two inches beyond the mouth, and drooping below the lips. *En face* it resembles a human tongue. It is furrowed lengthwise in the middle, and the nostrils are large and oval. This large nose is peculiar to the males. The females have only a very small nose, quite in proportion to the other features. The nose and face are naked, and of a reddish yellow colour. The nose, like the eyes and ears, seems all the larger from the fact that the head is very small in comparison with the size of the animal; the eyes are of bright Vandyke brown colour, but inexpressive, lacking the lustre and keenness which is so striking in most species of quadrumana. Another facial appendage which adds to the curious appearance of the animal is the beard, below which is a sort of collar round the neck and shoulders, composed of hairs of a whitish yellow, or often, in old animals, light grey colour. The hairs round the face are by nature brushed backwards, while under the chin they grow forward. The forehead is covered with thick and short hairs of the same colour as the rest of the body, viz. of a foxy or reddish brown colour. The arms and legs and underside of the body are of a yellowish grey colour, and the nails and the inside of the hands and the feet are greyish black. Just above the root of the tail is a triangular patch of a light yellowish grey colour, the apex of which is towards the tail. The caudal appendage, which is often nearly as long as the whole length of the body, is of an ash grey colour and somewhat bushy at the point. When resting, the tail always hangs perpendicularly downwards. These monkeys feed on wild fruits and leaves, and attain a large size, frequently equalling that of the orang utan. Of all the apes, excepting, perhaps, the orang utan, the *Nasalis larvatus* is the most difficult to keep in captivity. First, there is the difficulty of getting them to eat rice; and then, although not naturally active in their native home, they seem to pine under imprisonment. They appear exceedingly melancholy, and I have watched them sitting in the same position for a long time without making the slightest movement, and hardly ever attempting, even when teazed, to make any grimace or sign of anger. At Buitenzorg, Mr. Theismann showed me three, which he had managed to keep over two years; for a long time he had to give them fresh leaves from the forest, but he eventually induced them to feed by degrees on rice. While at Bandjermasin, my friend, Lieutenant Ouwens, who was a great lover of animals, bought a splendid full-grown nose-monkey, and put plenty of leaves in the cage, but the animal would not eat, sitting like a stuffed specimen in the British Museum, and died of sulkiness two days after.

Of other *Semnopitheci*, in different parts of Borneo, I saw *S. frontatus*, *S. rubicundus* (this is also extremely common in Sumatra), *S. chrysomelas*, *S. pruniosus* (called by the Koetei Malays, Loetong), and *S. cristatus* (called by the Dyaks in Koetei, Boehis). The two last-named monkeys are specially hunted by the Dyaks on account of the bezoar stones (*galiga*) found in them.

I have frequently seen in captivity, in the houses of Malays, the pretty gibbon, or malaat as it is called by the natives (*Hylobates conbolor*). It is easily tamed, and may be seen running free about the houses and plantations, never attempting to go back to the forest, even when captured close by the spot where it is kept. The same is the case with the *H. leuciscus* or Wa-wa. The natives say they are afraid of being killed by their associates if they return to their native home. I never, however, saw the gibbon in its native forest, though I have often heard in the forests the unmistakable "wa-wa" of *H. leuciscus*—the well-known noise from which it takes its familiar name; but the only place at which I actually saw these animals wild was at Mindai.

The Kukang (*Loris tardigradus*) is common everywhere. The Malay boys often keep it in captivity—for amusement, they say, though it is a nocturnal animal, and sleeps all day! The kukang is the most difficult animal to kill that I have ever seen. To get life really extinct in a kukang is a very painful sight to witness. I thought it horribly cruel; and after I had secured a couple of skins in Sumatra I resolved not to buy any more, for that reason. One day I wounded one, and knowing its tenacity of life I strangled the little animal, then cut it open and pierced its heart. An hour elapsed before I wanted to skin it, and when I took down its body I found it still alive, its lovely eyes wide open. When, hoping to finally despatch it, I pierced its brains with a needle it began to shriek, and still some minutes elapsed before it was actually gone. Inside the skin is a thick layer of fat, of an intolerable odour.

The rhinoceros is found in south-east Borneo, but very rarely captured. The Sultan of Koetei has a fine horn in his possession, from one killed not far from Tangaroeng. Wild cattle are very common in all the mountainous parts of Koetei, and in the Doesoen district. The horns are kept by the Dyaks in Doesoen and used for drinking purposes, only on state occasions. The jungles everywhere swarm with wild pigs; and deer are plentiful especially the *Cervus russa*, the flesh of which is highly esteemed both by

Malays and Dyaks. In the low-lying and open districts near Martapoera, the nobles make quite a sport of hunting this deer, which the Bandjermasin people call *Minjangan djawa*—the species having been introduced from Java about two centuries ago. There is also a large species of deer, *Cervus equinus*, which is, however, much rarer, and only frequents the thick forests. Deer horns are eagerly sought after by Dyaks and Malays, who carve the handles of their swords from the lower portion of the horn. The *kijang* (*Cervus muntjac*) is not common. I saw one above Long Wai, and disturbed it drinking on the banks of the river. The graceful chevrotains are represented by the *Tragulus javanicus*, which is caught in snares, as the natives are fond of its flesh.

Of reptiles the most common is the *Crocodilus biporcatus*, which may be seen in all parts of the Mahakkam and the Barito, or basking in the sun on the muddy banks. Many persons lose their lives whilst bathing, and yet the Dyaks pay great respect to these reptiles, and are very unwilling to let them be killed.

A smaller species is also found, frequenting the banks and smaller streams near the houses, and making considerable havoc among the poultry.

Of snakes I came across but few specimens, chiefly the poisonous black and yellow water-snake, and the boa-constrictor. There are, however, several other species in the island, many of them poisonous. The boa-constrictor is much sought after by the Dyaks for the sake of its fat, which is used as an ointment. At the same time these reptiles are valued by both Dyaks and Malays on account of the service they render in destroying the rats which infest the rice plantations. I may mention that at Padang I saw a large boa, fifteen or sixteen feet in length, kept in the warehouse of a Dutch merchant, who never allowed it to be touched or to escape, since it performed the duties of half-a-dozen cats in keeping the premises clear of rats and mice.

On the 15th February I left Mindai for Biraijan, taking with me a very fair collection of natural history specimens. After the difficulty I had experienced in getting the natives to carry my luggage here, I readily acceded to Lora's proposal that we should return by water instead of by land. Tomongoeng and his men constructed eight small bamboo-rafts, for which I paid him eight guilders; and with this miniature flotilla, with two coolies on each raft to steer, I bade adieu to the chief of the Orang Bukkit. There were several small kehams, or rapids, which we "shot" without difficulty, and in the afternoon we reached Biraijan. Here I stayed a week with Lora, seeking to add to my collection, but was not fortunate in securing much of value. Then I retraced my course to Barabai again, where my friend, Dr. Cohen, hospitably received me.

Barabai had during my absence made an acquisition in the advent of a fair Danish lady, my friend the doctor's intended bride, who had come out to this uncivilized region at the call of love, and was now looking as fresh and beautiful as a flowering rose, her natural charms enhanced by the unlovely surroundings. Dr. Cohen, needless to say, was in the happiest mood possible. The whole place, indeed, seemed the brighter since the arrival of the bride, and it was not without regret that I left Barabai on the 25th February.

Hiring a prau to take me back to Bandjermasin, I was soon in the centre of a district of morass, very different from the wooded and undulating country in which I had so lately been staying. A vast tract of country here—most of the Bandjermasin district in fact, but especially the country watered by the river Nagara—is entirely flooded in the rainy seasons, and numerous streams and lakes are formed, which to some extent disappear in the dry season. My men proposed to make a short cut to the village of Nagara, by going down one of the many small streams that flow into the main river. Only one of them had made the journey before, and, after we had wasted four hours in the creeks and lagoons, he calmly confessed he did not know the way: he had forgotten; and no wonder! for it was a perfect net-work of waters, crossing in all directions, and running through an endless mass of high grass.

Although it was in the middle of the day, the air was full of mosquitoes, which were so great a plague to all of us that we had to keep a smoking fire all day; still they came in such myriads that it was impossible to drive them away. We met several praus, the occupants of which were fishing, chiefly for cray-fish, prawns, and shrimps, which were here in millions. None of the natives seemed to remember the " short cut " across to Nagara—though they knew well the way up to Amontai and Barabai, from whence they had come. Many of the natives in these districts are wholly engaged in fishing, the produce of their industry being one of the great articles of trade. They generally fish with nets, or a kind of fishing weir or trap made of stakes. This is a common method. The Dyaks and Malays also practise *toeba* fishing, which I often heard spoken of, though I never was fortunate enough to see the process. Dr. Solomon Müller describes it as follows :[2]—

" In the neighbourhood of Moewara Lampoer, at the mouth of the lake of that name, we met a prau with two natives in. They informed us that they would go to the forests to gather '*toeba akar*,' or toeba roots, for a fishing-party. The roots, bark, leaves, and fruit of very different plants of different species, mostly of the leguminosæ family, and especially of the species *Dahlbergia*, *Pongamia*, and *Milettia*, are used for that purpose in Borneo, Java, and Sumatra. The roots and slender twigs of these plants are stamped upon and bruised with a piece of wood, and the sap or juice thus obtained is mixed with lime and thrown in the water where it is intended to fish. This serves the same purpose as the well-known—though for such a purpose forbidden—*cocculus Indicus*, and ' stuns ' the fishes, or makes them giddy, so that they come to the surface of the water powerless, and can be taken with the hand. Although afterwards used as food, they do not appear to have any ill effect on the health. The Malays call this *menoeba ajer*, also *menoeba ikkam*. (The first of these expressions means ' to poison the water,' thereby to catch fish ; the second means to ' stun ' or ' poison the fish.') In this way a great quantity of fish can be got in a few hours.

" This mode of fishing, however, seems to be seldom practised by the natives, who prefer to make inclosures or weirs near creeks and rivers, or to use nets.

" In former years," adds Dr. Müller, " when the country was

[2] "*Reizen in den Indischen Archipel.*"

independent, the Sultan used to farm out the lakes and rivers for fishing, especially the lakes Danau Paminggir, D. Panggan, and D. Talaga, situated about 2° 13′ S. latitude, between the rivers Negara and Doesoen. The yearly rent was 100*l.*"

The fish are mostly dried in the sun, salted, or smoked.

At last we came to a broader stream, and could in the distance see the thickly populated village of Nagara. Presently we came to Moeara Bahan. Just before entering the main stream very boisterous weather set in, the squalls bursting with great violence over the great river Barito, and the waves dashing against the banks as on the seashore. More than once we thought our prau would capsize, and I had the greatest difficulty to persuade my men to continue our journey and reach Bandjermasin that night.

My stay here this time was short. I was homeward bound, and only remained long enough to securely pack my collections.

On the 3rd of March I left Bandjermasin in the mail-steamer "Vice-President Prins," and arrived at Soerabaija on the 5th March, where I enjoyed the hospitality of my friend Mr. James Waddell till the 15th, when I left for Batavia, arriving there on the 19th.

On the 27th I took passage in the splendid mail-steamer "Princess Amalia," commanded by the popular Captain Fabritius, as fine a sailor and gentleman as ever sailed beneath the flag of Holland. There were many passengers, and still more friends to see them off. Among the crowd there was one whose name I cannot refrain from mentioning, who had come specially to bid me farewell from Java's shores—one who, having first crossed the great island of Borneo from Bandjermasin to Pontnianak, could sympathize with a fellow-traveller just returned from a similar, though less arduous, expedition—I mean the veteran Von Gaffron. Notwithstanding his years, he was still full of the youthful ardour of a born explorer, and talked enthusiastically of his adventures among the savages in the heart of Borneo, even hinting that he would still be prepared, if opportunity offered, to go through all the hardships of another such a journey again if his adopted country should profit by it. Since then my noble friend has started on his last journey. He died at Sindanglaya in October, 1880.

Of the voyage home I have as much to say as of the voyage out, but, for, the same reason that I refrained from attempting a description of the latter, I am silent now about the former.

It remains for me but to offer my tribute of thanks to the captain and officers of the good ship "Princess Amalia" for their courtesy and attention on the homeward trip. Officers and crew alike did their utmost to maintain the reputation which the fine fleet of the Nederlands Steamship Company has earned for itself; and, next to the skill with which the vessel was handled by captain and crew, my fellow-passengers must be especially grateful for the manner in which their personal comfort was studied by the purser, Mr. Jütte, on whose arduous exertions so much of their happiness depended.

The voyage home, with its attendant pleasures, was a grateful compensation for the dangers and hardships of a tour among the Head-Hunters of Borneo.

END OF PART I.

Part II.

JOURNEYINGS IN SUMATRA.

CHAPTER I.

A Dutch convict settlement—A cargo of criminals—Padang as a military station—The war in Acheen—Unhonoured graves—Monkey mountain—A colony of Nias islanders—More head-hunters—Friends in a far land—Uses of the buffalo—Ajer Mantjoer—A romantic waterfall—Signor Beccari—Padang Pandjang—An aged pensioner—Tanar Datar—A grotto at Boea—An underground river—Educated monkeys—The feast before the fast—Graves of the old Rajahs.

On the 6th August, 1878, the steamer "Atjeh" left Batavia for Padang, with over 700 Dutch troops bound for the seat of war in Atjeh, or Acheen, and a number of convicts—Malays, Chinamen, and a few Europeans—who were being sent from various localities in the Indian Ocean to expiate their crimes in the useful work of road-making, harbour-building, forest-clearing, and otherwise opening up the Dutch settlements in Sumatra. They were an evil-looking crew. Some of them wore round their necks a heavy iron collar, the presence of which was not needed to prove that they were the *crême* of the criminals—the murderers, and others whose history was even blacker than that of the average blackness of their associates in crime. Such, with a few ordinary travellers, were my companions in the three days' trip along the beautiful, rugged, mountainous coast of Sumatra.

Padang is the most important town on the west coast of Sumatra, situated in 0° 57′ S. and 100° 20′ E., at the mouth of the river of the same name. It is regularly built, with broad streets lined with stately chimara-trees, a species of pine, whose needle-like foliage gives a melodious humming sound when fanned by the slightest breath of air. The houses, mostly of wood or bamboo, are hidden beneath the luxuriant vegetation in the gardens surrounding them. There is a large garrison here, and the town was the scene of a good deal of painful excitement during my stay, owing to the incessant movements of troops, and the continual arrival of sick and wounded sent down from the seat of war. I cannot say much in praise of the bearing of the troops, who had little soldierlike appearance. Most of them were foreigners, runaways from Belgium, France, and Germany, tempted by the high pay and the prospect of something "turning up" in the Far East. The pick of the troops were said to be Swiss. The officers, on the other hand, were all men of capacity and personal courage, as attested by the number who wore on their breast the coveted Wilhelms Order—corresponding to the English Victoria Cross—for valour in the field.

It is a fact worthy of some notice that the Dutch have not been able to draw upon the vast numbers of natives in their eastern possessions for military service, though experience shows that these people are not without military capacity. The Malays will never voluntarily enlist in the army, though tempted by a small bounty. The few who have joined the ranks have been induced to do so as a *dernier ressort*, after having gambled away wives, house, clothes, and everything they possessed. Their nature rebels against the restrictions of military service.

The large military hospital at Padang contains more than seven hundred patients, whose numbers were augmented by arrivals brought twice a month by the transport "Graaf Bylandt;" one day this vessel had no less than 172 invalids on board. I am surprised that the Dutch war in Acheen has not attracted more notice than it seems to have done in Europe. It has cost the Dutch Government large numbers of men and vast sums of money, her troops having to fight part of the year against the natives, who offer a determined resistance in their mountain fastnesses, and against a still more ruthless enemy in the unhealthy climate during the rest of the year, when active operations were impossible.

The climate of Padang itself is considered good; the average temperature is 78° Fahr., though in the middle of the day 90° is frequently registered, while at night the thermometer falls to 68°. The breezes from the mountains on the one hand, and the sea on the other, serve to temper the heat of the equatorial sun. Along the beach are numerous tiny boats with outriggers, belonging to Malay fishermen, who go out daily to fish. The ocean here is specially rich in fishes and cuttle-fishes; the latter are dried, and sold to the Chinese and Klings, who eat them with great gusto.

On the beach, almost in front of the Sumatra Hotel, which was my headquarters, are three graves, nameless, said to be those of three Englishmen, whose mortal remains, "unwept, unhonoured, and unsung," are buried here.

On the left bank of the river, close to its mouth, is the Apenberg, or Monkey Mountain, or "Bukkit Monjet" of the Malays. It is 330 feet high, and affords from its summit a fine panorama of Padang and the neighbouring coast, with the ocean on the one hand, and the mountains in the distance on the other. It is called Monkey Mountain because it is said to be inhabited by these animals, but I never saw any there.

Close by is a village inhabited exclusively by more than 4000 people from Nias Islands, who were formerly slave-debtors, apparently a very industrious and harmless set of people. The number of pigs surrounding their dwellings showed at once that they were not followers of the prophet of Islam; and, looking into several of their bamboo cottages, I could see by the number of wooden idols or *adjoes*—rudely carved representations of human beings—that they were idolators. I was attracted to one dwelling by hearing music and singing going on inside, and found half a dozen men performing a sort of incantation. Against the wall of the bamboo hut stood some bundles of fresh maize leaves, before which sat a Nias man holding in his right hand a live fowl, with a banana leaf round its neck. He was apparently the officiating priest, and, undisturbed by me, continued his monotonous singing. To the man's right sat a pretty little Nias girl, and next to her two Nias men, one of them playing on a wooden drum; and behind him sat another, striking a Chinese gong. Over the door hung five wooden idols. All these performers joined in singing a slow and solemn hymn-like tune. Gathered round them was a group of onlookers, who occasionally entered into conversation with each other, some of them speaking Malay. One of the men offered me a glass of arrack, having first filled the vessel and drunk the contents, to show that it was not poisoned. On my asking what the ceremony was for, they told me that there was a person very ill in the village, and that they were engaged in driving the evil spirit away. This custom is, I am told, very common at Nias.

The god of these people is Loeboelangi. From him comes everything that is good; under him are the good spirits; and besides these are a number of "Begoes," or evil spirits, to drive which away they offer fowls and pigs. Pigs are greatly valued amongst them. Mr. Kraijenhoff, long resident at Nias, informed me that a pig has the same value as a girl; and it is considered a great honour to receive a pig as a present.

A Nias man is permitted to have one or more wives, and these are always obtained by purchase. Whenever a poor man wants to contract a marriage he borrows the money, say from fifty to a hundred florins, to buy his wife, and becomes the slave-debtor for the time being to his creditor. There used to be a wholesale export traffic in girls, carried on from the Nias Islands. They were sold for a few dollars each to the Acheenese or Chinese; and the Chinese in Padang are still mostly married by purchase to the fair damsels from Nias. Even now many Europeans who are not married secure a good-looking Nias girl as housekeeper.

The Nias and Dyaks are evidently descended from the same stock, even if they did not originally form one race. Their great resemblance in physique, complexion, and features tends to show this. Again, in their religious customs and general habits they have many things in common, such as "head-hunting"—the more skulls the men possess the more honoured are they; the practice of incantations; their belief in one God, and in good and evil spirits; the use of wooden idols; their burial ceremonies, and their mode of sepulture; their dress and ornaments. In all these particulars are they so nearly alike that it is difficult to doubt their common origin.

During my stay in Padang I received much valuable assistance and information from Mr. W. B. Pearson, of the firm of Messrs. Dummler and Co., whose attention and kindness to a stranger in a foreign land were unremitting. By him I was introduced to the Governor, who advised me to go to Mount Sago, as the most favourable locality for collecting natural history specimens. Mr. Pearson also helped me to engage a young Chinaman, Tjia Tjou Bie by name, who could speak Dutch. This was a great advantage, for, coming fresh from Europe, and having never before travelled in the East, I was wholly ignorant of the Malay language, which it is essential to learn. Tjia Tjou Bie agreed to follow me wherever I went for twenty-five florins per month; he proved himself very useful, soon learning to skin birds, and was always polite and attentive.

My next business was to get all my luggage transported. All heavy traffic with the interior is carried on by means of buffaloes—or "karbaus," as the Malays call this most useful domestic animal—harnessed to a cart of peculiar construction called a pedatti, not unlike, as a friend of mine suggested, a Noah's ark. The karbau is of the utmost service to the Malays, and he knows it too. Without his assistance the produce of the country could not be so easily brought to the coast, especially during the wet season. He ploughs the ground for the rice crops, grazing on the fields after the harvest has been gathered. He is, in fact, the cart-horse of the country. A well-trained karbau is worth from 120 to 150 florins, the best kind coming from Korinthji. The natives will never sell a cow, disposing only of the oxen, in order to keep the breed to themselves. Led by a nose-band, *i. e.* a rein attached to a ring passed through the nostrils, the animals are easily driven, and patient under subjection. The yoke is made of solid wood, so clumsily contrived that ninety per cent. of the creatures suffer from terrible sores on the neck, with the flesh more or less laid open—a source of intense suffering, which might easily be remedied by the use of better made harness. Occasionally a Malay gets fined when he drives a karbau whose neck is more than usually full of sores; but there is a large field here for the Society for the Prevention of Cruelty to Animals.

The yoke or collar is part and parcel of the cart, being a permanent fixture to the shafts. When the Malay takes his buffalo to the pedatti, the animal steps over the shafts, without needing a word of direction, lifts them from the ground with one of its horns, gets its head in position, meekly and submissively passes *sub jugo*, and does his duty without the need of a whip, slowly but surely. Only one buffalo is harnessed to a cart, not a number, as is the case with South African ox-waggons. The work is mostly done at night or early in the morning, the drivers letting their animals rest—as they rest themselves—during the hot hours of the day. All along the main roads are numbers of *lappoes*, or native inns, where grass can be bought for the beasts, and the drivers can get their meals of rice, with a little dried fish and a variety of fruit, for a few coppers.

One of these buffalo carts I engaged on the 14th August to take my luggage to Fort Von der Capelle, or Tanar Datar as the Malays call it, meaning Flat Land. The distance is seventy-two palen, or nearly eighty English miles. I left the following day at ten a.m. with Tjou Bie, in a dog-cart harnessed to two spirited ponies, whose pace reminded me of driving in Finland—always galloping. The road, a splendid specimen of mountain engineering, lay along the right bank of the Batang Aneh, which tortuously pursues its way, rushing along its rocky bed with a perpetual seething and roaring sound, to the sea. We changed horses every five or six miles, and arrived about seven in the evening at Ajer Mantjoer, one of the wildest and most romantic passes in the highlands of Sumatra. "Ajer Mantjoer" means waterfall; and here is one some sixty feet high, where a tributary stream, the volume of which varies according to the season, takes a perpendicular leap down a trachyte rock into the Batang Aneh.

Signor Beccari, the well-known Italian traveller, was collecting here, and, as my buffalo cart had not arrived, I stayed with him three days. The little hut he occupied was crammed with botanical and other specimens, but I just found room to hang up my hammock. In front of the window or opening Beccari had constructed a sort of reserved stand, in order to prevent the children from coming too near or intruding. Here the children, who proved themselves useful in collecting specimens, were permitted to stand and watch. Although their visits impelled by curiosity were not always convenient, the children would come at all hours of the day with beetles, butterflies, snakes, shells, frogs, and other specimens, sometimes bringing rare objects, for which they received an extra gratuity. Signor Beccari had been very successful on the whole, owing in great measure to the richness of the locality, and to the efforts of his renowned hunter, Sinen, whom I was fortunate enough to engage after Beccari left Sumatra. In twelve days he had collected 112 specimens, in addition to a large number of dried plants; while at the foot of Mount Singalang, an hour's drive further north, where a stream of the same name falls into the Aneh, he had collected in forty days 210 bird-skins of 125 different species. At Ajer Mantjoer I engaged a hunter named Kajuhan, brother to Sinen, and on the arrival of my cart, on the 18th, I left for Padang Pandjang. The road, making great curves, still creeps up the sides of the mountains, which are covered to the top with virgin forest; and after two hours' sharp drive we emerged on to a large plateau at an elevation of 2570 feet above the sea, on which the important town of Padang Pandjang is situated. The whole plateau is a vast expanse of cultivated rice-fields. It is open only on the north-east, the volcanic cone of Merapi, which occasionally discharges smoke, rising in the north, the extinct volcano of Singalang rearing its stately head towards the west, and the Ambatjang closing the view to the south.

The climate, owing to the elevation, is very agreeable, and one can hardly fancy the place is in the tropics. The thermometer during the middle of the day rarely rises above 70°, and at night I have more than once suffered from cold. The country is very thickly populated; and twice a week, on market-days, the "passar" or market-place of the town, is crowded with thousands of natives, bringing all the products of the country, except coffee, the trade in which is the Government monopoly, and offering for sale their beautiful native-made cloths interwoven with gold and satin, and delicate gold and silver filagree work.

A notable example of the healthiness of the place is Captain

Schultze, an old pensioned Dutch officer, who now keeps the hotel here. He came to Sumatra in 1825, the year I believe in which the island was handed over by the English to the Dutch, and is the type of good health, carrying his eighty-one summers like a youth.

My next stage was to Tanar Datar, where, my cart still lingering behind me on the way, I stayed for a week with the Assistant Resident, Mr. Van Hengst. Here again the country is devoid of forest, the land being laid out in terraces, for convenience of irrigation, and devoted to rice-fields and coffee-plantations, while here and there the eye is arrested by a rice-mill standing out above the level of the cultivated area. The coffee grown here is of superior quality to that produced in Java. The trade in the produce being a Government monopoly, each native planter is bound to deliver up his crop to the Government stores or warehouses, which are established in nearly all places, and to sell it to the Government at a fixed rate of fourteen guilders per picol for the first quality, and seven guilders for the second quality. All coffee is eventually sent to Padang, where it is offered for sale at public auction. The price at the time I was in Sumatra, in 1878-79, was from sixty to sixty-two florins per picol. At Tanar Datar is a small fort, with a garrison of fifty men, under the command of a senior lieutenant. Some fifty years ago the Dutch had some severe fighting with the natives in this neighbourhood. While I was staying with Mr. Van Hengst, Mr. Twiss, the Controlleur from Boea, came to Tanar Datar; and, as it was in his district I wanted to begin working, I took the opportunity of going with him to Boea, where he kindly offered me hospitality till I had engaged men and got ready to remove to the grand mountain of Sago, 6625 feet high, which rose in front of his house, apparently quite close, but really distant some fifty miles. From daylight till eight o'clock every day the view of the mountain was obscured by a dense fog, which gradually cleared, to be followed, however, by heavy rains, frequently falling in torrents. The thermometer showed from 78° to 80° Fahr. in the middle of the day.

Still waiting for the laggard pedatti, and having engaged a Malay cook and a second hunter—Sikundo by name, and with a local reputation as a good shot—to accompany me to my future quarters on Mount Sago, I had leisure to see some of the sights of the district. Mr. Twiss told me of a grotto or "Ngalau," about two miles off, which he said was worth visiting, and he kindly supplied me with a guide, and twelve coolies with torches, to accompany me in the subterranean chambers. The way to the grotto lay through a most picturesque mountain pass. At some places the rugged cliffs overhung the path, which was strewn with enormous boulders, rendering the walking difficult, if not dangerous. At last, after stumbling along the rugged path with no worse results than a few bruised shins, we reached the mouth of the grotto, through which flows a stream called Ajer Pangean, connecting the Lima Kaum with Boea. Wading through the cold water, on a pebbly bottom, we reached the first chamber of the grotto, a large and lofty cavern, from whose roof depended long stalactites, which, when lighted up by the torches held by the coolies stationed at different points of the great natural vault, glistened and gleamed with a fairy-like splendour, which was heightened rather than dimmed as the smoke from the torches floated upwards and played round the pendent clusters, or became lost in the deeper recesses of the roof. The effect of the lights reflected on the rippling surface of the water as the stream flowed rapidly over its shallow bed, reproducing in broken outlines the irregular formation of the ceiling overhead, and the partial veil of smoke floating like dark clouds from point to point, added to the glamour of the scene.

As we advanced further our lights and voices startled vast numbers of birds, whose cries and the flapping of whose wings we could hear in the darkness overhead, though we could not see them. Presently one of the men crawled up a crevice and brought down a nest, with the parent bird inside. It proved to be a species of swallow (*cypselus*), the structure of the nest being similar to that of the common European swallow.

The current of water seemed to get stronger the further we advanced, and after proceeding about a hundred yards I thought it well to return. It was, perhaps, fortunate we did so, for on our way back we met an unpleasant evidence that the exploration of the cavern is not unattended with danger. On a stone at the edge of the stream lay a large black-and-yellow water-snake, a poisonous brute, whose room was preferable to its company. One of the coolies rather incautiously struck it with a stone, partially disabling though not killing it. I offered fifty cents. to whoever would catch it, but they all hesitated to go near it; so I increased my bid to a rupee, when several of them made an effort to secure it with a noose run in a bit of cord, and after some difficulty succeeded in making it captive. The grotto was swarming with crickets and grasshoppers—good food for the swallows!

One day when driving to market to buy rice and other necessaries for my stay at Mount Sago, I met on the road a Malay with a large monkey, secured by a cord more than fifty feet long. I had thought that monkeys led in this fashion were a *specialité* of itinerant barrel-organ grinders in London, who, to make up for the defects of a more than usually decrepit and tuneless instrument, are in the habit of attracting attention and ensuring the popularity of the crowd by letting a small half-starved monkey, with a cord fastened round its loins, enjoy as much liberty as can be obtained within a radius of three or four yards, and then exciting a semblance of activity in the wretched creature by tugging violently at its tether.

Here, however, was no barrel-organ, and monkeys were pretty common objects everywhere. On my inquiring whether the monkey was trained to "perform," and promising a few cents for the entertainment, the man spoke a few words in Malay to the animal, which immediately began to climb a tall cocoa-nut palm close by, which I roughly estimated to be from forty to fifty feet high. When about one-third the distance up the tree he stopped, and looked down at his master, who as a signal pulled the rope, when again master Jacko nimbly climbed a few feet higher, again stopping to rest and indulge in playful tricks. At last he reached the crown of the tree, felt at several nuts, one after the other, till he came to a ripe one, which he pulled off and threw down to the ground. Still carefully testing the fruit, he pulled several ripe ones, tossing them down in a quiet business-like manner, till a nod from his master told him he had enough, when he quietly came down.

I was told the Malay went from village to village, and made his living by employing the monkey's cleverness to collect the cocoa-nuts in the plantations as a regular business. He wanted twelve florins for his pet, a low price for so clever an animal. I afterwards found that monkeys so trained were not at all uncommon.

During my stay at Boea the Poeasa, or fasting-time of the natives—corresponding to the Turkish Ramadân, or month of abstinence—commenced (29th August). Mr. Twiss told me that the period of fasting would be preceded by a great feast, for which great numbers of buffaloes would be killed; and on the 26th, in company with a guide and Tjou Bie, I went to the nearest village to witness the preparations. By the roadside, under the shadow of a venerable varingin or banyan-tree, were gathered together about 100 natives, while five buffaloes stood tied to the tree awaiting their doom. Among the group were many children, gaily dressed, and richly laden with silver bangles on arms and legs, and some with necklaces of coral, to which all Malays are partial. Before the tree lay a mass of large leaves called *daun anau*, on which the meat was presently to be laid. The animals were not slaughtered without difficulty. The *modus operandi* was to pass a noose round the right fore leg and left hind leg, and then to secure all the feet, after which it was easy to throw the animal on its back—loud yells and shouts, especially from the children, accompanying the operation, and frightening and exciting the poor beast not a little. A board was then placed between the karbau's legs, five men standing on it to prevent the animal from attempting to rise; and its head was finally fastened to a long pole, by means of which, amid kicks and struggles, and other natural manifestations of impatience, the beast's neck was stretched to its full length, so that the butcher's knife might be the more skilfully applied, and then—the end.

Not far from Boea are the graves of the old Rajahs of Boea. There is nothing particularly noteworthy in them, except that they are sacred, together with the dead trunk of a tree which stands on one of them. The Malays are rather fanatical here. No one goes near the graves, as they are considered places of evil omen, and ill-luck would befall any one who approached the spot.

CHAPTER II.

On Mount Sago—A new shell—Crossing the Ambiling—Washing for gold—Gold and squalor—A colony of bats—Market-day at Sidjoendjoeng—Dress of the natives—The matrimonial market—A Hadji—Personal characteristics of the Malays—A model native "officer of justice"—The Malay character—Degraded state of the women—European influence.

On August 30th I left Boea, for my destination at Ladanglawas, on Mount Sago.

To judge by the length of the name, this should be a place of some importance. It consists, however, of a solitary hut in the forest, on the south-eastern slope of the mountain, at an altitude of 2135 feet. For the last mile or two the road was rather steep, and the coolies complained that their burdens—some forty or fifty pounds each—were rather heavy, especially as it was fast-time!

The solitary hut, which was erected for the convenience of officials who occasionally come here to inspect the coffee plantations, contained one sitting-room, with a verandah in front, and a small bed-room by the side, with plenty of space for skinning animals and storing provisions, collections, &c. The roof was anything but waterproof, but I got a couple of coolies to repair the damage with some palm-leaves, and so effectually kept out the continual pouring rains, which, with consequent fogs, were a great hindrance to me in my search for natural history specimens.

Every day we went into the forest, Kajuhan and Sikundo to shoot birds, while I looked for insects and shells. I found several species of *helix*—one a large and fine specimen, which I took to be new, unless, indeed, Beccari had already found it elsewhere[1]—and in the

[1] This shell I have since ascertained to be newly-discovered. It is described in the Appendix.

ponds and streams were plenty of *melania* and *ampullaria*. The forest was also full of small leeches, which made their presence felt in a very unwelcome manner, fastening themselves to the feet and legs *sans cérémonie*. But birds were scarce, or, at least, owing to the incessant fogs and rains, difficult to get; and altogether my stay here was not crowned with success. Added to this, my men complained bitterly of the cold at night; and, as none of them were provided with blankets, they begged of me to go down into the valley, where "birds could be got in thousands." So I determined to remove to Sidjoendjoeng, which was represented to be a favourable locality, and ordered eighteen coolies for the 9th of September to take my luggage back to Boea, there to be transferred to a buffalo cart; while on the morning of that day I started to march direct to Sidjoendjoeng, a distance of over fifty English miles.

For the greater part of the way the road was excellent; and as we were without *impedimenta* we got over the ground quickly. Towards evening on the first day we came across six or eight wild boars, feeding in the low bush by the wayside. These animals generally make their appearance at dusk. On the afternoon of the second day we came to the River Ambiling, a tributary of the Quantum, which finds its way to the sea on the east coast. We crossed this river by means of a ferry, consisting of two long canoes, across which boards were laid. On the left side of this stream is the village of Tandjoeng Ampalo, whose inhabitants sometimes find gold in the bed of the stream.

In the Soepajang and Tanar Datar districts gold is also found in the river beds, but the "washing" for the precious metal is not carried on to any great extent. The methods adopted are primitive, and there is no doubt that if European appliances and skill were introduced the yield of alluvial gold would be very much greater than it is.

Korinthji, a small independent state in the interior, is the principal gold-producing district of Sumatra. The natives hate the whites, and have so far maintained their independence. In appearance they are a miserable, poverty-stricken people—at least such of them as I have seen, and I have seen hundreds of them going to and from Padang, half starved and clad in rags, but with perhaps thousands of guilders' worth of gold-dust concealed on their persons. This they sell at Padang, at the price of from sixty to seventy guilders a thail (one thail equals 39·225 grammes).

The fact that the Malays are fond of gold ornaments, and many of them are excellent goldsmiths, shows that the metal is plentiful in the island. Not only is it manufactured into buttons, earrings, bangles, and other ornaments, but fine wire is often woven into the cloths of which the slendangs and sarongs are made.

On arriving at the village of Tandjoeng Ampalo, I observed two large trees, called koebang, entirely dead and devoid of leaves, but covered with many hundreds of large bats (*Pteropus edulis*). I discharged my gun into the midst of the colony, when two fell down dead, and the rest, suddenly awakened from their day-dreams, took to flight amid loud screams and the flapping and fluttering of several hundred pairs of wings, which could be heard for some distance. During the daytime these bats hang head downwards from the trees, keeping a firm grip of the branches with their sharp claws, and wrapping their long wings round the body like a cloak. They have beautiful brown eyes, with a really intelligent look, and sharp teeth, with which they can inflict a bite that is not easily forgotten. I had one of these creatures—a young one—captive for some time, and succeeded in making it quite tame.

At nine a.m., on the 11th September, Sidjoendjoeng was reached, and weary and footsore, the soles of my boots utterly gone, I was thankful to receive the kind assistance of the Controlleur, Mr. Maarseveen, who gave me permission to use an empty house belonging to the village—a sort of public property—containing one good room with a verandah, and three smaller apartments.

In front of this house were two long covered open buildings—simple structures, consisting merely of rows of brick pillars supporting a thick thatched roof, surrounded by groups of smaller covered sheds, mostly with an elevated floor. This was the market-place, where every Thursday the Malays and a few Klings gathered together to sell their produce and articles of commerce.

"Passar," or market-day, was quite the event of the week here. In company with my Chinese servant I used to attend the market regularly, and buy the week's provisions.

Rice, the staple food, was to be bought in abundance at from six to eight rupees a picol. Some stalls in the market were piled up with heaps of bananas and durians, and other tropical fruits in great variety; while at others were displayed cakes made of rice flour, bananas fried in cocoa-nut oil, and other confections. Women, old and young, offered for sale salted eggs and fowls—the latter not particularly fresh—at from fivepence to sixpence a-piece. Many of the younger girls struck me as being excessively bashful. Whether their modesty was occasioned by the presence of a stranger or not, I will not venture to say.

The most attractive stalls were those devoted to the display of flowers—the beautiful boenga kananga (*uvaria*), and boenga melur, a sort of jasmine of delightful fragrance, being especially abundant, their sweet perfume pervading the whole atmosphere in the immediate neighbourhood. Different kinds of oils and scent were in great demand, especially the grease from the tangalong, or civet cat (*viverra zibetha*). Many people in the district keep these animals, and make quite a profitable trade by extracting the perfumed secretion from the double sac under the tail, and selling it either pure or mixed. In the former state, an atom the size of a pin's head is sold for twopence, or a minute quantity, mixed with cocoa-nut oil in a piece of bamboo some four inches long, may be had for the same price.

Leaving these sweet-smelling stalls, one comes upon a series whose odour is quite the reverse, where heaps of stinking dried fish are displayed; and beyond these, again, others where *minia tana* (literally "earth oil"), or petroleum, with a hardly less unpleasant smell, is offered for sale. The use of this mineral oil is rapidly superseding the smoke-producing damar or resin torches.

Some of the well-to-do merchants make a large display of Manchester goods, Boegis cloths, and Javanese sarongs, for which there is a large demand.

In the grassy plain surrounding what may be called the permanent market-buildings are grouped hundreds of Malays, selling cocoa-nuts and cocoa-nut oil, the ever-present betel and lime, beeswax, plaited mats, earthenware of such brittle construction that some of the pots fall to pieces at the slightest touch, salt, native tobacco, vegetables, and various other products. To my surprise I found potatoes of good quality, and bought some at the rate of a penny for eight small tubers.

On Passar day the place presents quite a gay appearance, the market being attended by perhaps a thousand Malays, men, women, and children, all arrayed in their best attire. The women wear a black calico or print dress, or a sarong, an open piece of cloth of native make, or imported from Java or Celebes, fastened round the waist and reaching to the feet. Over the upper part of the body they wear a jacket or *badjoe* of calico, or, in the case of the better classes, of satin or silk. This jacket fits closely round the neck, and has sleeves so thick and stiff that it is sometimes a work of some difficulty to get the *badjoe* on. The front is often ornamented with gold buttons or other ornaments. At Kotta Baroe, especially, I noticed the *badjoes* worn by the damsels were laden with gold jewellery, of workmanship so fragile, no thicker than tissue paper, that it would break with the least touch.

When out of doors the ladies wear a slendang across the shoulders, or over the head and shoulders so as to conceal the face. This slendang or shawl is, as a rule, the most expensive garment, being often of silk, frequently interwoven with threads of gold or silver wire. Some of these slendangs are of exquisite pattern, and would compare favourably with any European designs. Their price varies from 1*l.* to 10*l.*, or even more. Fort de Kock, Padang Pandjang, and Sinkarah are famous districts for the manufacture of these becoming cloths.

Sometimes the women wear a head-dress consisting of a gaily-coloured cloth, folded round and round; but most of them seem to prefer to walk bareheaded, priding themselves on their magnificent long jet-black hair, tied loosely in a large knot (*koendei*) at the back, which they take pleasure in displaying, and to the care of which a Sumatra *belle* devotes much time and attention, keeping it in order with perfumed oils. The eyebrows and eye-lashes are often dyed, or rather painted, to increase the feminine charms. Gold pins or scented flowers are never wanting in the hair. Round the neck are strings of glass beads or coral, and in the ears are circular gold earrings, or rather plates of immense dimensions; and, on the arms, a profusion of bracelets.

Rice-powder is lavishly employed by many of the women—not with the object of "preserving the complexion" or reducing the colour, but to prevent perspiration by closing the pores of the skin.

These elegantly dressed ladies are by no means merely housewives marketing, or pleasure seekers idling away the time. There is an immense deal of rivalry between the women, which they make no attempt to conceal, and many are the heartburnings and jealousies awakened on Passar day among the "fair sex" in Sidjoendjoeng. It is no secret that, among the many "bargains" made at the weekly fair, not the least important are those made in the matrimonial market. Many a heart is lost, many a wife is won, amid the turmoil of the more commonplace business of the day.

The men present a striking contrast to the women. Perhaps I am a prejudiced observer, but it certainly seemed to me that they are mostly stupid-looking, plain, and uninteresting, especially when the head is clean shaved, utterly devoid of every particle of hair, the bare skull being only partially concealed by the *detta* or turban. A different mode of folding the detta, or toedoeng, seems to prevail in each county or district. Many men wear conical brimless hats, woven of vegetable fibres. Their other clothing consists of a short sarong round the waist; a loose badjoe or jacket of white, black, or blue calico, mostly without buttons, but embroidered or inlaid at the sides or on the sleeves with silver or gold patterns; and a very wide pair of trousers, sometimes of the same material as the jacket, but more often of many-coloured prints. Stuck in his sarong, or in a belt, every Malay carries a *kris* or knife, to the ornamentation of which more attention seems to be devoted than to any other part of the male outfit, those belonging to the chiefs especially being of beautiful workmanship, the handle of carved ivory, embossed silver, or even of gold, and with embossed gold sheaths. The blades, I may add, are generally poisoned.

All classes go barefooted, though occasionally some of the richer people may be seen wearing sandals, and even bright patent-leather dress shoes, though I never yet saw a native who walked at his ease in the last-named products of civilization.

Here and there in the crowd may be seen a hadji, easily recognizable by his white muslin turban. He wears occasionally a waistcoat with an endless number of buttons; and when he goes to his devotions in the mosque he puts on a loose robe of black cloth, or striped silk or satin, and carries a string of beads in his hand—a *souvenir de Mecca.* No matter where a hadji is—in the mosque, in his private dwelling-house, in the forest, on the road, on board ship—he never forgets the duties of prayer to Allah five times a day. He stands, lifts up his hands, kneels and kisses the ground, with mingled resignation and pride, and with a sense of duty which commands admiration. It is true he murmurs the prayers in quick succession, but he is never ashamed to perform openly those duties which his religious belief imposes upon him.

In personal appearance the Malays are, as I have said, as a rule anything but prepossessing. The facial characteristics are—very prominent cheek bones; eyes slightly oblique, in colour varying from dark-brown to black; forehead somewhat rounded but fairly good. The teeth are as black as ebony from the habit of betel chewing, and many men add to the repulsiveness of their appearance by having the teeth filed almost level with the gums. I have heard from Dutch officials that in some parts of Sumatra the teeth are filed to a point like sharks' teeth, but I never saw any thus disfigured. In complexion they are darker than the Javanese, the colour being a yellowish brown, with an olive tint, and coming under Nos. 30, 36, and 37, of Professor Broca's colour-types in "Anthropological Notes and Queries," whereas those of the Javanese would fall under Nos. 44 and 45.

The face is mostly devoid of beard. Not that Nature has entirely deprived them of that facial ornament, though beard, whiskers, and moustache, are naturally scanty; but from early manhood till old age it is the custom for the men to extract any hair that may from time to time appear on their faces, using for the purpose a pair of pincers, called *sappi*, without which no Malay is ever seen.

Their character coincides with the sly and suspicious expression of their faces. They are very reserved, hardly ever expressing surprise at anything; very slow, and apparently careful in answering a question, though all of them are addicted to falsehood, and fond of exaggerating. They are extremely indolent, especially the men; the women being regular beasts of burden, and performing all the menial, and often very heavy, work. I have continually met a file of women carrying loads of rice or coffee on their heads, while the men would follow, lazily lounging along, with a long stick in their hands, like shepherds driving a flock of sheep. They are not naturally quarrelsome; but if they have a grudge against any one they will nurse their malice a long time, and are sure to revenge themselves for an offence, even if years elapse before an opportunity offers for retaliation.

A Malay's passion for gambling and cock-fighting is almost proverbial; and although in the Dutch settlements both these modes of recreation are forbidden they are by no means abolished. If a party of Malays cannot indulge in these amusements at home, they will go to the beach or the country roadside; if they are disturbed, then they will betake themselves to the forest. The *Kapala kampong* (head of the village) or the *Jacksa* (native officer of justice) has to look after the morals of the people in this and other respects, and see that the rules laid down by the Government—or "Kompanie," as the Malays call it—are duly enforced.

The Jacksa at Moeara Laboe afforded a fine example of how scrupulously these duties are performed. That worthy officer was a pious Mohammedan, regular in his attendance at the mosque, repeating verses from the Koran at every turn, and apparently an excellent servant of the state. But the law against gambling was the stumbling-block in his path of duty. He officially gave notice that the forbidden amusement was to be suppressed: the people, no more to be purged of their passion than they were to be washed white, approached him with bribes. The Jacksa, however, was above such temptations; but, while he refused the filthy lucre himself, he saw no objection to his wife eking out her pin-money by receiving the bribes. She could not jeopardise her future peace by such a practice, since women are not, according to the Koran, entitled to a seat in Paradise. So the official prohibition of gambling was made to harmonize with its public recognition in Moeara Laboe as elsewhere in the country.

Still the influence which European customs are having on the national character of the people is very great. Where Dutch officials are permanently stationed there is a vast improvement in the general tone of the people. At Padang Pandjang, Fort de Kock, and other places where several European families, besides garrisons and officials, are located, the general tone of the people is far superior to that prevailing in the districts left more exclusively to native rule. The Malays, for instance, have little or no innate politeness. Their treatment of the women is a proof of this. I have seen a man go into his house, where his wife was lying asleep on the bed, rudely wake her, and order her to lie on the floor, while he made himself comfortable on the cushions. But in the larger towns, where European example has long been exerting a silent influence over the natives, their innate boorishness is gradually giving place to a little outward polish.

Although the Malay is seldom a strict follower of the Prophet, Mohammedanism has much to answer for in respect to the inferiority of women. Their seclusion prevents them from rising from their state of degradation, and, although the Dutch Government is doing much to encourage education, the unfortunate women are debarred from the advantages of the Dutch *régime* in this respect.

CHAPTER III.

Scientific dining—Parting company with my servants—A Hadji's visit—Fate of an elephant-hunter—Bears to skin—Rhinoceros horn as medicine—"New-year's feast"—Festivities at Tandjoeng Ampalo—A familiar English sport—Government monopoly of cheap coolie service—Robbery by means of anæsthetics—View from Mount Silampung—Karimon's scars—Paio—A hunter's Paradise—A corps of volunteers—A surreptitious cock-fight—A giant flower, growing a foot in two days—Forest fare—Screaming hornbills.

It was still the Poeasa, or fasting time, and meat was consequently difficult to get. The natives, however, brought in plenty of wild fowls, which they caught in snares, and which served the double purpose of affording me an excellent dinner and of adding to my collection. Among other kinds that were offered me for sale were several beniols (*tetrao viridis*), puyus (*tetrao luzoniensis*) and kuaus or Argus pheasants; and once I got a wild peacock.

Meanwhile I was having troubles with my servants. My Chinaman, Tjou Bie, fell ill of fever, complicated by a violent attack of home sickness. Every week he received letters from his relations at Padang, his father imploring him to come back, fearing that the tigers would kill him, and his wife representing that she was very ill, and requiring his immediate return. I cured him of the fever in a day or two, but the other disease was more difficult to prescribe for, for I was loth to lose Tjou Bie's services, as the stock of Malay words which I had so far picked up was very limited, and his services as interpreter were more valuable than his bird-skinning skill, or his other accomplishments; so I reminded him that his agreement was to follow me wherever I went, and return with me to Padang, and that I had given him an advance on the faith of this undertaking. He said he must go, and that he would repay me; there was a countryman of his here who would lend him the money. So to secure peace, and rather than have an unwilling servant, I let him go, and two days later he started to walk back to Padang. My hunter Kajuhan too was very disobedient; my powder had an irresistible attraction for him, so I discharged him; and my cook displayed a similar weakness in regard to the fowls and eggs, so that he next had to part company. I then made arrangements to have my meals at the house of the native schoolmaster, whose wife, a Javanese girl, was a first-rate cook, having been brought up in a Dutch family.

One day while we were at dinner a venerable and stately hadji came in, accompanied by a slave servant. He seated himself quietly in a chair, while the slave sat on the floor by his side, when the schoolmaster offered him some rice. After having partaken of the food, the priest stood for five minutes reciting some prayers aloud, holding his hands before his face, and occasionally bowing. The schoolmaster gave him a few coppers, when he lighted his cigarette and disappeared as unceremoniously as he had entered. Meanwhile one of the neighbours, having heard of the venerable hadji's visit, had sent for him to come to his house and pray. The priests are in great demand during the Poeasa to come and pray, and give thanks for the past. There is a general belief prevailing that when a Malay dies during the Poeasa he is sure to go to heaven.

In Sikundo's place I engaged another hunter, named Bagindo Radin, who had the reputation of being the best shot in the district. His sporting ability he had inherited from his father, who was a Rajah of bad repute, and had met his death in the pursuit of his favourite occupation—hunting elephants. These pachyderms are very numerous in the forests here. The Rajah had mortally wounded an elephant, which in his fury and agony charged and tore open the Rajah's stomach. My arrangement with Bagindo was to give him ten cents for every bird not too much damaged that he brought me, and to supply him with powder and shot.

Birds and animals now began to come in in numbers. Civet

cats are numerous here, and are eagerly hunted by the Malays on account of the havoc they work among the poultry. Among other quadrupeds I had two large siamangs (*hylobates syndactylus*) in one day, and the work of skinning the larger animals was not easy. In consequence of the great heat the animals began to decompose within twelve hours after being shot; and the smell in the neighbourhood, in spite of large quantities of carbolic acid, was somewhat unpleasant. The Malays, notwithstanding the equanimity with which they suffer the smell of their decaying fish, and the still greater gusto with which they eat the putrescent food, professed to have a great abhorrence of the bad smell occasioned by my animals, and complained to the Controlleur about it, and I had to pay the penalty in increased gratuities to those who brought me specimens.

Bagindo, though not directly in my service, went out nearly every day to shoot birds, in order to earn a few coppers; he was generally accompanied by a friend; and one day at noon he came hurrying back, telling me he had shot two honey-bears, a male and a female, close by in a cocoa-nut plantation, while the animals were up in a palm-tree feeding. Having summoned some friends to his assistance, he went off to fetch the big game; and presently a crowd came, carrying the animals on four poles, and laid them down in front of my house. So great was the excitement that the boys literally spoiled the skins by cutting holes all over, merely for fun. I could do nothing to prevent them, and the men were so delighted at the death of the two bears that they took no heed of the possible value of the skins. Bagindo sold the hearts and gall-bladders of the beasts to a Chinaman trader for ten guilders. They were to be used in medicine—for what complaint he would not tell.

Among other large animals seen in the neighbourhood of Sidjoendjoeng was an occasional rhinoceros, which the natives killed for the sake of the horns. A Malay offered me a fine specimen, for which he wanted eighty florins. This fancy price was occasioned by the demand which existed for rhinoceros horns among the Chinese, who use them as medicine, or, rather, ointment for healing wounds, and especially snake bites.

On the 28th September the Poeasa came to an end, and was followed by a feast, corresponding, apparently from the date, to the Little Bairam of the Turks. The natives, however, assured me that it was the commencement of the New Year; and I record the fact as another example, as it seems to me, of the manner in which times and seasons, religious observances, moral customs—everything, in fact, is out of joint in these Eastern lands. Everybody, men, women, and children, arrayed themselves in new clothes for the occasion. The damsels of the village spent the day in paying visits to their friends, passing from house to house in long processions in Indian file, and returning home laden with presents of rice, bananas, and cakes, which they carried in baskets on their heads. There was no work done on this day, but general feasting and a continuous round of pleasure succeeded to the prolonged fast.

In the evening there was an incessant discharge of powder, which, by the way, it was hinted to me came from my stock, for the Government regulations were very strict as to the sale of gunpowder. The boys amused themselves by letting off Chinese crackers, or added to the general din by beating the monotonous drums and gongs, which were heard in almost every house, while an occasional discordant song from a Malay, in the peculiar high-pitched key favoured by these people, rose above the general hubbub.

Ten days afterwards another feast took place. This was an annual *fête* held at Tandjoeng Ampalo as a token of respect to the Controlleur. Mr. Maarseveen kindly invited me to accompany him and his family, and we drove off on the afternoon before the festival, to find Tandjoeng Ampalo in a state of effervescence. A great covered place, or stand, had been erected in the middle of a field where the weekly market was held, and the village was already full of visitors from the neighbouring kampongs preparing for the festivities.

On the morrow the formal proceedings opened with the reception, by the Controlleur and his "council" of native chiefs, of the representatives of the different districts, who passed in Indian file before them. First came the Laras (heads of districts) wearing rather old-fashioned black European coats, with heavy gold embroidered collars, white waistcoats with gold buttons, and sarongs round the waist, with a belt in which was stuck a fine *kris*. After them, following in order of rank, came the *Panghoelo kapala* and the *Panghoelo kampong*, and other native great functionaries; then a crowd of men of the general public; and lastly, walking stiffly, yet with rapid step, and downcast eyes, the women, profusely ornamented with mitre-shaped crowns, earrings, bracelets, and belts, all of gold. A band of native musicians brought up the rear, the orchestra consisting of a few *tingkahs*, or drums, of native manufacture, played with the knuckles, constructed of a hollow cylinder of wood, across both ends of which a piece of goat's-skin is stretched; a bamboo flute, called a *soeling;* and a European fiddle.

Thus ended the formal reception. The women and children now seated themselves beneath two large sheds, while the men indulged in dancing, fencing, and other amusements, and trials of skill on the grass plain outside. The women never dance, and the men's performance consists of a series of slow movements by two men *vis-à-vis*, attitudinizing before each other, with head bent forward, and hands and arms—the hands spread out flat all the time—slowly assuming various set positions.

I was very much amused to find here the familiar "greasy pole" of English rural sports, up which the Malay youths were as eager to climb as any English lads, in the hope of reaching the sixpenny toys and other prizes at the top. There was no "sweep" there to carry off the prizes by virtue of his sooty clothes; and it was not till the day was well advanced that the grease was transferred from the pole to the skins and clothes of the early competitors, and the later ones were able to mount the pole in triumph.

At one p.m. a feast was given to the people in the sheds, after which the crowd gradually dispersed, Mr. Maarseveen receiving with a sigh of relief the *slaamat jallans* of the people, and driving back home.

In the district of Sidjoendjoeng are some immense rich coal-fields, which have of late years been brought into prominence by the scheme proposed by a mining engineer (Mr. Cluysenaer) to construct a railway across Sumatra, from Soemnahan through Sidjoendjoeng to Sigoentoer, on the river Batang Hari, whence the coal could be brought to the east coast in lighters or steam barges. The plan would assuredly prove a costly one; and it is doubtful if the Dutch capitalist will venture to sink his money in such an undertaking, in the face of the competition which Sumatra coal would meet with in Australian and English coals, to say nothing of the cheap Borneo article. The coals are of the best quality, and Mr. Cluysenaer has shown in a report that he could deliver them at Singapore and over the whole Archipelago at 2*l.* per ton, while according to the statement of the Batavia Commercial Society the prices for English coals are 30 fl. (2*l.* 10*s.*) per ton, and the Australian coal cannot be delivered for less than 2*l.* per ton.

Still the coal-fields are not the only portion of the wealth of Sumatra that would be opened up by such an enterprise as Mr. Cluysenaer proposes, which could hardly fail to enormously develope the resources of the island.

On the morning of October 12, having hired a horse for the journey, I left Sidjoendjoeng to seek a station further inland. The Controlleur kindly furnished me with thirty-three coolies for the transport of my luggage, a favour which was really much greater than it appears on paper, for, although the Government officials are entitled to call upon each village to furnish coolies for transport whenever required, civilians and ordinary travellers are frequently unable to secure the services of these indispensable servants. The Government levies on the population a compulsory service called "Heerendiensten," under which the chiefs are required to see that certain work is attended to in each district, such as keeping the roads in order, or making new ones, building bridges, &c. The transport of Government luggage comes under this regulation, and the coolies are paid at the trifling rate of a few halfpence a mile. This sum is quite sufficient to remunerate them, and the law is a wise one, as obliging the natives to render services which they would otherwise probably refuse to do, even for high wages. But I think it would be only just that ordinary travellers should be allowed to engage coolies at the fixed Government rates. Notwithstanding the large population, the native character is such that there is little or no competition, for the reason that the people will not work at all if not obliged. It is to their own advantage, as well as that of the country at large, that their services are compulsory in certain cases. But the Government should not have a monopoly of cheap service, and all persons should be entitled at least to coolie labour at the same rate as the Government. I have been in districts where the officials have told me "You cannot get any free coolies." "Well," I have said, "what am I to do? I am at your mercy, and I trust you will be kind enough to help me." It is only fair to say that in nearly every case in my own experience I have met with the courteous reply, "Certainly; I will give you Government coolies; but, strictly speaking, I am not allowed to do so."

Soon after leaving, my party received a not unwelcome addition in the person of a half-caste named Jan, son of the clerk to the Controlleur at Sidjoendjoeng, who, having been somewhat harshly dealt with by his father, had run away from him, and came and offered his services to me as interpreter—an offer which, as I was making but slow progress in my knowledge of the Malay tongue, I was glad to avail myself of.

The way lay through mountainous country, clad with magnificent vegetation, the forest swarming with siamangs (*hylobates syndactylus*), whose curious howlings, almost amounting to a roar, could be heard at intervals throughout the day. Nine miles from Sidjoendjoeng we came to the river Palanki, which we crossed on a small raft, the road being still through dense forest, if the word "road" can be applied to an ill-defined track thick in mud, and often entirely undistinguishable. Still this was nothing to what was to follow. At Kotta Baroe, where we stayed for the night, I had to leave my horse, which had fallen lame on the road, and the next twenty miles, to Soepajang, had to be travelled on foot. The Laras, or chief of the district at the former place, told me the locality was noted for tigers and robbers; man-eating tigers were by no means rare, but he did not know whether it were worse to fall a victim to man or beast. So he kindly furnished me with a guide, as well as a fresh set of coolies.

A curious mode of robbery is practised by the natives in the districts around Solok and Tanar Datar. Taking the fruits and roots of a plant called "katjoeboeng," they grind them to a fine powder; and when the person they want to rob is asleep the powder is blown into his nostrils. Another method is to mix it with the coffee or tea to be taken by the victim. In either case it acts something like chloroform, with the wonderful difference that the person sees what is going on, and can take note of all the movements of the thieves, but is utterly helpless either to speak or move. I met a European who had been under the influence of this katjoeboeng, and who quite endorsed the correctness of the statements that I received from the natives to the above effect.

We had to cross the Silampung mountain, and although the road was as difficult as it is possible to conceive—a steep ascent through an almost trackless forest, the ground strewn with stones—the view from the summit was sufficiently fine to repay the labour of the ascent. The district of Soepajang lay at my feet, with that of Sidjoendjoeng beyond, the cultivated lands standing out in strong contrast to the rugged, wooded country in the immediate neighbourhood. The country was intersected by two large rivers and numerous streams, several of which are impassable during the rainy season.

At Ajer Loeo the Laras kindly accommodated me with a pony, but I am not sure that I should not have been wiser to have trusted to my own powers of locomotion. The path ran along the side of a chain of hills, at a height of from 100 to 800 feet above the valley, and the available foot-track was never more than three feet wide, sometimes barely one, running on the brink of a deep precipice. A single false step would be fatal to horse and rider. The aspect of the country changed here; the whole range of hills was crowned with high grass and tall pines, with here and there a patch of forest. I found a species of pitcher plant in great abundance, most of the flowers containing water. It was a small species, not one-third of the size of the fine Nepenthes Rajah of Borneo. The whole district was very sparsely populated till we reached Soepajang.

Here the Controlleur advised me to continue my journey to Solok, the neighbourhood of which was rich in *fauna*. As he was going to Allahan Pandjang, a distance of about thirty-five miles, I had the advantage and pleasure of his company. The road now improved, and we traversed a fine, broad, well-kept highway, at an altitude of from 4500 to 5000 feet. We were still in a region practically devoid of forest, but covered with high grass and scrub.

The first village of importance is Siroekam, embowered amid flourishing cocoa-nut plantations. Its people are noted for being good blacksmiths, manufacturing different kinds of knives and other weapons.

Soon after passing Sikindjang, the next settlement, the road attains its greatest elevation, gradually descending in an almost straight line into an immense plateau, of which Allahan Pandjang is the centre, crowned with rice-fields and other plantations.

From Allahan Pandjang to Solok there are two roads, one the highway, a distance of thirty-two miles, the other a narrow path across the mountains some six miles less. I chose the latter road, which follows the steep banks of two large lakes, called Danau Atas and Danau Baroe, at the foot of the smoking Mount Talang. A tropical thunderstorm, which lasted three hours, did not improve the walking, and the paths lower down in the valleys became transformed into temporary rivers, the water rushing over a bed of pebbles and boulders. At Kotta Anan, a flourishing village embedded in cocoa-nut plantations, the Pakhuysmeester, or keeper of the Government coffee store, lent us his horse and cart to enable us to reach Solok that night. When I asked the Pakhuysmeester his charge for the use of the vehicle, he replied that he did not want any pay, so long as I would reckon him among my friends! Such a condition I willingly accepted, and if my friend should chance to read these lines he will see that I have not forgotten him. He, indeed, proved his friendship in the truest sense of the word, for both Jan and I were footsore and worn out, and neither of us could have walked the eight miles that separated us from our destination that night. I had eaten nothing all day but a couple of bananas; and a glass of vermouth with which the Pakhuysmeester filled the cup of friendship was accepted as a refreshing stimulant.

An hour's sharp drive brought us to Solok, the chief town of the XIIIth kotta in the island of Sumatra, and held by a small garrison, so that it is quite a lively place for the interior. The Assistant Resident, Mr. Braam Morris, advised me to take up my quarters at Paio, about nine miles distant in an easterly direction, as a suitable locality for zoological research. Waiting for my coolies, and afterwards packing my collections, to be conveyed to Padang and thence shipped to England, occupied a week. Here I engaged a local hunter named Karimon, a good shot, and noted as having been a skilled hunter from childhood. Like all Malays, Karimon was given to boasting, and could tell some wonderful tales of his adventures with tigers, elephants, and other big game. If I seemed sceptical about the authenticity of any of his narratives, he would point to scars and wounds on all parts of his body, inflicted by various beasts. Among other things I told him I was particularly anxious to get some *kambing utan* or wild goats (*capricornis. Sumatrensis*), a sort of mountain antelope peculiar to Sumatra. Karimon at once pointed to two deep scars on his legs, inflicted by one of these animals, which he had wounded. They were, he said, very difficult to hunt, keeping to the most inaccessible parts of the mountains, and very dangerous when brought to bay.

The road to Paio lies through a succession of rice-fields. Paio itself is a small native village, surrounded by scanty forest, on the slope of the mountains, over 2000 feet above sea level. The climate is consequently delightful. I hired an old house, somewhat similar to the hut at Ladanglawa, though without a verandah, but fortunately with a waterproof roof, for it rained daily during my stay, and sometimes in torrents. Every morning the mountains were enveloped in mist, which, as the rays of the rising sun illumined their summits, looked like a mantle of snow, reminding me of the snow-clad plateaux of Norway, while the dewdrops on the leaves of the trees sparkled like brilliants. In the north-west rose the volcanic peaks of Merapi and Singalang, with the lake Sinkarah nestling as it were at their feet; to the east lay Solok, beyond which, on clear days, even Sidjoendjoeng could be distinguished.

Close to my hut was a large Government coffee plantation, in which I was fortunate enough to find many rare beetles and shells. In the early morning the woods echoed with the voices of birds, singing their song of praise before the business of the day began; during the heat of noon their notes became hushed, but the busy flutter of their wings, as you stood motionless against the trunk of some mighty forest giant, could be incessantly heard, showing that the happy creatures were engaged in the construction of their delicately wrought homes, taking food for their young ones, or teaching their fledgling family to fly. It seemed a sin to shoot the beautiful creatures in their peaceful homes; and Karimon and

MY HOME AT PAIO.

Bagindo were careful to obey my orders not to needlessly destroy more than were necessary to complete my series of specimens.

The siamangs made the woods echo again with their loud roar, while the pretty and active simpais (*semnopithecus melalophos*) would come in troops quite close to my hut, gambolling about in the trees, and occasionally making predatory incursions into the fruit plantations. A gunshot would startle them back for a time into propriety, but they would soon return, unabashed, to their antics. One day Karimon brought me a live young simpai, whose mother he had shot. The little thing kept looking up and stretching out its arms, as if searching for its mother, and kept piping and crying so miserably that I was constrained to consign it to the spirit jar. Its colour was white, with a broad reddish-brown band along the back, a red tail, and a greyish tuft of hair on the crown of the head. Squirrels were plentiful, and the village inhabitants begged me to assist them in clearing the woods of these graceful but destructive creatures, owing to the damage they did to the cocoa-nut plantations.

The first two days my two hunters shot thirty-seven birds, one simpai, one flying lemur (*galeopithecus variegatus*), and three squirrels. The third day's work comprised twenty-three birds, two simpais, and two flying squirrels.

From sunrise to sunset I was kept fully occupied, in a state of pleasurable excitement, in skinning the specimens brought to me, and in searching the wood for insects, shells, &c. Butterflies were abundant. I would recommend the chase of these beautiful insects amid the tangle of a Sumatran forest, as a cure for most of the bodily and mental infirmities which are fostered by an east wind in England.

On returning home at night I would find a corps of volunteers waiting outside my hut; little urchins, anxious to show their diligence by bringing something, however common or useless, rather than come empty-handed, and always ready to impose on my credulity if they could. One would carefully hold a bamboo, in which he said was a rare beetle, that turned out to be a common centipede. Another would offer a bamboo filled with stag-horn beetles (*lucanidæ*) which, during their short confinement in their narrow prison, had been fighting amongst themselves till some of them had lost their powerful jaws. A third little rascal stood waiting his turn for me to relieve him of his contribution, a large weevil, held by a noose of fine fibre fastened round its body, and fighting with all its might for liberty; "*Bagus, bagus, toewan*" (Good, good, sir), cried the little lad as he held out his captive at arm's length. It was a fine specimen of *protocerus colossus:* the thorax black, the elytra orange-red, and the whole surface plush-like to the touch: these insects are very destructive to the palm-trees. Others again had in pieces of banana leaves a number of snails (*helices*) and *clausilia*, or would hold in their fingers by the wings some more or less common butterflies, of course utterly spoiled. Occasionally a lad, thinking to surprise me with a more than usually varied assortment, would come with his sarong alive with bats, lizards, frogs, and other active creatures, carrying them quite as a matter of course in that very convenient receptacle.

Unexpected assistance in the task of bird-skinning arrived a few days after settling down here. Sutton, the bird-skinner employed by Dr. Beccari, having followed me from Tanar Datar to Boea, thence to Sidjoendjoeng and Soepajang, and then again to Solok and Paio, presented himself at my hut one day, saying Dr. Beccari had left Padang, and offering me his services, which I was only too glad to secure at the rate of fifteen guilders a month. "*Chapé, toewan; sakit kakki!*" said he (Tired, sir; sore feet!); and no wonder, for he had walked over 150 miles, without a day's rest. This man's name has a very English sound, but he was a Malay, his patronymic being Maharalaut. Whence he got his other name I know not, but it had the advantage of brevity and familiarity.

One day, when walking through the forest, butterfly-net in hand, in company with Jan, I came unexpectedly to an open grass plain, where several hundred Malays were gathered together in the surreptitious enjoyment of a cock-fight. In the midst of a ring, lined with eager onlookers, two birds armed with long spear-blades were in mortal combat, one of them shortly after succumbing to a deep wound inflicted by its adversary, whose owner's face was flushed with excitement as he seized the victorious bird, and proceeded to collect the bets he had won over the fight. A Malay woman who kept a refreshment-stall was driving a rare trade in boiled rice and chicken, and native drinks. This scene of excitement was too much for Jan, who mysteriously disappeared on the return walk, and only turned up next day, suffering from a bad attack of fever.

In the damp and shaded places in the forest, where the sun's rays never penetrated, the giant flower *amorpophallum titanum*, which Dr. Beccari had found at Ajer Mantjoer, grew in fair abundance. The natives here called it *sikaribut*, while at Ajer Mantjoer it was known as *grubué*. The first specimen I saw was pointed out to me by a native, who carefully dug it up; it was a young plant, the bulb measuring eleven inches in diameter. The next was a mature specimen, but almost dead, with a straight stem five feet ten inches high, and measuring three and a half inches in diameter at the base, with a fruit resembling the ear or head of maize, twenty-five inches long, and four inches in diameter at the base, tapering somewhat towards the top; the stem was one foot in the ground, and the bulb measured ten inches in diameter.

Since then I have frequently seen the plant in different parts of the highlands of Sumatra, but the flower and fruit are rare. Of the former I have seen only three, and of the latter only five specimens. It quite puts the great *Rafflesia* in the shade; it grows to a height of from five to six feet, when it throws out three large leaves, which may almost be called branches, from their size, and from the fact that they are covered with small subsidiary offshoots, which may be called leaves. The stem, which is cellular and contains a large quantity of water, is of a beautiful bright green colour, mottled with spots of yellowish white. Its growth is remarkably rapid. I have watched the young plant, and found it grow no less than one foot in two days, so that it attains its maximum height in about twelve days, when it stops growing and the leaves or "branches" are formed. The flower, which always appears before the leaves, grows close to the ground, seldom more than one foot from the surface. It consists of a single petal, very thick and leathery, and of the colour of the red cabbage. The three flowers that I have seen all differed in form.

The fruit is a solitary oblong head, covered when ripe with rows of brilliant red berries, to the number of from 420 to 440. The bulb sometimes attains enormous dimensions. At Ajer Mantjoer I have seen some gigantic specimens; one of them so large that it took five men to carry it from the forest to my hut.

Meanwhile my collection was growing apace. During three weeks my hunters collected altogether 352 birds and forty-nine quadrupeds. Some of these had the not unimportant advantage of affording a change of diet. A young male kidjang (*cervus muntjac*) one day supplied a good steak for dinner, which tasted like venison; now and then my old cook would make a pie of the meat from the breast of a hornbill (*rhyticeros plicatus*); while a roast pigeon or two formed a pleasant change from the everlasting wild fowl and rice.

Hornbills were common in the forest, but were difficult to get, owing to their habit of sitting at the top of a lofty tree or flying high in the air, the flapping of the wings making a rushing noise, which can be heard at a considerable distance. Of one variety (*buceros rhinoceros*) Karimon brought me one specimen alive, having broken its wing. He had tied up its bill to prevent it from biting with its powerful beak. I removed the string, and kept it a couple of days; but whenever any one approached it, it screamed most frightfully, more like the screams of a pig being killed than the voice of a bird.

The small wild cat, *rimau bulau*, was common here; the natives caught it in a trap.

CHAPTER IV.

From Solok to Moeara Laboe—A narrow escape—An extraordinary animal—Satan in the water-mill—A hot-water spring—Unpleasant visitors—The siamang—Malay pets—The denizens of the forest—Bitten by a beetle—A sickly settlement—A night-march through the forest—Bill of fare at the native inns—Lolo, a mountain sanatorium—Robbing Malay dwellings.

On November 14th I returned to Solok, and then moved southwards to Moeara Laboe, nearly eighty miles distant. The district was thinly populated, and I should have had difficulty in getting coolies to go so far without great expense, if at all, had it not been for the kindness of the Assistant Resident, who furnished me with sets of Government coolies to perform the three stages from Solok to Allahan Pandjang, thence to Soerian, and finally to Moeara Laboe.

The journey was performed by easy stages, chiefly on horseback, but it was very nearly signalized at the outset by a catastrophe. While riding along the edge of the cliff which overhangs Lake Baroe I was overtaken by a heavy thunderstorm, and bethought myself of my native umbrella. Every native either carries an umbrella, or wears a broad-brimmed hat of grass or thin wood, as a protection against the rain, for hardly a day passes without a shower. If he is overtaken by a sudden storm, he improvises an umbrella out of a large banana leaf. The native umbrellas are durable, and eminently useful, and may be bought at Sidjoendjoeng for a shilling apiece. While in the interior I saw an umbrella neatly made from the scales of the ant-eater (*manis javanica*), and the novelty of the idea struck me so much that I offered to buy it, but the owner declined to part with it. He had bought it in Quantum, an adjoining independent state, for one rupee.

To return to my umbrella. It was a large green affair,

eminently well calculated to keep the bearer dry, but as I opened its spreading ribs my horse took fright, and galloped incontinently away with me. A false step might have precipitated us both into the lake lying some 300 feet below; and as all my efforts to rein in the frightened steed were unavailing, I deemed prudence the better part of valour, and—shall I admit it?—sprang from the heedless horse, leaving him to seek a watery grave if he liked, preferring not to jump myself from the "frying-pan" of the rain into the "fire" of the lake. Fortunately the animal recovered his senses with his freedom from restraint, and was presently recaptured, and consented to convey me in a dignified manner into Allahan Pandjang.

Here I stayed for the night, starting again the next day for Soerian, the road gradually falling from 4500 to about 3000 feet, and the mountains on all sides covered with thick forest. At Soerian Mr. Stebbler, a Swiss coffee lord, kindly offered me hospitality, and on the following day he lent me one of his horses for the last stage of my journey to Moeara Laboe.

Moeara Laboe is situated in the fertile valley of the Silitti, a branch of the river Batang Hari. It is the most advanced post in Dutch territory, adjoining the independent state of Korinthji, and is used as a convict-station. In a south-south-easterly direction can be seen the giant mountain of Sumatra, the Goenong Korinthji, better known on the coast as Mount Indrapoera, a volcano of 11,100 feet in height. It stands on the frontier-line between the highlands of Padang and the independent countries. This mountain is visible from the sea, and within a circuit of from sixty to seventy miles inland. It has been lately ascended for the first time by two of the members of the Dutch geographical expedition.

The Malays here told me of an extraordinary animal, said to be living in the forest on the mountain, which no one had seen, although every one had heard of its existence. It went by the name of *Goeda arré*, and was said to resemble something between a horse and a buffalo.

The Malays of Moeara Laboe speak a dialect so entirely different from the ordinary tongue of the country that it may almost be said to form a distinct language; none of my servants from the northern districts could understand more than an odd word here and there.

Provisions were very cheap here, although the village had a poor appearance, and the people were indolent. A pensioned European soldier some years ago thought to take advantage of the indolent habits of the people to his and their joint advantage, and erected a water-mill, where the natives could get their rice ground the more easily and quickly at a small charge. It was with great difficulty he got some Malays to give his mill a trial without payment; but the foolish natives, who could not comprehend how water could work the mill and grind the flour, came to the conclusion that *Satan* was in it; and so they said, "If we send our rice to your mill, then next year there will be no crop in the fields!" The speculative soldier had consequently to abandon the mill, losing the money he had invested in the enterprise.

If the old soldier had been a little less scrupulous, or a little more persevering, he might possibly have turned the fanaticism of the people to account, by falling in with their views, and getting them to make a slaamat, or offering, to drive the evil spirit away. It is the natural impulse of a Malay, when anything does not go quite right, to conclude that Satan is in it, and to propitiate the evil genius by an offering. I once saw a man at Singalang burning stones for lime, who gave a slaamat when the stones did not produce lime, because, as he said, Satan was in them. Yearly feasts, called *slaamat soedal potong paddi*, are given after the rice-harvest, and on various social occasions, or when a child is born, or named, or when a death occurs. These feasts are really developments of the principle of an "offering" to propitiate Satan. Each guest pays his share of the expenses, the women often bringing contributions to the feast, in the shape of cakes, fruits, wine, &c.; buffaloes are slaughtered, and there is a general feasting—the result of which is that the Evil One is kept at arm's length. Thus are pagan customs engrafted on the Mohammedan system of religion; and the people, after a slaamat to drive away Satan, will go to the mosque and pray to Allah, and then get up a cock-fight in the temple itself.

The Rajah of Soengo Paga, who was Twanko or chief of the district of Moeara Laboe, advised me to go to a place called Ajer Angat—literally "warm water"—some ten miles from here, as a suitable locality for collecting, and gave me leave to engage an experienced man in his service, Katti by name, as hunter. The Rajah had a more than usually extensive acquaintance with the district, having accompanied the late Lieutenant Schouw Santwardt during the first half of his journey across Sumatra from Padang to Palembang.

To reach Ajer Angat the river Silitti had to be crossed; over it was suspended an elastic bambo "bridge," which swayed to and fro to such an extent, apparently threatening to collapse altogether at each step, that I retreated before reaching half-way, and preferred finding a shallow place where I could ford the stream to taking an involuntary header from a height. My servants followed my example; and as we were wading through the water several Korinthji people came across the bridge bearing heavy burdens on their back, and passing as lightly and easily as Blondin on the tight-rope.

At the small village of Trata Boea Kras the thick forest began. A new road was being constructed by the Dutch, right through the heart of the forest to Korinthji, and they had completed the work to a point three miles beyond Ajer Angat. Eighty convicts, under the charge of a half-caste Englishman, were at work on the road, which runs parallel with the river Soengei Kapoer. Ajer Angat is nothing more than the site of two hot springs, with water nearly at boiling-point. The only shelter available here consisted of two deserted bamboo sheds which had been constructed by the road-making party. Possibly when the road is completed, and the warm springs are rendered accessible, the place may one day become an important settlement. Strings of Korinthji people passed my hut, going to sell their gold-dust at Padang. Some of them came into the hut, of course without asking permission, unloaded their parcels, and were making themselves comfortable for the night, when Jan told them I did not wish for any companions in the narrow quarters. Their appearance was by no means prepossessing—most wretchedly dressed, with only a rag of calico round their loins in the form of short trousers, stuck in the waistband of which they carried a big knife. They said that their Rajahs knew what this road-making of the Dutch meant: it was simply to enable the soldiers to march through to get possession of their country; but the Rajahs in Korinthji were also busy making preparations—not roads, but fortifications. For themselves, they said, they were willing to be under Dutch sovereignty, as the country would then be opened up for cultivation; whereas at present they were oppressed by their Rajahs, who lived by robbery and extortion. This opinion of their own country and rulers coincided with that of the Malays in Dutch territory, who are afraid to enter Korinthji or Tabo.

Everything seemed favourable for zoological research. Ears, eyes, and nose, all bore witness to the abundance of animal life. The very smell of the place betokened the existence of the larger carnivora. In whatever direction I turned, I inhaled an odour exactly resembling that which pervades the lion-house at the Zoo. The Malays all said the forest was full of tigers, and the scent confirmed the statement. Footprints of deer, as well as traces of tigers and elephants, were visible. All day long the roaring of the siamangs (*hylobates syndactylus*) could be heard on every side, reverberating through the forest. The peculiar and tremendous noise made by these animals is not less remarkable than their appearance. The first feature that struck me was the extraordinary length of the arms, which reach nearly to the ground; these powerful arms allow them to swing from branch to branch with astonishing velocity. The hind limbs are short, and when a siamang is once on the ground it is almost helpless. The animal is adapted to an arboreal life, and its construction is just that which fits it for the circumstances of its existence.

Its body is covered with long glossy hair, which is longest on the back and limbs; the face, particularly in the older animals, is surrounded with a grey or white beard. Its average size is smaller than that of the orang utan. The following are the dimensions of the largest I have measured:—

No. 1.—Height from crown of the head to sole of the foot, 3 feet 3 inches; girth of the body, 2 feet 7 inches; stretch from fingers to fingers across body, 5 feet 9 inches; breadth of face, 6 inches.

No. 2.—Height from crown of the head to sole of the foot, 2 feet 10 inches; girth of the body, 1 foot 8 inches; stretch from fingers to fingers across body, 5 feet 1 inch; breadth of face, 5 inches.

THE SIAMANG (*Hylobates syndactylus*).

Both these were males. The females are always smaller in size.

The siamangs belong to the division of apes called Gibbons, and are peculiar to Sumatra and Malacca, where they live in companies in the lofty trees, in the depths of the forests, feeding on fruits and leaves, and particularly a kind of leaf known as *daun simantoeng*. The popular belief among the Malays is that the animal is descended from a woman who had turned her son away from home, and was punished by being transformed into an animal.

Although exhibiting such agility in its native home, swinging from branch to branch with the skill of a Leotard, the siamang is slow and stupid in captivity, displaying none of the activity so amusing in other apes, and seeming deficient in intellectual capacity. It is strange that no one has ever yet succeeded in bringing the siamang alive to Europe; but even in Sumatra the natives say it never lives long in captivity, but seems to pine for the freedom of its native home.

A curious observation made by Malays who have kept these animals in captivity is that they always use their hands as spoons when drinking.

If the Malays cannot keep the siamang in captivity, I doubt if any one could succeed in doing so, for they are very fond of animals and kind to their pets, even though not always as considerate towards their domesticated animals as they ought to be. In most native houses and huts may be seen a pet of some kind. That most commonly seen is the turtle dove (*Turtur tigrinus*), called *Ballam*, or in some places *Perkoetoe*. These birds are highly prized, in fact are held almost sacred; the prices given for them vary, according to perfection of colour and shape, from five to twenty guilders each. Each bird is kept separate in a small bamboo cage, of circular shape, with a conical roof, with a cloth cover over the top. Very often these cages are stuck up on high bamboo posts, but when the owners go out to the rice-fields, or to market, they generally take their pigeons with them. The birds are perfectly tame, and never attempt to fly away, the natives daily taking the birds out of the cage and caressing them. One of my servants spent a month's salary in buying a ballam, and took it with him wherever we travelled; and on his return to Padang he sold it for double what he gave for it.

Besides these birds, many Malays keep a small green parrot, which they call Selindit (*Loriculus galgulus*), a lovely little bird, that always sleeps like a bat, head downwards; the average price of these birds is sixpence each. Sometimes I have seen the beautiful ground-pigeon (*Chalcophaps indica*), which the Malays call

Punei tanar, and the Beo (*Gracula religiosa*), which can talk as well as a parrot. Cats are kept everywhere, the variety with the short knobbed tail being the most common.

Neither night nor day did there appear to be any intermission of the varied sounds with which the forest re-echoed. When travelling in Norwegian Lapland, in 1877, beneath the glorious light of the aurora borealis, silence reigned everywhere; the grand and varied scenery seemed the grander for the very absence of all noise. Here it was the very reverse. From early dawn till sunset the feathered tribes sang or screamed, as they flitted about from leaf to leaf, or soared with loud flapping wings overhead, or sat beneath the thick foliage holding converse in their own language, either in slow and solemn fashion like a deliberative assembly of rooks, or in loud and excited tones, as if in mortal combat. The incessant howling of the siamangs, especially demonstrative at sunrise and sunset, was followed at night by the equally characteristic cries of the geckos, calling to each other all through the hours of darkness, just like so many "whistling thieves," signalling to each other in the streets of London. Butterflies of large size and brilliant colours were very common, especially the genus *hestias*, which, though slow of flight, it was almost impossible to catch, owing to the height at which they flew. At the riverside swarms of butterflies were flying about in pairs, settling for a moment now and then on the rocks and stones, probably courting each other. Beetles, too, were plentiful. I got one beautiful specimen of the *Sagra buquetii* of a lovely golden green colour, slightly tinged with yellow. The peculiarity of all *sagrides* is the extraordinary development of the hind legs, especially the thighs, which are of monster size, and armed with sharp spines. As I was admiring my treasure in my hand it wanted to make its escape, and crawled up my forefinger but I held it firm again, when it suddenly "bit" me keenly, by squeezing the hind legs together and letting me feel its sharp hooks, affording ample proof that what the mandibles are to the *lucanidæ* as a means of defence the hind legs are to the *sagrides*.

But while I was congratulating myself on having fallen on such splendid hunting-ground, the unhealthiness of the place made itself painfully manifest. The first evening Jan got an attack of fever; then Katti, Karimon, and Sutton followed suit. Karimon only got on his legs again to be replaced on the sick-list by my cook. The heat during the day was oppressive, 110° Fahr. in the shade, while the nights were cold and damp. The elevation of the place was about 950 feet above sea level.

On the fifth day I fell ill myself; and as only one of the party still remained in health, and the ordinary quinine remedies seemed ineffectual, I sent a letter to Mr. Van Geuns, the Controlleur at Moeara Laboe, describing the plight we were in. The next day my pulse was as low as thirty-eight, and none of the party seemed much better, at one moment shivering with cold, and at the next burning hot. So we lay consoling each other with the reflection that the tigers had not put in an appearance, and anxiously counting the hours till a messenger should come from Moeara Laboe.

Late in the evening we heard the cheering tramp of feet outside, and presently the welcome figure of the Controlleur himself, accompanied by the overseer of the road, appeared in the doorway of the hut, stating that he had with him a number of coolies, ready to carry us "bag and baggage" bodily back to Moeara Laboe. A couple of hours sufficed to pack up all our baggage, while some of the coolies cut stout bamboos, to which the hammocks of those invalids who were unable to walk were slung, and we were carried away from the sickly place. It was raining fast, and the night was dark; the coolies had provided torches, but they were wet and would not burn. A light of some sort was deemed indispensable to keep off the wild beasts of the forest, and the overseer led the way, vainly trying to illumine the darkness with a box of matches! The supply of these was soon exhausted, when fortunately, about eight p.m., the moon—that lamp in the vault of heaven—made its appearance through a rift in the thick clouds, and shed its beams through the occasional openings in the forest. When about half the distance was accomplished we were met by a relay of coolies, who, like the wise virgins, had taken care that their lamps were ready to burn; and shortly after eleven we reached the hospitable roof of Mr. Van Geuns. Already I felt better, and in a day or two both my servants and myself were up and about.

Still I could not shake off the fever, and so determined to go to Lolo, a sanatorium some twenty-eight miles distant, stationed up among the hills at an elevation of 3420 feet, and with a climate resembling that of Southern Europe. For the journey the luxury of a dog-cart was afforded me by the kindness of Mr. Stebbler, whose residence at Soerian was about half way between Moeara Laboe and Lolo. Swarms of butterflies were playing about all along the road, and I caught a few while driving slowly up-hill. At Lobo Sampir I stopped, being tempted to enter one of the *lappoes*, or native refreshment-houses, as I already began to feel the bracing effects of the cooler mountain air.

These lappoes are to be met with at intervals along every road in the highlands of Padang, and often have I enjoyed some of the dishes to be had there at all hours of the day. The bill of fare always comprises curried rice, with a small piece of dried or salted fish, and vegetables of different kinds, particularly the popular *sajoer*, smoked maize, and bananas either fresh, or fried whole in cocoa-nut oil, or made into cakes with rice-flour and fried. Cocoa-nut milk, with water, and occasionally tea or coffee, form the sole beverages of the Malays; but sometimes a glass of vermouth or Christiania *bier* may be had at these refreshment-houses. The majority of the natives do not care for coffee made from the berry, but drink *copee daun*, that is, an infusion of the leaves of the coffee plant, which, to my mind, has a most disagreeable flavour.

The above dishes form the ordinary diet of the Malays. Ducks and fowls are plentiful, especially in the Padang Pandjang and Fort de Kock districts; but they are reared mostly for the consumption of the European residents, both poultry and buffalo meat being reserved, so far as native use is concerned, for *slaamats*.

Opposite the lappoe at Lobo Sampir stood a lofty tree, to which my attention was attracted by a continuous screeching, proceeding from a troop of hornbills.

At Lolo I was authorized by the Assistant Resident of Solok to take up my quarters in the Government house erected for the use of the Controlleur when he visits the place. The house is built of wood and raised on posts; the rooms are lofty, eighteen feet high—too lofty indeed for this cold place, where really a stove is wanted in the afternoons and evenings.

This was quite a palatial residence compared with the huts to which I had lately been accustomed.

The ordinary Malay dwelling-house is constructed of wood, or more often of bamboo on a wooden frame work, and roofed with *atap*, *i.e.* split nipa palm leaves—or *idjoe*, *i.e.* the fibres from the stem of the anau palm; these look like horsehair. The houses are all raised on posts from two to four feet from the ground, and the space between the ground and the floor is made into an enclosure for the fowls and ducks, being surrounded with a fence of plaited bamboo. Some of the chiefs have the gables of their houses ornamented with carvings. It is a favourite custom to build the house in the midst of plantations of bananas and cocoanut-trees, so that from the roadside only the roofs of the houses are visible. In many districts rice-sheds, called *rangkiang*, are attached to the dwelling-houses; some of these are prettily painted and carved, the owners priding themselves on the appearance of these storehouses. Near Tanar Datar and Solok I saw several which must have cost the owners over 100*l.* each.

The floor is of split bamboo, very slippery and elastic to walk on, and the ordinary furniture comprises a number of mats, and a bedstead consisting of a mattress raised a few inches from the floor, covered with a mat, with two or three cylindrical head-cushions filled with cotton wool, and the ends often ornamented with silver plates. It is only in the houses of the upper class among the natives that chairs and tables are found, and these are never used except on the occasion of a visit from a European. The only household ornaments are a pair of deer horns.

Such is the "living room" of a Malay dwelling. Looking into the "kitchen," we find every family possesses a series of earthen pots called *prioek*, while the richer classes have iron pans called *koewali*. No other utensils are required except a kettle, which is not found in every house. The poorer classes cook their rice in bamboo cylinders. A number of saucers and small cups lie on shelves, or are stored in basket-work suspended from the ceiling. The hearth is mostly a heap of sand or ashes, surrounded or supported by three or four stones. The water is kept in stout bamboos called Parian, or in *kendis*, vessels made from the *laboe* fruit, or gourd, which serve as a decanter.

At Boea and Soepajang I noticed a large open house, standing by itself on a plain, and erected on higher posts than the ordinary buildings. This is called a *bali*, and corresponds to the European town hall.

A curious contrivance which strikes the traveller's eye in almost every village is the trunk of a large tree, hollowed out, and covered at the top with a piece of goatskin stretched tight across. This is called a *taboeh*, and is used as a public alarm.

CHAPTER V.

Wild beasts at Lolo—A hurricane—The wild goat of Sumatra—Market-day—Lazy natives—Woman's work—Rice cultivation—Coffee and other produce—A Christmas-bo x—Work without wages—The smallest antelope in the world—A struggle with a snake—Back to Ajer Mantjoer—Sinen the hermaphrodite tiger-hunter—A tiger trophy — An Albino siamang —The mormolyce—Cupid appears on the scene—A Malay wedding —Women's rights and wrongs—Education among the Malays—A small menagerie—Leaving Ajer Mantjoer—Results of collecting tour—Lost in the Red Sea.

WILD boars were plentiful at Lolo; they used to come in parties of from three to eight, quite close to the road. One afternoon Karimon shot one about a hundred yards from the house, but no one would take the trouble to bring the animal in, and I could not even persuade my old cook to go and cut off a piece for my dinner.

Tigers used to be common here, but of late, the natives told me, they had not seen or heard of any. A couple of years ago they were very troublesome, and several horses and buffaloes were killed by them. Mr. Maarseveen had told me that when he was Controlleur here he had often seen them near the house, attracted, no doubt, by the scent of his horses; and Mrs. Maarseveen had related how one evening, when her husband was away visiting another district, she was sitting under the verandah, when she saw a big tiger creep from within a few feet of where she was and return quietly to the forest. The animal had no doubt been into the stables, to seek a horse there for his supper.

Karimon went up into the mountains with two coolies to shoot, but in less than a week he returned, very ill with dysentery and fever, and complaining of the great cold up on the hills. "*Stenga mati, toewan*" (Half dead, sir), was his cry as two Malays brought him into the house, and laid him on a mat and put a blanket over him: but with doses of chlorodyne, twice daily, I got him on his legs again in four days.

The next week was a week of storms, and it was well Karimon returned when he did. For six days it blew a most terrific gale, making every plank in the house rattle again, and we all thought the house would have been blown to pieces. Much damage was done in the neighbourhood, many of the frail native residences being utterly destroyed; but the Government house weathered the storm without appreciable injury.

As a compensation for this enforced idleness, I heard on the day after the storm that a Malay, up in the hills about two miles away, had caught a young "kambing utan" or wild goat, (*Capricornis*

HEAD OF KAMBING UTAN, OR WILD GOAT (*Capricornis sumatrensis*).

sumatrensis). Ever since my arrival at Lolo two men had been specially employed setting snares in various parts of the forest in the hope of catching one of these creatures but without success, so I set off with Sutton at once to find out the man and try to buy the animal. After nearly an hour's rough walk, over stones, through tall grass, and across several streams, we came to the hut, with the kambing utan in a small enclosure alongside.

When I first saw it, it struck me as not being like a goat at all: its form and outlines more resembled those of a young reindeer. It was a young male of perhaps ten months or a year old. It was covered with long, coarse hair of jet black colour, and had a mane of stiff hair of a whitish grey colour, the length of the hairs being from three to four inches. Its ears, which were of a brown tint, mixed with black, were sparingly covered inside with white hair; the ears were remarkably long and erect, but were bent forward, reaching in front of the horns when listening for any sound. The eyes had rather the appearance of revenge than that gentle and mild expression so common among the deer species. An inch below the eye was a lateral glandular opening or lachrymal passage, from which now and then, especially when the animal was irritated, an oily substance of a white colour was secreted, which hardened and became dark when exposed to the air. There were slight traces of beard coming. I was told by the Malays that the old males have a long beard. The horns were straight, and deeply furrowed from the root to about the middle. In the old animals, the horns (of which I purchased several) are curved, and half way up furnished with a number of rings, which again are striated longitudinally. All the horns I have are more or less covered with earth and bark, firmly rooted between the wrinkles, but the apex is quite smooth. The owner asked twenty florins for the animal, which was absurd, as the Malays had told me the value of them here was only six florins; and after a considerable amount of bargaining I obtained the goat for six florins—ten shillings English.

I named my new pet Lolo, and soon got him tame enough to take bananas from my hand. He had an ugly habit, however, of striking the hand that fed him, or attempting to do so, when the last banana was gone; and I brought into requisition a small whip, for which he learnt to have the greatest respect. He was a powerful animal, but by no means active in his movements, and before I had had him many days he began to look fatter and sleeker. His ordinary food consisted of leaves and young shoots of trees. Before commencing to eat, he would blow and sniff at the food for a few minutes, and I noticed he always liked to lick a certain stone. He would not drink any water, but I always let my cook throw a quantity of water over the leaves before feeding him.

The Malays catch the kambing utan in nooses made of strong

fibre; the flesh is eaten by them, and said to be superior to that of the domesticated species.

Every Monday is market at Lolo. The market was held not 200 yards from my house, and I always attended with my cook to buy provisions. Rice was plentiful at the market, but fowls were scarce and very dear. The dealers were mostly women, and a more ugly set of Eve's daughters I don't think I ever saw in my life. The majority of them had large wens in the neck, resembling the throat of the South American howling monkey. As for the men, they were the most indolent lot I had as yet met with, even in Sumatra. Even the little boys were too lazy to look for beetles or butterflies for me, though they delighted in watching what my men and I were doing.

It puzzled me to discover what the men really do to earn their living in Sumatra; the only occupation I have ever seen the natives engaged in all over the highlands is looking after the coffee plantations. To the women is transferred all the heavy manual labour; they keep the rice-fields in order, and get them ready for sowing—dirty work, in which they have to work to their knees in mud; they also gather the rice when ripe, and dry it in the sun; they take the husks off—a slow operation; and finally carry it to the market, to sell what they do not require for home consumption. A few men are engaged in trade, and may always be seen at the *passar,* where they sit under a shed and sell cotton cloth, sarongs, dull razors, tobacco, &c.

The highlands of Sumatra are very fertile, and the soil adapted for the growth of many valuable products. The island might be another Java for the Dutch, if the natives were of a similar type of character to the Javanese. Were it not for the pressure put upon them by the officials, the culture even of the staple product, rice, would be neglected, and would yield only enough for their own consumption. As it is, the province of Padang practically supplies the northern parts of Sumatra with rice.

The mode of cultivation principally adopted is that of sawahs, or terraces, which can be irrigated at pleasure by the waters running down from the mountains. The only work which the men attend to is the ploughing of the soil, which is done by buffaloes, which, when the harvest is over, are permitted to graze in the fields on the "stubble" which forms an abundant and excellent food.

Coffee is the next product of importance. As I have already mentioned, the native cultivation is a Government monopoly. The natives have to deliver the produce up to the Government stores built all over the country; these are kept by native storekeepers—a position much coveted, as the "Pakhuysmeester" always knows how to weigh the coffee so that his pockets get a little lined as well as the Government's! The coffee harvest in 1878 was estimated at 100,000 picols.

Cassia is cultivated at Tanar Datar and Soerian, and nutmegs especially near Padang and Priaman; indigo, gambier, and pepper are also cultivated. I must not omit tobacco, which in certain districts, especially Sinkarah and Paiecombo, is grown on a large scale. The plant thrives at an elevation of from 1500 to 2000 feet, but sufficient is not yet grown for export. The Government has of late years planted chinchona, but with what success I do not know.

The depressing fever still clung to me, and I was not able to get out so much as I wished; but Karimon and Sutton were not idle. On Christmas Day a severe feverish attack kept me in bed all day, but the following morning I was well enough to receive a Christmas box in the shape of the head of a full-grown male tapir, or, as the natives call it here, Tjipan, which Karimon had sent to me from Loebo Sampir, a place about eighteen miles to the south, to which I had sent him for a few days. Not having a kettle large enough to boil the head in, it was a difficult question how to get it rid of all fleshy matter. I found under the house a large ant's nest, in which I deposited the head, and in a few days it was dug out, scraped perfectly clean, and no wages to pay for the labour!

Among other zoological specimens I found two of the small species of deer, the napu and the kanchil, which were not uncommon here. The latter, the *Moschus kanchil*, is the smallest known species of deer, and inhabits the dark forests of Sumatra, where the sun does not penetrate. The sketch, which is drawn from life, represents the animal, one-fifth natural size, in its favourite position

The kanchil is a genus of ruminants allied to the antelopes. Its name Kanchil means "Little," and the beautiful creature measures only fifteen inches in length, and about ten in height. The body is of red-brown colour, a well-defined black line running down the back, while inside the legs and on the belly it is white. Like the very closely allied species, the napu, it has three white stripes on the breast. The tail is from one and a half to two inches long, white underneath and at the tip. The kanchil has spurious hoofs.

THE KANCHIL (*Moschus kanchil*).

I have never seen this graceful animal in the forests, either on Mount Sago or at Sidjoendjoeng, though at the latter place it is by no means rare. The natives cannot shoot it, but the animal is caught in snares. In this way three living specimens were captured and brought to me; but they none of them lived long, for, however roomy a place is built for them, they soon pine and die in confinement. One died the day it was brought to me; and as the small house I occupied at Sidjoendjoeng was full of bird-skins and other natural history specimens, and the air in consequence not exactly so fresh and invigorating as in the forests, the Controlleur was kind enough to take charge of the other two in a spacious enclosure under his house. One, however, died the next day, and the other lived only ten days longer.

While lying fever-stricken one afternoon, half asleep and half awake, I was disturbed by Sutton shouting, "*Ulor gadan, toewan*" (Big snake, sir); so I hurried out and saw the unwelcome guest, which was of a venomous species, under the house. Half a dozen Malays were looking on, but they were afraid to do anything, and would only remain as spectators, while Sutton and myself set to work to capture the brute. This was no easy matter, for he was very agile; but after some little trouble Sutton caught him by the head, with a noose fastened to the end of a long bamboo. Thus secured, he was hauled out in triumph, coiling his body in vain attempts to break the noose. The second operation, of getting him into the tin of spirits, was even more difficult. No sooner had the reptile tasted the spirit than he used every effort to get out, splashing the spirit as he writhed his body into every conceivable contortion, and succeeding half a dozen times in getting entirely out of the tin. At last he was securely imprisoned, and on making an incision in the belly to allow the spirits free access to the inside, I found the snake had only just swallowed his last meal—a rat.

This was almost my last acquisition here. On the 18th January I bade farewell to Lolo and returned *viâ* Allahan Pandjang and Kotta Anan to Solok. The women were busy in the fields sowing the rice, and here and there a team of buffaloes or zebus lazily dragged the plough across the easily worked ground. From Solok I ultimately went to Padang Pandjang, and from there again visited the romantic district of Ajer Mantjoer.

I had some two months previously engaged Sinen, the famous hunter whom I had seen here before with Professor Beccari, and on arriving at Ajer Mantjoer I inquired what success he had had in collecting specimens for me. He replied that he had been unable to go out shooting, in consequence of injuries he had received from a wounded tiger. One day when hunting he had met a huge tiger in the jungle, and had lodged no less than six balls in him, the last one bringing the noble animal to the ground with a tremendous howl. Sinen concluded the tiger was dead, and approached to skin him, when the animal in his death-agony got up and furiously attacked him, biting him severely in his right arm, and lacerating his shoulder in a frightful manner with his claws. Sinen managed to get away, and, although weak from loss of blood, succeeded in getting to his home. His mother and brother dressed his wounds on the arm, but those on the shoulder were of so serious a nature that they were obliged to send the wounded man at once to the nearest hospital, the Sanatorium at Kajoe Tanoem, where the doctor sewed up the wounds; but he had been incapacitated ever since. Thereupon he bared his arm, and showed me the marks of the terrible wounds he had received.

To look at, Sinen was the last person in the world you could expect to find tiger hunting. The portrait in the annexed wood-cut, from a photograph taken at Padang during my last stay in the town, is an admirable likeness of this local celebrity. His face, with its broad forehead and beautiful, mild, expressive eyes, is really handsome; it has a rather sad expression, and quite a feminine appearance, with which the tone of voice entirely harmonizes. His long hair, which is inclined to curl, is carefully concealed in a shawl, which he wears over his head like a hood. Instead of trousers he wears a woman's sarong, fastened round his waist with a belt. This peculiar dress adds to the general resemblance to a woman; in fact it was long before I could bring myself to believe that Sinen was not a woman, and I do not know whether I received with greater incredulity or faith the statement which was afterwards made to me that Sinen is an hermaphrodite. This assertion was repeated to me again and again by different persons in the neighbourhood, and I have little doubt that it is correct. Sinen's arms are very muscular, and he is possessed altogether of great bodily strength, being noted for his courage and power of endurance.

In manners he was calm and dignified, but exceedingly shy, and it was not till we had been associated together for several weeks in mutually congenial enterprises that he threw off his reserve and became quite at ease with me. He was polite, thoughtful, and eminently trustworthy; and when I was attacked with fever for a few days he nursed me with the greatest care and tenderness. I have never come across a better and more faithful servant than Sinen, and I am convinced that a more genuine and honest Malay

SINEN, THE HERMAPHRODITE TIGER-HUNTER.

could not be found throughout the length and breadth of the archipelago.

Sinen's fame as a tiger-hunter was known far and wide. About three weeks after my arrival at Ajer Mantjoer a messenger came from Kajoe Tanoem, six miles off, saying that a tiger had been killing two buffaloes, and begging Sinen to go and kill the brute. Sinen quietly asked permission to go, which was readily accorded to him. One would have thought he had had enough of tiger-hunting for a time, after his recent narrow escape, but he went off as calmly as if he had received an invitation to join in a pigeon-shooting match, and three days afterwards he returned, carrying the head of a magnificent female tiger on his head, and followed by a crowd of men and boys, shouting "Matjam! matjam!" (Tiger! tiger!)

Sinen laid his trophy at my feet, and then sat down by the side of it and told me the history of his expedition. When he came to the place where the buffaloes were grazing which had been the object of the polite attentions of the tiger, he built a rude shed, in which he watched from dusk to dawn. For two nights the royal beast did not make its appearance, but on the third Sinen saw it creeping slowly and cautiously through the jungle directly towards his hut. Two bullets brought her dead to the ground. This made the fourteenth tiger that Sinen had killed single-handed. He had taken the skin to the Controlleur at Kajoe Tanoem, in order to receive the Government reward of thirty guilders (2*l.* 10*s.*).

A few days later another messenger came from the same place, to say that another tiger was in the neighbourhood, and had killed a buffalo. Again Sinen went in search of the game, but returned empty-handed, the tiger having left the neighbourhood.

Meanwhile the more prosaic work of collecting such smaller prey as birds, the lesser mammalia, reptiles, and insects went on apace. Sinen one day brought in an albino variety of the siamang, which was very rare. Troops of boys daily brought me beetles, grasshoppers, and butterflies in endless abundance and variety, and now and then one or two of the wonderful mormolyce—that curious flattened insect, with an oval body as large as a penny, but as thin as a piece of paper—so thin indeed that it was sometimes difficult to conceive that it was endowed with life, and able apparently to creep between the pages of a closed book without difficulty.

I also had the assistance of Sinen's brother, Kajuhan, whom I had discharged at Sidjoendjoeng; he came to me, however, and begged me to re-engage him, so I did so, paying him by results, being anxious to get as many rare specimens as possible from this favourable locality.

But Diana was not to have the field all to herself. Venus and her attendant Cupid came on the scene, personified by a pretty young Malay woman, with a young child, to whom, amid the pleasures and perils of the chase and its attendant duties, Sutton found time to pay his addresses. The fair charmer was already the wife of another man, by whom she had had a child; but her husband had left her for two months, and according to the local customs or laws she would be able to marry again if her faithless spouse was absent for three months altogether. Sutton himself had already twice become a widower, or a *divorcé*, after this easy fashion. Before we had been at Ajer Mantjoer a month he confided to me the secret that if all went well, *i.e.* if Siumen's husband did not turn up within the stipulated period of three months, they had agreed to find solace for each other's bereavement in matrimony.

So, on the 18th March, the amorous bird-skinner came and asked me for an advance of twenty guilders, saying the wedding was to come off that evening, and inviting me to the ceremony. With part of the money he purchased a nice petticoat for his bride, and the remainder went towards paying for a slaamat. The house where the wedding was to take place was just across the road, and in the evening about seven I went over, to find Sutton, his brother, and four Malays all seated cross-legged on the floor, while a priest stood by ready to tie the nuptial knot. He was a most curious-looking old man, with a remarkably long "beard" for a Malay, composed of perhaps a dozen hairs at the utmost, projecting from the point of his chin, and hanging downward in the form of the letter S.

Having asked for his fee beforehand, on the amount of which depended the length of his prayers, he uttered a series of invocations, standing with closed eyes and upraised hands, while the bridegroom and his five "supporters" sat at his feet. Sutton was very quiet and bashful all the time: but where was the bride, that most necessary and interesting member of the wedding party? She was shut up in the *tampat tidoer*, or bedstead, which stood at one side of the room, enclosed for the occasion with a white cloth with a gay-coloured border at the top, from which were festooned loops of red, blue, and white fringe, with large tassels and balls of the same colours. These ornaments are always suspended to the bedstead of a newly married Malay, being hired for the occasion. They remain there for a month, *i.e.* during the "honeymoon," when they are removed. Such a bedstead with its bridal trappings is shown in Plate 30.

Sweetmeats and tea were presently handed round, but the fair if frail Mrs. Sutton did not put in appearance. I had, however, the pleasure of taking her portrait the next day, in all the glory of bridal array. This was a great privilege, for I had had great difficulty in inducing the ladies of other households to allow me to sketch them. Through the intervention of Mr. Maarseveen I obtained leave to sketch a pretty young woman at Sïdjoendjoeng with her infant. She sat with a nervous feeling, and two days later her child fell ill with convulsions, while a companion, who favoured me with a sitting on the following day, had a premature confinement. Both these mishaps were attributed to me.

The marriage tie is not held very sacred among Malays, as is shown by the ease with which it is dissolved. The early age at which it is contracted is an obstacle to any real affection between married couples: for girls to be wives at fourteen is a common occurrence; indeed that age may be put down as the average age of first marriages. The girls are then frequently good-looking, but hard work and the cares of maternity soon stamp their faces with the marks of age, and spoil their figures, and then the Malay husband forsakes his wife—if, indeed, he keeps her so long. As long as his affection lasts he guards her jealously, and is generally content with one wife in the same village, wisely keeping his establishments separate, for fear of quarrels! Marriage, in fact, is a pure matter of £ s. d. If a young woman gets separated from one husband she soon finds another, who gains her affections by a plentiful supply of jewellery and new clothes.

And so it was with Mrs. Sutton; before she had enjoyed her new title six weeks a coolness sprang up between her and her husband. I inquired the reason, and she naively confessed that her husband had no more rupees to give her, and so she did not care for him any longer!

Although the girls are thus treated as chattels, to be bought and sold, to be taken up and forsaken at will, the natives appreciate the advantage of education among the boys, which the Dutch are promoting in every possible way. According to Dr. Hollander, in his "*Land en Volkenkunde van Nederlandsch Oost-Indie*," there were already, some twenty years ago, twenty native schools in the highlands, the pupils being mostly sons of chiefs and well-to-do Malays. Now, native schools are to be found in every village of any importance, to which the parents take great pride in sending their sons. I visited the native school at Padang Pandjang twice. All the arrangements were perfect, and the boys exceedingly well behaved, better so perhaps than in a European school. They were all being taught to write Malay, in Dutch as well as in Arabic characters, and some specimens of handwriting I saw were beautiful. The boys were, however, slow at arithmetic.

To get his sons in the college at Boekit Tingih is the ambition of every Malay father. The students have to pass an examination before being admitted, but then they receive a money reward if successful, and a good education superior to that which can be obtained elsewhere. When they have finished the course there, they are looked upon as very learned, and begin their career in life as writers or copying clerks in the office of an Assistant Resident, first as volunteers, and afterwards as paid officials, eventually rising to the office of coffee-store keeper, or native officer of justice, or to some similar position.

I was very loth to leave this hunter's paradise, especially as I had the good fortune to meet with another European—Mr. Edwin Sachs—bound on an errand similar to my own. Such a born butterfly-catcher as Edwin Sachs I never saw. No butterfly seemed to be able to fly too high, or too low, or too quickly, for him. If he saw a specimen, and set his heart on catching it, that butterfly's fate was sealed. He also was possessed of a most remarkable faculty for engaging the attention and affection of animals. Among my captives was a young bat, which accepted with a bad grace any familiarities on my part. But the sound of Mr. Sachs' voice, his very footfall, was sufficient to attract the creature's attention, and with him it was as tame as a kitten.

My menagerie also included a fine binturong, "Jack" by name, which quickly became quite docile; some of the favourite Malay ground-doves; a white musang (*Paradoxura*), which was a great rarity; and three parrots from the Moluccas, amongst which was a red lory, the admiration of every one from its affectionate disposition and its cleverness in talking. Unfortunately the only language it was well versed in was the Boegis tongue.

At last, with many regrets, I quitted Ajer Mantjoer, with its waterfall, its glorious wooded hills, its romantic vales, leaving for Padang, in company with faithful Sinen, on the 12th May. Altogether, in three months and a half I had collected at Ajer Mantjoer 321 bird-skins, 24 mammalia, and 575 lepidoptera and neuroptera, besides a great number of serpents, lizards, and frogs. The whole of these specimens, as well as those I had gathered at Lolo and Ajer Angat, were so much labour lost. They were wrecked in the Red Sea on the voyage to England, and utterly destroyed. The principal general results are shown in the Appendix.

My live animals and birds were more fortunate, though these did not altogether escape disaster. Leaving Padang for Batavia, on the 2nd June, 1879, I went to the Dierentuin or Zoological Gardens at the latter place, intending to deposit the animals there; but on the way thither the musang broke loose, and I never saw it again. All that I could gather later on concerning its career was that it had been amongst the fowls belonging to the Java Hotel, killing some of the birds and robbing their nests. The greater part of my living collection, however, I ultimately succeeded in bringing to Europe, on my return, ten months afterwards, from my expedition among the Head-Hunters of Borneo.

APPENDIX I.

THE DYAK ARROW POISON.

The publication of this book has been delayed several months in the hope that experiments would have been undertaken by a competent physiologist, with a view to ascertaining the action of the Dyak arrow poison referred to in the body of this work, and that the results of these experiments might have been published in an Appendix. Owing, however, to the "obstruction" which the Vivisection Act places in the way of scientific research involving experiments even of the most painless kind with living animals, it has been found impossible to make any investigations into this important subject. Three eminent physiologists and chemists have found themselves precluded by the operation of the Vivisection Act, as administered in accordance with the views of an unscientific and fanatical faction, from undertaking the smallest experiments which would throw any light on the nature and action of the Dyak arrow poison, and lead to the discovery of a possible antidote. Professor T. R. Fraser, F.R.S., Professor of Physiology at Edinburgh University —than whom there does not exist a man less open to a charge of inflicting unnecessary pain—at last applied for the "licence" which is necessary before a scientific man can prick a vertebrate animal with a pin in the cause of science and the avoidance of human suffering; but after considerable delay the licence was refused to him. It has been consequently impossible to obtain any information on the important questions how far the arrow poison is fatal, or likely to be injurious, to human beings, and whether an antidote is to be found.

This, unfortunately, is by no means the only instance, though it is one of the most striking examples, of the arbitrary refusal of the only legal means of making physiological researches of the kind. It is hardly within the province of this book to discuss the general question of the necessity for vivisection carried on by skilled operators, but the aspect which the matter has assumed under the particular circumstances referred to is so striking as to justify a lengthened reference to the facts of the case. Dr. Fraser himself, in his address before the recent Medical Congress as President of the Section on Pharmacology and Materia Medica, drew particular attention to the subject. After referring to several cases in which investigators to whom the necessary licence had been granted had been assailed with unbridled invective for performing experiments on living animals, and to some recent instances of the refusal of a licence where the objects were of the highest interest, and in which the importance of the result could not be predicted, Dr. Fraser says :—

"I do not make this statement unadvisedly. The instances are within my own knowledge, and in one of them I have the best of reasons for knowing the facts, as only the other day I experienced the mortification of being refused a licence. In this case, permission was requested for performing a few experiments on rabbits and frogs with a reputed poison used by the natives of Borneo to anoint their arrows. If this be an active substance it is impossible to predict what advantages might be gained from its use in the treatment of disease; but, apart from this, it is surely important to discover in the interest of travellers whether it really possesses toxic properties, and, if it does possess such properties, what are their characteristics, and what is the best method of counteracting its effects. I am obliged to conclude, however, that those who are now authorized to decide such questions for us entertain a different opinion, and consider that these objects and the interests of science are insufficient to justify the most trivial infliction of pain upon rabbits and frogs. That the infliction of pain would be only trivial will, I think, be apparent when I state that the only operation for which permission was requested was the subcutaneous injection of the poison; for the question of the possible infliction of pain by the action of the supposed poison does not arise, as the substance might, without any infringement of the Act, be placed in the stomach or in contact with any absorbent surface, provided no wound was inflicted. The absurd position has now been assumed by the State that an operation implying merely such a wound as can be produced by a needle-point is not justifiable so long as it is performed for the purpose of acquiring knowledge and in the hope of benefiting the human race.

"To us the matter bears a most serious aspect. To us it is as clear as the light of day that the action of remedies cannot be ascertained otherwise than by experiments on the lower animals. If this method of research be denied to us, what means are we to adopt for increasing the resources of our art? How are the rich treasures which the enterprise of travellers and the never-ceasing discoveries of chemists place at our disposal to be applied, as hitherto they have in so many instances been most beneficially applied, to the treatment of disease? How are we to discover antidotes to the poisonous action of toxic agents? Experiments on man with substances regarding whose properties no knowledge exists will ever be repugnant to medical science; and on that account, as well as because of their entire insufficiency, they cannot be adopted as substitutes for experiments on the lower animals."

The unsatisfactory state of things thus brought about by the Vivisection Act as at present administered is the less to be tolerated when it is remembered that the very poison which a skilled physiologist is thus debarred from investigating for scientific purposes may be used by any person, scientific or unscientific, licensed or unlicensed, for the purpose of taking the life of an animal, provided his object is merely to kill, and not to seek a means of preserving life.

That the Dyak arrow-poison is fatal to the smaller mammalia and to birds is verified by the observations of the author of this book. That wounds inflicted by an arrow anointed with this poison may result in the loss of valuable lives, may be inferred from the analagous case of the death—to quote the most recent notable example—of Commodore Goodenough in the South Seas; for the projected extended colonization of Borneo by Europeans may easily lead to conflicts with Dyaks, in which poisoned arrows may play a prominent part. And all this time our acquaintance with the nature of this poison is practically *nil*, and is likely to remain so as long as the Vivisection Act is made so formidable an obstacle in the way of research.

In 1864 Dr. P. M. Braidwood received from Prof. Du Bois-Reymond, in Berlin, a minute quantity of arrow poison from Borneo, which he called Dajaksch, and which had been brought to Europe by a doctor who had been in that island. Dr. Braidwood's experiments with this specimen were made in the pre-obstruction days; but the quantity of material with which he had to work was so limited that his observations (which are recorded in the *Edinburgh Medical Journal*, August, 1864) established nothing beyond the fact that the poison, when injected beneath the skin of a rabbit, was fatal.

"The first noticeable evidence of the working of the poison," he writes, "when administered subcutaneously, is restlessness and signs of irritation. These reflex movements are not those resulting from excessive pain, but resemble such as are produced by a mild local irritant. This is followed by a state of languor—the animal lying perfectly still and the respiration being slow but not laboured. . . . This condition is interrupted by several fits of convulsions, which increase in intensity from time to time. By degrees paralysis . . . sets in. . . . Lastly, the respiration is noticed to become heaving and irregular."

Dr. Braidwood's conclusion is that the poison produces death by paralysis of the heart; but, owing to the small amount of poison at his disposal, his researches were incomplete. He adds, "A very important element wanting in the above sketch is a prefatory notice respecting the natural history of this interesting poison: but this is not as yet attainable, the poison being comparatively, if not quite, new. The peculiar action of dajaksch on the heart may well recall the well-known Java arrow poison, Upas Anthiar. But these two poisons, though perhaps allied in their natural history, differ in other respects from one another. Upas Anthiar is properly a Java poison, and, if met with in Borneo, it is only found and used there to a slight extent; whereas dajaksch is the name of a well-known native tribe in Borneo. In chemical characters these poisons show themselves also not to be one and the same. Lastly, these poisons seem to differ from one another in the physiological effects they produce on the animal organism. For, as Prof. Kölliker, of

Würzburg, stated as the result of his investigations in a paper read before the Medical Society of Würzburg in 1857, Upas Anthiar produces paralysis of the heart by acting directly on its muscular fibres; whereas dajaksch produces cardiac paralysis by acting on the sympathetic ganglia of the heart."

The specimen of poison examined by Dr. Braidwood was "stale;" it was in the form of an extract, wound round a small piece of stick and dried thereon, and it is described as fragile, and of a dark iron-grey colour. When finely pulverized it was partly soluble in water, and then emitted an odour resembling "organic matter decaying in a moist place."

It is more than probable from this description that the poison was of a different character from that made by the Orang Poonan, as described in the body of this book, and the failure to obtain accurate scientific observation of the most recent specimen of Dyak arrow poison brought to Europe is consequently the more to be regretted.

C. E. F.

APPENDIX II.

LIST OF LAND AND FRESHWATER SHELLS COLLECTED IN SUMATRA AND BORNEO, WITH DESCRIPTIONS OF NEW SPECIES.

(*Prepared for the Zoological Society, by* CARL BOCK.)

THE specimens were collected in the highlands of Padang, Sumatra, and in the eastern and southern portions of Borneo.

In determining the species, and comparing the specimens with those in the British Museum, I have to acknowledge the assistance received from Mr. Edgar Smith.

I have not ventured to make out the species of so difficult a form as *Melania*, but have forwarded my specimens for determination to Dr. A. Brot, of Geneva, who is the highest authority on this kind of freshwater shells.

I.—LAND SHELLS COLLECTED IN SUMATRA.

HELICIDÆ.

Nanina, Gray.

1. *Nan.* (*Ariophanta*) *foveata*, Pfr. Of this fine sinistral *Helix* I found two adult live shells at Sidjoendjoeng.

2. *Nan.* (*Hemiplecta*) *densa*, var. Ad. and Reeve.

Nan. (*Hemiplecta*) *Schumacheriana*, Pfr. Three specimens at Mount Sago and Sidjoendjoeng. Mr. Wallace found this species in Borneo.

3. *Helix* (*Camæna*) *tomentosa*, Pfr. Only two specimens found: one adult at Sidjoendjoeng.

4. *Nan.* (*Xesta*) *malaccana*, Pfr. This brittle shell I found very abundant in the coffee plantations at Paio.

5. *Helix* (*Plectotropis*) *sumatrana*, var. Martens. At Ajer Mantjoer—scarce.

6. *Helix* (*Nanina*) *granaria*, sp. nov.

Shell thin, sinistral, conical, depressed, of an olive-brown colour, becoming pinkish grey at the apex; narrowly umbilicated; whorls six, oblique arcuate; sculptured with lines of growth, and concentric finely granular striæ, producing a shagreened appearance, especially on the last whorl, which is also considerably wrinkled and bears a somewhat raised ridge or keel at the periphery, which, however, does not produce an angle, not descending in front. Whorls of the spire only a little convex; the last, large, rather ventricose. Spire shortly conical, with the apex obtuse.

Aperture large, broadly obliquely lunate, of a somewhat mauve tint within. Peristome thin, simple, only very shortly expanded over the umbilicus.

Greatest diameter forty millims.; height thirty-one millims.

Hab. Mount Sago, at an elevation of 2000 feet. Only one specimen found, in a decayed trunk. Like the rest of *Nanina* I found in Sumatra and Borneo, this is also sinistral.

7. *Helix* (*Nanina*) *maarseveeni*, sp. nov.

Shell perforate, sinistral, depressly trochiform, thick; of a light-brown horn colour, somewhat paler round the umbilicated region. Spire conical, depressed, with the apex obtuse. Whorls seven, sculptured with feebly granulated, obliquely arcuate, lines of growth, and increasing slowly; last whorl with a very acute pale keel about the middle, below the carina somewhat concave then convex, sculptured like the upper surface, the lines being rather flexuous.

Aperture oblique, angularly lunate. Peristome thick, upper margin above the keel short, oblique rectilinear, the basal margin very arcuate, towards perforation somewhat expanded.

Greatest diameter thirty-three millims.; axis fourteen millims.

Hab. Sidjoendjoeng. I have associated the name of Mr. Maarseveen, the Assistant Resident at Sidjoendjoeng, with this shell, of which I found only three specimens.

A near ally in form and colour is the *H. hugonis*, Pfr., from Labuan; but the *H. maarseveeni* has an extra whorl, is umbilicated, and the spire is considerably less elevated, and the granular sculpture in *hugonis* is much stronger. The *H. maarseveeni* comes much nearer the *Helix mindaiensis*, found by me in Borneo, but that has only six whorls.

8. *Helix smithii*, sp. nov.

Shell thin, orbicular, umbilicated, flatly depressed; semi-transparent, of a greyish-white colour, covered with a thin epidermis of a light horn colour; spire flattened. Whorls four, flattish, sculptured with fine lines of growth, the last slightly descending at the mouth, broad, with a strongly-marked obtuse keel and a broad, distinct groove above; below convex, obtusely ridged round the deep umbilicus.

Aperture large, subquadrangular oblique. Peristome thin; outer margin expanded, reflexed, especially in the umbilical region.

Greatest diameter twenty-one millims.; height eight millims.

Hab. Paio, Sumatra; two specimens found.

The *Helix smithii* is nearly allied to *H. caseus,* Pfr., from Siam; but the latter differs in having a less acute keel on the last whorl, which descends considerably, while the peristome is almost continuous and ovate.

I have associated with this shell the name of Mr. Edgar Smith, the distinguished conchologist at the British Museum.

9. *Helix* (*Geotrochus*) *rufo-filosa,* sp. nov.

Shell shortly conical, narrowly umbilicated, thin; semi-transparent, of a greyish or horn colour; sometimes with a thread-like red line, bordering the sutures and encircling the last whorl at the periphery. Spire with rectilinear outlines, converging at an angle of about thirty degrees, rather obtuse at the apex. Whorls seven, very obliquely striated, slowly increasing, keeled beneath immediately above the suture; three or four uppermost rather more convex than those beneath, which are but slightly so; last volution acutely carinate at the middle, and convexly flattened beneath.

Aperture small, oblique. Peristome thin, outer margin above the keel scarcely expanded, beneath it feebly thickened and narrowly reflexed, in the umbilical region more expanded, and partly concealing the perforation.

Length from ten to eleven millims.; greatest diameter of base also ten to eleven millims.

Hab. The forest at Paio, 1500 feet above the sea; only six specimens found —rare.

10. *Helicarion sumatrensis,* Schepm.

Hab. Paio, very rare.

STENOGYRA.

11. *Bulimus paioensis,* sp. nov.

Shell elongate, subulate, imperforate, of a dirty-greyish white colour, covered with a somewhat deciduous and coarsish olive epidermis. Whorls twelve, apical ones obtuse, glossy, vitreous; these and the few succeeding rather convex and slowly enlarging; the five last proportionally longer and flatter, increasing more in length than breadth, and separated by a rather oblique deepish suture. Sculpture consists of coarsish, oblique, flexuous, indistinctly subgranose, raised lines of increment.

Aperture elongate, subpyriform, acute above, occupying rather more than one-fifth of the entire length of the shell. Outer lip (viewed laterally) oblique, a little excurved near the suture, simple, thin. Columella whitish, slightly arcuate, and thickened, oppressed to the whorl, connected with the extremity of the labrum by a very thin callosity.

Length forty millims., diameter seven and a half millims.; aperture nine millims. long, and three millims. broad.

Hab. Paio, Sumatra, 1500 feet above the sea.

The animal is of a yellow colour; has a short foot, and carries its shell in an oblique position.

I never met with this interesting species in any other spot in the highlands; and even at Paio it appears to be rare, for after close search I found but fourteen specimens in all.

12. *Bulimus* (*Amphidromus*) *adamsii*, Reeve.
Hab. Sidjoendjoeng, Paio, &c.

13. *Vitrina hyalea*, sp. nov.

Shell depressly globose, subauriform; olive-brown, glossy, sculptured with very fine lines of growth and microscopic spiral striæ. Spire small, pale, hardly raised above the last whorl. Volutions two to three, depressly margined at the suture, last very large.

Aperture very large, subhorizontal or only a little oblique, lunar rounded. Outer lip, seen from above, feebly incurved near the suture; the somewhat excurved columellar margin of the peristome thin, membranous.

Greatest diameter twenty millims.

Hab. Ajer Angat, near Korinthji. This species is darker in colour than most others of this genus, but somewhat lighter than the Tasmanian *V. milligani*.

14. *Clausilia sumatrana*, Martens.
Hab. Common in the coffee plantations at Paio.

CYCLOSTOMACEA.

15. *Pupina superba*, Pfr. I collected three specimens at Paio.

CYCLOPHORUS, Montf.

16. Section *Myxostoma*, *planorbulus*, Lam. In the dense forests at Sidjoendjoeng, with the aid of some natives, I secured some fifty specimens, all living, with opercula. They are rare, and require a close search amongst the decayed leaves and in the damp soil. They vary considerably in size.

17. *Cyclophorus eximius*, Mousson. Of this glorious shell, the pride of the Sumatran forests, I succeeded in collecting some sixty specimens at Sidjoendjoeng. I first found dead shells in the immense forests there pretty common, and, being determined to exhaust the place of live ones as much as possible, I put a number of natives to work every day, to pull down the decayed trees that were filled with earthy matter, also to look amongst the masses of dead leaves on the ground. The former, especially, seemed to be their favourite resort. We succeeded in finding from two to three live perfect specimens every day; but when I looked over the whole collection, over fifty per cent. were dead, white specimens with hardly any colour at all; thirty per cent. were shells in various stages of growth, but without a lip, and in most cases the last whorl near the mouth had been broken and repaired; twenty per cent. were fine full-grown examples with the bronzy shining epidermis complete.

Hab. Mount Sago and Sidjoendjoeng.

One specimen near Silago, one at Soengei Aboe, two near Moeara Labœe, one at Mount Korinthji at a height of 1000 metres, four at Loeboe Gadang, and two at Ajer Boesoek.

N.B. The Dutch Sumatra Expedition found eleven specimens, all dead; they were, however, interesting as indicating the locality, all being found in places with immense forest vegetation.

18. *Cyclophorus tuba,* Sow. Mount Sago and Sidjoendjoeng. Rarer than the foregoing species.

19. *Megalomastoma sectilabrum,* Gould. I found eight specimens at Paio.

II.—FRESHWATER SHELLS COLLECTED IN SUMATRA.

The ponds are teeming with many varieties of *Melania, Ampullaria,* and *Paludina.* These I could not make out. The *Melaniacea* and *Clea* have been determined by Dr. Aug. Brot of Geneva.

20. *Ampullaria ampullacea,* Linn. All over the highlands in natural ponds, and in the "sawahs" or rice-fields.

21. *Paludina ingallsiana,* Lea. One specimen, from Boea.

22. *Paludina hamiltoni.* The specimens vary from those in the British Museum, by being more rounded at the top.

23. *Paludina sumatrensis,* Dunker. Common in the "sawahs" or rice-fields at Boea, and in the rivers.

Melaniacea.

Genus *Melania,* Lamk.

24. *Melania datura.* Found at Boea.

25. „ *semigranosa,* Busch. Found at Boea and Tanar Datar.

26. „ *lirata,* Bens; *granosa,* id. var.

27. „ *lævigata.* Found at Boea and Tanar Datar.

28. „ *malayana,* Issel. Boea and Tanar Datar.

29. „ *sumatrensis,* Brot. One young specimen from Boea.

30. „ *boeana,* sp. nov. }
31. „ *provisoria,* sp. nov. } Locality Boea.
32. „ *bockii,* sp. nov. }

The new species of *Melania* will be described by Dr. Brot in M. Crosse's *Journal de Conchyliologie.*

33. *Corbicula gracilis,* Prime. Abundant in all the lakes in Sumatra,

especially lake Sinkarah. The shell is fished in quantities, and used for making lime for betel chewing.

34. *Unio dimotus*, Lea. Abundant at Boea.

III.—LAND SHELLS COLLECTED IN BORNEO (IN KOETEI, AND THE AMONTAI AND BANDJERMASIN DISTRICTS).

HELICIDÆ.

1. *Nanina* (*Rhyssota*) *brookei*, Adams and Reeve). I found dead specimens in Koetei. The Dyaks use them as ornaments on the top of the lid of their arrow cases. Six live specimens at Mindai (in Amontai district). It is however rare. Keeps in the decayed layer of leaves.

2. *Nanina* (*Xesta*) *consul*, Pfr. I found two specimens at Mindai.

3. *Helix Mindaiensis*, nov. sp.

Shell very slightly umbilicated, sinistral, convexly conoid; semi-transparent, of a reddish-brown colour, with a white-tipped lip. Spire conical, with somewhat convex outlines, and the apex obtuse. Whorls six, but slightly convex, sculptured with finely granulated radiating striæ, regularly increasing, the last acutely keeled.

Aperture oblique lunate. Peristome sharp, slightly thickened; upper margin short, oblique; the basal, seen from beneath, rather sinous.

Greatest diameter thirty millims.; axis thirteen millims.

Hab. Mindai (Amontai district). Very abundant amongst the decaying leaves in the forest. This species is of a darker colour than *Helix maarseveeni*, has one whorl less, has more convex outlines to the spire, is not so sharply keeled around the last whorl, and more narrowly umbilicated. Its sculpture too is rather more coarsely granular.

4. *Helix* (*Videna*) *Metcalfei*, Pfr. One specimen, collected at Mindai.

5. *Helix* (*Videna*) *planorbis*, Lesson. Mindai; scarce.

6. *Bulimus* (*Amphidromus*) *interruptus*, Müller. This shell was very abundant in Bandjermasin, both the dextral and sinistral forms, and variously coloured. After the heavy rains the trees were quite spotted with them. Of the rare pure white variety I found only one specimen.

7. *Scarabus borneensis*, A. Adams. Only one specimen, found at Bandjermasin.

PTEROCYCLOS, Benson.

Borneo is especially rich in this genus; in some places, particularly at Mindai, the ground was literally swarming with them

8. *Pterocyclos mindaiensis*, nov. sp.

Shell depressed, orbicular, rather solid; dark reddish-brown, varied with zigzag narrow white markings both above and below; covered with a greenish-brown velvety epidermis, bearing two series of close-set short hairs, one above and the other beneath the periphery, the former winding up the suture. These cilia are invariably worn off in adult shells. Whorls five, rounded, divided by a deep suture, marked with distinct spiral striæ and lines of growth. Peristome double, outer margin considerably expanded, especially at the upper part where it joins the body-whorl but less reflexed than towards the base. Inner margin simple. Operculum very concave exteriorly, consisting of seven narrow whorls, which are coarsely obliquely striated, with the outer margins exserted at the sutural line.

Greatest diameter nineteen millims.; axis five millims.

This species very closely resembles *P. Lowianus*, Pfr., from the island of Labuan. It is however rather larger, has a darker and thicker epidermis, which is ciliated—that of *Lowianus*, as far as we know, lacking that peculiarity—and the peristome is more expanded and reflexed. The opercula of these two forms present such differences of character as to distinguish at once their specific distinctness. That of *P. Lowianus* has exteriorly a deep groove, separating the whorls, which stand up erect and lamelliform. In *P. Mindaiensis* the whorls rest one upon another, and the surface is regularly concave.

Hab. Mindai (Amontai district). Exceedingly common amongst the decaying leaves.

9. *Opisthoporus euryonphalus*, Pfr. Only two specimens, from Long Wai, Koetei. One has the tube directed the opposite way. Two specimens from Mindai.

Leptopoma, Pfr.

10. *Leptopoma, lowi*, Pfr.
11. „ *duplicatum*, Pfr.
12. „ *barbatum*, Pfr.
13. „ *subconicum*, Pfr.
14. „ *massenæ*, Less.

(10–14:) All from Mindai. Only two specimens of each found.

Cerithidea, Sow.

15. *Cerithidea obtusa*, Lam. Abundant at Bandjermasin in the swamps. They were more on land than in the river. Amongst the numbers collected I only found one with apex perfect.

16. *Cerithidea charbonnieri*, Petit. Found at Bandjermasin, but not so common as the former.

Melanidæ, Lam.

17. *Clea nigricans*, Bens. Common at Bandjermasin. Only in young shell

is the apex perfect; in the old ones the spire is broken and eroded. Dr. Brot makes out two varieties, the *Clea maxima*, H. Ad., and *Clea fasciata*, H. Ad.

18. *Clea bockii*, sp. nov. (will be described by Dr. A. Brot in M. Crosse's *Journal de Conchyliologie*).

NERITIDÆ.

19. *Neritina depressa*, Benson. Common in the brackish waters at Bandjermasin.

20. *Neritina* (*clithon*) *aculeata*, Gmelin. Found at Bandjermasin. Rather rare. Six specimens found, with the spines only feebly developed.

21. *Neritina piperina*, Chem. Exceedingly abundant at Bandjermasin, and ornamented in great varieties.

22. *Auricula Judæ*, Linn. *Hab.* Koetei, on the coast amongst the mangroves and casuarinas.

APPENDIX III.

LIST OF BIRDS COLLECTED IN THE HIGHLANDS OF THE WEST COAST OF SUMATRA.

I FIND from Mr. Wardlaw-Ramsay's Paper (in the proceedings of the Zoological Society, January 6, 1880) that my first collection of birds, made and sent home to the late Lord Tweeddale, consisted of about 800 specimens referable to 166 species. Of these Mr. Ramsay says thirty-two are not included in the lists of the Marquis of Tweeddale (*Ibis*, 1877, pp. 283—323), or of Count T. Salvadori (*Ann. Mus. Civ. Gen.* 1879, pp. 169—253). The latter are as follows:—

1. Neopus malayensis (Temm. ex Reinwardt).
*2. Accipiter stevensoni (Gurney).
*3. Milvus govinda (Sykes).
4. Caloramphus hayi (J. E. Gray).
5. Anthracoceros malayanus (Raffles).
6. Hydrocissa convexa (Temm.).
7. Merops philippinus (Linn.).
8. Cypselus subfurcatus (Blyth).
9. Collocalia francica (Gmelin).
10. Eurylæmus javanicus (Horsfield).
*11. Niltava grandis (Blyth).
*12. Xanthopygia cyanomelæna (Temm.).
13. Bhringa remifer (Temm.).
14. Phyllornis media, (Bonap. ex Müller M.S.)
15. Criniger gutturalis (Müller).
16. Ixidia squamata (Temm.).
17. Ixidia leucogrammica (Müller).
*18. Turdus sibiricus (Pallas).
*19. Turdus obscurus (Gmelin).
20. Ianthocincla lugubris (Müller).
21. Phylloscopus borealis (Blasius).
22. Erythrura prasina (Sparrm.).
23. Limonidromus indicus (Gmelin).
24. Analcipus cruentus (Wagler).
25. Carpophaga ænca (Linn.).
26. Euplocamus vieilloti (G. R. Gray).
*27. Twenix pugnax (Temm.).
28. Rhynchæa capensis (Linn.).
29. Hypotænidia striata (Linn.).
30. Bubulcus coromandus (Bodd.).
31. Ardetta cinnamomea (Gmel.)
32. Dendrocygna arcuata (Horsf.).

Out of this list, seven species, to the names of which an asterisk (*) is prefixed, have, as far as Mr. Ramsay knows, not been before recorded as occurring in Sumatra. In addition to the above-named species there are three which appear to be new, viz.:—

1. Dicrurus sumatranus (ten specimens collected at Ajer Angat, Paio, and Mount Sago).
2. Turdinus marmoratus.
3. Myophonus castaneus (Mount Sago).

This collection was made between August, 1878, and January, 1879. One of the chief points Mr. Wardlaw-Ramsay remarks is that it contains examples of several migratory species, such as Turdus sibiricus (Pallas), and Phylloscopus borealis (Blasius), which would only occur in the winter season.

My second collection of birds, consisting of 571 specimens—collected at Lolo and Ajer Mantjoer—and containing by far the finest and rarest specimens, together with mammalia and reptiles, had the misfortune, through the sinking of the steamer, to be buried in the Red Sea. My friend, Professor Odoardo Beccari, has kindly forwarded me a catalogue of 506 specimens of birds belonging to 179 species, collected by him during June, July, August and September, 1878, in the same locality as that in which my collection was made. They are described by Count Salvadori as follows:—

1. Falco melanogenys (Gould).
2. Microhierax fringillarius (Drap.).
3. Limnætus caligatus (Raffl.).
4. Spilornis bacha (Daud.)?
5. Haliastur intermedius (Gurney).
6. Elanus hypoleucus (Gould).
7. Ninox scutulata (Raffl.).
8. Glaucidium sylvaticum (Müller).
9. Scops lempiji (Horsf.).
10. Scops rufescens (Horsf.).
11. Bubo sumatranus (Raffl.).
12. Ketupa javanensis (Less.).
13. Pyrotrogon flagrans (Müller).
14. Pyrotrogon duvaucelii (Temm.).
15. Hapalarpactes mackloti (Müller).
16. Psilopogon pyrolophus (S. Müller.).
17. Chotorea chrysopogon (Temm.).
18. Choterea mystacophanes (Temm.).
19. Cyanops oorti (S. Müller).
20. Xantholæma hæmacephala (Müller).
21. Iyngipicus fusco-albidus (Salvad.).
22. Xylolepes validus (Reimo.).
23. Hemicercus sordidus (Eyton).
24. Lepocestes porphyromelas (Boie.).
25. Callolophus mentalis (Temm.).
26. Callolophus malaccensis (Lath.).
*27. Chrysophlegma mystacalis (Salvad.).
28. Tiga javanensis (Ljungh.).
29. Meiglyptes tristis (Horsf.).
30. Micropternus badius (Raffl.).
31. Vivia innominata (Burt.).
32. Surniculus lugubris (Horsf.).
33. Penthoceryx pravatus (Horsf.).
34. Cacomantis merulinus (Scop.).
35. Hiracococcyx fugax (Horsf.).
36. Rhinortha chlorophæa (Raffl.).
37. Rhopodytes diardi (Less.).
38. Rhamphococcyx erythrognathus (Hartl.).
39. Carpococcyx radiatus (Temm.). ?
40. Centrococcyx javanensis (Dum.).
41. Centrococcyx eurycercus (Hay).
42. Anorrhinus galeritus (Temm.).
43. Rhytidoceros undulatus (Shaw).
44. Rhinoplax scutatus (Bodd.).
45. Buceros rhinoceros (Linn.).
46. Merops sumatranus (Raffl.).
47. Nyctiornis amicta (Temm.).
48. Alcedo bengalensis (Gm.).
49. Alcedo meninting (Horsf.).
50 Alcedo euryzona (Temm.).
51. Pelargopsis fraseri (Sharpe).
52. Caridagrus concretus (Temm.).
53. Sauropatis chloris (Bodd.).
54. Lyncornis temmincki (Gould).
55. Caprimulgus affinis (Horsf.).
*56. Caprimulgus pulchellus (Salvad.)
57. Macropteryx comata (Temm.).
58. Collocalia linchi (Horsf. et Moore).
59. Chætura coracina (S. Müller).
60. Calyptomena viridis (Raffl.).
61. Psarisomus psittacinus (Müller).
62. Eurylaemus ochromelas (Raffl.).
63. Cymborhynchus macrorhynchus(Gm.).
64. Corydon sumatranus (Raffl.).
*65. Niltava sumatrana (Salvad.).
*66. Stoparola ruficrissa (Salvad.).
67. Muscicapula maculata (Tickell).
68. Muscicapula hyperythra (Blyth).
69. Rhipidura javanica (Sparrm.).
*70. Rhipidura atrata (Salvad.).
71. Cryptolopha trivirgata (Jard.).
72. Artamus leucogaster (Valenc.).
*73. Pericroctus montanus (Salvad.).
74. Lalage terat (Bodd.).
*75. Graucalus melanocephalus. (Salvad.)
76. Irena cyanea (Begbie).
77. Chaptia malayensis (Hay).
78. Dissemurus platurus (Vieill.).
79. Buchanga leucophæa (Vieill.).
80. Hemipus obscurus (Horsf.).
*81. Hemipus intermedius (Salvad).
*82. Hyloterpe bruneicauda (Salvad.)
83. Lanius bentet (Horsf.).

84. Lanius magnirostris (Less.).
85. Dendrophila azurea (Less.).
86. Prionochilus percussus (Temm.).
87. Prionochilus maculatus (Temm.).
88. Cyrtostomus pectoralis (Horsf.).
89. Arachnophila simplex (S. Müller).
90. Æthopyga siparaja (Raffl.).
91. Æthopyga temmincki (S. Müller).
92. Anthothreptes malaccensis (Scop.).
93. Chalcoparia phœnicotis (Temm.).
94. Arachnothera chrysogenys (Temm.)
95. Arachnothera modesta (Eyt.).
96. Arachnothera longirostra (Lath.).
97. Arachnothera crassirostris (Rchb.).
*98. Zosterops atricapilla (Salvad.).
99. Ægithina scapularis (Horsf.).
100. Ægithina viridissima (Bp.).
101. Phyllornis sonnerati (J. et S.).
102. Phyllornis cyanopogon (Temm.).
103. Phyllornis icterocephala (Less.).
104. Trachycomus ochrocephalus (Gm.).
105. Ixus bimaculatus (Horsf.)
106. Ixus analis (Horsf.).
107. Brachypus euptilosus (Jard. et Selb.)
108. Brachypus plumosus (Blyth).
109. Brachypus pusillus (Salvad.).
110. Rubigula dispar (Horsf.).
111. Ixidia cyaniventris (Blyth).
112. Brachypodius melanocephalus (Gm.).
113. Hypsipetes malaccensis (Blyth).
114. Timelia striolata (Müller).
115. Timelia larvata (Müller).
*116. Stachyris bocagei (Salvad.).
117. Mixornis gularis (Raffl.)
118. Macronus ptilosus (Jard. et Selb.).
*119. Turdinus rufipectus (Salvad.).
*120. Rimator albo-striatus (Salvad.).
121. Brachypteryx epilepidota (Temm.).
*122. Brachypteryx saturata (Salvad.).
*123. Brachypteryx flaviventris (Salvad.).
124. Pnoepyga pusilla (Hodgs.). ?
*125. Myophonus dicrorhynchus (Salvad.)
*126. Arrenga melanura (Salvad.).
*127. Cochoa beccarii (Salvad.).
128. Cissa minor (Cab.).
129. Platylophus coronatus (Raffl.).
130. Garrulax bicolor (Müller).
131. Garrulax palliatus (Müller). ?
132. Leiothrix mitrata (Müller).
*133. Leiothrix laurinæ (Salvad.).
*134. Heterophasia simillima (Salvad.).
*135. Pteruthius cameranoi (Salvad.).
136. Eupetes macrocercus (Temm.).
137. Henicurus velatus (Temm.).
138. Henicurus ruficapillus (Temm.).
139. Orthotomus borneensis (Salvad.).
140. Prinia familiaris (Horsf.).
*141. Prinia hypoxantha (Salvad.).
142. Cittocincla macroura (Gm.).
143. Copsychus musicus (Raffl.).
144. Calobates melanope (Pall.).
145. Munia maja (Linn.).
146. Munia acuticauda (Hodgs.).
147. Munia punctularia (Linn.).
148. Ploceus maculatus (S. Müller).
149. Calornis chalybæa (Horsf.).
150. Gracula javanensis (Osbek.).
151. Oriolus coronatus (Su.).
152. Oriolus xanthonotus (Horsf.).
153. Dendrocitta occipitalis (Müller).
154. Platysmurus leucopterus (Temm.)
155. Corvus tenuirostris (Moore).
156. Treron nepalensis (Hodgs.).
157. Treron nasica (Schleg.).
158. Butreron capellei (Temm.).
159. Osmotreron vernans (Linn.).
160. Sphenocercus oxyurus (Reinw.).
161. Sphenocercus korthalsii (S. Müller). ?
162. Ptilopus jambu (Gm.).
163. Ptilopus roseicollis (Wagl.).
164. Carpophaga badia (Raffl.).
165. Spilopelia tigrina (Temm.).
166. Geopelia striata (Linn.).
167. Macropygia leptogrammica (Temm.)
168. Macropygia ruficeps (Temm.).
169. Chalcophaps indica (Linn.).
170. Chalcurus inocellatus (Cuv.).
171. Argusianus argus (Linn.).
*172. Acomus inornatus (Salvad.).
173. Gallus ferrugineus (Gm.).
*174. Peloperdix rubrirostris (Salvad.).
175. Caloperdix oculea (Temm.).
176. Rollulus rouloul (Scop.).
177. Tringoides hypoleucus (Linn.).
178. Erythra phœnicura (Penn.).
179. Ardea purpurea (Linn.).

Of these, twenty-four are new species, which are marked in the list with an asterisk. I obtained the following eight of them :—

Chrysophlegma mystacalis.
Rhipidura atrata.
Hemipus intermedius.
Heterophasia simillima.
Pteruthius cameranoi.
Myophonus dicrorhynchus.
Arrenga melanura.
Peloperdix rubrirostris.

APPENDIX IV.

A SHORT VOCABULARY OF THE LONG WAI (DYAK) DIALECT.

AIR, langet.
Ant, wooliang.
Arm, gui.
Ashes, awaah.

Bad, ák.
Bananas, petoi.
Belly, saa.
Bird, monok.
Black, mendong.
Blood, lahá.
Boar, owoi.
Boat, halók.
Body, óng.
Bone, tuluang.
Bottle, jonggun.
Box, tung, or tong hólo.
Breast, bang.
Breasts, wé.
Butterfly, jipodoä.
Buttons, segát obing.

Cat, njéou.
Child, mopeng.
Chopper, nenjáp.
Cocoa-nut, njo.
Cold, hengám.
Comb, njon.
Come, kehá.

Day, deou.
Deer, pedjú.
Dog, sau.
Door, gong molong, or gong poonóng.

Ear, song kinin.
Egg, kolo.
*Eye, matén.

Face, njong.
Fat, menjé.
Father, mek, or men.
Feather, belun.
Finger, hangeo.
Fire, poä.
Fish, tok.
Flesh, sen, or saïn.
Flower, lip.
Floor, mek mäsau.
Fly, lengeau.
Foot, tais pelen, or tes.
Forest, metená.
Fowl, jip.
Fruit, gua.

Go, komité.
Gold, meas.
Good, kas.

Hair, wook.
Hand, gué, or goé.
Hard, mahéng.
Hat, tapán.
Head, dau.
Hen, jib, or jip.
Honey, wonjoe.
*Hot, panés.
House, mesâ.
Husband, laká, or lon laká.

Infant, netsoe.
Iron, maleat.

King, hopoi.
Knife, peit.

Large, pun.
Leaf, hatteng kadjâ.
Little, amok.
Louse, tâ.

Man, lon.
Mat, pen.
Monkey, jook.
*Moon, bulum, or úlun.
*Mosquito, njamok.
Mother, men, or nin.
Mouse, owäo.
Mouth, pangbosung.

Nail, hulún, or holón.
Nest, hining.
Night, njohóp, or dam.
No, nda.
Nose, gonglóng.

*Oar, dajung.
Oil, njé, or ninjo.

Partition, ding.
Pig, owoi, or jim.
Plank, wijak.

Rain, sidn, or sin.
Rat, howeó.
Red, seék.
Rice, hés, or mä.
River, long.
Road, län.
Roof, sepäu.
Root, woké.

Saliva, loá.
Salt, sedjâ.
*Sea, milaut.
Silver, plak.
Skin, les, or leás.
Smoke, sōn.
Snake, pâ.
*Sour, sam.
Spear, tapáng.

Spoon, lés.
Squirrel, telás.
Stag, pedju.
Star, téng.
Stomach, sáh.
Stone, uttau.
Sun, matéu deou.
Sweet, manés.
Swallow, pengles.

Thigh, sepé.
Tongue, toléh.
Tooth, keu.

Urine, hängét.

War, pedjap.
Water, hongói.
Wax, leä

What?, non.
White, smohong.
Wife, ledóh.
Wind, hwås.
Window, ding pedja.
Wing, maléng.
*Wood, kadjāū.

Yellow, mansäu.

1. Sie.
2. Ungo.
3. Atlau.
4. Pet.
5. Må.
6. Nam.
7. So.
8. Tojout.
9. Septin.
10. Soan.
11. Sie hoan soan.
12. Ungo hoan soan.
20. Ungo plo.
30. Atlau plo.
100. Matus.
1000. Sie jemlen.

In the few words collected I find some are of Malay origin: these are marked with a *. The absence of the letter *r* is peculiar to the Dyak language.

The Dyaks have no names for the days of the week, and none for the months; those Dyaks who can speak Malay use the Malay terms.

APPENDIX V.

LIST OF SUMATRA BUTTERFLIES.

THROUGH the kindness of Mr. Henley Grose Smith, I am enabled to add a list of the principal species of Diurnal Lepidoptera known to inhabit Sumatra.

Ornithoptera.
Brookeana.
Minos.
Amphrysus.

Papilio.
Nephelus.
Memnon.
Coon.
Priapus.
Antiphus.
Helenus.
Palinurus.
Pammon.
Payeni.
Brama.
Eurypilus.
Bathycles.
Agamemnon.
Delessertii.
Sarpedon.
Demoleon.
Polytes.
Caunus.
Paradoxa.
Leptocircus.
Curius.

Pieris.
Nero.
Albina.
Nathalia.
Enarete.
Cardena.
Lyncida.
Paulina.
Glauce.
Alope.
Lelage.
Var Naomi.

Hebomoia.
Glaucippe.

Callidryas.
Scylla.
Crocale.
Pyranthe.

Terias.
Hecabe.
Eumide.

Gonepteryx.
Gobrias.

Hestia.
Lynceus.

Danais.
Melaneus.
Grammica.
Agleoides.
Similis.
Vulgaris.

Euplœa.
Ochsenheimeieri.
Egyptus.
Menetriesii.
Midamus.
Ledercri.
Novaræ.
Mazares.
Modesta.
Rhadamanthus.
Tyrianthina.

Cirrochroa.
Orissa.

Atella.
Sinha.
Aruana.

Cethosia.
Hypsea.

Terinos.
Robertsia.
Atlita.

Argynnis.
Niphe.

Vanessa.
Cardui.

Junonia.
Asterie.
Vellida.

Cyrestes.
Periander.
Nivea.

Neptis.
Duryodama.
Hordona.
Peraka.
Nata.
Susruta.
Ormeroda.
Soma.

Athyma.
Idita.
Kresna.
Reta.
Larymna.
Abiasa.
Subrata.
Nefte.

Apatura.
Parvata.

Diadema.
Anomala.

Limenitis.
Dudu.
Bockii.

Prothoe.
Franckii.

Amnosia.
Decora.

Charaxes.
Hebe.
Borneensis.

Herona.
Sumatrana.

Adolias
Palguna.
Supercilia.
Pulasara.
Aruna.
Laverna.
Cocytina.

Diardi.
Coresia.
Adoma.
Merta.
Dirtea.

Amathusia.

Luxerii.
Aurelius.
Phidippus.

Thaumantis.

Odana.

Clerome.

Arcesilaus.
Busiris.

Cœlites.

Epiminthia.
Euptychoides.

Debis.

Arcadia.
Mekara.

Neorina.

Lowii.

Mycalesis.

Diniche.
Maianeas.
Orseis.
Lalassis.
Megamede.
Diniche.
Medusa.
Hesione.
Samba.
Janardana.
Mnasicles.
Ostrea.
Anapita.
Bockii.
Asophis.

Yphthima.

Baldus.
Fasciata.

Erites.

Madura.

Elymnias.

Panthera.
Penanga.
Sumatrana.
Ceryx.
Lais.

Eurytela.

Horsfieldii.
Castelnaui.

Amblypodia.

Buxtoni.
Anartes.
Agnis.
Atrax.
Anunda.
Eumolphus.
Aroa.
Atosia.
Agesias.
Metamuta.
Inornata.
Perimuta.
Hypomuta.
Apidanus.
Capeta.
Anita.
Amisena.

Dendorix.

Nasaka.
Orseis.
Var Chozeba.
Domitia.

Loxura.

Pita.

Myrina.

Travana.
Nedymond.
Malika.
Estella.

Ravindra.
Thesmia.
Amrita.
Freja.
Burbona.
Chitra.
Tharis.
Marciana.

Iolaus.

Isæus.
Vidura.

Hypolycaena.

Etolus.

Poritia.

Erycinoides.
Philota.
Sumatræ.

Hypochrysops.

Superba.
Elegans.

Lycaena.

Augusta.
Atrata.
Celeno.
Akasa.
Ethion.
Rosimon.
Dionisius.

Lycaenopsis.

Ananga.
Cylinde.
Lohita.

Miletus.

Horsfeldi.
Symethus.
Zymna.

Temeros.

Emesoides.

Abisara.

Susa.

Taxila.

Thuisto.
Telesia.
Orphna.

Iomene.

Badra.

Eudamus.

Phaneus.
Calathus.
Thyrsis.

Hesperia.

Elia.
Avesta.
Irava.
Schœdia.
Aria.
Marsena.

Isoteinon.

Phiditia.
Ogygia.
Pertinax.
Merja.
Zema.
Vermiculata.
Mœsa.

Pterygospidea.

Trichoneura.
Folus.
Simula.

Astictopterus.

Sindu.
Salsala.
Xanites.
Fuscula.
Verones.
Ficulnea.
Ladana.
Diocles.
Harmachis.
Jama.

Pamphila.

Cinnara.

INDEX.

THE END.

Some other Oxford Paperbacks for readers interested in Central Asia, China and South-East Asia, past and present

CAMBODIA

GEORGE COEDÈS
Angkor: An Introduction

CENTRAL ASIA

PETER FLEMING
Bayonets to Lhasa

LADY MACARTNEY
An English Lady in Chinese Turkestan

ALBERT VON LE COQ
Buried Treasures of Chinese Turkestan

AITCHEN WU
Turkistan Tumult

CHINA

HAROLD ACTON
Peonies and Ponies

ERNEST BRAMAH
Kai Lung's Golden Hours

ANN BRIDGE
The Ginger Griffin

PETER FLEMING
The Siege at Peking

CORRINNE LAMB
The Chinese Festive Board

W. SOMERSET MAUGHAM
On a Chinese Screen*

G.E. MORRISON
An Australian in China

OSBERT SITWELL
Escape with Me! An Oriental Sketch-book

INDONESIA

S. TAKDIR ALISJAHBANA
Indonesia: Social and Cultural Revolution

DAVID ATTENBOROUGH
Zoo Quest for a Dragon*

VICKI BAUM
A Tale from Bali

MIGUEL COVARRUBIAS
Island of Bali*

BERYL DE ZOETE AND WALTER SPIES
Dance and Drama in Bali

AUGUSTA DE WIT
Java: Facts and Fancies

JACQUES DUMARCAY
Borobudur

JACQUES DUMARCAY
The Temples of Java

JENNIFER LINDSAY
Javanese Gamelan

EDWIN M. LOEB
Sumatra: Its History and People

MOCHTAR LUBIS
Twilight in Djakarta

MADELON H. LULOFS
Coolie*

ANNA MATHEWS
The Night of Purnama

COLIN McPHEE
A House in Bali*

HICKMAN POWELL
The Last Paradise

E.R. SCIDMORE
Java, Garden of the East

MICHAEL SMITHIES
Yogyakarta

LADISLAO SZÉKELY
Tropic Fever: The Adventures of a Planter in Sumatra

EDWARD C. VAN NESS AND SHITA PRAWIROHARDJO
Javanese Wayang Kulit

MALAYSIA

ABDULLAH ABDUL KADIR
The Hikayat Abdullah

ISABELLA L. BIRD
The Golden Chersonese: Travels in Malaya in 1879

PIERRE BOULLE
Sacrilege in Malaya

MARGARET BROOKE RANEE OF SARAWAK
My Life in Sarawak

C.C. BROWN (Editor)
Sejarah Melayu or Malay Annals

COLIN N. CRISSWELL
Rajah Charles Brooke: Monarch of All He Surveyed

K.M. ENDICOTT
An Analysis of Malay Magic

HENRI FAUCONNIER
The Soul of Malaya

W.R. GEDDES
Nine Dayak Nights

JOHN D. GIMLETTE
Malay Poisons and Charm Cures

JOHN D. GIMLETTE AND H.W. THOMSON
A Dictionary of Malayan Medicine

A.G. GLENISTER
The Birds of the Malay Peninsula, Singapore and Penang

C.W. HARRISON
Illustrated Guide to the Federated Malay States (1923)

TOM HARRISSON
World Within: A Borneo Story

DENNIS HOLMAN
Noone of the Ulu

CHARLES HOSE
The Field-Book of a Jungle-Wallah

SYBIL KATHIGASU
No Dram of Mercy

MALCOLM MacDONALD
Borneo People

SOMERSET MAUGHAM
The Casuarina Tree*

AMBROSE B. RATHBORNE
Camping and Tramping in Malaya

ROBERT W.C. SHELFORD
A Naturalist in Borneo

J.T. THOMSON
Glimpses into Life in Malayan Lands

RICHARD WINSTEDT
The Malay Magician

PHILIPPINES

AUSTIN COATES
Rizal

SINGAPORE

PATRICK ANDERSON
Snake Wine: A Singapore Episode

ROLAND BRADDELL
The Lights of Singapore

R.W.E. HARPER AND HARRY MILLER
Singapore Mutiny

JANET LIM
Sold for Silver

G.M. REITH
Handbook to Singapore (1907)

J.D. VAUGHAN
The Manners and Customs of the Chinese of the Straits Settlements

C.E. WURTZBURG
Raffles of the Eastern Isles

THAILAND

CARL BOCK
Temples and Elephants

REGINALD CAMPBELL
Teak-Wallah

MALCOLM SMITH
A Physician at the Court of Siam

ERNEST YOUNG
The Kingdom of the Yellow Robe

**Titles marked with an asterisk have restricted rights*

DISCARD